Year
of
Peace

Register This New Book

Benefits of Registering*

- ✓ FREE **replacements** of lost or damaged books

- ✓ FREE **audiobook** – *Pilgrim's Progress,* audiobook edition

- ✓ FREE information about new titles and other **freebies**

www.anekopress.com/new-book-registration

*See our website for requirements and limitations.

Year
of
Peace

*a daily
devotional*

Jason Pettus

ANEKO
PRESS

Aneko Press

www.anekopress.com

Aneko Press, Life Sentence Publishing, and our logos are trademarks of

Life Sentence Publishing, Inc.
203 E. Birch Street
P.O. Box 652
Abbotsford, WI 54405

RELIGION / Christian Living / Devotional

Paperback ISBN: 978-1-62245-716-8

eBook ISBN: 978-1-62245-717-5

10 9 8 7 6 5 4 3 2 1

Available where books are sold

Contents

To my precious children: I pray that you will always have the peace of God that comes through faith in Christ and allows you to say in every season, "It is well with my soul."

Preface

The goal of this book is to encourage people to read the Bible. I pray that this book will help you on your spiritual journey whether you have never read the Bible before or if you have been studying it for years. God's Word is a trusty guide. It has blessed the lives of billions of saints throughout the centuries, but many followers of Jesus today find it difficult to spend time studying and meditating on the Bible. This book will help. The great news is that God speaks to us through the Bible no matter where we may be in our spiritual journey. Those who know the Word of God are better able to discern the will of God and to walk in the way of Jesus. This is the great need of our day.

The reading plan for each day listed at the top corner of each page is from the "M'Cheyne Reading Plan" developed by Robert Murry M'Cheyne (1813-1843). He was only twenty-nine years old when he went to be with the Lord, but he left behind a great legacy of faith and a wonderful tool for reading the Bible. This plan allows for a person to read the Psalms and New Testament twice a year and the Old Testament once a year.

While reading all four chapters is preferred, those reading this devotion can limit themselves to reading one chapter a day. The underlined chapter is the one being written about for that day. If a choice must be made between reading the devotion or reading the chapter of the Bible, please read the Bible.

The intent of the book is to help readers gain an overall understanding of the Bible by guiding the reading using the central theme of "peace." *Peace is the personal experience of knowing that all is well with your soul no matter the circumstance.* That is the simple definition that is used throughout this volume.

There was silence for four hundred years between the Old and New Testaments. God's perfect plan to bring salvation to the world through the line of Abraham and David seemed impossible, but it began to be realized in Matthew 1. God promised Abraham that the world would be blessed through his family (Genesis 12:1-3). God promised that He would build an eternal kingdom through David (2 Samuel 7:16). God promised Mary that she would be the mother of the Messiah who would fulfill God's ultimate plan of salvation.

At first glance, the genealogies in Matthew 1 do not seem very exciting, but they remind us that God is at work in the lives of real people like you and me (vv. 2-17). This list has the names of several women: Tamar, Rahab, Ruth (v. 5), Bathsheba, the wife of Uriah (v. 6), and Mary (v. 16). Listing women like this was unusual in Jesus' day. Each has a story that reveals God's grace and mercy. God's plan has always been and will always be to work through those who are willing to humble themselves and trust Him.

God's gift of salvation is miraculous. The birth of Jesus occurred through the womb of a virgin (v. 18). Mary and Joseph were humble people with faith in God (v. 19). The divine involvement through angels points to the uniqueness of their calling (vv. 20-25). The coming of God in flesh was a miracle. It happened in real time and space with real people.

Myths and stories in ancient times did not have heroes who were as marred and meek as those who fill the pages of Scripture. The truth of the Bible reveals how God chooses ordinary, sinful people to accomplish His extraordinary plans. The Bible is unique. It reveals the author, God Himself, who stepped into space and time to save His people.

The Bible is filled with promises God has yet to keep. Although Jesus has come, the Bible promises that He will come again. Until then, we have the opportunity to serve Him and join in on the adventure of seeing salvation come to every nation.

Is your life a part of God's eternal story and purpose? Have you turned to Jesus in faith and been saved by grace? Are you willing to do what God says no matter what?

Those who believe God and act in faith live with peace.

Genesis 2; Matthew 2; <u>Ezra 2</u>; Acts 2

Lists of names don't make for fun reading, but they matter. There is a great list of names in heaven in the Book of Life (Revelation 20:15). Each name listed reminds us that God pursues His people because of His unending desire to be with them. Even though it was their sin that caused Judah to be sent into Babylonian captivity, God never stopped loving them. The list in Ezra 2 reveals the providence, the purpose, and the plan of God.

The Babylonian exile is a picture of the fall of humanity. God's people disobeyed and were expelled from His presence and protection. In the brokenness of their own sin, God's people suffered. By His grace, God provided salvation. The people were called home to Israel. Today, God's children are called to new life in Christ. Salvation is found by grace in Christ alone. God used an unbelieving king named Cyrus as part of His plan to release and provide for His people. More than one hundred years before Cyrus was born, God said that Cyrus would do this (Isaiah 44:28)!

The Lord rescued His people first and foremost for the glory of His great name. Those listed in Ezra 2 and those listed in the Book of Life can only boast in the grace of God. None of us deserve new life, but God gives it for the praise of His name and to reveal His eternal love and kindness. The beneficiaries of grace are compelled to praise God. The God of grace is the reason and the object of praise. God's glory is the purpose.

Those whom God calls, He equips to accomplish His plan. He has chosen to work in the world through His adopted children. Every child of God has a particular purpose. Just as God had a plan for every person who returned to Jerusalem from Babylon to rebuild the temple, so He has a plan for each and every one of His children today. It is a plan designed by our loving Father (Ephesians 2:4-10). The Lord gifts each person and providentially provides so that His children know and do His will. By faith, we work with God and fulfill His loving purpose for us.

Have you entered into a personal relationship with God through faith in Jesus? Is your name written in the Book of Life? Are you pursuing God's purpose for your life?

Those who pursue their destiny in Christ live with peace.

Genesis 3; Matthew 3; Ezra 3; <u>Acts 3</u>

It is amazing how God chooses to work through His people! God ushered His kingdom into the world with power. Not only did Jesus perform great miracles, but the apostles did as well. This was to fulfill the promises of God and to help people see that the Lord was at work doing a new thing. Along with the miracles, there was a simple message: peace with God is possible.

Having established a local church by the power of the Holy Spirit (Acts 2), Peter and the other apostles began to establish a new way of life within the old order of Judaism (Acts 3). God works through His people in the culture where He sends them. The New Testament is filled with many different methods for making disciples because the cultures that were infiltrated with the gospel were different. Within the framework of Jerusalem's culture, Peter performed a miracle and pointed to Jesus' power (vv. 1-10). Disciples are made as God's people meet needs with love and point people to the gospel of Jesus.

Peter did not just heal this man, but Peter gave glory to God and preached the gospel (vv. 11-16). The right response to the gospel is faith revealed in repentance (vv. 17-21). God always meets us where we are in our sin, but He loves us too much to leave us there. God changes His people's lives with the truth. The truth sets them free and inspires their obedience. Through faith in Christ, a person gains peace with God, which changes their heart and mind. God's grace makes it possible to live in peace.

This peace was promised long ago, when God told Adam and Eve that a Savior would come and crush Satan's head (Genesis 3:15). Throughout the Old Testament, God consistently spoke of a coming time of peace. He raised up Moses and the prophets to tell of Christ's coming and that Jesus would suffer for sin (Acts 3:18, 22-24). This Savior would bless all the families of the world. He would come through the line of Abraham, as promised (Genesis 12:1-3). Jesus has come (Acts 3:25-26). He saves sinners.

Do you have peace with God? Is Jesus transforming your life each day by making you more like Him? Are you a peacemaker who cares for people and shares the gospel with a hurting world?

Those who in faith look to Jesus Christ have eternal peace.

Genesis 4; Matthew 4; Ezra 4; Acts 4

Life on earth is hard, but God is good. He will see us through. He has a plan we can count on and trust. As a part of the original plan in the garden of Eden, God had already promised Eve that she would give birth to children (Genesis 1:28), but now, because of sin, doing so would be painful (Genesis 3:16). Eve also heard God curse the serpent, promising that through her line a Savior would be born (Genesis 3:15). Genesis 4 tells us that Eve had two sons: Cain and Abel. They were born with a sin nature and were incapable of saving themselves, much less the world. They needed peace with God, like we all do.

When the two boys grew up, they became aware of their need for peace with God. To have peace with God, there must be a sacrifice made for sin (Hebrews 9:22). God prescribed what was needed for the sacrifice (Genesis 4:1-4). Cain was angered that God had no regard for his offering (v. 5). Cain wanted peace with God on his terms rather than on God's terms. The Lord warned Cain that he must repent and pursue Him according to His word (vv. 6-7). Cain did not respond in faith, and he lived without peace with God.

Without peace with God, peace within is impossible, which also makes peace with others impossible. Once jealousy and frustration set in on a heart, conflict always comes. Cain killed his brother Abel (v. 8). God called him out for his actions, which was an opportunity for Cain to repent, but Cain refused (vv. 9-10). Sin is devastating. By the second generation of humanity, murder was committed. Like all sin, it had serious consequences. Cain was cursed and was forced to wander the world without God's blessing (vv. 11-14). He kept the dignity that all human beings have and received a protective mark (v. 15). Cain continued in his sin, and his children followed in his footsteps (vv. 16-24).

God blessed Adam and raised up another child to replace what was lost in Abel (v. 25). Seth grew up and enjoyed peace with God, and he passed it on to his son, Enosh (v. 26). God's peace comes through grace and is to be passed on to others.

Do you have peace with God through faith in Jesus, the Savior who sacrificed His life for your sin? Are you passing on God's peace to others? Are you living in peace with God and others?

Those who seek God in accordance with His way live with peace.

Genesis 5; <u>Matthew 5</u>; Ezra 5; Acts 5

Oh, to have been among the crowds that day Jesus preached! The sermon that Jesus preached that begins in Matthew 5 is likely the most famous in the world. Beginning with descriptions of what leads to blessedness and calling people to be attentive to their hearts' desires, Jesus reveals the way the redeemed of God are to live. Even though we may not realize it, the blessings of God are desired by all people. We all want to be heirs of God's kingdom, to be comforted and satisfied, to have mercy, to see God and be called a child of God, and to stand with the righteous people of God's heavenly realm (vv. 1-12). Those blessings are found only by faith. The way of God seems strange to the world, but those who know Jesus understand the power of humility and kindness.

Those who know God's way are a light to the world. It is critical that those who have peace with God reveal the means to that peace so that others can shine (vv. 13-16). The will of God is to have His church shine within every city in the world.

The church shines brightest when God's people obey His law from their hearts and not just through mechanical willpower. Jesus fulfilled the law (vv. 17-20). Those who repent and believe in Jesus are not only forgiven of their sin, but they are also given a righteous standing with God that allows them to keep His law with the love of God that lives in them. Those who know Jesus love Jesus. Those who love Jesus obey Jesus. Love for Jesus overcomes anger, lust, marital strife, lying, and vengeance (vv. 21-42). God's love allows God's people to have and make peace.

Peace begins with love. Even though we are born in sin, Jesus' love and sacrifice heal our relationship with God. Because Jesus loved His enemies, His children can love their enemies too (vv. 43-48). Those who love as Jesus loves are being sanctified in love. This is a transformational process that glorifies God and blesses His people.

Are you a child of God by grace through faith in Jesus? Are you living a life that loves Jesus and obeys Him gladly from the heart? Are the blessings of God evident in you to a watching and hurting world?

***God wants what is best for people, and those who
choose to trust and obey Him live with peace.***

Genesis 6; Matthew 6; <u>Ezra 6</u>; Acts 6

God has always been and always will be in control of all things, including the workings of all governmental systems. Although government officials at all levels make millions of decisions for which they are completely responsible, God is at work accomplishing His will through each and every one. In Ezra 6, we see that God provides for His people through a government system.

Having had to halt the construction of the temple, the people of God were cared for. The governor of the province sent an inquiry to Darius, king of Babylon, to determine if the people of God were acting rightly in building the temple of God. In Ezra 6, we see God provide and the people grow. In both the letter that was sent in Ezra 5 and the response in Ezra 6, there is a favor shown to the people of God. That was God's kind provision.

The first thing the king did was to search the legal records of Babylon (v. 1). A scroll was found with the historical background *concerning the house of God in Jerusalem*, explaining the legality of rebuilding the temple (vv. 2-5). Given the facts, Darius commanded that God's people would be allowed to continue with their work (vv. 6-7), which was nice, but God inspired more. Darius commanded the governor to do something *for these elders of the Jews for the rebuilding of this house of God* (v. 8). Provisions were also made for sacrifices so that prayers could be offered for the king and his family (vv. 9-10). The king also threatened harm to any who interfered with the work being done (vv. 11-12). God provides for His purpose. God's people never need to be anxious.

The temple was built, and the people celebrated (vv. 13-17). They also began to worship according to the Bible's directives (vv. 18-22). The people did more than accomplish their task. They grew in their faith. God's people can often get so caught up in doing God's work that they forget the importance of their relationship to God. The returned exiles served and sought the Lord.

Are you engaged in serving God in such a substantial way that the intervention of God is needed? Are you praying for miracles? Are you growing in your faith through your service?

Those who trust in God's provision and pursue His purpose live with peace.

Sometimes the sacrifice for being a Christian is huge. Stephen was the first Christian we know of to be martyred for his belief in Jesus. Much like we do now, he lived in a world hostile to the gospel of peace. As recorded in Acts 7, he preached the gospel of peace, and the response was anger by people who lashed out in hate.

Stephen was not a mean-spirited man. He was an anointed leader filled with great faith and the power of the Holy Spirit (Acts 6:5). He was the first person mentioned in Scripture to be able to perform signs and wonders who was not an apostle (Acts 6:8). He was also a wise, kind man (Acts 6:10), and was willing to tell the truth in love and call the religious leaders of his day to faith.

He began his discourse with a simple history lesson (vv. 1-50). The things he said were well-known by his listeners. They would have agreed with what he said. These historical facts were used to build Stephen's case for the gospel. Stephen pointed to the promises of God and the hope of the Messiah who had come.

Having laid a solid biblical foundation that his listeners understood and agreed to, Stephen turned the message toward the sinfulness of his listeners (vv. 51-53). The gospel is given in love and established in truth. The truth is that we are all sinners. Stephen made it abundantly clear where these men stood spiritually based on how they had treated Jesus. They were lost.

The religious leaders did not appreciate what Stephen had to say about them. As long as the message is historical, interesting, and emotionally uplifting, people are happy to hear it. However, as soon as it points to the reality of their situation and the need for salvation in Christ alone, many become hostile. These religious leaders did just that (v. 54). Stephen was able to see past their hate to Jesus *standing* by the throne (v. 56). Jesus is usually seen seated in heaven at the right hand of God the Father, but He stood for this saint. Stephen was martyred, but his dying words were like those of Jesus. He died with peace (vv. 57-60).

Do you have the faith to share the gospel with a hostile world? Are you able to forgive and ask God to forgive those who hurt you? Will you die with eternal peace?

Those who stand for Christ live and die with eternal peace.

Genesis 8; Matthew 8; Ezra 8; Acts 8

God does not forget His people. It may feel at times that the Lord has forgotten our plight and pain, but God knows. God sees. God has a plan. In Genesis 8, the nature of God and the plan He has for His creation is revealed.

That God *remembered Noah*, his family, and all of the animals does not mean that the all-knowing God had allowed Noah, his family, and the beasts of the world to slip His almighty mind. It meant that God was ready to act (v. 1). The water from the deep and from the sky ceased to flow. The ark rested on Ararat, a mountain in Turkey, and other mountaintops began to be visible (vv. 2-5). Those who wait on the Lord see the Lord's provision from a unique perspective that inspires faith and produces peace.

Noah first sent a raven, an unclean animal, to test the conditions of the earth (vv. 6-7). He then sent a dove that returned with nothing, but then seven days later it came back with a leaf from an olive branch (vv. 8-12). The olive branch has become a universal symbol of peace. It showed that God's wrath had been abated and that there was now peace on earth. God is both loving and just. He is perfect. He is God.

When Noah and his family emerged from the ark, they entered into a new earth (vv. 13-19). This is a picture of the coming of Christ seen in Revelation 21. In that day, the wrath of God will have been satisfied. All of the earth will have been purified with fire, and heaven and earth will be one. This is the future of God's people.

The world of Noah was not perfect like the earth will be when Christ returns. This world is filled with sinners. The first thing Noah did was to offer a blood sacrifice (v. 20). This provided him with peace with God (v. 21a). God determined to never again curse the ground because of sinners. Humans are sinful and experience brokenness because of this sin, but God still loves us (v. 21b). The world now goes on with days and nights and seasons (v. 22). Peace on earth is not yet fully here. Christ has come, but the new heaven and earth have not. We now await our conquering Savior.

Do you have peace with God? Are you living for the coming of Christ? Do you trust God to provide?

Those who believe in the God of the Bible and
trust and obey His Word live with peace.

Jesus came into the world to rescue sinners from His just wrath and punishment. In Matthew 9, Jesus performs both physical and spiritual miracles, and the chapter finishes with an overarching explanation of reality. God is at work in the world.

After Jesus returned to the city He was from, several people brought their paralytic friend to Him. Jesus first addressed his spiritual problem and healed him of his sin. Our spiritual problem is our greatest problem. Then, by healing the man of his physical brokenness, He demonstrated His power to forgive sin (vv. 1-8). This man was healed by the grace of God because of the compassionate ministry of his friends who took him to Jesus.

Matthew was most likely not a very popular man when Jesus first met him. He was among the tax collectors, whom many hated, but Jesus did a work in his heart and called Matthew to follow Him. The first thing Matthew did, having been saved by grace, was to introduce his friends to Jesus (vv. 9-13).

When Jesus was asked about fasting, He revealed the importance of that moment in history. He was the promised Messiah who had come to make a new covenant. Jesus' new covenant could not fit into an old system. Jesus had come to bring new life (vv. 14-17). This new life comes to those who experience Him. When the woman touched His garment, she was healed (vv. 18-22). When Jesus touched the dead girl, she was made alive (vv. 23-26). When Jesus touched the eyes of the blind men, he was miraculously healed (vv. 27-31). When the demon-possessed man came into contact with Jesus, he was healed (vv. 32-34). Everyone who has an experience with Jesus is changed.

Jesus is still changing lives. The world is filled with brokenness. Those who are touched by Jesus find healing for their souls and sometimes for their bodies. The harvest is still plentiful, but the workers are still few (vv. 35-38). The need of the day is for those who know Jesus to help others come into contact with Him. Through prayer and sharing the gospel, lives are changed.

Are you helping people meet Jesus? It takes work! Are you praying for people you know to be saved and physically healed? Many people mocked Jesus. Are you willing to serve God no matter what?

Those who join God in His work in the world live with peace.

Genesis 11; Matthew 10; Ezra 10; Acts 10

Life on this broken planet is messy! Even doing the right thing can often create a mess. In Ezra 10, the newly returned exiles were called to take huge sacrificial steps that would put them in a right standing with God. These steps would require hard decisions to be made and heavy consequences to be felt.

Those who had returned from Babylon to Israel had done many good things. They had rebuilt the temple and had committed to obey the law of God. Yet there were still temptations and people living in sin. Some of the men had married women who were not of the covenant community. This was intolerable. Rather than just rail against them, Ezra taught them the Word of God, prayed, and wept in appalled grief (v. 1a). Sometimes the best thing a leader or parent can do is teach, pray, and cry.

Ezra had prayed fervently for the people with strong words of conviction (Ezra 9:6-14). The people now gathered around him and joined him in his grief (Ezra 10:1b). They repented and encouraged Ezra to lead them (vv. 2-5). A leader can take people no further than they are willing to go. God blessed the people to follow Ezra.

All the leaders of the nation were summoned to meet with Ezra to discuss the faithlessness of the people and the steps that would need to be taken to repent and remedy the situation (vv. 6-8). The people came and stood in a mess – both spiritually and physically. They were spiritually in conflict with God, and it was pouring down rain (vv. 9-13). Our circumstances can often tell us a great deal about our spiritual condition.

The leaders acknowledged the need for reform, and they determined a practical plan (vv. 14-17). A plurality of leaders is often needed to accomplish God's purpose. These leaders identified the changes needed, and the people made them (vv. 18-43). The changes would require divorce, which would lead to more messes. Sin creates messes. It is best to trust and obey God in order to avoid the pain and suffering that sin always brings.

Are you walking faithfully with God? Do you need to make changes in your life that will enable you to live a life that honors Jesus? Are you willing to obey God no matter what?

Those who trust and obey God no matter what live with peace.

It is easy to lose sight of what is most important and to settle for what tradition or cultural norms tell us. Peter was all too willing to remain a happy, faithful Jew who knew Jesus. Jesus had bigger plans for Peter. God is so good to cause His people to get beyond their preferences and on to what is best.

When the word got out that Peter had eaten with gentiles and evangelized them, the *circumcision party* was not at all happy. They criticized Peter for his departure from the Jewish customs they still held (vv. 1-3). Those who obey Jesus will often be criticized by those outside of the church for their beliefs and criticized by those inside of the church for their actions. Disciples of Jesus must be faithful to their calling regardless of what others think.

Peter could have been offended and criticized his criticizers, but he took a mature stance. He simply told the truth with love and allowed those who did not appreciate his work to make their determination as to how they would respond (vv. 4-16). There is great freedom in simply obeying Jesus. Life will not always be easy for faithful followers of Jesus. People will not always support their efforts, but those who are looking to please Jesus will enjoy peace in their own hearts.

To their credit, the people responded humbly and happily. They confessed that what they had in Christ was a gift (v. 17). It was not something they earned. They celebrated God's grace to the gentiles and happily embraced their place in God's family (v. 18).

Meanwhile, the church was being scattered (v. 19). The gospel was spreading and was accomplishing God's plan that had been outlined in Acts 1:8 (vv. 20-26). These new believers were equipped, and when a famine was prophesied, they began to give toward the needs of their Judean brothers (vv. 27-30). People from different backgrounds were loving each other in the peace of Christ!

Are you driven by the mission of Jesus, or have you been neutralized by tradition and cultural expectations? Are people coming to saving faith through your witness? Do you support using different methods in order for others to hear the gospel?

Obeying Jesus can make life difficult, but those who are willing to share the truth in love will live with peace.

Genesis 13; Matthew 12; Nehemiah 2; Acts 12

Like many of God's children, Abram had to learn to trust God the hard way. The lessons Abram learned in Egypt (Genesis 12) provided faith for the next phase of his journey.

In Genesis 13, a dispute broke out between Abram's men and the men of his nephew, Lot (vv. 1-7). They had a big problem. They were rich with livestock, but their ability to keep the animals watered and fed was limited. These limited resources led to strife. Having wealth is not always easy. It creates challenges that only the wise are able to navigate. Few succeed at having wealth and maintaining a humble love, a grateful heart, and a godward life.

Rather than fight for his right to choose what was seemingly best, Abram trusted the Lord and invited Lot to choose the land he preferred. Instead of letting things rankle him, Abram chose the way of peace, which always demands sacrifice (vv. 8-13). Lot chose the land that was lush, but which was also filled with wicked people. Those whom we associate with impact our lives in significant ways. The wise do not choose to live as the wicked or with the wicked (Psalm 1). Godly people are called to live as light in the darkness. Lot's decision to choose the attractive land would cost him dearly in the end.

After Lot escaped Sodom, God appeared to Abram and renewed His covenant promise (Genesis 13:14-17). Abram received this promise and acted in faith. God always directs the way of those who trust in Him rather than in their own understanding. Abram settled near the capital city of the Canaanite kingdom, Hebron, where he had allies. Unlike Lot, Abram went to his new dwelling intent on honoring God and being a light to the world. He set up an altar and worshipped God. He made no secret of his faith. His peace came from God, who had made an eternal covenant with him. His life was in God's hands, and Abram gladly served God.

Are you defined by your wealth or lack of wealth, or do you live with a higher sense of calling? Are you willing to trust God and give up what seems to be best from a worldly perspective? Are you living as light in the darkness?

Those who trust God rather than their own personal, selfish inclinations live with peace.

Genesis 14; <u>Matthew 13</u>; Nehemiah 3; Acts 13

Personal responsibility is a burden shared by everyone. Regardless of what we have, we are completely accountable for it. In Matthew 13, Jesus spoke in parables and pointed to the purpose of God and the responsibility of people.

The heart of humanity is a great mystery. Only God truly understands the heart of a person. Some hearts are hard toward God, and some are tender and receive God's Word (vv. 1-9). The Lord Jesus spoke in parables, and the Word of God speaks today, but not all people apprehend God's meaning. God's grace is a glorious mystery. Those enabled to believe are truly blessed (vv. 10-16). Not all who hear believe (vv. 17-23). Those who can receive the Word of God are very grateful. Gratitude is a fruit of the gospel. All who are saved produce it in abundance.

Those who do not receive the gospel of God are like weeds in the garden of God (vv. 24-30). They grow up alongside the redeemed, but will be revealed, judged, and burned. The righteous are recognizable by their beliefs and behaviors. They are changed by the truth (vv. 31-33). They value the truth above all else (vv. 34-46). They look forward to the return of Christ and His judgment (vv. 47-50). They recognize their responsibility, and they desire to be found faithful in the eyes of God (vv. 51-52).

Those who are raised to know Jesus and those who become accustomed with the reality of Jesus must be careful to avoid becoming immune to the effects of His presence and power. Those who spent years with Jesus and saw Him grow up in Nazareth were resistant to His message of hope. They heard His wisdom and were astonished, but their hearts were hard toward Him and they took offense at Him. They did not honor Him (vv. 53-57). Their lack of faith limited the work of God (v. 58). It is easy to judge them and think of them as strange for their lack of faith, but there are many raised in the church with access to the gospel who reject the Lord.

Is your heart tender toward the Word of God? Do you have a deep sense of gratitude in your soul for God's grace? Are you cold toward Jesus and offended by His demands?

***Those who are wise stewards with what they have will give
to what matters for eternity and will live with peace.***

Genesis 15; Matthew 14; <u>Nehemiah 4</u>; Acts 14

The way of God will rarely be celebrated by worldly people. God's way is a threat to the desires of the flesh and the evil ways of the world. Those who belong to God should expect to be attacked and intimidated by those who do not walk with God. It is spiritual bullying, and its true source is evil.

In Nehemiah 4, God's people were being intimidated by worldly people. Sanballat and Tobiah were the main voices of opposition. Sanballat was the governor of Samaria and probably had assumed authority over Jerusalem. Nehemiah's coming and leading the people there to rebuild Jerusalem's wall was a threat to him. When Sanballat heard that the people were organized and committed to work, he began to intimidate them (vv. 1-3). That is a typical trick that the evil darkness of this world uses.

In response to their attacks, Nehemiah prayed and asked God to curse them (v. 4). He also got busy building the wall, which is what God had called him to do (v. 5). The best way to deal with demonic and human attacks is to trust God in prayer and to get busy doing what God said to do.

Seeing that the work continued, Sanballat and Tobiah upped their game and created rumors and lies. They even convinced some of the faithful in the land to demand that their relatives stop building the wall and go home (vv. 6-12). Nehemiah wisely placed people around the wall among their family and friends and set up a defense system (vv. 13-19). When under any evil attack, the people of God must defend each other. God's people can know that God will fight for them as they live wisely by faith (v. 20).

Nehemiah never let the people get complacent or let their defenses down (vv. 21-23). It is crucial that God's people always remember what they are living for and keep themselves armed and ready for battle. The darkness never gives up, so the children of the light must always be ready for battle.

Are you walking in God's way and building His kingdom? Are you defended by and defending other believers? Are you armed with God's Word?

Those who are faithful may not always be comfortable, but they will always have peace.

Disagreements abound. We are all either in a conflict, coming out of a conflict, or about to get into a conflict. The church is filled with people, and people will not always agree. In Acts 15, we see that the church was in conflict and had to come to an agreement. There was a great need for Jesus and His truth, grace, and wisdom. Thankfully, God gave them peace – and the world is better for it.

Having come from their first missionary journey during which many had come to saving faith and during which they had faced many painful challenges (Acts 13-14), Paul and Barnabas were bound to have been tired and in no mood for a theological controversy, but that is what they found waiting for them when they returned home. A group had come from Judea teaching that a person had to first embrace a Jewish lifestyle before they could be saved (Acts 15:1). Many people still think they must live up to a certain moral code before coming to faith in Jesus. That has never been the case. People are not saved because they behave a certain way. People behave a certain way because they are saved.

The debate must have been heated. Rather than run in circles, which many disagreements can lead to, the leaders at Antioch sent a delegation with Paul and Barnabas to have the matter settled in Jerusalem (v. 2). They were welcomed warmly, and both sides – those who said the ceremonial law of Moses must be kept and those with Paul who said it did not have to be kept – were presented (vv. 3-12). Truth with grace was shared by both sides. This is how godly people speak to one another.

After both sides were presented, James stepped forward to settle the matter (v. 13). It is significant that James, not Peter, was the apparent leader of the church in Jerusalem and of this theological council. He sided with Paul and Barnabas, and a letter was presented that was to be shared with all the churches (vv. 14-29). Paul and Barnabas left content, but then they fell into a conflict. It ended with them deciding to go their separate ways (vv. 30-41). Even in their separation, the gospel work continued.

Are you handling conflicts well? Are you honoring Jesus? Are you remaining on mission for Jesus despite the conflicts?

Where Jesus is present with His benefits, there is peace.

JANUARY 16

God's grace changes everything. Left to ourselves, we human beings flounder in folly and brokenness. In God's grace, people's lives, along with their destiny, are changed. God's plan is worked out through those who receive His grace and honor Him.

Abram was shown God's grace. He was saved from a pagan way of life. He became a worshipper of the one true God and was promised to be the leading part of the line through which the promise of God would be fulfilled (Genesis 12:1-3). In Genesis 17, we see that plan taking shape. God sanctified Abram and Sarai and provided for His purpose.

God does more than give His people a right standing. God transforms His people into the likeness of Christ. God made Abram and Sarai into His conduits of grace. He changed their names to correspond to His purpose (vv. 1-16). A name change corresponds to a life change. All who walk with God by faith are made holy, and their new lives are realized in the real world.

Abram became Abraham – father of a multitude. Sarai became Sarah – the one through whom the blessing of the nations would come. The promised son would be called Isaac, which means laughter (vv. 17-21). Abraham laughed when he understood he would become a father at a hundred years of age. Who wouldn't? What was about to happen was supernatural. This was not the normal way of things. God worked in such a way that Abraham and all who would come through his family line would know that they were a part of a supernatural plan.

Abraham acted on his belief (vv. 22-27). God's plan demanded obedience. Abraham and all the males of his household had to be circumcised, and they were. Faith without action is useless (James 2). God was establishing a covenant with Abraham and his descendants. They were to look different from the rest of the world. Their way of life was to be uniquely godly. The purpose of all that God was doing was to reveal His glory and grace to the world. He was showing His love through an unworthy man made righteous.

Have you received God's grace? Is your lifestyle changing by God's grace? Are you living out your faith through obedience to God's Word?

Those who live out God's plan live with peace.

The life of a disciple of Jesus is lived in the real world, or it is not real at all. Christianity is not an ideal, a philosophy, a demographic group, or an institution. Christianity is a way of life that is experienced by those who have received new life by the power of the Holy Spirit through their reception of Jesus.

A few different events are recorded in Matthew 17. Peter, James, and John saw Jesus transfigured on a mountain. All the disciples saw Jesus do a miracle that required faith. The chapter ends with Jesus teaching His followers what it means that He has come into the world with His kingdom to bring freedom. This was a radical revelation.

Six days after telling His followers that some would see Him coming in His kingdom, Jesus was transfigured, and Elijah and Moses showed up (vv. 1-3). Peter misunderstood and thought this would be the new kingdom: Elijah and Moses alongside Jesus. God the Father interrupted Peter to make it clear that Jesus was uniquely His Son (vv. 4-6). When God spoke, Peter, James, and John fell to their faces, but God assured them (v. 7). When they looked up, only Jesus remained (v. 8). Jesus is not a religious leader. He is the Savior and King over all.

This person, Jesus Christ, revealed His divinity through many wonders and signs. One of these wonders was when Jesus healed a boy His disciples couldn't heal (vv. 14-18). The disciples later asked why they couldn't heal him, and Jesus explained the importance of faith (vv. 19-21). God's work is not about positions of authority. It is about service by faith.

Following Jesus is not easy. Jesus died on a cross at the hands of religious leaders. He made no secret that this was His destiny, which distressed the disciples (vv. 22-23). What they could not yet see was that God had sent the Son to bring about a new kingdom of liberty. The old ways that pointed to Him were passing away. The new was coming, but they were not to be disrespectful of the old (vv. 24-27). God's new way is the way of grace.

Are you looking to the coming of Jesus that He promised? Are you living by faith and seeing God change lives? Are you serving the kingdom of God respectfully?

Those who live the life of a true disciple of Christ will see
their lives changed by faith and will experience peace.

Genesis 19; Matthew 18; <u>Nehemiah 8</u>; Acts 18

There is nothing like the Bible. The Bible is a single story with four parts: creation, fall, rescue, and restoration. It is the Word of God, and it will accomplish the purpose for which God has sent it (Isaiah 55:11). In Nehemiah 8, we see that the power of the Word of God was experienced by the people of God. Ezra read it. The Levites taught it. The people obeyed it.

The people had gathered at the Water Gate to be refreshed with the Word of God (vv. 1-6). Ezra stood over the people and read the Pentateuch, the first five books of the Bible, the foundation of the Scriptures. The Word of God is to reign over the people of God and is to be the source of their understanding of reality.

Reading the Bible is not like a magical incantation. To be blessed, people must know what the Scriptures mean. The Levites explained the meaning so the people could ascertain who God is, who they were, and what grace can do (vv. 7-8). What a great picture of discipleship! Those who were trained were training those who would be able to live out the meaning and instruct others.

Hearing the Word of God is not always easy. It takes time and commitment. These people stood outside for hours listening and seeking to learn the meaning of God's Word. When they understood the meaning, they were grieved (vv. 9-10). The Bible reveals that all have failed God and cannot restore what they have broken. The good news is that God has done all that is needed to save His people through Jesus. Although the people of Nehemiah's day did not understand all that God intended to do in terms of rescuing people from sin, they had faith. That faith led them to trust in the mercy of God and rejoice in His visitation of truth upon them (vv. 11-12). The joy of the Lord was their strength.

Obedience always follows repentance. Having received the message, the people sought to obey God. They kept the festival, as commanded (vv. 13-18). What peace must have filled their souls as they experienced what it is to have a right standing with God!

Are you a student of the Scriptures? Are you making the necessary sacrifices to understand and obey the Bible? Are you experiencing the peace that comes with being right with God?

Those who read, understand, and obey the Bible live with peace.

How are we supposed to fight and have peace at the same time? Interestingly, there is a peace that God gives to those who fight the good fight of faith. Jesus said, *Do not think that I have come to bring peace to the earth. I have not come to bring peace, but a sword* (Matthew 10:34). This world is not as it should be. It is occupied by an ancient evil that Jesus came to vanquish. In Acts 19, God reveals His will and how He fights darkness.

Paul was a great man of war! During his missionary travels, he made disciples and saw many people set free from darkness. In Ephesus, a dozen men were saved (vv. 1-7). This was during the time when there was an overlap between the old and new covenants. Those who were saved had repented and had been baptized by John, but had not yet received the Holy Spirit. Today, all who believe are made alive by the Spirit and sealed by Him (Ephesians 1:13-14).

Having made disciples of some, Paul continued to teach, but he faced opposition (vv. 8-9). Soldiers of Christ should always anticipate opposition, but must continue in the work, as Paul did, until everyone has heard the gospel (v. 10).

Spiritual warfare was common in the first century. Demons revealed themselves plainly in order to intimidate and gain worshippers. This led to an industry of itinerant exorcists among the Jews. The sons of Sceva sought to use the names of Paul and Jesus to gain power over the darkness, but their faith was not genuine, and they were severely wounded (vv. 11-20). This caused Jesus and *the Way* (Acts 9:2; 19:9; 24:14) to gain more respect in the region.

The Way of Jesus became so prominent that the idol makers of Ephesus began to lose money (vv. 21-27). True revival will transform how a culture invests resources. A riot was stirred up (vv. 28-40). Thankfully, cooler heads prevailed (v. 41). This kind of disruption makes governments nervous. Spiritual victories in the name of Jesus will shake the pillars of society. Those who fight those fights live with peace, knowing they are doing God's will.

Are you fighting the good fight of faith? If you died today, would the enemies of God say, "I am glad that one is gone!"? Are you making disciples and praying for cultural change?

Those who battle under the banner of Jesus live with peace.

Genesis 21; Matthew 20; Nehemiah 10; Acts 20

Sometimes life is very scary. As long as a child of God is walking with God, according to His Word and in His will, the child of God can overcome any fear. The people mentioned in Genesis 21 were scared. God cared for them. He cares for all of His children.

Abraham and Sarah were given what God promised. Their life was filled with laughter. The name of their son Isaac means "laughter" (vv. 1-7). God provided for them in such a way that everyone had to agree that Isaac's life was miraculous. Only God could enable a man and woman near one hundred years old to have a child. God often provides in such a way that everyone knows it was He who did the work. God's goal is always His glory. Those who live to glorify Him will see God provide.

Where there are people, there will always be conflict. Even in the midst of this great blessing, Sarah saw Hagar's son laughing, and she assumed the worst, which led to Hagar and her son being cast out into the desert (vv. 8-10). God promised to provide for Hagar and her son, and He did (vv. 11-21). Things do not always go the way we want them to in life. Through all the conflict, loss, and pain, we can trust God to provide for His purpose.

God's miraculous provision gave Abraham all he needed, including the protection he needed for his family so he could accomplish God's purpose. He was in a vulnerable position compared to Abimelech, who approached Abraham with his commander, Phicol (v. 22a). They sought a treaty with Abraham, not because Abraham was great, but because his God is great (v. 22b). They entered into a covenant as equals (vv. 23-24).

Again there was conflict. This time it was regarding a well. Abimelech clarified his lack of knowledge of the issue, and the two men made an agreement (vv. 25-32). This well, Beersheba, "well of oath," became the name of this famous town, which marked the southern border of Israel (Genesis 26:33). This town was a reminder of God's provision for His purpose (vv. 33-34).

Are you pursuing God's purpose for His kingdom with your life? How have you seen God provide for you in the past? Can you trust God to provide for your future?

Those who live in God's will live with peace.

Genesis 22; Matthew 21; Nehemiah 11; Acts 21

We are inconsistent creatures. We can be happy and excited one day, and miserable the next. It is never wise to let other people's demeanor or actions determine our own. Regardless of what others say and do, God's people can confidently follow Jesus.

Sometimes Jesus will lead us in a triumphant parade where people gather and celebrate His presence (vv. 1-11). In those moments, the followers of Jesus must not rejoice in the crowds, but in the exaltation and the joy of following Jesus.

Sometimes Jesus will lead us to disrupt practices that distract from God's purpose and glory (vv. 12-17). In those moments, the followers of Jesus must be careful that their actions are not prideful or selfish, but truthful with love – tough love.

Sometimes Jesus will lead us to pursue difficult things (vv. 18-22). God expects His people to be fruitful and to live by faith. God expects us to pray for His purpose, even if it means praying that something we like must come to an end. In those moments, the followers of Jesus must be careful to walk by faith, trusting in what the power of God can do.

Sometimes Jesus will lead us to be strategically combative with our words (vv. 23-27). We must recognize the enemy and deal with evil in a direct and forceful way. In those moments, the followers of Jesus must be wise as serpents.

Sometimes Jesus will lead us to confront hypocrisy (vv. 28-32). God calls us to look beyond words and make judgments based upon deeds. In those moments, followers of Jesus must be extremely practical in their thoughts and judgments.

Sometimes Jesus will lead us to speak of the coming judgment of God (vv. 33-46) through Christ, when He will hold everyone accountable for their deeds. In those moments, we followers of Jesus must be assertive and creative in communicating the truth so that others will listen and under-stand our meaning.

Are you willing to say and do the hard things that Jesus demands of His people? Are you seeking the affirmation of Almighty God or of fallen people? Do others see and hear in you the heart of Jesus?

Those who follow Jesus will live with peace.

Genesis 23; Matthew 22; <u>Nehemiah 12</u>; Acts 22

It is not always easy to serve God, but it is almost always a joy. The priests who served during the days of Nehemiah served during difficult but glorious times. The list found in Nehemiah 12 reminds us that these were real people (vv. 1-26) who were serving a real cause (vv. 27-43) and were depending on real resources (vv. 44-47).

The listing of priests here is a reminder to all those whose names are listed in the Lamb's Book of Life (Revelation 21:27). All those who come to saving faith in Jesus Christ become members of the royal priesthood who serve under Jesus, as a holy nation (1 Peter 2:9). The redeemed of God now have direct access to the throne of grace through Jesus Christ (Hebrews 4:16). Each saint, having believed in Jesus, is now serving as a priest.

Those who served in the day of Nehemiah had a significant responsibility. It was not just the tasks they performed that were significant, but the One whom they represented was significant. Through their presence and work, the priests reminded the people that God was with them. As they sang and stood among the leaders, they celebrated the greatness of God. The sacrifices caused all to rejoice (v. 43). When God's people serve, there is much to celebrate.

The priests could not work for free. They had families to feed and care for. They were dependent upon the faithfulness of God's people to give. The Levites were not given land when they came into the land under Joshua (Joshua 18:7). They were to be provided for by the twelve tribes. In the days of Nehemiah, the people gave so that the Levites could serve (v. 47). A sign of a healthy church is generosity. When God's people give, the Lord is able to provide servant leaders who minister to the people. One of the issues that Nehemiah had to deal with later was the lack of provision for the Levites and their absence because of it (Nehemiah 13:10). When God's people will not provide for God's purpose, evil creeps in, and death is the result. Healthy congregations have generous members.

Are you serving God faithfully as one whose name is listed among the ransomed of God? Do you stand as a good representative of God to your family and friends? Are you generous in your giving?

Those who serve God live with peace.

We were made for harmony and peace. Chaos is what we are experiencing. There will always be disagreements on this planet. Conflict is the way of the world. The way of God is peace through love, understanding, and forgiveness. In Acts 23, the way of the world is seen in contrast to the way of God.

Paul was wrongly arrested and accused by the same people who wrongly arrested and accused Jesus (Acts 22). Because of Paul's arrest, the Roman authorities needed to know what charges to bring against him, so they sent him to the Sanhedrin, the ruling body of the Jews, to be questioned (Acts 23:10). The Sanhedrin was made up of Pharisees and Sadducees. The Pharisees believed in an afterlife and angels, but the Sadducees did not. Paul, a trained Pharisee, used their divided allegiances and proclaimed that his beliefs in an afterlife were the reason for his arrest. Paul believed that Christ would return and that all the saints will be gathered in glory, while sinners will be sentenced to eternity in hell.

God granted Paul peace in that moment. The words of Jesus must have been a great comfort to him (v. 11). God often calls His people to be in hard places and to do difficult things. The good news for God's saints is that He has a plan, and we simply need to obey Him.

Given the extreme threat that Paul represented to the religious leaders in Jerusalem, it is not surprising that a plot was put together to kill Paul (vv. 12-15). Paul's nephew acted heroically and made the plot known (vv. 16-22). God often uses the small and weak things of the world to accomplish His purpose.

Because of the threat to Paul, a Roman citizen, Paul was sent to Felix, the governor (vv. 23-35). The hand of God was all over this situation. The goal was to get the gospel to the ends of the earth. God provided Paul with Roman citizenship, Pharisaic education, and protective care. God's people can always have peace knowing that God is always providing for His purpose.

Are you living in God's purpose, or are you caught up in the divisions of the world? Do you sense God's approval and presence in your life? How has God provided for your path in life?

> *Those who pursue God's purpose, trusting in God's provision, live with peace.*

Genesis 25; Matthew 24; Esther 1; Acts 24

All relationships are complicated. Family relationships are the most crucial, but can be the most difficult. It is vital that disciples of Jesus do all they can to foster a culture of peace among their family members and choose to be peacemakers.

The first one hundred years of Abraham's life involved a lot of waiting. The last seventy-five years were significant in setting a trajectory for biblical history. Abraham's actions recorded in Genesis 25 provide an example of wisdom. He did all he could to foster peace in his home and to honor God's purpose (vv. 1-4). He had more children, but he designated Isaac, the child of promise, as his heir (v. 5). While he was alive, he sent the children he had with Keturah away from Isaac (v. 6). It is not always easy to define a family estate, but wise planning provides the best opportunity for peace.

At his death, Abraham's sons Isaac and Ishmael buried him (vv. 7-9). He was buried with his wife Sarah (v. 10), which communicated his desire to honor God and point to the blessing God had given Sarah (Genesis 17:16). That funeral could have been bitter, but it seems the boys both understood their place and honored their father. Both boys were blessed (vv. 10-18). This is the hope of every parent – that their children would be able to have peace with their siblings and be blessed in their lives.

The fact that Isaac's family becomes the focus of the story reminds us that God's plan is on track and will be realized through Isaac, as God promised. Just because Isaac is in God's will does not mean life will be easy. The birth of his sons was hard on his wife (vv. 19-26). The boys seemed to be at odds from birth (vv. 27-28). Jacob gaining the birthright was not random (vv. 29-34). Esau chose stew over divine blessing. His choice was under the sovereign hand of God. Jacob was the one through whom God would accomplish His purpose (Romans 9:13). We are all responsible for our decisions, but God's plan cannot be stopped.

Does your family enjoy peace among its members? Are you helping to foster peace within your family? Is God's plan for your life coming into focus, or is it a bit fuzzy?

Those who promote peace honor God and live
with peace in their hearts and minds.

Genesis 26; <u>Matthew 25</u>; Esther 2; Acts 25

The world is not as it should be, but it soon will be. Jesus will return! When Christ comes back, He will make all things new. Everything will be as it should be. Matthew 25 is a reminder to all the saints to be looking for Jesus (vv. 1-13), to be living in light of His judgment (vv. 14-30), and to help as many people as possible escape His righteous wrath (vv. 31-46).

The Lord has not kept His plan a secret. Jesus Christ came the first time, as promised, to save sinners. He will come a second time to judge the world and make everything as it should be. Those who know this truth are preparing for His return. It was the custom of the Jews to have the groom and groomsmen gather at the groom's house and then go to the bride's home for the wedding at night. The entire party and guests would then go to the groom's home to celebrate. Each person would need a lamp and would be responsible to have enough oil to keep it lit. Only those who are filled with the Spirit of God will enter into eternal life with Christ. Those who are Christ's look intently for His coming. Those who die without the Spirit will be cast out into the darkness forever.

God has invested His blood and Spirit in the saints of God. He has provided each one with gifts, talents, and opportunities. Jesus will judge each person for their work. The wise are living their lives in preparation for that great day! There is a great peace that resides in the heart of the person who is fulfilling God's will. It is liberating to live under God's righteous rule.

That great day of judgment will be a time of celebration for the redeemed of God, but those who have not been forgiven of their sin will not celebrate, but will suffer. The judgment of Jesus is a serious thing. The righteous will be brought into glory with their Master, while sinners will be cast out with Satan. No one will be able to alter their situation after the judgment of Jesus.

Are you prepared for the second coming of Christ? Are you using your gifts, talents, and opportunities to serve God's kingdom purpose? Are you helping sinners become saints in light of the judgment of Jesus?

Those who live for and are making preparations for
Christ's return and eternal reign live with peace.

Genesis 27; Matthew 26; <u>Esther 3</u>; Acts 26

From the beginning, the devil has sought to destroy the people of God. Having seduced the human race to surrender to his lies, he now has great power. He uses that power to make war against God and against God's most loved creation – people.

Anti-Semitism is not new. In Esther 3, we see that God's chosen people were once again in a foreign land and in grave danger. Haman was an Agagite (v. 1). The Agagites were an ancient enemy of Israel (Exodus 17:8-16). Agag was the king of the Amalekites. Saul defeated them, and the prophet Samuel killed Agag (1 Samuel 15) – but the people group was not wiped out. The hatred between Mordecai and Haman was intense. Mordecai refused to bow to him (v. 3:2). The people of God must never partner with injustice and hatred.

This put Haman, a very proud man, in a challenging position (vv. 3-5). His power was being questioned. This infuriated him and inspired him to want to kill all of the Jews in the world (v. 6). This conflict was under God's sovereign care. The Lord often allows His people to enter into threatening situations in order for His ultimate will and glory to be revealed.

Haman hatched a political plan that would have eradicated the Jews (vv. 7-14). He convinced King Ahasuerus that the Jews were a serious threat. The king did not seem at all concerned about who the people group was. He heard that there was a threat, and he trusted Haman and gladly submitted to the plan to have the Jews put to death throughout his kingdom. Wise people trust advisers, but they should always look to motive and consequences before acting.

The decree went out, but it was not well-received by the people of Susa (v. 15). They did not share Haman's hatred for the Jews. Apparently, the exiled Jews had obeyed Jeremiah 29:7 and had earned a good reputation. Followers of Jesus, who obey His commands, are a blessing to the society in which they live.

Are you mindful of the spiritual battle you are in because you are a child of God? Do you believe that God is truly in control and has a plan for every challenge you face? Do you have peace in every circumstance?

Those who love and serve God will be hated and threatened by God's enemies, but they will live with peace.

Genesis 28; Matthew 27; Esther 4; <u>Acts 27</u>

The way of Christ is not always easy or safe. Paul was called to take the gospel to Rome. He did this as a prisoner. Acts 27 shows how treacherous it was for Paul to get to Rome from Israel, but God was with Paul. This narrative reveals the challenge of life, the gift of leadership, and the provision of God for His people in tough, dangerous times.

Paul made his way to Rome with God's favor (vv. 1-12). Not only did he have Aristarchus, a trusted friend, along with him (v. 2), but he was also treated kindly by the centurion who was in charge over Paul (v. 3). Although Paul perceived danger and shared the centurion's concerns, his warnings were ignored and the lives of all of the passengers were placed in danger. God's people never need to feel as though they are victims in life. God is in control and always has a plan – a perfect plan that will produce what is best.

The boat carrying Paul went through a terrible storm (vv. 13-38). Life is very much like this journey Paul had – with treacherous circumstances and difficult people. God provides peace to those who are willing to look for Him in their difficulty. An angel spoke to Paul. God's Word speaks today. All who believe can stand with hope and call others to believe. Paul not only showed great strategic leadership, but he also showed compassion. He called on the men to eat and to have faith. Those who trust in God are able to rest in Him and share their peace with others.

The moment came to abandon ship, and God was gracious to Paul and to all who were on board (vv. 39-44). The Lord had used Paul in the midst of the storm to steady the minds and hearts of those in charge. When the soldiers were ready to kill the prisoners, the centurion stepped in for Paul's sake, and all made it safely to land (vv. 42-44). God has sent His Son, Jesus Christ, to save sinners. It is the responsibility of every saint to do all that is possible to share their hope in Christ and be of help to people in the world.

Has God seen you through a difficult storm in life? Are you a person whom others respect and listen to? Is God using you to be a blessing to others?

Those who trust in God's purpose and pursue His
plan in every circumstance live with peace.

Genesis 29; Matthew 28; Esther 5; Acts 28

Every good thing is not necessarily a blessing, and every hardship is not necessarily a curse. Good things can become replacements for God. Pain often pulls us toward God. God has a plan for everything His children go through. In Genesis 29, Jacob discovers his wife. We see that the fourteen years it cost him were a blessing, but those years were hard.

Jacob was on a journey seeking his destiny, as we all are. His specific pursuit at that time was a wife, and he met her at a watering well (vv. 1-12). Most of God's provisions come through very ordinary ways in ordinary places among ordinary people. We often want to experience something spectacular in our significant discoveries in life, and God will do that at times. Our destiny is usually found in normal life where ordinary things are occurring.

When Laban heard of Jacob's presence, he rushed to meet him. The two men came to an agreement concerning his payment for his work, as well as the cost for Rachel to become his wife (vv. 13-20). God was teaching Jacob a lesson through Laban, his uncle. The name *Jacob* means "swindler." He had swindled the birthright and blessing from his brother, Esau. Laban was a master swindler who took advantage of Jacob (vv. 21-30). God often allows us to experience pain and difficulty so we learn to trust and obey Him.

Jacob married both Leah and Rachel, but he only truly loved Rachel. God intervened and provided children through Leah only (vv. 31-35). This gave Leah hope that she would receive Jacob's love. We must be careful with our expectations. We often imagine that specific actions will produce certain outcomes. This is not always the case. We don't always get what we want. God knows what is best for us. God's will is that we find our identity and meaning in His love and grace. When we do, everything else is just a nice addition to what is needed. We need to know that we are loved and are valuable to God. This knowledge produces a deep, abiding peace so that we pursue our destiny free from the bondage of human inconsistency and aware of the world's weaknesses.

Are you pursuing your destiny with passion, or are you just floating from thing to thing in life? Do you trust God to provide for you in His way and in His time? Is Christ your identity and peace?

Those who honor God and trust His unseen hand live with peace.

Genesis 30; <u>Mark 1</u>; Esther 6; Romans 1

God does not promise that life will be easy, but He does promise to be with us every step of the way. In Mark 1, we read about how God was at work in the world through Jesus. That same Jesus is risen and alive in His people. He is taking care of them.

The ministry of Jesus was prepared for by John the Baptist (vv. 1-8). God promised through His prophets that He would send a messenger ahead of the Messiah who would announce the coming of the Son of God. John, Jesus' cousin, was given a unique ministry. It was not incidental. John and his parents were clear on what he was to do. He was to prepare the people to receive the Savior of the world. God provided.

Jesus was prepared for the ministry (vv. 9-13). First, He was baptized. This is now the first step of obedience for every disciple of Jesus. Jesus' baptism did not make Him anything. It announced who He already was. That is what baptism does. It announces who we are so we can stand in Christ, who was baptized and then went to war with the devil. Jesus did what Israel failed to do. He overcame temptation and lived a holy life that God provided.

Having been announced, baptized, and prepared for ministry, Jesus began to do His miraculous work of announcing the coming of the kingdom of God, raising up leaders, and healing the sick (vv. 14-45). He preached the good news that God had come to save sinners and transform lives. He called disciples to follow Him so they would be prepared to take leadership once He was crucified and raised. He changed people's lives through His miraculous healing power.

That is what Jesus is doing in the world now. Through His body, the church, He is announcing the coming of the kingdom of God into the world. Leaders are being trained up and prepared to oversee His sheep. Lives are being transformed by the grace of Jesus. Through the power of the resurrected Christ, people are being saved from sin, renewed with hope, and healed from the brokenness of sin. God is providing.

Have you accepted Jesus Christ as the Savior of your life? Are you serving as part of the body of Christ in the world? Are you fulfilling your calling and seeing people transformed by Jesus?

Those who look to the Lord to provide live with peace.

Genesis 31; Mark 2; Esther 7; Romans 2

Sometimes life is just not going to be easy. There is no permanent comfort here. Thankfully, we have an intercessor – Jesus Christ. He offered Himself to free us from destruction. Esther 7 pictures the work of Christ through the life of Esther.

Haman thought he had finally arrived in life. He was the king's trusted servant and was using his power to destroy the Jews he hated so much. Going with the king to his second feast that was provided by the queen assured him of his strong position (v. 1). This is the weakness of evil – pride is always followed by a fall, and evil cannot help but to be proud.

Having established herself as a trusted and true wife, Esther was prepared to use her position to serve God's purpose. At just the right moment, Esther risked her life and revealed her identity as a Jew (vv. 2-4). As a Jew, she had been sentenced to be killed by the king's own decree (Esther 3:9-11). She revealed that Haman had devised this scheme and was determined to destroy her and her people. Like Jesus, she risked her life so others could be saved.

The king left the room to determine what to do (Esther 7:7). When he returned, he found Haman on the couch with his wife (v. 8). He was perhaps begging for mercy, but it looked far less innocent to the angry king. It was reported to the king that the gallows that Haman had constructed upon which he intended to have Mordecai hanged (Mordecai was Esther's Jewish uncle who had earlier saved the king's life [Esther 2:19-23]) was available to serve justice against Haman (Esther 7:9). The king ordered that Haman be hanged, and after justice had been administered, the king's wrath was abated (v. 10). Through the sacrifice of Jesus, the wrath of God has been fully satisfied. Those who trust that the cost of their sin has been paid on Jesus' cross and that Jesus has been raised to give new life are saved. They have peace with God. One day the wrath of God will finally and fully fall on the devil and all who side with him. Only those who trust in Jesus have peace with God.

Do you believe that Jesus the Son of God, was sent by God, and that His death paid for your sin? Is His resurrected life alive in you? Do you believe that Christ is your advocate? Are you willing to sacrifice your life to serve God's purpose?

Those who trust in Jesus live with peace.

We are all struggling with our failures and hurts. Without grace, we have to do that alone. The gospel is the good news that we do not have to figure out life on our own. The gospel tells us that God has come to rescue us from our brokenness. Every person on the planet is in desperate need of the gospel. Everyone needs to be freed to pursue and recover God's original design for us by gaining a new life in Christ by faith. The gospel can heal us.

In the third chapter of Romans, Paul dealt with an important question concerning the gospel: If it is the gospel that saves, was there any value in his day to being Jewish (v. 1)? The answer is yes, for the Jews had been given the Old Testament (v. 2). Although they were not all faithful to this holy truth, God remained faithful to His promise of salvation (vv. 3-4). Grace does not make sin permissible. Grace brings about salvation (vv. 5-8). Salvation creates peace with God and produces a life that honors God and is victorious over sin.

Sin destroys all that is good in the world and in every person – both Jews and Greeks (v. 9). The seriously depraved situation that human beings are born into is sad (vv. 10-18). God is gracious to give the law so that people can see what God demands. Everyone will give an account to God for their sin (v. 19). No one can truly keep the law. The law reveals sin. It does not justify anyone (v. 20). The law reveals the need for what only the gospel can do.

Thankfully, the righteousness of God that was promised in the Old Testament is now available through faith to those who believe in Jesus Christ (vv. 21-22). All have sinned, but all can be justified through faith in Jesus (v. 23). The just wrath of God is satisfied in Jesus. Jesus is the propitiation – the sacrifice that appeases God's justice (vv. 24-26). Now all who trust in Jesus are made right with God – not because they keep God's law, but because they are justified by faith (vv. 27-31). The gospel is the power of God to set sinners (both Jews and gentiles) free from the power of sin.

Have you come to terms with the fact that you are a sinner in need of salvation? Are you trusting in Jesus or in your own merits to be saved? Is your life being changed by the gospel as you experience more and more freedom from sin?

Those who look to the gospel of God experience peace.

FEBRUARY 1
Genesis 33; Mark 4; Esther 9-10; Romans 4

Anger is a part of the human condition. Holding grudges and refusing to forgive others is not good. It hurts our relationship with God (Matthew 18:21-35). It also ruins relationships with other people. Genesis 33 tells us that Esau and Jacob were reunited and experienced peace. They have something significant to teach us. They were able to overcome hate for and fear of one another.

Jacob had every reason to fear Esau. Not only was Esau stronger and in possession of an intimidating armed force, but Esau had every reason to be angry with Jacob and to want to cause him harm (Genesis 27:42). By the time these two men met again, almost two decades had passed. Uncertain of how Esau felt about him, Jacob did what con men do. He sent bribes. He also humbled himself before his brother (vv. 1-3). Showing respect toward a person is a good first step in resolving conflict with that person.

Esau showed forgiveness toward his brother (v. 4). What a touching scene this must have been as these two men wept together! Tears of regret were probably mixed with tears of happiness. But was it genuine? As Esau questioned Jacob, there were probably doubts in Jacob's heart as to Esau's true feelings (vv. 5-11). Again, showing respect is a wise step in the process of making peace.

Having settled themselves into their relationship, Esau suggested that the two men begin to make their way home (v. 12). Jacob wisely pardoned himself from this plan and offered another way forward (vv. 12-16). Rather than traveling together and opening the door for potential future conflict, Jacob urged Esau to go on his way. Jacob then took a turn and made his way in the opposite direction. Sometimes space is the best way to keep peace. When two strong individuals who are set in their ways spend a lot of time together, sooner or later there is conflict. Jacob wisely chose to get some space between him and Esau.

Is there someone you need to forgive or seek forgiveness from? Are you being humble in your dealings with those with whom you have conflict? Are you being a peacemaker?

Those who are humble and wise have the best
opportunity to live with peace.

Everyone lives by faith in something. The object of our faith defines who we are and determines how we perceive and understand life. God is gracious to intervene in our lives and free us from whatever keeps us from Him. God wants us to experience truth and to be set free from lies and deceit. In Mark 5, God's power to liberate people is on display.

Having crossed the Sea of Galilee and performed a miracle on the way, Jesus encountered a demon-possessed man and healed him (vv. 1-13). The world is filled with demons, and there are instances of demon possession. This is a very serious condition and one that people would be wise to avoid. This person was in very bad shape, but no one is ever beyond the power of God to be healed. The demons in the man requested to be allowed to remain in the region and to be cast into some nearby pigs. Jesus complied, and the pigs drowned themselves. This reminds us of the goal of the devil – to steal, kill, and destroy (John 10:10).

The response of the people was sad. Rather than run out and worship Jesus, they asked Jesus to leave (vv. 14-17). The power of God is an awesome thing. Those who do not trust Jesus find it unappealing. They prefer Jesus to leave them alone. The liberated man wanted to go with Jesus, but the Lord sent him on a mission to share his hope with his family and friends (vv. 18-20). This is God's will for all who have been saved (Matthew 28:18-20; Acts 1:8).

Crossing to the other side of the sea, Jesus found more needs, including a dying girl and a woman who had suffered from a discharge of blood (vv. 21-26). Jesus was being rushed to the dying girl when the woman touched Him and was healed. Jesus stopped the entire procession to honor this woman and her faith (vv. 27-34). As He prepared to go heal the girl, word came that she had died. Jesus challenged her father to believe, and they continued to his home, where Jesus healed the girl (vv. 35-43). No one is beyond God's healing power. *What is impossible with man is possible with God* (Luke 18:27).

Has God healed you from sin and eternal death? Are you living by faith in God? Do you truly trust in God's power?

Those who are set free through faith in Jesus live with peace.

Genesis 35-36; Mark 6; Job 2; Romans 6

We all know that the world is messed up. The question is: Why? Why is there pain and suffering in the world? The simple answer is that the world is filled with sin and evil. God made the world to be perfect and in harmony, but because of the sin of humanity, the world is filled with suffering and pain. In Job 2, the spiritual battle taking place behind the scenes of the world stage is revealed.

Satan is a glory thief. He fell from heaven because he wanted to be worshipped in God's place (Isaiah 14:12-14). Since his fall, Satan has sought to take what is rightfully God's – all praise, glory, and honor – and secure it for himself. One of the ways he seeks to do that is by deceiving humanity into betraying God. He did this in the garden of Eden (Genesis 3). He also tried to do this with Job. Having taken the people and things that Job loved most, Satan expected Job to turn against God, but he didn't (Job 1). Job remained faithful to God to the praise of God's great name.

Having come before God again, Satan accused God of keeping Job in His holy hands by keeping Job physically comfortable (vv. 1-5). Unbeknownst to Job, God allowed Satan to strike Job's flesh (vv. 6-8). This put Job in physical agony. His wife told him to curse God and die because of his circumstances (v. 9). Job was faithful. He rebuked his wife and honored God (v. 10). He gave testimony to his faith. He was willing to receive from God whatever God determined to give him. Job did not sin against God. He remained faithful to God to the praise of God's great name.

In the midst of sorrow, one of life's great blessings is a circle of good and godly friends. Having heard of Job's suffering, some of his friends came to him (vv. 11-13). He was so marred from his sores that they did not recognize him at first. For seven days they sat with him and grieved. That is what good friends do. They recognize our pain and console us with their presence. If they had just sat with Job, they would have been a blessing.

What might tempt you to turn your back on God? Are you willing to receive the good and difficult things from God's hand? Do you belong to a group of faithful friends?

Those who choose to trust God's good-
ness no matter what live with peace.

Genesis 37; Mark 7; Job 3; <u>Romans 7</u>

Before I became a Christian, my heart was very hard. Grace gave me a new heart. One of the great transformations that occurs in the life of a person who is born again is the ability to care. Jesus gives believers new hearts. While every human being has a conscience, not every person is aware of the damning effects of sin. Those who believe in Jesus understand the seriousness of sin and hate it. In Romans 7, Paul speaks to the spiritual mindset that exists in every true disciple of Jesus.

Everyone is born under the law of God (vv. 1-3). That law condemns us all because every person who has ever lived on the planet, other than Jesus Christ, has broken God's law. Those who are in Christ are released from living under the law and are made free to live under the grace of Jesus in the Spirit (vv. 4-6). This is an entirely new way of life that is received by faith.

God's law is not bad. It is good. Without the law, we would not know what sin is (vv. 7-14). With that knowledge of what is good and evil, our flesh found enticement. Thankfully, Jesus liberates sinners from both the punishment and the power of sin. Without Jesus, people remain subject to sin and are slaves to sin's power. Without Jesus, people will be punished for their sin.

In His grace and for His glory, God gives those who are saved by grace through faith in Jesus a new desire. Although we continue to sin, we do not want to. We continue to do what we do not want to do because we are still in fallen flesh in a fallen world (vv. 15-20). The new life that comes through Christ enables a person to recognize sin for what it is and provides a new desire to honor Jesus and live in peace with God.

Followers of Jesus are stuck in a tough spot (vv. 21-25). They are free to live in the way of Jesus, but sin is still at work. Thanks be to God, Jesus Christ has come. We can now live by the power of the Spirit and have peace in our soul. We can know we are right with God in our hearts, even though we still struggle with sin.

Are you giving in to sin or are you struggling with sin? There is a difference.

Do you desire to honor God with your life? Have you been given new life in Christ by grace through faith?

Those who hate sin and pursue Jesus have peace with God.

<u>Genesis 38</u>; Mark 8; Job 4; Romans 8

God is mysteriously glorious and beyond what we human beings can comprehend. God gives us the faith to believe He exists and rewards those who seek Him. Faith in God is not blind. It is based upon what God has made known of Himself in creation (Romans 1), His Word (Psalm 119), and His Son (Hebrews 1).

Judah did not live a life of peace. He was a man plagued with problems – many that were of his own making. Like most people, Judah imagined himself capable of accomplishing greatness by doing things as he pleased. Genesis 38 tells that the failure of Judah and his progeny to trust God caused catastrophe. When God is not honored and His law is ignored, problems abound and pain persists.

Judah went his own way, away from the family of God, and formed a family with a Canaanite (vv. 1-5). Getting away from God's family and walking with those who do not know God never ends well. Judah's sons walked in the ways of their father. One son was killed, and the others refused to take responsibility for their brother's widow, Tamar, which led to another death. Judah's unwillingness to put any of his other sons in harm's way resulted in Tamar going back home with her parents and having no hope (vv. 6-11). When men won't lead, women suffer for it and are required to fend for themselves.

Rather than remain alone and forgotten, Tamar deceived Judah and became pregnant by him (vv. 12-23). Trapped in his folly and with his sin revealed, Judah did the right thing. He took Tamar as his wife. She bore him two sons, Perez and Zerah (vv. 24-30). These three people – Tamar, Perez, and Zerah – are listed in the family line of Jesus Christ (Matthew 1:3). This is another reminder of the goodness and power of God to work all things for good according to His divine purpose and eternal plan.

Life would have been easier for everyone if Judah had just trusted and obeyed God. People who are living faithfully to God have peace in their lives.

Are you trusting God with your life, or are you going your own way? Do you make decisions based upon your own thoughts and feelings void of the Word of God? Are you doing what is right by others according to the Word of God?

Those who trust and obey God live with peace.

Genesis 39; Mark 9; Job 5; Romans 9

In Mark 9, God the Father spoke of His Son in very specific terms and exalted Him above all others. Jesus revealed His identity through His healing power, His victory over death, and His call to holiness. Jesus truly is glorious, powerful, and terrifying.

Peter, James, and John were blessed to know Jesus in special and unique ways. Having promised that some would see the kingdom of God with power (v. 1), Jesus allowed these three to see Him transformed in His glory (vv. 2-3). Moses and Elijah showed up, and it appears that Peter imagined that Jesus was their equal (vv. 4-6). God the Father made it very clear that there is none like Jesus. He is God's Son. They were to listen to Him (v. 7). They were awestruck with terror, but Jesus comforted them and assured them that God's plan was on track (vv. 8-13). The world was raging, but God was implementing His promised plan, as He always does.

Meanwhile, the other disciples were at the bottom of the hill struggling to cast out a demon (vv. 14-18). Jesus stepped in and healed the boy (vv. 19-27). Afterward, the disciples asked Jesus why they were not able to heal him (v. 28). *And he said to them, "This kind cannot be driven out by anything but prayer"* (v. 29). In this fallen world, prayer is the ultimate power and the means by which God's will is accomplished. God's people must pray!

Having seen Jesus' displays of power, the disciples began to do a very human and sinful thing. They ignored the fact that Jesus had just explained that He was going to die and be resurrected (vv. 30-32). Their focus was too much on themselves and on who among them was the greatest (vv. 33-34). Jesus explained that the greatest one is the servant of all who cares for the least and for the seemingly insignificant in the world (vv. 35-37), who looks to partner with kingdom-minded people (vv. 38-41), and who hates sin and is willing to do hard things to live a holy life (vv. 42-50). Those whom God blesses are sacrificial saints who care more about the glory of Jesus, prayer, helping others, and being holy than about themselves.

Are you living to exalt the name of Jesus? Do you gladly serve others? Is your primary aim to live a holy life that honors God?

Those who honor Jesus and live for Him have peace.

Genesis 40; Mark 10; Job 6; Romans 10

True, fulfilling peace is found in Christ alone. There are many comforts that a Christian can occasionally count on, such as the comfort of a spouse (Ecclesiastes 4:9-12), the reliability of friends (Proverbs 17:17), and a God-honoring life (Psalm 1). Along with the physical suffering that Job endured, he also had to deal with emotional and spiritual pain caused to his heart and mind by his circumstances and counselors. Job 6 tells Job's response to the attack of Eliphaz, his so-called friend (Job 4-5).

Job's friends believed that those who suffer are in their plight because of their sin. The fact is that the righteous do suffer (Psalm 73), but not like the unrighteous. Job suffered because he was right with God. God chose to use Job's life for an eternal purpose. Job was like Jesus in this. He was able to do what Peter commanded (1 Peter 3:14-17). God's people can go through pain and still have peace because they know that God is good and that His plan is perfect.

Job did not want to go through this suffering. He wanted to die (vv. 8-9). Job knew that he had not sinned against God (v. 10). He lost His appetite and his desire to live (vv. 1-7). His strength was gone (vv. 11-13). His friends were of no help (vv. 14-27). His desire was for his friends to turn away from him (vv. 28-30). God will often allow His children to suffer so that they no longer look to find comfort in created things.

Job's experience is unique, but those who suffer can certainly identify with him and learn his lesson. Job learned that God is always good. Even when we hurt, God is good. Now in heaven, Job can look back on His life and rejoice at the honor that was his. He was allowed to suffer and to stand for God in a most horrendous battle. He won! He kept his faith (2 Timothy 4:7). There is no greater honor or victory than to win the fight of faith. Job provided a picture of the coming of Christ, who would suffer for God's glory to bring about salvation through His suffering.

Are you able to trust God, even when every earthly comfort is taken from you? At your death, will you hear Jesus say, *Well done*? Will you keep the faith?

> **Those who rely on God completely are able
> to experience authentic peace.**

We all have good days and bad days. Over time, everyone chooses a rhythm for their life – when they do what they do, and how they do it. Without a passionate pursuit of God's truth, human beings tend to fall into an unwise way of life. This is certainly true of faith communities. At times, God's people have lost sight of God and have replaced Him with a system of their own making.

The Jews abandoned the God of the Bible and became enamored with their own rules and messianic expectations. Romans 11 outlines the outcome of their lack of dedication. God allowed them to wander from the biblical promises and pursue their own identity and desires. These zealots put Christ to death. They were unwilling to look to their Bibles and believe the miracles of Jesus. Even though they rejected God, God did not reject the nation outright. There was a remnant (vv. 1-10). Just as there was a remnant at the time of Elijah, so there was a remnant at the time of Jesus and Paul. There is a remnant now. Many will be lost by pursuing false religion and things other than Christ, but yet some will be found faithful. Those who are faithful to Christ will have lasting peace.

The rejection of Israel was anticipated by God. His plan was always to graft in the gentiles and to bless the whole world (Genesis 12:1-3; John 3:16). The branch of the Jews that was broken off was used by God to graft in the gentiles (vv. 11-24). God's family tree is magnificent to behold. It is made up of all nations! The colors and languages that will be in heaven will be part of the glorious praise to our saving God (Revelation 7:9-10).

The Jews have not been forgotten. God's Word stands. Although there has been a partial hardening for the purpose of God, the Lord will move among the Jews and will save a people from among them for Himself (vv. 25-36). The gospel has the power to change minds, hearts, and lives. Even those from the most rigid, unaccepting theological systems can be saved. Even those with the most apathetic hearts can be saved. Even those with the most sinful lifestyles can be saved. This is the power of God!

Have you come to saving faith in Jesus? Are you a member of God's family tree through faith in Jesus?

Those who remain faithful to God live with peace.

Genesis 42; Mark 12; Job 8; Romans 12

Deep emotional wounds can sometimes be hard to heal. When those closest to us cause us harm, the pain is intense. Finding peace is possible with God. Holding grudges and living with hate destroys the soul.

Genesis 42 describes when Joseph was given his first chance to exact revenge on his brothers for selling him into slavery. These men had done a horrible thing to him. They had robbed him of a life with his beloved father. They had robbed him of a life of comfort. Because of them, he had to live as a slave, a prisoner, and an Egyptian. Like Jesus, Joseph was taken from his home, from his father, and from his comfort in order to serve, struggle, and suffer so others could be saved.

While his actions were understandable, it is not clear why Joseph treated his brothers the way he did. When he saw them, he remembered the dream that they would bow before him (v. 9). He understood their conversation, and he wept (v. 24). There was a lot going on with Joseph mentally and emotionally in that moment. In His grace and for His glory, God gave Joseph a plan. The goal of the plan was to provide opportunities for more interaction with his family to ascertain their character and how he would relate to them. God does the same with His children. He has a plan that requires them to live by faith. It challenges their character. How the children of God respond to their circumstances and to God determines how God relates to them.

Ultimately, Joseph showed mercy to his brothers (Genesis 45 and 50). Genesis 42 describes Israel and his sons being very concerned about their circumstances. Simeon had been imprisoned by Joseph (v. 24), the money had been put back in their bags so it could be said that they had stolen from Egypt (v. 28), and their father was desperate to keep Benjamin from harm, having lost Simeon and Joseph already (v. 36). We cannot understand much of what happens to us in life, but we can know that God has a plan for everything we face.

Do you trust God with the plan of your life? Are you willing to forgive those who have hurt you, or are you determined to harm yourself with hate by holding grudges?

Those who are able to forgive others because Christ has
forgiven them will be freed to live with peace.

There is a lot that can distract and rob a child of God from having peace. The world is broken. People are hurting. Social systems and structures fail. Nothing is certain – except the love and grace of God.

Jesus made it clear in Mark 13 that this world is headed to a cataclysmic end. This is not difficult for some to imagine, but others are like the disciples in Jesus' day who looked in wonder at the temple edifice and thought it was amazing (v. 1). Jesus shattered their exhilaration and said plainly, *There will not be left here one stone upon another* (v. 2). This prompted the disciples to ask about the end of the world and the signs that would lead up to it (vv. 3-4). Jesus explained that there will be lots of confusion, lies, disasters, and famines (vv. 5-8). He warned them to stay on guard (v. 9). The gospel would first go to all nations (v. 10), but in the process, the disciples of Jesus would be persecuted (vv. 11-12). Those who endure to the end will be saved (v. 13). Life is going to be hard here, but God is with us and will provide. He is our peace.

When the Antichrist comes, as Daniel prophesied (Daniel 9:27; 11:31; 12:11), the people of God will need to flee (vv. 14-18). This will be a terrible time (v. 19). God will be gracious for the sake of His people (v. 20). There will be great confusion, and people will claim to be Christ (vv. 21-22). God's people will have to be wise (v. 23). This is true of the end, and it is even true now. Be wise!

After a time of struggle, there will be signs in the skies, and the Lord will return (vv. 24-27). The explanation in 1 Thessalonians 4:13-18 is helpful. God will make plain what is happening (vv. 28-30). Thankfully, God's Word will always guide the faithful (v. 31). The day of Christ's return is not known (vv. 32-36). What is known is that God is in control. God not only knows what is going to happen, but He has a plan for each of us. We do not need to worry. We can walk with Jesus and trust Him. He is our peace.

Do you trust Jesus Christ as your Savior and ruler? Is He your peace at all times? Are you living in light of His second coming, when He will judge the world?

Those who look to the Lord in faith and trust Him at all times and with all things will experience peace.

Genesis 44; Mark 14; <u>Job 10</u>; Romans 14

When life does not go as we planned, it is easy to question God and His intentions toward us. It may seem at times that the Lord is against those He has saved by grace, but He is never against His people. He is for His people. Because He loves us as children and desires to bring glory to His name through our lives, He will allow us to go through difficult days. These days are intended to strengthen us.

Job had lost his peace. He could not understand God's intentions toward him. In Job 10, Job outlines his concerns. It is such a blessing to know that God truly understands and empathizes with us. Although He is God, He became one of us, so He knows what it is to suffer and struggle as a human. We can talk with God about our struggles (Hebrews 4:15-16). Job shared his heart with God. He did not understand why God was against Him (vv. 1-6). He knew that he needed a deliverer (v. 7), he knew that God had made him (vv. 8-11), he knew that God loved him and cared for him (vv. 12-13), and he knew that nothing is hidden from God (vv. 14-17); he just couldn't figure out why God was doing what He was doing (vv. 18-22).

We will not always understand why God allows and does what He does, but we can always know that if we knew what He knew, if we had the power and love He has and could work out a plan with providence as He can, we would completely agree with Him. Job did not agree with what God was doing. Job was physically, emotionally, and spiritually exhausted. Strangely enough, when we suffer for Christ's sake, that is when we ought to consider ourselves the strongest (2 Corinthians 12:10).

The world, the flesh, and the devil despise weakness. It is a fatal flaw to the powers of darkness. For children of God, weakness is a strength. When we have given up on our own abilities and trust ourselves to God completely, then God's power is released. There is no limit to God's power! He gives us His strength when we surrender ourselves to Him completely.

Are you completely trusting God's love and plan for your life? Can you endure suffering with peace? Has God taught you to trust Him in difficulty before?

Those who are assured of God's love for them and are confident that He has saved them live with peace.

In helping others, we help ourselves. Serving the needs of the world is the way and will of Jesus. The greatest blessing in all of the world is to be a blessing. God's glory is seen in His blessings given with grace to sinners. We are most satisfied when we are able to trust God and choose to be helpful to others in the name of Christ. In Romans 15, believers are commanded to pursue the deep satisfaction of being like Jesus and to choose to serve others.

Brothers and sisters in Christ are to constantly look out for one another. Each believer is susceptible to sin in different ways. Those who are free from addictions and sinful habits must be sensitive to those who struggle (v. 1). The goal of God's people is to build others up and assist them in their lives in Christ (vv. 2-3). This is what it means to be like Christ.

This way of Christ is not new. The Old Testament speaks to it just as well as the New Testament does (v. 4). Those who heed the Word of God and endure by faith have hope. This faith leads to harmony in every aspect of a saint's life (vv. 5-6). The blessing comes by being like Christ and putting the needs of others first. The secret to happiness is blessing others (v. 7).

God's plan from the beginning was to save a people for Himself, so He chose Abraham and the patriarchs. Through these very flawed people, God's grace was made manifest and His sovereign power was displayed in bringing Christ into the world through Israel (vv. 8-12). Born-again believers (John 3) are able to experience joy, peace, and hope in the Holy Spirit (v. 13).

Paul was convinced that the Romans were mature, Christlike believers, and he shared his ultimate vision with them (vv. 14-21). He invited them to join in the work he was doing by supporting him in his effort (vv. 22-33). Having established the need and theology for his mission, Paul invited these godly people to gain an eternal blessing by helping him.

Are you putting the needs of others before your preferences? Are you experiencing the happiness of being a blessing? Is God working in and through your life?

Those who bless the church have peace with God and others.

Genesis 46; Mark 16; Job 12; Romans 16

Regret is a terrible thing! We only have one shot at life, and it is crucial that we waste no time lamenting what could have or should have been. All we can do is live as best we can now by pursuing God and trusting Him to provide for the future. In Genesis 46, Israel (Jacob) and his family showed great wisdom.

Having heard that Joseph was alive and that resources had been made available for him and his family, Israel chose to move to Egypt. Rather than getting mad about what had been missed, Israel took a moment to praise and worship God (v. 1). God honored his heart of worship and met with him and spoke to him. God gave Israel hope and a future (vv. 2-4). God is sovereign. The world and the people in it are broken. Despite all of the sin and evil in the world, God's will is done. Life may not be as we want it to be, but we can trust that God is at work and will provide for His people.

Although Israel had experienced loss, he had been blessed. He had great resources and a large family. When they moved to Egypt, it was not a quick or uncomplicated event. There were a lot of people and livestock to move (vv. 5-7). The names listed remind us that God knows every person and cares for every single one of us (vv. 8-27). We may just be a number to the world, but to God we are precious. He knows our names. Our lives matter to God.

Judah took the lead (v. 28). He would soon receive a great blessing, and the Messiah would come from his family line (Genesis 49:8-12). Joseph made preparations and went to his father and cried and cried (v. 29). Rather than get angry, Israel rejoiced in the moment and honored Joseph with love (v. 30). Then Joseph prepared his father and brothers to receive the blessing of Pharaoh. The plan was to put space between the Egyptians and the Israelites so Israel could thrive as a people distinctly set apart as people who were the recipients of the promises of God (vv. 31-34). God's people must always be wise and must be in the world, but not of it.

Are you able to be content and thankful for what is and for what can be? Do you wallow in regret? Can you look to God with hope and live wisely?

Those who can embrace the moment and go forward by faith live with peace.

Genesis 47; Luke 1:1-38; Job 13; 1 Corinthians 1

We will not always understand how God will provide and accomplish His purpose in the world. He does not expect us to. God expects us to simply receive His Word by faith and believe. In Luke 1, Zechariah and Mary received a message from God. One of them questioned, and the other one simply believed.

Luke, the physician and friend of Paul, was chosen by God to write one of the four Gospel books in the Bible, as well as the book of Acts. His historical account is considered one of the greatest writings in all of Greek literature. His Gospel was given so that both Jews and Greeks could know the hope of the world (vv. 1-4). Each of the four Gospels was inspired by the Spirit and was given by God to help us know the truth and to be set free by grace.

Zechariah was a Levite. He and his wife, Elizabeth, were not able to conceive (vv. 5-7). He was selected to enter into the holy of holies to burn the incense. This was a high honor (vv. 8-9). While there, an angel appeared to him and promised that he and his wife would have a blessed son (vv. 10-17). Rather than just receive this blessing, he asked for a sign and became unable to speak (vv. 18-23). Elizabeth conceived and was very happy (vv. 24-25). When God speaks, we must trust and obey. We might not understand how or why, but that's okay. We must believe without doubting.

Mary received a similar promise (vv. 26-33). She did not ask for a sign. She believed, but she wondered how God's will would be done (v. 34). Gabriel provided her with an explanation, but it was an explanation that neither she nor we could possibly fully comprehend (v. 35). We cannot comprehend the incarnation, but we can believe it. God also told Mary of Elizabeth's blessing as proof of God's power and promise (vv. 36-37). Mary gladly submitted. This is what God expects of His children. We might not fully grasp God's ways, but we can trust Him and choose to honor and accept His will.

Are you willing to receive God's Word and obey it no matter what? Can you trust that God is bigger than any circumstance you may face and is able to accomplish His purpose? Do you believe that God really is all-powerful and good and can be trusted?

Those who choose to trust God and happily submit to His will and way of life live with peace.

Genesis 48; Luke 1:39-80; <u>Job 14</u>; 1 Corinthians 2

Satan will often tempt us to despair. The Evil One no longer has dominion over the lives of the redeemed, but he does have the ability to accuse us of sin and cause us to doubt God's redemptive love and our ability to live out God's redemptive plan. Zophar, Job's so-called friend, criticized Job for his apparent lack of faithfulness by stating that if Job had truly been faithful to God, his life would have been bright and happy instead of dark and painful (Job 11:17). As seen in Job 14, this honest and honored saint stood his ground and spoke to the reality of all people.

Job was not under any delusion that he was better than anybody else. He knew that he was human and frail (vv. 1-2). What he found interesting and clarifying was that he was being judged by those who were no different than him (v. 3). There is no place for pride in any human heart (vv. 4-6). The best we can do is try and make life a little easier for others by not condemning them and making them feel uniquely cursed. We are all weak, sinful creatures doomed to live a short, troubled life and die a physical death. That fact is also liberating. We are not experiencing something strange when we suffer; this is the way of the world.

There are opportunities for renewal and reconciliation in life, but not in death (vv. 7-17). A tree that is cut down can sprout again with water. People who are cut down in death can only remain in their condition for eternity. Job looks to the hope that is to come in Christ through His resurrection (v. 12). He also looks to the hope of redemption in Christ (v. 14). Those who are redeemed in Christ and are looking forward to the second coming of Jesus can see life's trials as momentary afflictions and can look forward to eternity (2 Corinthians 4:17). Hope in heaven is where real peace is found.

Those who seek to find meaning and peace in this life will always be disappointed (vv. 18-22). The Evil One tempts us with this and accuses us when we do seek to find meaning and peace in this life. God's people find hope in grace and enjoy meaning in God's love and the promise of eternity.

Is your hope in heaven? Do you see your trials in light of eternity? Are you confident in your salvation?

Those who can trust God despite the painful realities that exist in this life live with peace.

Genesis 49; Luke 2; Job 15; <u>1 Corinthians 3</u>

What does it mean to be a mature Christian? There are many opinions on that. Some think that maturity is having Bible knowledge. Some think that maturity is having certain spiritual experiences and abilities. Some think that spiritual maturity is having a certain level of discipline that produces a distinct ethical lifestyle. In 1 Corinthians 3, Paul mapped out what it means to be mature in Christ. His words will surprise some religious people.

At the time when Paul wrote this letter, he had hoped to be able to address the church at Corinth in a spiritually mature way, but unfortunately, they were not ready for that kind of conversation (vv. 1-3). The church was still looking at life from an earthly perspective, and each person was focusing on following the church leader whom they preferred (v. 4). The truth is that God uses people for His purpose, but only God can bring about life change (vv. 5-9). Those who make idols of Christian leaders rather than focus on following Christ are not mature.

Every Christian has a job in God's plan (v. 10). Paul was used by God to lay the foundation, which is Christ (v. 11). The people were being formed into the building that houses Christ (vv. 12-17). Each person will have to give an account for the life they built. If they lived for Christ, then their reward will survive the flaming judgment that is to come. Mature believers live to become beautiful Christ-dwellings that honor Jesus.

The world offers a kind of wisdom that is actually foolish in light of the coming of Christ (v. 18). Godly, mature disciples of Jesus live in light of heaven, which the world thinks is a crazy way to live (vv. 19-20). The world is crazy! Disciples of Jesus do not boast in the things of man or trust in the things of man (vv. 21-22). Mature disciples look to Christ and find their life in Him alone. He is the provider and sustainer of life. Jesus is the plan, purpose, and power!

Are you a mature Christian? Do you find your identity in the person and work of Christ, or are you defined by your allegiance to a man-made system or personality? Are you living wisely in light of the coming of Jesus?

Those who know what it is to be mature in Christ and consistently seek to attain and sustain that life live with peace.

Genesis 50; Luke 3; Job 16-17; 1 Corinthians 4

God made us to be in families. Our family connections have the capacity to create some of the most precious bonds, as well as some of the most painful experiences. Joseph loved his family, but he was hurt by them. Having been sold into slavery by his brothers and forced to live in a faraway country on his own (Genesis 30-49), he could have become a bitter man. He had professional success, but the familial hurt was there. In Genesis 50, Joseph's faith is revealed.

Having secured his family in Egypt, there was peace. Joseph was able to be with his father when he died. He wept for his father (v. 1). He cared for his father's remains (vv. 2-3a). The Egyptians wept for seventy days with Joseph (v. 3b). Israel had made his desires known as to how his remains were to be cared for, and Joseph did what was requested (vv. 4-6). When Joseph buried his father, he did not go alone. The leaders of Egypt, along with all of Israel's household, went to weep and bury Israel, and then they all returned (vv. 7-14). In this world, there is death when a loved one is lost, and those who enjoy peace endure a time of weeping.

Once Joseph's brothers returned to their homes in Egypt after burying their father, they prepared for the worst. They assumed that Joseph would turn on them now that their father was dead (vv. 15-18). Those who have wicked hearts often assume that others will do to them as they would do to others if they had the opportunity. Joseph had come to trust God and to see His hand in what had occurred (vv. 19-20). Those who can look at their lives from the perspective of God's eternal purpose can endure great suffering, yet still have peace.

Joseph lived a long and blessed life. When it came time for him to die, he gave specific instructions for his remains. He did not want to be buried immediately with his father. He wanted to be a testimony and reminder of the covenant of God. He was embalmed, and his body was placed in a coffin to await the day the people of Israel would return to the promised land (vv. 21-26). One day, Christ will return. All who are in Christ will be raised and, by the power of God, taken into heaven – the promised land.

Are you at peace with God, yourself, and others? Are you a peacemaker? Do you need to seek or give forgiveness?

Those who trust God and see life from a
divine perspective live with peace.

Exodus 1; <u>Luke 4</u>; Job 18; 1 Corinthians 5

Having established that Jesus is the Son of God (Luke 3:22), and having established His genealogy to Adam (Luke 3:23-38), Luke describes in chapter four of his Gospel how Jesus was led into the desert to be tempted. This is how Jesus began His ministry. He went into the desert to do what only He could do. He was tempted, but never sinned. From there, Jesus went on to heal the sick and preach the gospel.

When Jesus encountered the devil in the desert, He was weak. He had eaten nothing for forty days, and then the devil came after Him (vv. 1-2). Each temptation revealed the schemes of the devil. Satan wants God's people to depend on physical strength alone. Jesus made clear that we are to live by the Spirit and not by bread alone (vv. 3-4). Satan also wants God's people to avoid taking up the cross, and instead just worship him and try to make the world a better place. Jesus made clear that we are to worship God alone and continue in the way of God that leads to salvation by faith (vv. 5-8). Satan wants God's people to try to force the hand of God to do as they want rather than as God wills. Jesus made clear that we are to let God lead us rather than try to manipulate and test God (vv. 9-12). Satan did not succeed, so he waited for another opportune time to tempt Jesus (v. 13). The devil is never done with us. He is always looking for ways to trip us up.

Victoriously, Jesus went in the power of the Holy Spirit and began to fulfill His ministry assignment. Word about Him spread (vv. 14-15). They rejected Him in His hometown of Nazareth (vv. 16-30). Despite their rejection, Jesus continued in His purpose. We must never let people determine who we are or what we do. We must obey God. Jesus obeyed the Father's will. He healed people of demon possession (vv. 31-37) and sickness (vv. 38-41), and He also preached (vv. 42-44). God's people are to bring hope and healing by proclaiming the gospel and living in the power of the Holy Spirit.

Are you defined by God and His grace? Do you know the Bible well enough to fight temptation? Are you spreading the gospel?

Those who overcome temptation and bring healing and
light into the world as Jesus did live with peace.

Exodus 2; Luke 5; Job 19; 1 Corinthians 6

Jesus Christ suffered and died so that sinners can have peace with God. The just punishment humanity deserved was placed on Him. Jesus is holy. He, who never sinned, was condemned. Jesus suffered to save us from our sin. In Job 19, the suffering of Christ is pictured in Job's life. Job was not holy, but his sin was not what caused His suffering. God's will was for Job to suffer for God's glory. This is not an easy truth to understand or experience.

Job was accosted and tormented by his friends (vv. 1-5). Jesus was confronted by the religious leaders of His day and tormented by them when He was dying on the cross. They mocked Him and said, *He saved others; he cannot save himself. He is the King of Israel; let him come down now from the cross, and we will believe in him* (Matthew 27:42). Jesus could not come down if He was to save sinners. He chose to suffer so we could be saved.

Job cried out to God, but felt the Lord's wrath and abandonment (vv. 6-12). It was nothing like what Jesus experienced. Job only felt abandoned, while God the Father actually turned away from Jesus. Jesus cried out, *My God, my God, why have you forsaken me?* (Matthew 27:46). The wrath of God was poured out on Jesus so that the righteous requirements of the law would be met and sinners could be saved.

Job was also abandoned by his friends and family (vv. 13-22). Jesus knew this pain as well. His brothers doubted His identity (John 7:3-5). The disciples of Jesus abandoned Him when He was arrested in the garden of Gethsemane (Matthew 26:56). Christ had to die alone to redeem His people.

Job was not hopeless. He had the faith to look beyond his circumstances to God (vv. 13-29). He believed that his Redeemer lived and that he would see God. Jesus also had hope. He knew that He would die, but would be raised victorious on the third day to reign at the right hand of God (Matthew 26:64). Jesus and Job suffered because they were righteous in accomplishing God's will.

Do you trust in Jesus to save you from sin? Is Jesus your delight? Are you walking in the way of Jesus gratefully?

Those who believe in God's grace and love that made Jesus to suffer so that sinners can be saved experience ultimate peace.

Exodus 3; Luke 6; Job 20; <u>1 Corinthians 7</u>

Relationships make life meaningful. At the same time, relationships are the cause of much of the anxiety and pain in life. When people are involved in each other's lives, conflicts are bound to arise. It is sad, but true, that everyone is at all times either in the midst of, getting into, or coming out of a conflict. In 1 Corinthians 7, Paul spoke to the challenges that exist in family life and in kingdom responsibilities. Marriage, vocation, and service to God are not easy, but we must not let the difficulty keep us from enjoying the blessings they bring, even though they are hard.

Paul was not against marriage, but he encouraged those who could remain single to do so since time is limited. Christ is soon returning. Paul's reasoning was charitable. He said in verse 32, *I want you to be free from anxieties.* Relationships, especially marriages, are stressful. God made marriage to be a blessing; Paul in no way condemned it. Paul's message was clear: if you have to get married, then be married well and be a godly spouse (vv. 1-5). Marriage is a picture of the gospel (Ephesians 5). It is a blessing to society, but it is not easy. The person who chooses to be married chooses a good thing, yet Paul would have liked everyone to be single even more (vv. 6-8).

God made humanity with sexual desire, and a marriage between a man and a woman is the only condition in which sexual intimacy is appropriate. Paul encouraged those who could not restrain their sexual desire to marry (v. 9). To those who marry, Paul gave clear expectations as to how they were to live (vv. 10-16).

God has a particular purpose for every person's life. Paul encouraged people to fulfill their destiny and pursue God's perfect plan for them in the place God puts them (vv. 17-24). Rather than wish for a different life, we each must make the most of the life that God has given to us. It will be difficult at times, especially for those who lose their spouse (vv. 25-40). Each widow and widower must carefully consider whether or not to remarry.

Is God calling you to be single or married? Are you being faithful in your calling? Do you see your place in life as God's plan and as a mission field?

Those who pursue what God wants will live with peace.

FEBRUARY 21

Exodus 4; Luke 7; Job 21; 1 Corinthians 8

Every child of God has a particular calling for their life that God has given to them. To fulfill God's plan, the redeemed of God must live by faith. The journey we must take is unique, but not altogether different from what all of God's people are required to endure. All Christians will face trials and will be called to deal with thorns and carry crosses. This is the way of Christ. Exodus 4 shows that God was graciously dealing with Moses and preparing him for the next leg of his journey.

Moses did not have peace about going back to Egypt to lead the people to the freedom God promised. He did not have peace because he was focused on what he could do rather than on what God could do. God had to convince Moses of the divine power that would be at work in and through him (vv. 1-9). God has the power to do all that He has determined. The faithful only need to trust, believe, walk in the way of God, and obey His Word.

Having seen the miracles of what God could do, Moses was still unsure about obeying God because of his lack of oratorical skills (v. 10). God assured Moses that he had been made just the way God wanted him to be. God wanted Moses to speak with the mouth He had made for him (vv. 11-12), but Moses was insistent that God should send someone else, which made God very angry. In His grace, God provided for His plan (vv. 13-16). Aaron, Moses' brother, was already coming. God always provides. He knows what is needed.

With affirmations and further clarifications from God, Moses made all the preparations to go. He took his wife with him and headed to Egypt to do God's will (vv. 17-23). Along the way, God would have put Moses to death if his wife had not stepped in and provided the blood of the covenant (vv. 24-26). It is only by grace in God's blood covenant that we can live and fulfill our destiny. Moses met Aaron, and the Lord provided – just as He said He would. The children of Israel believed, and the battle with Egypt began (vv. 27-31).

Are you living under the blood covenant of Christ? Do you have the faith to do what God has planned for you? Who are the people God has provided to help you on your journey?

Those who trust and obey God rather than
rely on self will live with peace.

Exodus 5; Luke 8; Job 22; 1 Corinthians 9

Everyone believes in something beyond themselves. Everyone, in some sense, lives by faith. A big difference between a Christian and someone who is not a follower of Jesus is the object of their faith. We see in Luke 8 that Jesus trained His disciples to live by faith, tested His disciples' faith, and taught His disciples what faith can do.

God always provides for His purpose. Jesus' mission was costly. It not only cost Jesus His life, but many people provided financially for the ministry (vv. 1-3). One of the great joys of the Christian life is to be able to give generously to the Lord's work. Those who gave were able to hear much of the teaching of Jesus. Jesus taught His disciples the importance of faith and how the Word of God works in the real world (vv. 4-18). Faith in God changes relationships and priorities. Those who trust in Jesus gain a new family and identity in Christ (vv. 19-21).

Having taught the disciples what faith is and how it works, He tested them (vv. 22-25). We often expect life to go in a certain way because Jesus is with us, but it can sometimes appear that Jesus is unaware of or does not care about the challenges we are facing. God knows. God sees. God does not expect us to always understand why or how He chooses to work, but He expects us to simply believe that He will not fail and will always provide what is best.

The Lord has the power to transform and heal. He not only controls the winds and waves, but He has authority over demons, sickness, and death (vv. 26-56). All the demons of hell must yield to His every command. The people who reach out to Him in faith can be healed of sickness. God can raise the dead. Jesus performed these miracles trusting in the Father's will. It is by faith that the redeemed can see and experience the miraculous power of God. One day there will no longer need to be miracles. When Christ returns, the world will be as it should be. While we live on this broken planet, we must live by faith. Faith is the victory!

Are you giving generously to the Lord's work? Do you understand what faith is and how it works in the real world? Can you trust God's plan when life is not going the way you thought it would or when God does not act the way you think He should?

Those who have genuine faith in Jesus have peace.

Exodus 6; Luke 9; Job 23; 1 Corinthians 10

We should never think we have a full understanding of what is happening in and through our lives and why it is happening. We are very limited in what we can know, and what we do know is tainted with sin. Our hearts are never as pure and our motives are never as upright as we allow ourselves to believe.

In Job 23, Job's ignorance and faith are showing. His ignorance says as much about us as it does about him. We are all very much like Job in terms of how we think. Job truly thought that he was right and God was wrong (vv. 1-2). Job thought that if he could just sit down with God, explain his position, and have God hear him out that God would realize how wrong He was and that God would do as Job willed (vv. 3-7). In that moment, Job's view of God was off. He was thinking too little of God. We humans have a tendency to minimize God in our thoughts and affections and to maximize our view of ourselves. This obstructed and erroneous view leads to sin and robs God of the glory and honor He deserves.

Job recognized his inability to ascertain and experience the purpose and presence of God (vv. 8-9). We cannot always perceive what God is doing in the world. The Lord is mysterious and glorious. He is spirit. Only those who are living in the Spirit and keeping in step with the Spirit (Galatians 5:25) can discern God's presence and purpose and produce the life and attitude that honors God. Job was thinking in the flesh.

Although Job was off, he was not completely lost. He still knew that God knew where he was and what he was going through (vv. 10-12). He saw his trial as a means to be sanctified. Job also recognized the sovereign right of God (vv. 13-17). Not only does God have the right, but He is right in all He does. Job believed in the greatness of God and found hope, even though his perception of God was darkened by his circumstances. Giving God praise when there is no earthly reason to is one of the greatest ways we can glorify God and be His witnesses.

Are you perceiving yourself and God rightly? Is God big to you? Do you trust God?

Those who have a balanced view of their life and
faith in the grace of Jesus have peace.

Exodus 7; Luke 10; Job 24; <u>1 Corinthians 11</u>

If everyone who knows you lived the way you live, would their lives and the world be better for it? God has called His redeemed people to be examples to others and a light in the darkness. We will often be tempted to excuse our own behavior and to make others feel shame for theirs. God wants us to be free to truly love Him and others. In 1 Corinthians 11, Paul spoke about how we are to live as Christ.

Paul was able to say what all Christians need to be able to say: *Be imitators of me, as I am of Christ* (v. 1). This was not the statement of an arrogant man, but it was the statement of a godly man who was living in Christ. Paul was not perfect, but he was faithfully following Christ Jesus. Any Spirit-filled Christ follower can live with confidence and be an example to others.

The ultimate quality of a lifestyle of Christlikeness is love. God is love, and those who live to love God and others live as Christ. Corinth was filled with broken people. There was a temple to the goddess Aphrodite. The female temple prostitutes were recognized by their shaved heads. When some of these prostitutes came to saving faith in Jesus, they would wear head coverings to cover their shame. Paul commanded all the women to wear head coverings (vv. 2-16). Covering shame and being united in love is a sign of a Christ-honoring church.

Like all churches, Corinth was not perfect. It was like all churches – filled with saints who struggled with sin. Paul had to come down on them hard for dishonoring Christ in how they received the Lord's Supper (vv. 17-34). The Lord's Supper is a time to celebrate Jesus in the unity of the body of believers. It is a time to serve one another by waiting for one another. The rich Corinthians were able to get to worship early, and some of them were eating and getting drunk. When the poorer working-class members showed up, they found no food or wine with which to remember Christ. God's people must serve each other in love as they remember Jesus.

Are you a model of Christ whom others can follow? Do you make it easy for saints to put off their shame and pursue Christ? Is your worship of Jesus honoring to Him and other believers?

Those who live a life of love, living as Christ, experience peace.

Exodus 8; Luke 11; Job 25-26; 1 Corinthians 12

It matters. What you are going through matters to God. God does not waste our trials and challenges. He uses them to grow us and enable us to love Him and trust Him more. There are certain things we could never learn about God or ourselves without difficulty. We see in Exodus 8 that Moses learned many vital things about God that all of God's children need to know: God is sovereign, He answers prayer.

God led Moses to Egypt to lead the people to freedom. Moses foreshadows Jesus. He is the one who was miraculously born, gifted, and called to lead God's people. Unlike Jesus, Moses was not divine. Like Jesus, Moses depended on God the Father. God was determined to not only rescue His people, but also to reveal His sovereign might. He did not have to bring about the plagues of frogs (vv. 1-15), gnats (vv. 16-19), and flies (vv. 20-32), but God chose to do so in order that His people and the world would know His power.

In the midst of each plague, Pharaoh requested Moses to ask God to relent. Pharaoh did not have a personal relationship with God. He could not call on God. Moses knew God, and God knew him. God was with Moses, and Moses was able to speak to God through prayer. Prayer is a supernatural conversation in which God's people speak to God, and God speaks to His people. Prayer is a gracious privilege to all who believe in Jesus.

After God answered Moses' prayer and each plague was lifted, Pharaoh would harden his heart. Throughout the battle with Pharaoh, the Bible says that God hardened Pharaoh's heart and also that Pharaoh hardened his own heart. Apart from God's gracious hand, the heart of humanity is hard and gets harder toward God the more a person sins and rejects God's authority. The children of God must be sensitive to the Spirit of God, respond in faith to the Word of God, and keep a tender heart toward Jesus.

Do you trust in the sovereign power of God to guide you and provide for your life? Are you seeking God through prayer and seeing His hand move according to His Word? Is your heart tender toward God?

Those who trust that God is using their hardships to
make them holy have peace in every circumstance.

Exodus 9; Luke 12; Job 27; 1 Corinthians 13

Everyone thinks, but not everyone thinks wisely. Those who are made alive by the Spirit of God and are saved by the grace of Jesus have the mind of Christ (1 Corinthians 2:16). Those who are alive in Christ have a spiritual mindset that is liberating and inspiring. In Luke 12, Jesus speaks about the mindset His followers are to have.

Those with the mind of Christ think rightly about God. He is the omniscient, righteous judge who sees and knows all things and will uncover all sin (vv. 1-3). Those who think they can fool God are only fooling themselves. God is the gracious giver of all good things to those who love and trust Him so that those who trust in Him never need to fear (vv. 4-7). God is wise and knows what is best, and in love He cares for those who trust and obey Him.

Those with the mind of Christ think rightly about their circumstances. They know that God has the perfect plan for their lives and will guide them in what to say and do in every situation (vv. 8-12). They know that this world, along with all of its temporal pleasures, is passing away, so they do not hope in this world (vv. 13-21). They know that God will provide for their needs, and because He is faithful, they never need to be anxious (vv. 22-34).

Those with the mind of Christ think rightly about their purpose. They know that Jesus is returning soon and will bring their recompense with Him (vv. 35-48). The reward that God gives is eternal. It will never spoil or fade. It is given to all who believe and live to do God's will. Believers know that Christ did not come the first time to bring peace, but to bring war against sin and darkness (vv. 49-53). There will be spiritual strife, but children of God have hope. They know to keep watch for the coming of Jesus (vv. 54-56). Like the coming weather, the coming of Christ has clear signs. They know to be practical (vv. 57-59). Life is complicated, and it is wise to keep things simple and not get tangled up in lawsuits.

Do you know and believe in the God of the Bible? Can you seek God's purpose in whatever circumstance you find yourself, or must things go your way before you will serve God? Are you pursuing God's purpose for your life?

Those who think like Jesus live with peace.

Exodus 10; Luke 13; <u>Job 28</u>; 1 Corinthians 14

Every person is a part of the story of God. The world is filled with people who have stories that are filled with brokenness. While people with power, fame, and resources appear to have the best things in life, Job 28 reveals reality. Worldly things are not better than wisdom. Without wisdom, we cannot have peace.

Peace does not come to those who can dig out, uncover, and take control of the things of the earth (vv. 1-11), yet that is what most people spend their lives doing. Most people live to get things that they cannot keep and that will not satisfy. The ingenuity of humanity is truly amazing. God has blessed people with the intelligence and dexterity to pursue and discover the wealth of the world, and even change the landscape of the planet by their work. Yes, humanity can do great things, but few live wisely.

Wisdom produces peace. Those who know that their decisions are wise live free from anxiety and shame. The wisdom that produces peace cannot be purchased and cannot be found among the living things or depths of the seas (vv. 12-19). Although the world is filled with schools, and people have access to seemingly unlimited amounts of information through technology, few live truly wise lives. The pride that comes from education, professional accomplishment, and comfort blinds humanity.

There is only one source of wisdom that gives peace. Although it is hidden from sinful humanity (vv. 20-23), it is accessible – but only by grace. God alone gives the wisdom that produces peace (vv. 24-26). The wisdom that produces peace comes by fearing the Lord and turning from evil. This wisdom is found by those who repent of their sin and trust in Christ for forgiveness and His leadership. It is in acknowledging our need and looking to God's provision of grace that we gain the wisdom that produces peace. Without Jesus, there can be no peace. Jesus saves and liberates. Jesus makes us wise.

Do you have a personal relationship with Jesus Christ? Are you seeking the wisdom that produces the peace that is found in the grace of Jesus? Is your life defined by Jesus, or is it defined by your accomplishments and pursuits?

Those who are wise live with peace.

Exodus 11:1-12:20; Luke 14; Job 29; <u>1 Corinthians 15</u>

This world is not as it should be, and we are not what God made us to be – but thankfully, that is all going to change one day. Jesus is going to come back! When He returns, He will create a new heaven and a new earth. At that time, those who belong to Christ will be raised with resurrected bodies. First Corinthians 15 tells us about the blessed hope of the resurrection.

It is by the gospel of Jesus that peace can be experienced (vv. 1-11). Through the life, death, and resurrection of Jesus, sinners are made into saints by grace through faith. The proof of Jesus' authority to redeem sinners is His resurrection. The resurrection was attested to by hundreds of eyewitnesses who would have been available at the time of Paul's writing to deny what he wrote and denounce the gospel of Jesus. But rather than deny it, those who saw the resurrected Jesus announced it with great enthusiasm.

Getting people to deny the resurrection is one of Satan's most ardent endeavors. Those who deny the resurrection have no basis for their faith, and their hope is only in this world (vv. 12-19). Thankfully, Jesus did rise from the grave! It is through Adam that death came, and it is through Jesus that life comes (vv. 20-23). Once Jesus' enemies have been deposed, the end will come (vv. 24-28). God's people are to live in light of the coming of Jesus (vv. 29-34). Holy living is not incidental. Holy living comes from an intentional life motivated by allegiance to and appreciation of Jesus.

The resurrected body that will house the soul of a redeemed saint will be like the raised body of Jesus (vv. 35-49). It will be glorious! This coming victory gives God's children peace. We can know that death has lost its sting! Jesus has won the war over sin and death (vv. 50-58). All who believe and follow Jesus have peace in all circumstances, for they know that in time, all results of the fall will pass away. All that will remain is in Christ.

Do you have peace with God through faith in Jesus Christ? Are you making decisions about how you live in light of the resurrection? Can you see past the problems of this life by keeping your eyes on Jesus and His coming kingdom?

Those who believe in Jesus and choose to live in the
light of His coming resurrection live with peace.

MARCH 1

Exodus 12:21-51; Luke 15; Job 30; 1 Corinthians 16

Sin is serious business because the holiness of God is intense. God deals justly with sin. Because God is loving, He has provided the means for the just requirements of sin to be satisfied by an atoning sacrifice. In Exodus 12:21-51, the love and just demands of God are put on display.

God had revealed His power through the plagues of natural disasters He had poured out on Egypt (Exodus 7-12). Now He was going to bring about a supernatural disaster – the judgment of God. The Lord was about to pass through Egypt and strike down the firstborn of every creature. To be saved from this judgment, the children of Israel were commanded to cover the lintel and two doorposts of their homes with blood and then enter and remain in their homes until morning (vv. 21-23). Jesus calls for belief in His sacrifice on the cross and faith in His grace until He returns. The Israelites were to commemorate this event with the Passover meal (vv. 24-28), just as Christians now commemorate Christ with the Lord's Supper.

That night, the Lord passed through Egypt, and all the firstborn were killed except for those who were covered by the blood of a lamb (vv. 29-31). It was after this plague that Pharaoh allowed the children of Israel to go free (vv. 32-33). The people of Egypt were anxious for the Israelites to leave, and they gave them gifts, just as God promised they would. Also, the children of Israel provided for their own needs as God commanded them (vv. 34-36). God always provides, but we are also responsible to take care of ourselves as good stewards.

The children of Israel had been in Egypt for four hundred and thirty years, as God said they would be (Genesis 15:13). They went where God told them to go, and the statute of the Passover was established (vv. 37-51). God's plan is perfect. Those who trust in Him must follow His lead and obey His commands. Those who have peace with God through faith in the Lamb of God, Jesus, will be blessed.

Are you trusting in the blood of Jesus to cover your sin and provide salvation for you? Do you receive the Lord's Supper regularly and rightly with your local church? Is God guiding you, or are you trusting in another source?

*Those who trust in the grace of God to cover their sin and
to give them God's righteousness live in peace.*

Exodus 13; <u>Luke 16</u>; Job 31; 2 Corinthians 1

Is it well with your soul? There is nothing more significant than the condition of a person's soul. Those who are in a right standing with God by grace through faith in Jesus have peace with God. This peace comes with great promises and demands. Luke 16 teaches that the soul is made well when we trust in Jesus.

The world encourages people to pursue money as the means of their salvation, and many, if not most people in the world, put their faith and hope in money. The parable of the dishonest manager provides an illustration of how the world works and what the world values: shrewdness (vv. 1-9). Jesus commands good stewardship, but not idolatry (vv. 10-12). Only those who trust in Christ alone will be saved and live with peace in their soul (v. 13). Idolatry produces despair and pride. Faith in Jesus produces hope and gratitude.

Religious people who do not trust in Jesus appear to be in good standing with God, but the Lord knows the true condition of their souls (vv. 14-15). Those who trust in Jesus as the Promised One whom the prophets foretold pursue the kingdom of God with all vigilance (v. 16). They submit to the authority of God's Word (v. 17). They refuse to accept the way of the world as it pertains to divorce and remarriage (v. 18). Religious people pretend to be pious, but they always provide loopholes for their desires. The faithful in Christ trust and obey Jesus, and their souls thrive.

All people will give an account to God for their lives, just as Lazarus and the rich man did (vv. 19-23). The rich man suffers, while Lazarus rests (vv. 24-26). If the dead could speak to us, they would tell us to seek the welfare of our souls and of the souls of others (vv. 27-28). We do not need the dead to speak. We have the Word of God and the risen Christ (vv. 29-31). Those who have peace with God can rejoice and must help those who are perishing.

Are you tempted to make an idol of money and to spend your life pursuing what you cannot keep rather than to trust in Christ to gain what you cannot lose? Are you a disciple of Jesus and not merely a religious person? Are you ready to give an account to God for your life?

Those who look to Jesus and gratefully love and serve
Him live and die with their soul at peace.

Exodus 14; Luke 17; <u>Job 32</u>; 2 Corinthians 2

On the day humanity fell into sin, God's honor was being questioned. The serpent accused God of holding Eve back from having the life and moral insight she deserved. Unable to see past her own perspective, she accepted the accusation and turned against God. Every person born since has doubted the goodness of God, as Eve did.

Job was a good man, but God had offered him up to Satan for consideration (Job 1:8). Satan accuses humanity and seeks to rob God of glory by seducing people to sin and turn from God. Satan went after Job with God's permission.

God allowed Job to suffer. By the time we get to Job 32, Job had silenced his friends and had become righteous in his own eyes (v. 1). He had previously sought to have God answer his perceived righteous inquiries (Job 31:35). This angered Elihu (Job 32:2). What made him so mad was that Job was justifying himself rather than God. Job was not speaking to the goodness of God and the right of God to do whatever He pleases with His servant. Job was accusing God of being unjust by allowing him to suffer, when in his estimation he had done nothing wrong.

Elihu was not only angry with Job, but he was also angry with the three older friends who had not brought Job to a place of humble acceptance of God's sovereign will (vv. 3-19). Elihu had waited and listened patiently because the other men were older. His hope was that he would hear them give glory to God and bring Job to a place of humble submission to God.

When the other men had clearly failed, Elihu spoke up with full conviction. It was a message that was burdensome to him, and only by speaking would he find relief (v. 20). He would not be intimidated by any person's standing (v. 21). He feared God and would speak as a God-fearing man (v. 22). He would defend the honor and glory of God.

Are you in danger of thinking that you deserve better than God has provided? Do you doubt God's goodness when life gets hard? Can you truly trust God to always do what is best?

Those who believe in the love of God and defend
His dignity and honor live with peace.

Exodus 15; Luke 18; Job 33; <u>2 Corinthians 3</u>

We are all struggling. Sin is so easy. We don't have to try to sin, for sinning comes naturally – but so do the consequences of sin. We are all sinners in need of a Savior! None of us can alter our affections and change our identity. We love sin, even though it has cursed our race and has caused the brokenness in our soul. We need a change of heart and desire that only God can bring about.

Paul had a lot of responsibility. His ministry was to the gentiles. The Lord led him to Western Europe and blessed his efforts. The church at Corinth was a place where the Holy Spirit brought many to life and where a church was formed. Paul wrote 2 Corinthians 3 to the Corinthians because of a conflict that existed. People were doubting his authority. They said that because he was suffering, he was not a real apostle. He pointed to his ministry among them and reminded them that they were the proof of his calling (vv. 1-3).

The Corinthians' life in Christ gave Paul hope (vv. 4-6). He knew that the Spirit had done a work in them and through him. There was no doubt about who had done the work. Human beings cannot change the spiritual condition or heart of another human being. Only God can do that through the power of His Word and His Spirit. The Corinthians experienced that transformation, and their lives gave Paul confidence to carry on and fulfill his calling.

The work of God's Spirit is mysterious, but it is also plain. Those who are saved are able to admit their sin and see how atrocious sin is. This is what the law does. Paul reminded them how Moses' face would shine with glory after he had been with God (vv. 7-13). Even in the midst of that miracle, many of the Israelites would not and could not believe (vv. 14-15). That same hardheartedness exists in all who are without Christ. Those who receive Christ by the power of the Holy Spirit are transformed (vv. 16-18). This change is by the power of God and not of human doing. Paul knew this, and he counted on God to do the work that he was engaged in and committed to.

Are you encouraged with the hope of the gospel? Can you see how God has changed your life? Is God glorified, and are others encouraged, by your transformation in Christ?

Those who rely on God to provide for their lives and
join Him in His kingdom work live with peace.

Exodus 16; Luke 19; Job 34; 2 Corinthians 4

We ask, "What am I going to do?" Decisions. The world is filled with them. We will make many today. Everyone makes choices that they believe will be in their best interest or in the best interest of those they love and care about. Discerning what is best and choosing to do it is not always easy. We are flawed people.

Zacchaeus was in need of Christ. He had been stealing from people for years and was hated by his neighbors, but he genuinely hoped for a different life. In Luke 19, we read that he heard that Jesus was coming through town and that he sought Jesus. Being small in stature, he climbed up in a tree to see Jesus (vv. 1-4). Jesus saw him. Jesus called him. Jesus entered his life. Zacchaeus repented and believed (vv. 5-7). Zacchaeus was transformed, and Jesus proclaimed that he was saved (vv. 8-10). Zacchaeus had thought that gaining power and possessions was best – until Jesus gave him a better way.

Jesus then told a story about a nobleman and his servants (vv. 11-25). The servants were to invest the nobleman's money. The servant who had been given ten minas and the servant who had been given five minas each chose to invest the money, while the servant who had been given one mina hid the money. They each did what they thought was best. The two who invested were celebrated, but the one who hid the mina was cast out and disciplined with the enemies of the nobleman (vv. 26-27). We must all choose heaven or hell. Heaven and kingdom service is best!

When Jesus entered Jerusalem on Palm Sunday, He was greeted with praises from the people and with criticism from the religious leaders (vv. 28-40). Each did what they thought was best. Jesus wept over Jerusalem because the people of Jerusalem could not see the peace that had come or the destruction that would soon ensue (vv. 41-44). With zeal, Jesus entered the temple and cleared it of money changers (vv. 45-48). The mob, the religious leaders, the money changers, and Jesus all made choices. Jesus and those who glorified Him chose best. He is the way of peace. We all must choose either to make our own way or to follow Jesus in His way. Jesus will help us if we will look to Him in faith.

Are you making the best choices for your life? Do people see and celebrate your salvation? Is Jesus' way of life your way?

Those who rely on God's help and do His will live with peace.

Exodus 17; Luke 20; <u>Job 35</u>; 2 Corinthians 5

There are times when we can be tempted to think too much of ourselves. We can get trapped into thinking we are really good or really bad. Those who think of themselves as really good see little need for God's grace. Those who think of themselves as really bad see little hope in God's grace. In Job 35, Elihu made a sensible argument. While his overall premise was very strongly worded, what he said about the greatness of God was true.

Job did not have peace in his suffering. He knew that he had done nothing to cause his suffering. Job's friends saw his suffering and assumed he deserved it. Job had done a lot of thinking in his pain and had come to the conclusion that God is not always just because good people suffer and evil people don't always suffer. Although Elihu was young, he lectured Job and his older friends. Elihu's point was that God is always right (vv. 1-8). Elihu was right that God is always right. He is holy. He is righteous. He is self-sufficient. God needs nothing from us, and in His righteousness He is glorious and perfect and always does what is good.

People will often cry out in their suffering (v. 9). Elihu condemned the faithlessness of humanity for not seeking the God *who gives songs in the night* (vv. 10-11). Everyone wants their circumstances to be changed, but few want to be changed in their circumstances and find God's song of hope in their pain. There is peace for those who can look to God with faith in their suffering.

God does not hear the prayer of the proud (vv. 12-16). Elihu was right about that and was attempting to help Job see the extent to which Job was being presumptuous in thinking he was too good to suffer. Job was proud and was convinced that he was in the right and God was in the wrong. It is a true friend who seeks to silence sinful and silly words that are empty and without knowledge. Job was speaking ill of God, and Elihu sought to bring Job to a place of clarity and respect for God.

Do you always have confidence in the grace of God – both when you feel as if you are doing well and also when you feel as if you have failed? Can you seek God and sing His praise – even when life is hard? Are you looking at God rightly, as high and exalted?

Those who see God as glorious and over all live with peace.

Exodus 18; Luke 21; Job 36; <u>2 Corinthians 6</u>

Throughout the Bible, there is a consistent warning for Christians to be true to God and to be sure that their salvation is real. In 2 Corinthians 6, Paul appealed to the church to have genuine faith, and he explained what genuine faith looks like. Having outlined the ministry of reconciliation that is given to all of God's redeemed people, he concluded the previous chapter (2 Corinthians 5) with a stirring explanation of the gospel. Paul's concern was that there were some in Corinth who claimed Christ, but were not really saved.

Genuine faith joins God in His work in the world by recognizing the favorable time and the opportunity for salvation (vv. 1-2). God is seeking to reconcile sinners to Himself, and He calls all of His disciples to join in that effort. When the Spirit of God gives new life, which is experienced through conviction of sin, it is a favorable time. In that day, a person must repent and believe in order to be saved. To be saved is to be made eternally right with God.

Genuine faith often causes others to want to believe. Faith that endures hardship reveals the power of God in those who believe (vv. 3-10). Paul shared some of his own experiences and the qualities that he came to see in himself and his companions because of their relationship with Jesus. While not all Christians will have to endure the hardships Paul and his friends suffered, all Christians will experience the Holy Spirit and God's love. Paul and his companions shared their lives. They were transparent (vv. 11-13). This is one of the great freedoms believers enjoy with one another.

Genuine faith binds believers to Christ and His people. A Christian is to marry only another Christian (vv. 14-18). Believers are to be yoked with a marriage partner who is pushing toward heaven in Christ. They are to be holy and consecrated to the Lord and should reveal His grace in their lives. God's love is powerful and beautiful, and God is glorified when His love is manifested in marriage.

Is your salvation sure? Is your relationship with Jesus causing you to serve God, make disciples, and become more like Jesus? Are you consecrated to God?

***Those who have a personal relationship with God
by grace through faith in Jesus have peace.***

Exodus 19; Luke 22; Job 37; 2 Corinthians 7

God does not need anything from anybody. He is completely satisfied in Himself. Being Father, Son, and Spirit, He is filled with love and happiness. He does not need angels or image bearers, but He chose to create people to for His glory. Humanity has fallen into sin, and without grace, we stand condemned. By grace, God has chosen to save a people for Himself. God's grace is costly. Jesus lived a holy life on this earth, died for sin, and was raised. This is the gospel. Exodus 19 reveals the gospel of God and the opportunity that exists for those who believe in Jesus.

God graciously saved Israel from bondage in Egypt. He guided them to freedom and provided His presence and power on the journey to their home (vv. 1-4). God promised to bless Israel if they would trust and obey Him. Those who are saved by grace through faith in Christ alone, and who trust and obey God, are given a position and an eternal purpose with God. They are made into a kingdom of priests and a holy nation (vv. 5-6). This position and purpose is given to all who are saved by grace.

The people first had to be consecrated by God in order to fulfill their calling (vv. 7-15). This process of being set apart requires discipline by God's people, but it is accomplished by the gospel of God. Those who come to God must come on His terms (vv. 16-25). God has provided the means by which He can be approached. Only those who have been called and covered by God's grace can approach God and live. All who are outside of God's grace and stand in God's presence will be judged and condemned.

God is now at work in a special way through His church. What He did for Israel, He is now doing in the world. God is now saving people all over the world (Acts 1:8). The faithful in Christ are joining God in bringing peace in Christ to the world. This is the purpose of God's people. This purpose brings peace.

Are you a member of God's kingdom of priests through saving faith in Christ alone? Is God working in your life and changing your character through the consecrating work of the Word and the Spirit? Are you obeying God and joining Him in His work by spreading the good news of grace in the world?

Those who walk with God live with peace.

Exodus 20; <u>Luke 23</u>; Job 38; 2 Corinthians 8

Love is powerful. We all have love for something or someone. Anyone who comes to know Jesus as He really is and as He is revealed in Scripture cannot help but love Him. Love for Jesus changes everything about us and how we experience life. In Luke 23, the heart of God's enemies, the heart of Jesus, and the heart of Jesus' followers are seen.

The religious leaders, Pilate, and Herod had no love for Jesus (vv. 1-25). While Jesus was on earth, He was a problem to the people who were in power. Pilate and the religious leaders in Jerusalem were concerned that He would cause their downfall. Herod wanted entertainment, but Jesus was not willing to be Herod's clown. Herod did not understand Jesus. He could not understand the person, the power, the life, or the grace of Jesus. Herod was like so many people who are glad to have Jesus around, but if He does not give them what they want, they turn away from Him.

Jesus showed love to all, including His enemies (vv. 26-49). While He was dying on the cross, He prayed for those who were killing Him. Even in His suffering, He saved and comforted the thief at His side. God loved us enough to send Jesus to die for us while we were still sinners. He is gracious and willing to forgive. That is why Jesus died on the cross. He died to pay the penalty for the sin of others. Jesus is our only hope for salvation. The love of Jesus is amazing. He genuinely loved Herod and all who hated Him. How? How could Jesus love like that? The answer is grace.

After Jesus died, Joseph of Arimathea provided for the care of Jesus' body and its burial (vv. 50-56). He was a member of the organization of religious leaders who had conspired to put Jesus to death, but he did not agree with or support the decision. He believed in Jesus. He was looking to the coming of the kingdom of God under Christ. His decision would not be popular. This act of love for Jesus was costly, and it probably ruined his reputation among the religious leaders. That is the cost of discipleship.

Do you know the true Jesus of the Bible, and do you love Him with all of your heart? Can you discern who the enemies of Jesus are? Are you willing to sacrifice your life and reputation for Jesus?

***Those who know Jesus as Lord and Savior are able to
love, trust, and obey Him and live with peace.***

Exodus 21; Luke 24; Job 39; 2 Corinthians 9

Tough times are growing times. It is during difficult days that God's people are most prone to look to God for truth. God is God. He is who He says He is. Philosophical propositions, Bible inquiries, and theological discussions are helpful in many ways. However, in the day of testing, when trials come, we will either believe in God and who He says He is in the Bible – or we won't. In Job 39, God is in the midst of offering Job a selection of questions intended to remind Job that he is not God. Job, along with all human beings, are beneath God in every way. There is only one God.

Job wanted answers. He was so sure that if he could dialogue with God, He would understand that there had been a divine mistake and would clarify and rectify everything in Job's favor. Job, like all people, wanted to be able to put God in a nice, comfortable box and have God work the way Job wanted Him to.

Job liked the idea of a God who looked after the people who wanted to be good, and who scorned and punished the bad people who wanted to do bad. Like his friends and counselors, Job believed he was a decent man who had a pretty good sense of what was going on and how things should go. It was devastating for him to know in his heart that he had done better than most, yet was suffering like the worst.

Job needed to learn the most important lesson any person can learn: God is God, and we are not. It is vital to learn this lesson. Without this key fact of reality, people will either fall into pride because they consider themselves morally superior to others, or they will fall into despair because they cannot measure up.

With this list of interrogatives, God was putting Job in his place. God was revealing His sovereign power. God is in control, and He does what He pleases. He pleases to do good. In our fallen and broken world, God will use bad things, like a cross and a tomb, to bring about the best things, like salvation and resurrection.

Do you truly trust the God of the Bible? Are you able to go through hardship and know that God is in control and is working out what is best? Can you praise God in the storms of life?

Those who accept, love, trust, and obey God will go
through difficult days and will maintain peace.

Exodus 22; John 1; Job 40; <u>2 Corinthians 10</u>

What is real and true? This has been and continues to be one of the most important debates among human beings. Christians claim that the Bible is God's Word, that it is truth. Among some Christians, there is a pseudo-faith that reverses the reality taught in the Bible. The Bible teaches that we are made and redeemed by God for His glory. There is a destructive lie that was birthed in the United States and is being distributed around the globe that claims to be Christianity, but teaches that God made us and redeemed us for our glory. It teaches that God exists for us so that we can be happy, healthy, and wealthy. In 2 Corinthians 10, Paul exposes the attitude of false teachers and reveals what is real and true Christianity.

Paul was empowered by the Holy Spirit, and his ministry was conducted with humility. His confidence was in the power of God (vv. 1-6). He did not look to his abilities, but to the power of God. He wisely battled in the supernatural power provided by God through faith. He looked to demolish the strongholds of the flesh and the devil. He fought a spiritual fight. God was with him.

Paul's goal was to disciple those he had reached with the gospel to be faithful saints who would look beyond themselves and help the broken people of the world who needed Jesus (vv. 7-17). The most difficult thing to overcome in the Christian life is the selfish desire to want to be our own god rather than to honor and serve the true God. This challenge existed in Paul's day, and it certainly exists in our day. It is seen as men and women stand on stages and claim to be Christians, but lie to people by telling them that God's main concern in the world is their personal prosperity and making their dreams come true. This lie leads people to focus on their prosperity and what their flesh desires rather than to expand God's glory and build the kingdom of God. Christ came into the world to save sinners, not to make self-realized narcissists who care for themselves and their desires and dreams.

Are you a genuine Christian saved by grace? Do you live to glorify God or to glorify self? Are you living for God's kingdom or for your personal desires and dreams?

***Those who hold to the authentic faith of Christianity
taught in Scripture live with peace.***

Exodus 23; John 2; Job 41; 2 Corinthians 11

The Christian life is not complicated. However, we can make it complicated by our disobedience and pride and by ignoring the basic things God calls us to do. In Exodus 23, Moses was providing the law of God to Israel. In this section of the law, the people were taught how to relate to one another, how to schedule their lives, and how to relate to God.

Jesus said that the entire law of God could be summed up in two things: love God and love people (Matthew 22:37-40). When we love God and love people, those who do not know God will still consider how we live. The world needs people who demonstrate Christ through their actions as well as their words. There are a lot of hurting people in the world. God loves them and calls His beloved to love them. God's people are to be kind, forgiving, and helpful (Exodus 23:1-9). It is not complicated, but it does require focus and intentionality.

Given the challenges of life and how easy it is to be selfish, mean-spirited, and proud, God's people need constant reminders of the grace and mercy God has shown them so that they will show them to others. Christians must set up a rhythm or schedule in life that keeps them coming before God for instruction in His Word and for fellowship with and accountability from His people (vv. 10-19). Godly people become wise through daily steps of growth in Christ.

During Israel's journey from Egypt to the promised land, God was present with them. They were to remain faithful to God by focusing on Him and obeying Him (vv. 20-33). Their journey was filled with difficulties and challenges, and each one was used by God to teach them to trust and obey Him. The Christian life is also like that. God allows the followers of Jesus to go through trials, to feel the pain of thorns, and to carry crosses so that they learn to trust God's will and rely on His strength. This dependence leads to greater obedience. Life in our broken world is not easy. God empowers His people to praise Him no matter their circumstances.

Are you nice to people because of God's grace to you? Do you have a Christ-centered rhythm to your life? Is Christ gaining a greater influence in your life for His glory?

Those whose lives are disciplined and who do
what God commands live with peace.

Exodus 24; John 3; Job 42; 2 Corinthians 12

God is mysterious, but has made Himself accessible. Every person on the planet is born with a sin nature. We never have to teach children to lie or misbehave. They do that naturally. Sin is a natural function of fallen humanity. Thankfully, God has intervened to give us new lives. In John 3, Jesus explains how a person can get a new life with God.

Nicodemus was a good man. He was a powerful religious leader in Jesus' day. He liked Jesus and wanted to strike a deal with Him. He approached Jesus one night to figure out how Jesus and the religious leaders could get along and work together (vv. 1-2). Jesus was not willing to play his game. The religious leaders wanted to stay in power with their religious customs. Jesus came to bring life where there was death so that those who believe could be rescued from condemnation (vv. 3-18). Real Christianity, based upon the Scriptures, is unlike all other world religions. It does not offer a slightly better, yet still messed-up life. Jesus offers a new life that is free to love and live forever with Him.

Nicodemus had come at night. He wanted to keep his conversation with Jesus a secret and make an agreement that would have been, in Nicodemus' mind, mutually beneficial. Jesus was not willing to make that deal. Jesus came to bring light into our dark world. Those who choose to live apart from Christ remain in darkness. Darkness hates the light (vv. 19-21). The light of Jesus exposes the real motives of all people and either condemns or liberates.

John the Baptist was also not interested in playing the game of the religious leaders of his day. John was not interested in building his own kingdom. His job was to tell people about the coming of Jesus (vv. 22-30). Jesus Christ came to save sinners. Those who will turn from self-sufficiency and believe in the power of Jesus to forgive and to give new life will be saved. Those who are saved obey Jesus and are free of condemnation (vv. 31-36).

Is Jesus in control of your life, or are you trying to make a deal with Jesus to get Him in on what you want? Are you living in the light of God's Word? Are you free from condemnation?

> *Those who know and love Jesus are born again*
> *and experience eternal peace.*

Exodus 25; John 4; Proverbs 1; 2 Corinthians 13

Navigating life's many problems, pains, and opportunities is hard. We were made to know, love, and obey God and to be helped by angelic hosts. We were not made to live in a fallen world. We were never meant to be separated from God by a chasm of sin. Human beings are born broken. The world we live in today is broken. Thankfully, God has given us His grace, and His grace is sufficient to heal us and our broken world. Those who are redeemed by grace can discern truth. Proverbs 1 is a gift from God that helps His children know how they are to think, feel, and live.

Wisdom is not just knowledge, but we cannot be wise without knowing what is true. The book of Proverbs is a collection of sayings that provide insight into God, humanity, and life. Those who gain understanding and insight are better equipped to make wise decisions (vv. 1-6). This is God's will for His children. He wants His people to know what is true and to do what is best.

Wisdom begins with the fear of God (v. 7). If we do not acknowledge the power and holiness of God, we cannot be wise. Without a deep respect and awe of God, human beings fall into the same gutter as the demons of hell and assume that God is wrong and we are right. Without wisdom, humans do as their flesh desires rather than doing what is best based upon what is true.

God, in His grace, has given human beings His Word and His Spirit. God has also given us the gift of family. Those who follow Jesus have the gift of godly friends (vv. 8-19). The shared experience of a mom and dad is a great gift to children. Having godly friends rather than broken sinners as advisers is best.

The Lord has made plain His intentions and desires. He calls us to be wise. His revelation is in creation and Scripture (vv. 20-31). Those who are wise heed the wisdom of God and avoid the travesties that sin produces (vv. 32-33). Wise people listen to God and obey His Word.

Are you a wise person who knows the truth of God's Word? Do you have wise people advising you? Are you joining God in His work in the world, according to His Word?

Those who know the truth, fear the Lord, and obey God live with peace.

Exodus 26; John 5; Proverbs 2; <u>Galatians 1</u>

God promised that He would send His Son to rescue sinners. This is the gospel. Jesus Christ has come. He lived a holy life. He died an atoning death. He has been raised. He has sent the Holy Spirit. He is returning soon. In Galatians 1, the apostle Paul had to refute some people who were doubting the true gospel.

Peace is possible with God through faith in Christ alone. Apart from the atoning work of Christ, human beings are lost in sin. Paul wrote to the church at Galatia to help them discern God's will. In his typical introduction, Paul encouraged the believers in the grace that God gives and in the peace that comes to those who trust in Christ alone (vv. 1-5). This gospel is glorious and must never be taken for granted or contaminated with worldly accommodations.

Paul was not pleased with this church. They were falling into a trap. They were abandoning the gospel for something that seemed religious and gospel-like, but was not the true gospel of Jesus Christ (vv. 6-7). His calling down a curse on any who would proclaim a false gospel is shocking and should concern any person who would dare draw people away from Jesus (vv. 8-10). The gospel is from God and is consistent with all of Scripture.

Paul's encounter with Jesus Christ and his understanding of the gospel came in a miraculous way (vv. 11-12). Paul's experience on the road to Damascus was unique (Acts 9), but the truth he learned there was not. What Paul learned that day had been established over the centuries by the Scriptures. Paul was able to take time to relearn what the Bible taught. He had been trained to be a Pharisee (vv. 13-17). It was several years before he ventured to Jerusalem to consult with the apostles and Jesus' brother James (vv. 18-23). Having heard his testimony and his explanation of the gospel, they glorified God (v. 24).

The gospel is an objective reality revealed by the Bible. It is experienced by grace through faith in Jesus. There is no other way that a person can know God and be saved.

Do you know the gospel? Have you been saved? Can you defend the gospel?

> *Only those who trust in Jesus and remain faith-*
> *ful to the gospel live with peace.*

Exodus 27; John 6; Proverbs 3; Galatians 2

There is never a single moment in your life when God is unaware of your need. He cares about you and what you are going through. He knows what you need before you do, and He always provides what is best for His people. We often imagine ourselves wise enough to know what we need, but we are often wrong. In our fallen world and flesh, we are limited. God is not limited. He is all-knowing, all-powerful, and perfectly good and righteous. In Exodus 17, God outlined His plans for three important parts of the tabernacle: the altar, the court, and the lamp. His plan was good.

The world is a complicated place. It is difficult to know who to trust. God is vast and beyond our comprehension, but He has chosen to make Himself known and accessible to those who believe. While we will often struggle to trust others and ourselves, we can always trust God and His intentions.

The tabernacle was a gift from God that the people were to construct through sacrifice and obedience. The altar was to be made in a particular way (vv. 1-8). This is where the offerings would be made. This is where sin would be atoned for and where people would be made right with God. The tabernacle's court had a specific space dimension with a certain look (vv. 9-19). This was the sacred space people would enter into in order to do business with God and discover God's provision. The oil for the golden lampstand was to come from the people (vv. 20-21). This was to insure that there was always a light within the tabernacle.

All three of these things point to Jesus. He is the atoning sacrifice. Jesus came to give His life and to pay for the sin of the world (Hebrews 7:27). He is the place where people do business with God and discover God's provision. Jesus is the mediator for all who believe (Hebrews 9:15). He is the light that shines for all of eternity. Jesus is the light of the world (John 8:12). God has always provided for His people through Jesus. In the Old Testament, they looked forward to Jesus, and now we look back to Him.

Is Jesus your hope for salvation? Have you entered into His life by faith? Are you living in the light of Christ?

Those who trust in God's plans and purpose in
Christ experience the peace of God.

Exodus 28; John 7; Proverbs 4; Galatians 3

Sometimes we forget who we really are and what it is we are living for. Jesus had an amazing peace about His life and calling. There were many who doubted Him. John 7 reveals that His own half-brothers, the other sons born to Mary and Joseph, did not believe in Him, and neither did the religious leaders of His day.

Jesus' brothers did not believe in Him (vv. 1-9). That seems hard to believe. These men had seen Jesus in His perfection their entire lives, but they did not believe. They were sort of mocking Him in suggesting that He should go up and make a spectacle of Himself at the festival in Jerusalem. Jesus was confident in who He was and in God the Father's plan and timing for His life.

The religious leaders of His day did not believe in Him, and the people who gathered for the festival that year were not sure what to make of Him (vv. 10-13). When Jesus began to teach, He told the truth about the desires of the religious leaders to kill Him, but the people mocked Him (vv. 14-24). In the face of danger and doubt, Jesus sustained His confidence. All who live in the Spirit can face deterrents and remain faithful to God.

The teaching of Jesus was persuasive, and many believed in Him (vv. 25-31). Their belief made Jesus a threat to the religious leaders who wanted Him stopped. The religious leaders were powerless to stop Him from accomplishing God's purpose for His life (vv. 32-49). This is the power of Jesus. He cannot be stopped. His kingdom will advance no matter what!

There was one person among the religious leaders who believed – Nicodemus. He provided support for Jesus' ministry (vv. 50-52). By standing for Jesus, Nicodemus was opposing his friends. This probably put Nicodemus on the outs with the powerful people of his day, but what an honor he had to take a stand for Jesus! Those who believe in Jesus will often have to make the difficult choice to speak on His behalf and be rejected by the world.

Do you believe in Jesus? Are you standing for Him? Is your faith being ridiculed by the enemies of God?

Like Jesus, God's children can be assured of who they are, they can know what they are called to do, and they can experience peace no matter what others say about them.

Exodus 29; John 8; Proverbs 5; Galatians 4

Chaos is normal in our broken world. We should expect our relationships, work, and health to be a struggle. In Proverbs 5, a father was coaching his son in how to avoid unnecessary struggles and how to enjoy one of life's great blessings: marital intimacy.

God created sex. It is not bad. What is bad is when God's good gift is practiced outside of the boundary that God intended. Marriage is God's intended boundary for sex. When a man and woman unite their lives in a lifelong covenant, sex is appropriate, good, and satisfying. When human beings seek sexual pleasure outside of the covenant bond of a man and woman, they sin. This sin leads to chaos. People get hurt, and hurt people hurt other people – and a cycle of sin and sickness is created.

A man would do well to keep away from wanton women who have no respect for the dignity of marriage and the godly purpose of sex (vv. 1-14). A young man must be patient and must discipline his mind and body so that he does not fall into a trap. Young men and women need to get a vision for their life that includes being a faithful husband or wife. Husbands must look to find sexual fulfillment in their wives, and wives must look to find fulfillment in their husbands (vv. 15-20). Physical intimacy is not complicated or difficult. The challenge for a husband and wife is to maintain the mental and emotional focus that produces romance, which leads to an appreciation for marriage and satisfying sex.

God is watching (v. 21). He knows what we are doing and why. God wants our lives to be blessed, but if we choose sin, we will suffer the consequences of our sin (v. 22). Those who discipline their lives and maintain a commitment to God's purpose for sex and marriage will avoid much pain and sorrow. While movies, music, and television tempt us to distrust the way of God, a quick survey of history shows the wisdom of God's way.

Are you keeping yourself sexually pure? Do you have a vision for marriage that inspires you to be obedient to God's Word and way of life? Is God pleased with your way of life? Is your way of life one that God blesses?

Those who are able to navigate their desires and keep
chaos at a minimum will experience peace.

Exodus 30; John 9; Proverbs 6; <u>Galatians 5</u>

Religion can seem right, but it is wrong. Ignoring God's law seems liberating, but it actually enslaves. The path of false religion tells us that we can gain God's favor by our activity rather than by faith in the grace of Jesus. The other path, self-indulgence, tells us that we can do whatever our flesh desires and assumes that God does not demand holiness. Galatians 5 uncovers the treachery of each of these paths and shows God's way forward in the power of the Holy Spirit.

Peace does not come to those who try to earn God's favor. The church at Galatia had been deceived into thinking that God expects Christians to add the act of circumcision to their faith (vv. 1-2). Paul challenged them in this and pointed out that if they were going to depend on circumcision to solidify their salvation, they would have to keep the entire law and not just one part of it (v. 3). The gospel of Jesus is the only means of salvation (vv. 4-5). To trust in anything else is to fall away from grace. While there is nothing wrong with the Jewish heritage, it cannot save (vv. 6-12). The goal of a Christian is to always love by grace, which produces peace.

Peace does not come to those who disobey God's law (vv. 13-15). The law of God is to love. When we love God and other people, we keep the entirety of the law. It is difficult to sin when we are truly loving others as Christ has loved us. The way of love is found in the life of Christ, and His life is the way of peace.

Peace comes to those who live by the Spirit. The Spirit of God lives within all who are born again. As we abide in Him and follow His leadership in our lives, we produce the fruit of the Spirit (vv. 16-24). The way of the flesh produces the worst in us. The life of the Spirit produces the best in us. By keeping in step with the Spirit and crucifying our flesh, we find freedom and delight in the love and life of Christ (vv. 25-26). As we humbly submit to the Spirit of God, as we study and obey the Word of God, and as we love all the people of the world, we experience peace.

Do you trust in Jesus alone for salvation? Are you producing the fruit of the Spirit? Is your life filled with love for others?

> ***Those who live by the power of the Holy Spirit experience the power of the gospel and enjoy peace.***

God is Immanuel. *Immanuel* means "God with us." God is present and willing to work in the lives of His saints in wonderful ways. The way of God is not complicated. The world is complicated, and sin makes life extraordinarily difficult – but life in Christ is simple. Exodus 31 reveals the simple way of life that all saints can enjoy in God's presence. It is a life filled with the Holy Spirit. It is a life with healthy rhythms of work and rest.

The Holy Spirit is a great blessing to the people of God. We who live on this side of Pentecost have an even greater exposure and experience of Him in our lives than those before Pentecost. In the Old Testament, the Spirit would come upon people and work in them, but it was not in the same way that He does now. The Holy Spirit came upon Bezalel and filled him with abilities that served God's kingdom purpose (vv. 1-11). God now provides spiritual gifts to redeemed people (Romans 12; 1 Corinthians 12). These gifts are from the indwelling, life-giving presence of the Holy Spirit. He blesses every born-again believer with unique gifts that enable them to serve God's purpose with their lives.

The gift of calling and work is precious. Knowing that each day of our life has a purpose provides great peace to God's people. Thankfully, life in Christ is not all work. There is to be a day of rest (vv. 12-18). The day of rest has many good purposes. One, it allows us to acknowledge that God is our provider and that we trust in Him. By resting, we are showing that we are not driven to depend on ourselves, but are living by faith in God's provision. Two, it provides God's people with a day to remember God's grace and goodness and to be renewed with hope. Three, it unites God with His people and unites the people with God in worship. The day of rest is a God-honoring gift that blesses everyone.

Learning to exercise our gifts and to rest in God's grace are two of the most significant activities in our spiritual lives. These activities simplify our focus and strengthen us to pursue our destiny.

Are you serving God with your spiritual gifts? Is your life disciplined and scheduled appropriately so that you take a day to rest and gather with the church for worship?

Those who live simply according to God's Word live with peace.

Exodus 32; John 11; Proverbs 8; Ephesians 1

Nothing is impossible with God. God has the power to take what is dead and raise it to life. He takes dead souls, dead marriages, dead friendships, dead family connections, and dead dreams and raises them to life. Jesus Christ was raised from the dead. That was not difficult for God. Nothing is difficult for God. Everything is a small thing to God! John 11 reveals the resurrection power of God in Christ Jesus.

When Jesus heard the news, He did not immediately go and heal His friend Lazarus (vv. 1-6). He delayed for His divine purpose. When it was time to go, His disciples were afraid. He was leading them back to a place where they were wanted men (vv. 7-16). Jesus was not afraid. He had peace because He knew God's plan. He was walking in the light. He was walking in the power and presence of the Holy Spirit. Jesus left heaven for earth to be the way, the truth, and the life (John 14:6). He was pursuing the Father's plan.

Once He arrived, Jesus heard from Lazarus' sister, Martha. She was understandably upset (vv. 17-27). This sad experience was going to end happily, but Jesus wanted her faith to grow in the process. God never wastes our pain. He always teaches us in hard times, which trains us to live in peace in all circumstances.

Once Mary heard that Jesus had shown up, she went and wept at His feet and uttered her disappointment (vv. 28-32). Jesus wept, went to the grave, and commanded Lazarus to come out (vv. 33-43). The miracle happened! Lazarus came out of the tomb, and Jesus commanded them to unbind him from the death cloths (v. 44). When the Lord gives us new life, we must leave off sin and unbelief – the things that bind us. We must walk free in Christ and shine as light in the darkness.

The darkness hates the light. Jesus' enemies were not happy to hear about Lazarus being raised. They were even more committed to arrest Jesus and get rid of Him (vv. 45-57). The saints of God should never be surprised by persecution.

Do you trust God's plan for your life? Have you been raised from the dead to new life in Christ? Are you a threat to darkness?

All who are raised to life through faith in Jesus live
with confidence and an eternal peace with God.

Exodus 33; John 12; <u>Proverbs 9</u>; Ephesians 2

It is easy to be foolish in our fallen world. To be wise takes discipline, faith, and a strong desire to glorify God and enjoy Him. Proverbs 9 provides several pictures of what wisdom looks like and what it takes to live a wise life rather than a life of folly. The consequences of wisdom and folly are pictured clearly.

Wisdom is pictured as an organized life that provides for the basic necessities of life and offers hospitality to those who would like to join her (vv. 1-6). A wise person understands that shelter and food are fundamental to a healthy life. A wise person provides these things through hard work. A wise person does not keep these good things private. A wise person has a hospitable nature. Wisdom calls out to all people with the invitation to come and live a simple, pleasant life. Those who walk with Jesus enjoy His blessings and invite others to the feast.

Telling people who do not want to be wise to be wise is unwise (vv. 7-8). Only the wise want to be challenged to be wiser (v. 9). Wisdom begins with a proper understanding and awe of God (vv. 10-12). Those who trust in Christ live a holy life that is wise. Telling people without Christ to be holy is a waste of time. They don't want to hear it, and they cannot do it.

The way of the world is folly, which is pictured as a loud-mouthed woman with no discretion. She invites people who are without discipline and devotion to God to join her in her carousing and sin (vv. 13-16). Those who think that they are above God's law and beyond the reach of justice will live in sin, and sin will always have consequences (vv. 17-18). Those who walk humbly with God by grace through faith in Christ alone will live in peace, knowing that their life is where God wants it to be. Those who live outside of Christ will be deceived and will make choices that ultimately lead to their harm in life and destruction in death.

Are you a wise person? Is your life one that others can participate in and mimic, and in so doing find God's blessing and peace? How will God judge you in the end? Do you live in light of heaven, and will you enter those gates with thanksgiving?

Those who live wisely enjoy a deep peace in any and every circumstance.

Exodus 34; John 13; Proverbs 10; <u>Ephesians 3</u>

Just as fish rarely appreciate being born in water, few Christians appreciate the privilege of being raised in Christian homes with a God-centered heritage. Writing to gentiles in Ephesians 3, Paul spoke about the privilege he had and the privilege that all who hear the gospel have. It is the privilege to know the mystery of God and to be saved through faith by the grace God gives.

Paul had a unique testimony, and he used his story, training, and experiences to help gentiles understand the gospel of Jesus Christ (vv. 1-9). He made known to them the great mystery of God that generations before could not fully know, and that many on earth had never heard. Those who apprehend and receive the truth of the gospel experience a great blessing.

This blessing is meant to be shared. God has determined to share His gospel through His church (vv. 10-13). The church at Ephesus had been blessed to be taught not only by Paul, but also by the apostle John, and later by both of their apprentices. This church had to endure Paul's suffering, but he wanted them to be encouraged with the hope and honor that was theirs in Christ. This encouragement is the blessing of every generation of believers.

Paul prayed for them what we all need to pray for ourselves and those we love (vv. 14-19). There is nothing more important for a follower of Jesus than to be filled with the Spirit, to be rooted in the love of Jesus, and to be trained in the depths of God's Word. These blessings do not just happen. These blessings come through discipline and personal pursuit. These blessings are the foundation and goal of the Christian faith, and they give peace to the soul.

Having spoken about the privilege and then having offered a gracious prayer, Paul broke into a doxology that is a fitting benediction to his pastoral prayer (vv. 20-21). He praised God for all He can do by His power, and he glorified Him for His blessing in and through the church in every generation. This God of the Christian faith is a gracious and glorious God worthy of our worship.

Are you grateful to know the mystery of the gospel? Are you growing in Christ and glorifying God?

> *Those who know the gospel and receive it by*
> *faith live in God's eternal peace.*

Exodus 35; John 14; Proverbs 11; Ephesians 4

God does not need His people, but He loves them and wants them to be a part of His work in the world. Like a father working on a project who allows his small child to come along and "help," God allows His children to join Him in His work. Exodus 35 explains that God was being a good Father to Israel. He allowed them to be a part of what He was doing in the world.

Having come out of Egypt and having been established in God's plan and purpose, it was vital for Israel to have a sound and steady relationship with God. To provide for their spiritual needs, God commanded the people to set aside the Sabbath to rest (vv. 1-3). He had them construct the tabernacle so He could dwell with them. Through the ministry of Moses and the Levites, the people had their sins atoned for, and God provided direction for their journey into the promised land. It is in Christ that our sins are pardoned, and it is by His Spirit that God's people are led through life.

While God could have made the tabernacle on His own, He chose to allow the Israelites to contribute to its construction (vv. 4-29). God did not need their materials or their labor. He could have done it all Himself. Instead, God allowed His people to join Him and show Him their love. God's people show their allegiance to and affections for God by giving financially to God's work and by serving God's purpose with their gifts and abilities. This show of love demands sacrifice, and it brings glory to God.

Not only does God allow us to do His will and work in the world, but He gifts us to do it. Bezalel and Oholiab were gifted by God in craftsmanship, and they led the people in the construction of the tabernacle (vv. 30-35). They did not choose to be gifted the way they were, but they were willing to choose to use their gifts for God. Every Christian is gifted naturally and also spiritually by God. We must choose either to use our gifts for God's glory or to be foolish and miss out on joining in on God's work.

Do you set aside a day to worship and honor God? Have you been saved by Jesus? Are you giving your money, time, and abilities for God's purpose?

Those who sacrifice what they cannot keep in order to
invest in what will last forever live with peace.

MARCH 25

Exodus 36; John 15; Proverbs 12; Ephesians 5

Life is not always hard, but it is not always easy either. The world is filled with lots of pressure. While children are in school, they are under pressure to perform well academically in order to get into college. College students are under pressure to succeed and stand out in order to get good jobs. The workforce is filled with people under pressure to produce results. In John 15, Jesus blessed His disciples with the hope of the Holy Spirit, who helps with life's pressures.

The Christian life can become stressful if it is not lived in the Spirit. There are many miserable Christians in the world who are loaded down with guilt and shame, and there are many who are wearing themselves out trying to do better. Jesus has not called us to do better. He does not desire us to be a better form of our old, sinful self. Jesus came to give new life. Christians simply have to abide in Jesus, and His life will be manifest in them (vv. 1-11). Christians abide in Christ through the presence and power of the Holy Spirit. We experience Jesus through His Word and through gathered people.

Peace is enjoyed by Christians who have complete confidence in Christ's love. Jesus laid down His life for believers (vv. 12-17). There is no greater love than that! Those who receive His love are able to love others. It is in the love of the saints that God's people experience genuine friendship and find the comfort and encouragement to overcome the pressures of life. Followers of Jesus are never alone. Their friend, Jesus, is always with them and will guide them through the leading of the Holy Spirit.

While all of God's children are loved by Him, they are hated by the world (vv. 18-25). This should not surprise or concern a disciple of Jesus. Not only do we have the hope of eternal life and the knowledge that this world is not our home, but we also have the assistance of the Helper, the Holy Spirit (vv. 26-27). He will constantly remind the saints who Jesus is, and He will help them bear witness about the gospel. This produces peace.

Are you abiding in Jesus and producing the fruit of the Holy Spirit in your life (Galatians 5:22-23)? Is the love of Jesus the source of your hope? Are you living in the Spirit?

Despite life's pressures, those who abide in Jesus and walk in the power of the Spirit enjoy peace.

Exodus 37; John 16; Proverbs 13; Ephesians 6

All of us are being influenced by something and someone. What we do has a direct impact on how we feel and how we process life. Lives left unchecked will wallow in worldly ways. The way of the world is unwise. It leads to brokenness and pain. Proverbs 13 provides an overview of how a follower of Jesus is to live.

A follower of Jesus is to listen to wise counsel. One of the most important functions of parents is to teach their children to know what is right and wrong. This happens through biblical instruction. Children are truly blessed who learn the biblical faith lessons of their parents. Good parents not only teach their children the fundamentals of the faith, which provides them with the tools to live well, but they discipline their children when they do not live wisely and obediently.

A follower of Jesus is to focus on the ways of God and avoid the ways of the world. The ways of the world cause a person to live either in despair or in pride. The person who succeeds in worldly, temporary ways will typically be prideful, while the person who fails in worldly pursuits will tend to fall into despair. God's way leads us to humble contentment and confidence.

A follower of Jesus is to guard his words. The easiest thing to do is to say whatever we may feel. This is unwise. Unfiltered words cause great harm. Those who walk in the Spirit will produce the fruit of the Spirit, and their words will match their character. The words of the righteous honor God and build others up.

A follower of Jesus is to be a good steward. There is nothing wrong with gaining resources and having the benefit of possessions, power, popularity, and pleasure. What is wrong is when those things become the goal of a person's life rather than the tools we use to honor God. Dishonest gain destroys lives. When we work honestly and use the gain we get to serve the Lord and His purpose, we will experience peace.

The righteous gift of God satisfies the hunger of the soul, but those who dishonor God are never able to feel full (v. 25). Worldly people have a worldly appetite that is never satisfied.

Are you being wise? Is your life blessed? Do you have peace?

Those who walk in the way of God live with peace.

Exodus 38; John 17; Proverbs 14; <u>Philippians 1</u>

There is never a single moment when our lives are not under the sovereign care of God. We all must make decisions in life, and those decisions have consequences. It is a great comfort to all who are in Christ to know that God has the power to work all things for good (Romans 8:28). Philippians 1 is one of the great reminders of God's faithfulness to those who believe.

Paul was writing from prison to his beloved friends at the church of Philippi. Paul had planted that church years before through miraculous means (Acts 16). The church of Philippi had sent Epaphroditus on a short-term mission trip to help Paul. Paul was sending him back to them with news of his life and faith.

Paul was confident that God was working out the perfect plan for his life and was using everything he was going through to conform him to the image of Christ (vv. 1-6). God sanctifies all of His children and uses the perfect means to do so.

Paul was praying for his friends (vv. 7-11). This is one of the great favors Christians can do for one another. Paul's prayer is a perfect model. While it is good to pray for physical needs, it is important to remember that our spiritual needs are the most important.

Paul was encouraging his friends (vv. 12-18). It was probably disheartening to them, and maybe even embarrassing to them, that Paul was imprisoned. But Paul was able to see his circumstances through an eternal lens. He was not worried about worldly comforts. He was focused on expanding God's kingdom. This is the mindset that is needed today, and it is one that will always produce peace.

Paul was practical in his approach to life (vv. 19-30). While he would have preferred to die and go to heaven, he was confident that he would remain a while longer to serve God's purpose. He also encouraged his friends to pursue God's purpose through a united effort and commitment. Suffering is a part of God's plan, but it is also a part of the blessing. God's people are to love and help each other through struggles, and in so doing, they honor Jesus.

Are you confident in God's power and plan? Are you helping other believers grow in Christ?

Those who truly trust in God's power to accom-
plish His plan live with peace.

God is a God of order. He made all things in perfect harmony. It is because of the fall that there is so much chaos in our spiritual lives and in our relationships with other people. Those who are redeemed by God get to experience the power, unity, and purpose of God in their relationships, as pictured in Exodus 39.

The priestly garments worn by Aaron can seem strange to those of us living under the new covenant of Jesus. This description provides a beautiful picture of the grace and goodness of God. It is important to note the beauty (vv. 1-7), the community (vv. 8-29), and the majesty (vv. 30-43) that this clothing communicates.

Those who saw this masterpiece of fashion were awed by its splendor. That was the point. When God created the world, He made it beautiful on purpose. Our God is a God of wonder, and He makes things beautiful. Those who trust in Him can be made into new creations that are beautiful (2 Corinthians 5:17). This is the power of God.

Those who receive God's grace are born again into a new life as God's adopted children. The stones that represented the twelve tribes must have been a wonderful reminder to each Israelite that they belonged to a special people and inheritance. So it is for the redeemed of Christ. We are a special people saved for a special purpose that honors God (1 Peter 2:9-10). It is God's grace that makes us what we are and enables us to live holy lives.

Those who are redeemed by grace and made members of God's covenant people are restored in the image of Christ. God is holy. Those who are born again in Christ are given a holy standing with God that enables them to live holy lives. Without the grace of the Father, the redemptive blood of the Son, and the indwelling power of the Holy Spirit, we could do nothing to be holy. Because of who God is and what He has done for us, in us, and with us, we are changed and are becoming what God intended us to be. The more and truly we follow Jesus, the more holy we become.

Do you live in awe of God? Are you living as an active part of God's family in a local church? Is your life holy?

> *By aligning our lives under the love and leader-*
> *ship of Jesus, we enjoy God's peace.*

Exodus 40; <u>John 19</u>; Proverbs 16; Philippians 3

Grace is getting what we do not deserve. Mercy is not getting what we do deserve. Every one of us human beings deserves to live our lives empty and hopeless because we have all sinned. By God's grace and mercy, though, we are able to live lives filled with love, healthy relationships, and hope. John 19 describes the death and burial of Jesus. It is because of Jesus' sacrifice that we can have peace with God, peace within, and peace with others.

The death of Jesus was not an accident. It was promised and foretold by the prophets and Jesus. The torture that Jesus endured came at the hands of those whom Jesus came to save (vv. 1-9). Pilate was an evil man, but even he knew that Jesus was innocent. He did not want to have the blame for Jesus' death, and Jesus, in this moment of pain, gave Pilate hope and assured him that he was not to blame (vv. 10-11). Despite knowing the right thing to do, Pilate caved in to the pressure (vv. 12-16). Although each person was responsible for their sin that day, God was sovereign. The death of Jesus was the will of God, and nothing can keep the will of God from being fulfilled.

The process of Jesus' death was horrific (vv. 17-24), yet as He was dying on the cross, He looked to the needs of His mom (vv. 25-27). Having come in flesh, Jesus had a mom, and He loved her and provided for her.

Although Jesus was crucified, it was He who laid down His life and gave up His spirit (vv. 28-30). He could have come down off that cross and lived eternally, but that was not God's will. He died to save us. His death paid for our sin (Hebrews 9:22). This is the gospel. Jesus died to save sinners.

There can be no doubt that Jesus died. The Romans were experts at killing. The soldiers confirmed that Christ was dead (John 19:31-37), and Jesus' friends made sure He received a proper burial (vv. 38-42). His friends' act of kindness was costly. It was not just the grave and spices that were expensive, but these men identified with Christ, which made them enemies of the powers of the world. They showed Jesus their true love.

Have you trusted in Jesus' sacrifice to pay for your sin? Are you truly grateful to God? Do you live as a friend of Jesus?

Through Jesus, we can have eternal peace.

Leviticus 1; John 20; <u>Proverbs 17</u>; Philippians 4

The world is not as it should be. While everyone talks about changing the world, there has been very little change in the corrupted character and ruined state of the world since the fall of man. The human condition is sinful. The brokenness of the world is unrelenting. Proverbs 17 provides a realistic picture of the condition of the world and the impact wise people can have on it.

The best place to apply help and healing in the world is at home. The family is the backbone of society. As families go, so goes the culture. Homes that enjoy peace, even if they do not have riches, are blessed (v. 1). Homes with obedient children are blessed (v. 2). Parents would be wise to work on keeping a healthy marriage and training their children to be respectful and obedient (v. 25) so that future generations can bless and be blessed (v. 6).

God puts people to the test to help them know their true character (v. 3). The world is filled with liars and evildoers (vv. 4-5, 8-9, 11, 13, 15, 19-20, 23). Those who are poor and have limited opportunity will always be oppressed in societies that do not have an abundance of God's gospel and God's Word. The goodness of the gospel and the truth of God's Word inspire love. While the poor suffer, those who cause their pain are cursed.

The best way forward is to live like Jesus. Jesus is the manifestation of truth and wisdom. Proverbs 17 is filled with verses about the importance of saying the right things, doing the right things, and investing in key relationships so that a person can enjoy the best things in life. Wisdom is revealed in the way people choose to live. Those who are cursed are called fools. They lack discretion and humility, which leads to their downfall. Those who use kind words, choose to help others, learn from others and from their own mistakes, and are willing to make the hard choice of doing the right thing will live a blessed life.

Are you a person who is considered wise by those who know you best? Do people seek to understand your way of life because of the relationships you enjoy? Is God able to bless you and be praised for your way of life?

While none of us can make the world what it was made to be, we can make it better and can gain peace for ourselves in the process.

Leviticus 2-3; John 21; Proverbs 18; <u>Colossians 1</u>

The life of a disciple of Jesus is not easy, but it is peaceful. There is a great relief in the heart of every believer who knows that the life of Christ is being manifested in their relationships. Every believer is related to Jesus and to all of God's children, including the redeemed heritage of Old and New Testament saints. Colossians 1 reveals how saints function in the world.

God gives many gifts to His children, and three of Paul's favorites to mention are faith, hope, and love. Although Paul never visited Colossae, he loved the people. He shared with them a spiritual bond in Christ. Every person who claims Christ as Savior is connected to all other believers. As part of God's family, each member is responsible to love and pray for the others (vv. 1-14). By loving each other, praying for one another, and being a source of encouragement to the redeemed, we fulfill our calling in Christ.

We are called to love, obey, and follow Jesus. Who He is and what He has done is miraculous (vv. 15-23). He is the Son of God, and He has made Himself known to us through Christ so that we can relate rightly to Him. God is glorious and mysterious, and yet we can know Him and love Him. God loves us and has done everything necessary for us to have eternal life in Him if we pursue Him by faith. Salvation is a gift that comes with responsibilities. The redeemed must walk in a way worthy of Christ and must live by faith in all circumstances.

As we love one another and choose to live by faith, we will be witnesses to the world (vv. 24-29). It is not always fun or comfortable. The apostle Paul was in prison, but from there he could see God's hand using him. The mystery of God is His gospel and how such a holy and glorious God could endure and care for such sinful and broken people like us. God is truly gracious. His grace has been and is being made manifest through His redeemed people. The redeemed are called to warn the world of the righteous judgment of Jesus that is to come and to tell the world of the eternal grace that is available to all who believe.

Are you connected with other Christians in a local church? Is Christ the ultimate source of your decision-making? Do you regularly tell others about Jesus and His saving power?

Those who live rightly in Christ live with peace.

Leviticus 4; Psalms 1-2; Proverbs 19; Colossians 2

Nobody is perfect. Only one perfect person has lived on this planet, and He was God in the flesh – Jesus Christ. While we may pursue perfection, we will never achieve it on this side of heaven. For a follower of Jesus, sin is always only to be unintentional. Assurance of salvation comes from confidence in grace and a love the produces the fruit of faith. Keeping in step with the Spirit with a heart that desires and is disciplined to pursue holiness creates confidence in the Christian life. Leviticus 4 shows how serious sin is, but also how God gives grace to those who look to Him in faith.

God knows that we are living in the flesh in this fallen world and are being deceived by demonic foes. The grace of God that enables us to be filled with the Spirit and redeemed by the blood of Jesus inspires us to live holy lives. The Old Testament saints had to live by faith in looking forward to the cross of Jesus. Those of us who live on this side of the cross can look back by faith to Jesus' sacrifice that paid for our sin. Despite our best efforts, we will fall short of God's holiness. Thankfully, there is grace (vv. 1-12).

Not only can individuals fall short of God's perfection, but entire communities of faith can fall short as well (vv. 13-21). People are easily deceived and can be convinced that what is wrong is right. For centuries, Christians in the United States enslaved Africans and treated them as animals. Thankfully, God revealed His truth and the masses repented. The saints must be sensitive to injustice.

Confusion among the saints is often the fault of a leader. Leaders will fail (vv. 22-35). The Bible points to the fallibility of every leader who has ever lived. The only perfect leader is Jesus. The only means to know what is true and right is God's Word. Those who lead must be sensitive to the Spirit and repent of sin quickly. Every leader is blind to their sin to some extent and needs others for accountability. When a leader sins, that leader must seek forgiveness and stand in the gospel of God.

How are you tempted to sin? Are you humble enough to admit your sin and repent? What are the blind spots of your faith community? How can you pray for your leaders?

Those who genuinely pursue God's purpose of holiness in life will live and die with peace.

Leviticus 5; <u>Psalms 3-4</u>; Proverbs 20; Colossians 3

What we perceive is not always reality. We live in a physical world that is being controlled by spiritual powers. It is easy to live by physical sight and to grow weary and angry with the way things are on this planet. God calls His people to see beyond the physical world to the spiritual realities that are moving and influencing the physical realities. In Psalms 3 and 4, David is dealing with the pain of life and seeking help from his heavenly Father.

David was a great military leader and politician, but one of his sons, Absalom, turned out poorly. When David had to flee from him, it seemed as if he had many more enemies than friends; he was even told that God had abandoned him (3:1-2). Yet, David knew better. By faith, he looked beyond his circumstances to God in prayer (vv. 3-4). God's children always have hope. We can depend on the truthfulness of Scripture and talk with God.

The Lord was David's strength. David knew the truth, and the truth was that God was with him – and because God was with him, David had no reason to fear (vv. 5-8). He was able to sleep knowing that the Lord was His provider. David was not a fool. He was attuned to how serious his situation was, but he knew that God was bigger than his problems – and he experienced peace.

Having lived through trials and having depended on God in difficult times, David was able to call out to God with confidence (4:1). He was able to testify to the world about the greatness and goodness of God (vv. 2-3). Inspired by the Holy Spirit, David still commands humanity to avoid sin by honoring God and doing what is right (vv. 4-5). God does more than tell us to say "no" to sin. He calls us to say "yes" to His life and to pursue what is best. What is best is to trust in the God who puts joy in the hearts of the faithful (vv. 6-7). Those who trust in God are able to sleep in peace (v. 8). So many people needlessly struggle with anxiety. We can trust in God!

Are you able to look beyond physical difficulties? Do you pray with confidence knowing that God is your provider? Is your faith producing peace in your soul?

Those who look to God and find salvation in Christ
alone find peace in every circumstance.

Leviticus 6; Psalms 5-6; <u>Proverbs 21</u>; Colossians 4

Happiness depends on happenings. Everyone wants to be happy. God made us to be happy. The world is not as it should be. God made everything in harmony, but humanity spoiled it with sin. God has not abandoned us. We can experience some of what God intended for us. We can fulfill our design. Proverbs 21 points to the basic things that God graciously gives that lead to happiness.

God is in control (vv. 1, 31). This chapter begins and ends with that fact. While politicians and leaders thrive on power and seek their own good in their positions, they are still under God. God moves them as He pleases. The outcome ultimately depends on God. What comes to be is what He wills. While evil and destruction are certainly part of the perils of the planet, those who have eyes to see what God can do get glimpses of God's hand at work. God is at work in the world, and He can and does use evil for good. We only need to look at the cross of Jesus to know that.

What people choose to do is important. Our actions matter (vv. 2-8, 10-18, 20-30). We can fool lots of people, including ourselves, but we cannot fool God. He knows our hearts. Our actions reveal the condition of our hearts and souls. How we treat the least in the world and how we honor or dishonor God ultimately reveals the people we are and the people we will end up becoming. Caring for the poor, working hard and honestly, and honoring God authentically will lead to a blessed life and legacy.

One of the greatest legacies a life can leave is that of a godly marriage. When one man and one woman choose to honor God and live under Christ in a covenant of marriage, they are a blessing. When men refuse to lead, women will step in and do what must be done. Men and women living outside of their God-given roles cause confusion and frustration (vv. 9, 19). Husbands and wives living in their God-given roles with love for one another become a great blessing to each other and to all who know them.

Are you trusting God's power and plan to accomplish His purpose for you? Do you treat God and other people well? Are you living in or preparing to live in a godly marriage?

Those who trust God and pursue His ways will
enjoy His peace and will taste happiness.

Leviticus 7; Psalms 7-8; Proverbs 22; <u>1 Thessalonians 1</u>

There is nothing like the peace that enters a soul when a person trusts in Jesus Christ as the redeemer and ruler of one's life. That peace not only impacts the individual, but it also impacts those who already believe. They get to see God doing in others what God did in them when they were saved. In 1 Thessalonians 1, Paul praised God and encouraged the believers in Thessalonica regarding the saving faith that rescued the members of that church.

The people of Thessalonica were not unlike all of the other European people of their day. They were pagans. They did not know or believe in the one true God. All of that changed when God led Paul to their city. Paul preached the gospel, many people believed, and a strong church was formed (Acts 17:1-9). After leaving that city to preach in other cities, Paul continued to check in on them. He had heard that they were in distress, so he dispatched Timothy with his letter. He began the letter in his typical manner of honoring God's grace and rejoicing in the peace of Christ (v. 1).

He wasted no time before giving the Thessalonian Christians a strong word of encouragement and affirmation (vv. 2-3). Paul let them know that he and others were praying for them faithfully and were remembering them because of their faith and love. Being known for encouraging others is one of the best things a believer in Jesus can be known for. Being a person or a people who are known for their love and faithfulness is a great honor, and it is one that blesses all of God's people.

Paul encouraged them in their faith and assured them that they were indeed redeemed people in Christ (vv. 4-10). He pointed to the many proofs of their faith: the Holy Spirit had brought great conviction to them, their lifestyle had changed and now mimicked that of Paul and the other disciples of Jesus, their reputation was used to inspire other believers, and their rejection of paganism and acceptance of Jesus was well documented. When Jesus saves a person, there is always proof – or what the Bible calls *fruit*.

Has Jesus Christ saved you from your sin and given you a new life? Is your faith an encouragement to others? Can you note changes God is making in you?

> ***Those who are saved and those who get to see them***
> ***come to saving faith experience divine peace.***

Being transformed from a sinner into a saint is the greatest experience a human being can have. When a child of God is born again, everything changes. Redeemed saints are no longer on their own. Their sin is pardoned. God is in them, with them, and for them. Leviticus 8 describes the scene of the consecration of Aaron and his sons. What they went through is a picture of what all of God's redeemed children experience in salvation.

The work of God in a saint's life is personal, but it is never meant to be private. God had Moses bring the people together to see Aaron and his sons set apart (vv. 1-4). When God saves people from their sins, they are to be baptized. They are to make a public profession of what God has done in their lives. Having trusted in Christ and obeyed God's Word by being baptized, they are ready to be recognized as members of a local church and to live as witnesses of the gospel of Jesus (Acts 1:8).

The work of God in a saint's life is supernatural. It is by the power of the Holy Spirit that a person is able to believe and to be saved. Having trusted in Christ, a person is sealed by the Spirit until the day of judgment (Ephesians 1:3-14). Aaron and his sons were consecrated and blessed to know God's will and to walk in God's way (Leviticus 8:5-13). This is normal for all Christians.

The work of God in a saint's life makes the person holy. Through Christ's sacrifice alone, a person is saved (Ephesians 2:8-9). Aaron and his sons were made holy by a blood sacrifice that was a type and foreshadowing of Jesus' coming sacrifice (Leviticus 8:14-35).

The work of God in a saint's life ultimately leads to a life of obedience to Jesus. Having been sanctified, Aaron and his sons obeyed God's Word and will (v. 36). Those who are truly saved live a life of obedience to God (John 3:36). Salvation is affirmed through obedience to Jesus. It is impossible to know and love Jesus and to refuse to obey Him. Obedience is the fruit of real faith.

Have you been saved by Jesus? Are you living in the power of the Holy Spirit? Is your life marked by God's grace and your devotion to Jesus?

Those who live in Christ are blessed, and the blessings God brings produce peace.

Leviticus 9; <u>Psalm 10</u>; Proverbs 24; 1 Thessalonians 3

It can sometimes seem as if God is far away, but He isn't. God is not only transcendent, but He is also immanent. He oversees every galaxy, weather system, and life. He also holds together every molecule, moment, and soul. God is the one true God. There is none like Him. Psalm 10 seems to be something of a lament, something of an imprecatory plea, and something of a provisional prayer. The entire chapter reminds us that God knows what is best.

The Lord sees, and the Lord knows. The world is not as it should be. In this world, the wicked will prosper (vv. 2-11). Those with power must always choose how they will use their influence – whether for good or for evil. The psalmist is sad to see injustice, and he wonders where God is (v. 1). God has the power to use evil things for good. He does not create evil, but He has a purpose for it. In the end, all things glorify Him and accomplish His eternal purpose.

The best thing a child of God can do is to trust and obey God and pray for God's provision. The prayer of the righteous is possible because of the faithfulness and goodness of God. We pray to God by faith, trusting in God's holiness (vv. 12-14). The righteous can look back and remember the way God has helped in the past. They can pray for God to wreck the unrighteous and to pour out His wrath on them because of their sin (v. 15). The children of God must be careful to pray in humility and to not assume they are any better than the sinners they complain about. Seeking the will of God gives clarity and confidence in prayer.

God always provides for His people and His plan. The Lord's plans stand. His given goal is to save a people for Himself, and in so doing, to bring glory to His name. The Lord takes no pleasure in destruction, but because He is holy, He will bring justice (vv. 16-18). Those who are opposed to God have every reason to live in trepidation. Those who side with God can live with humble confidence in His goodness and grace.

Are you living a life that honors God and blesses others? Is the Lord free to do as He pleases with and in you? Are you praying rightly for God's will to be done in you and others?

*Those who trust in God's will and seek His guid-
ance and blessing live with peace.*

Leviticus 10; Psalms 11-12; <u>Proverbs 25</u>; 1 Thessalonians 4

Wise people don't have to learn the hard way through painful experiences. They can learn from others' experiences. To act wisely is to choose to do what is best at the right time. Blessed people are wise people who bless others. The wise sayings of Solomon that begin in Proverbs 25 were collected during Hezekiah's days to be used as a means of instruction and to call the people of God back into alignment with God's will.

Wise people enjoy peace under God-given leadership (vv. 1-10). There are certain things that God conceals from some people, but provides to those who are entrusted with authority. It is vital that people in leadership seek out the will of God. In seeking God's will, a leader can discern what is best. Those who are under wise leadership are fortunate, and they need to honor those whom God has placed them under rather than pester or distract them. Filling the courts with issues that can be handled among neighbors in a neighborly way is unwise. The godly must do what is right and be an example to others.

Wise people enjoy peace as they relate rightly to others (vv. 11-26). There is a right way and a right time for everything. Wise people not only know the right thing to do, but also they are mindful of the timing. When we do what is right in the right way at the right time, there is a blessed outcome. Wise people are able to challenge those who are in the wrong. It is the will of God for His people to be an example to others as to how to live.

Wise people enjoy peace as they discipline themselves (vv. 27-28). Hardship has a way of straightening out what is crooked. The better way is to trust God and obey His Word. In order to obey God, people have to be willing to subdue their flesh and avoid sin. The wise people of the world are those who seek the glory of God by setting biblical boundaries for their activities and in their relationships. God has given specific limitations. When we live within the bounds of what God has commanded, we are wise and blessed and are able to be an example to others.

Are you pursuing a wise path in life? Is God's Word your guide in determining what is best? Do you live in such a way that others can learn wisdom by following your example?

Those who seek to live wisely live with peace.

Leviticus 11-12; Psalms 13-14; Proverbs 26; <u>1 Thessalonians 5</u>

You are listening to someone, and believe it or not, someone is listening to you. We all are being led, and to some extent we are providing leadership. Who and what influences us and how we influence others reveals what we believe. In 1 Thessalonians 5, God tells us to be influenced by Christ, by His second coming, and by other godly leaders.

The Lord has not revealed when He will return. That is not our concern (vv. 1-3). It is enough to know that the day is coming and that we need to be prepared for it (v. 4). Being prepared means living as children of light who are wide awake to the reality of God and the spiritual battle we are in (vv. 5-8). Those who trust in Jesus have received His salvation and can be encouraged and give encouragement to others (vv. 9-11). It is not only the super-spiritual people who live in light of Christ's return, but average Christians also do so out of a deep sense of awe and faith in God's promises.

To prepare us and to help us look for the return of Christ, God places each of His children in a church family. In each church family, God raises up leaders who are to be respected and esteemed (vv. 12-13a). As the church lives under godly leadership, the people are to pursue peace (v. 13b). The leaders are to provide the proper guidance that matches each member's situation and need (v. 14). Wise leaders are able to discern those needs and to govern the church well (v. 15). Those who live peacefully under divinely called leadership in a local church enjoy God's blessings.

When God's children are living blessed lives under godly leadership, they are able to rejoice and pray without ceasing (vv. 16-17), be grateful always (v. 18), walk in the Spirit (v. 19), and obey the Bible (vv. 20-21). The Lord sanctifies His people and commands them to pray for not only their own church needs, but also for missionaries and other faithful servants (vv. 22-25). Saints being sanctified have a warm affection for God's Word. God is honored, and His grace is apparent in their lives (vv. 26-28).

Are you honoring God's leaders? Do you bless your church? Is God using your life to help the church?

Those who give and live happily under godly leadership live with peace.

<u>Leviticus 13</u>; Psalms 15-16; Proverbs 27; 2 Thessalonians 1

God is the perfect parent. He knows what is best. He provides laws to protect both our souls and our bodies. He did this for Israel. The Levitical laws that were specifically related to the nation of Israel or temple worship are no longer functional. Both the theocratic nation of Israel and the temple are gone. The laws still point to Jesus and the life He alone can give to all who believe in Him. In Leviticus 13, the manifestations of disease are described, and the effects and consequences are explained. Like sin, these diseases impact a person's body, relationships, and appearance.

Like sin, the diseases described in this chapter had the capacity to infect others. It is crucial that those who walk with Jesus are aware of temptations that can easily contaminate their lives. Like a disease, sin is not easily contained. It will often spread to other parts of the body and cause sickness. Sin is a pollutant to the soul. It sickens the mind and damages the heart. Those who are lost in sin have no hope because their souls are sick.

Like sin, the diseases in this chapter impacted relationships with others. Because people could contract the disease, it was crucial that space be created between the sick and the healthy. Those who are stuck in sin will infect their children and acquaintances. We are all in contact with those who are lost in sin, and we must be mindful of their sickness and take the necessary steps to keep us from falling into their sin. Sin damages relationships. It limits the depth of contact and the quality of the interactions.

Like sin, the diseases in this chapter impacted a person's appearance. Although not all sins will cause physical change, sin, over time, has a way of sickening both the soul and the body. Those who live hard lives separated from God often show the signs of it as time goes by. Those who die in sin will suffer for eternity in the pain their sin caused (Isaiah 66:24).

Are you washed clean in Christ by faith? Do you protect your life from sin by honoring Christ and obeying His Word? Will you live eternally pure with Christ?

Those who live clean in the purifying work of Christ
have eternal peace through faith in God's grace.

Leviticus 14; Psalm 17; Proverbs 28; 2 Thessalonians 2

Confidence in the Lord is powerful. Being sure of who God is and how much He loves us makes our prayer and our commitment to Him strong. In Psalm 17, David is praying with great confidence. He knows God. He knows His love. He is seeking God's provision in the midst of difficulties caused by his enemies. This psalm provides insight into who God is, who Christ is, and who God calls His children to be.

David was in a tight spot. He was surrounded by people who wanted to hurt him. David was not perfect. He knew that. Although he was not perfect, he was right with God. Knowing that he stood in the right gave him confidence to call out to God and claim that his cause was just (v. 1). His confidence was based on his belief that God knew him, loved him, and was for him (vv. 2-8). His enemies were dangerous (vv. 8-12). David called on God to intervene (vv. 13-14). David lived with an assurance of faith in God (v. 15). This is the way God desires all of His children to live.

To live with that confidence, God's children must look to Christ. This psalm could be seen as coming from the lips of Jesus. As He was praying in the garden hours before He would die for the sins of the world, He agonized in prayer. Jesus is the righteous One. He called on God to help Him. Having prayed, Jesus took His stand and gave His life for all who would believe. By being steadfast in His love, He won the victory over sin and death! Jesus knew who He was and lived out His purpose.

The children of God who live under Christ have every reason to live confidently in God. Not only can we look back to the life of David and see how God was faithful, but we can look at the sacrifice of Christ and know that all is well with our soul. Knowing that God is a great and mighty God who loves us enables us to pursue God's will and stand against the darkness. The darkness is our enemy. We are children of light. We should never be surprised that we are hated and hunted by the Evil One. God knows us, loves us, and is for us. We can trust God and fulfill our purpose.

Do you have faith in God? Are you confident in His plans for you? Can you stand against the enemy in prayer and faith?

Those who live confidently in Christ have great peace.

Leviticus 15; Psalm 18; <u>Proverbs 29</u>; 2 Thessalonians 3

Society is a strange thing. While what it is and becomes is based on the masses, the masses are made up of individuals who come from specific kinds of families. A society made up of godly and wise individuals and healthy families will be a blessing. Proverbs 29 speaks to the importance of the right choices of an individual and of individual families, and of the decision-making of leaders who oversee societal norms.

The collection of wise sayings in Proverbs 29 begins and ends with a focus on the individual (vv. 1, 27). The rest of the chapter is peppered with insights as to how individuals are to live and respond to godly, wise leadership and to unrighteous and godless influences. Each person has to make the choice to be godly or not. Once that choice is made, all other choices will be influenced by that choice. The person who chooses to follow Jesus has millions of decisions already made for life. Jesus calls us to love. It is liberating and always loving to obey Jesus.

Experts debate the exact percentage necessary for a society to be influenced by a single group. The fact of the matter is that if there are enough righteous people, a culture can be blessed; but if the wicked rule, there is suffering (v. 2). Proverbs 29 is filled with truth concerning leaders and their influence. Societies and cultures are influenced by a set of beliefs and values. Leaders of culture often determine what those beliefs and values are. Cultures that are influenced by genuine Christians will give help to the hurting and hope to all.

Individuals and leaders all come from families. People who are led by godly parents and who heed the good advice of their parents, rather than squandering their lives and resources, will make their parents glad (v. 2). All children need discipline. Those who learn from it become stronger for it. They gain a vision for what life should be, and they submit to God's law (v. 18). What people need most is restraint. Pursuing every feeling and desire leads to destruction. Freedom is found in godly pursuits that come from discipline.

Are you a wise person? Is your family producing offspring who will be helpful and encourage human flourishing? How can you lovingly help your culture?

Those who contribute to the health of a society live with peace.

Leviticus 16; Psalm 19; Proverbs 30; <u>1 Timothy 1</u>

There is a unique blessing that a Spirit-filled mentor can give. It is vital that we not only have godly mentors, but also that we be godly mentors. Timothy was mentored by Paul, and Timothy was mentoring the leadership and congregation at Ephesus. First Timothy 1 shows that a mentor in Christ is to remind, encourage, and model Christ. Being in a mentoring relationship requires faith and humility. Timothy seemed to have both.

Paul had a special relationship with Timothy. God used Paul to call Timothy and prepare him for the ministry (Acts 16). Ephesus was an influential city, and the church that gathered there was important. Timothy had been sent there by Paul to shepherd the people. Writing to Timothy, Paul first reminded him of his high calling and the blessings he had in Christ (vv. 1-2). What we have in Christ is all we need to enjoy this world and to succeed and thrive in it.

Having reminded Timothy of his blessings, Paul encouraged him in his work. Ephesus was a city filled with idol worship. It was a pagan city, and there would be a tendency and temptation among the people to attempt to synchronize the pagan faith with the Christian faith. Paul encouraged Timothy to train the people to be faithful to maintain sound doctrine (vv. 3-11). If sound doctrine is lost, the motivation and means for living a godly life are lost. We all live and make decisions based on what we believe. If we believe what is true according to God's Word, we will live like it.

Paul and Timothy had spent a lot of time on the mission field together. Timothy had seen Paul stand strong and be used by God to do many miracles and raise up several churches. Despite all of his success, Paul managed to remain humble. He shared with Timothy his testimony and his sense of self (vv. 12-20). Paul knew that since Timothy was young, he would be tempted to think of himself as incapable of standing strong and refuting those who would cause harm to the church. Paul reminded Timothy of the calling he had in Christ, and he challenged him to do the work God saved him to do.

Are you a godly mentor to someone? Who are the Christian mentors God has given to you? Do you understand your unique calling in Christ, and are you standing strong in and for Him?

Those who are mentored well in the Lord live with peace.

Leviticus 17; Psalms 20-21; Proverbs 31; 1 Timothy 2

Life is sacred. Human life is the most sacred because humans are made in the image of God and have been given authority over all other life on the planet. All life matters to God and is to be respected. In Leviticus 17, God makes it clear how He wanted the people of Israel to treat the blood of animals. Life in our fallen world is complicated. In His grace, God gave clear instructions. These instructions were intended to provide the proper means of worship and atonement, to enable the people to avoid paganism, and to instruct the people in how to show respect for life.

The children of Israel had been given a sacrificial system that pointed to Jesus Christ. They were to sacrifice animals in order to have their sin debt paid and to have their sinful ways revealed to them so they would refrain from them. They were to bring their sacrifices to the altar so that the priest could honor God with the sacrifices (vv. 1-4). Anyone who sacrificed wrongly was to be cut off from God's covenant and His people. Jesus Christ is the Lamb of God who takes away the sin of the world (John 1:29). All the sacrifices in the Old Testament point to Him. It is now by faith in Christ alone that we have access to God and membership in God's eternal family.

The children of Israel were being tempted to make sacrifices to demons (vv. 5-9). Darkness hates light and always seeks to rob God of glory. Those who look outside of Jesus Christ for hope are cut off from God, the pure means of love. Only Jesus can satisfy the soul with love. All other ways are idolatrous, and those paths dishonor God and do not lead to life.

The children of Israel were commanded to be humane. Human beings have a unique dignity given to them by God. As God's image bearers, we are to honor life. Drinking blood dishonors life and is detestable and wrong. God commanded His people to honor life and His will (vv. 10-16). Those who disrespect life, especially human life, at any stage or in any condition reveal a lack of understanding and a lack of respect for the Maker of life.

Are you in a right relationship with God through faith in Jesus Christ? Do you worship Christ alone? Are you honoring God and the life He has made?

Those who honor God live with peace.

Leviticus 18; Psalm 22; Ecclesiastes 1; 1 Timothy 3

God is gracious and merciful to those who repent and believe in Jesus Christ for salvation. To those who believe and obey, God gives what they do not deserve, which includes eternal life, hope, joy, and peace. He withholds what they do deserve, which includes hell, despair, bitterness, and strife. Psalm 22 shows what we should go through because of our sin and what Jesus went through to redeem us.

When David wrote Psalm 22, he was in a painful and desperate situation. God's people often find themselves in difficult situations in this world. Sometimes we end up in pain and suffering because of our sin. Sin has consequences that are natural and spiritual. There is also the discipline of God that often comes with sin that we believers must endure in order to learn the lesson our loving Father wants to teach us. No matter what we go through or why we go through it, the righteous can always trust in God and look to Him in times of trouble.

Jesus looked to God and cried out to Him what David cried out (v. 1): *Jesus cried with a loud voice, "Eloi, Eloi, lema sabachthani?" which means, "My God, my God, why have you forsaken me?"* (Mark 15:34). In that moment, *For our sake he made him to be sin who knew no sin, so that in him we might become the righteousness of God* (2 Corinthians 5:21). Jesus took our punishment so we could be saved. Jesus not only had to deal with God's wrath, but He also had to deal with the cutting hatred of humanity, as David did (Psalm 22:7-8, 12-13, 16-18). Jesus is now exalted, as David anticipated he would be (vv. 19-31).

Salvation comes at a great price. God does not merely forgive sinners. The Lord has come and has taken our punishment. The Holy One, the Almighty, the King of Kings and Lord of Lords, entered into our poverty and lived a holy life. He died for sins He did not commit. He has been raised and will now redeem. He will soon return and make all things new. He will restore His world and save His saints fully and finally.

Are you grateful for Jesus? Do you trust God in your suffering? Have you been saved?

Those who have gratitude for Jesus' atoning sacrifice live with peace.

Leviticus 19; Psalms 23-24; <u>Ecclesiastes 2</u>; 1 Timothy 4

The world keeps telling us that we can buy happiness, earn our personal value, and make life meaningful by succeeding in a worldly enterprise. That is a lie. The writer of Ecclesiastes put the world's promises to the test and determined that the things of this world are vanity. The words are practical and piercing.

The Bible is clear about what we must be on our guard against: *For all that is in the world – the desires of the flesh and the desires of the eyes and pride of life – is not from the Father but is from the world* (1 John 2:16). The writer of the book of Ecclesiastes, probably King Solomon, was a wealthy man. With his resources and wisdom, this man put the world to the test and found it wanting.

Pleasure and success could not satisfy his eternal soul (Ecclesiastes 2:1-11). He set out to fill his life with fun and good times. Rather than discipline his flesh, he sought to satisfy it. This led him to seek laughter and cheer. Both are good things, but they make terrible purposes for life. He desired to find meaning in success, but he only found frustration and disappointment. Satisfying the flesh won't help the soul. A satisfied soul can only find enjoyment in the flesh when the activity is within God's design.

Wisdom is good, but it is not the final answer to life's longing for fulfilment (vv. 12-17). While being wise is better than being foolish, both the fool and the wise die in the end. Believing that there is superiority in knowledge has been the cause of prejudice. What really matters is character and love. Those who are sincere and kind like Jesus are blessed by being a blessing.

Keeping busy is appropriate because there is so much that needs to be done in this world, but an active life does not equal a happy life (vv. 18-26). Being busy in order to store up treasure or to keep from being bored will lead to disappointment. The best thing to do is to enjoy what you have by honoring God with gratitude rather than trying to acquire what cannot be eternally kept.

What is your hope in life? Are you trusting in God or in self-gratification to give you peace? Do you believe that things or status will satisfy your soul?

Those who find their confidence, value, and mean-
ing in Jesus Christ live with peace.

Leviticus 20; Psalm 25; Ecclesiastes 3; <u>1 Timothy 5</u>

Life can be simple. Living a simple life is often a choice. Even though we may face struggles and difficulties, we can still choose to make life simple. Once we determine to live for God's glory rather than for our own comfort or prestige, life becomes much more simple. Once we choose to trust and obey God, all of our other decisions are basically made. First Timothy 5 provides examples of how to live a simple life.

Choosing to think about others and then treating them with dignity in purity makes life simple (vv. 1-2). When we try to impress other people or control them in some way, life gets complicated. God expects us to take responsibility for ourselves and then do what is right for other people out of respect for God. It's simple.

Looking after those who cannot care for themselves pleases God and makes life simple (vv. 3-16). Widows who are left without family are a perfect example of the kind of people God expects His followers to look after. Some widows can care for themselves or have family who can care for them. Those ladies and their families must be responsible. Those who can help should do so, and those who need help are to be looked after by those who can. It's simple.

Respecting leadership is crucial. It makes life simple (vv. 17-23). Those who are supported by the church in order to fulfill their calling to preach and shepherd God's flock must be provided for and honored. Shepherds must be given time to study, pray, and develop leaders who will serve the church. Leaders who reject God's Word and choose a life of sin must be disciplined publicly. Leaders must be trained well and released to serve. It's simple.

Looking to God as the ultimate judge, while being wise in making decisions about who to trust, is crucial and makes life simple (vv. 24-25). Some leaders will fail because of their sin. They may do good things, but their true character will be revealed in the end and they will be judged by God. Others will be blessed by God because of their faithfulness. Obeying God and seeking to honor Him is wise. It's simple.

Are you living a simple life? Do you do the things that God expects you to do? How are you serving as and under leadership?

Those who choose to live a simple life live with peace.

Leviticus 21; Psalms 26-27; Ecclesiastes 4; 1 Timothy 6

God is so good! His kindness and love are overwhelming. What He has done in the gospel is amazing! Everyone who has been saved by grace through faith in Christ alone has direct access to God (Hebrews 4:16). Every disciple of Jesus is a priest (Revelation 1:6). Jesus Christ is our mediator (1 Timothy 2:5), and through Him, we can speak to God. This is a gift. In the Old Testament, God raised up and provided priests to serve Him and His people. Some of the expectations for priests are laid out in Leviticus 21. Followers of Christ can learn a lot from these expectations.

The Old Testament priests were not to touch or go near a dead body unless it was a close relative (vv. 1-4). Attending to the burial rights of friends and servants was not allowed. Holiness is required of a priest. Death, which symbolizes sin, is not to be touched or to be a part of a priest's life. Disciples of Jesus must avoid sin at all costs and must live lives of holiness unto God.

The Old Testament priests were not to participate in any pagan activities (vv. 5-6). These men were called to provide the sacrifices that were presented to God. Looking like a pagan in any way dishonored the God they served. Disciples of Jesus must avoid pagan lifestyles and live consecrated lives committed to Christ.

The Old Testament priests were to be yoked in marriage with women of upstanding moral character and backgrounds who led their families to honor God (vv. 7-15). These men were to represent God to the people of Israel and to stand before God on their behalf. Disciples of Jesus are to be married only to those who are committed to Christ. A husband and wife are to pursue Christ together and raise children who know and love Jesus.

The Old Testament priests were to be pure when they came to serve God. They were to have no blemishes (vv. 16-24). Their task was holy, and there was to be nothing unseemly about them when they came before God. Disciples of Jesus are to serve God with pure hearts and consciences. There is to be no hint of disobedience or any ongoing sin in their lives. They are to be holy.

Are you living as a representative of God in the world? Is your family life God-honoring? Are you living a holy life?

Those who seek to meet God's expectations live with peace.

Leviticus 22; Psalms 28-29; Ecclesiastes 5; 2 Timothy 1

God has a great plan for each of our lives. Knowing what God wants us to be and then praying toward that end is vital to finding and fulfilling our destiny. There are two kinds of people in the world: those who walk with God by faith, and those who reject God by faith. Everyone lives by faith. Psalm 28 is a prayer, and Psalm 29 is a pronouncement made by a saint intent on honoring God.

David was confident in God's will and found peace in His personal pursuit of God. His prayer was intense (Psalm 28:1). He needed God to respond. He was certain that he would be cursed if God did not intervene. He asked God for mercy and help from His holy habitation (v. 2). He knew what God could do and where to find Him. Having prayed, he worshipped God (vv. 6-9). From the depths of their hearts, those who trust in God delight in who He is.

In between his request and his anticipatory praise, David spoke of what he did not want to be (vv. 3-5). He did not want to be like the wicked. He wanted to be true to God and to other people. He wanted justice. Those who live by faith in Jesus long to see Him return. When Jesus comes, He will make all things new, and those who rejected God will be rejected by Him. Those who accepted God will be accepted by Him. Heaven will be glorious!

Those who know who they are in Christ and find confidence in His Word and in prayer are able to call others to attribute to God the qualities of His excellency and the characteristics of greatness for which He deserves credit (Psalm 29:1-2). God is like a mighty storm that thunders and shakes the earth (vv. 3-4). He is like thunder that breaks what is seemingly unbreakable (vv. 5-8). God causes all things to happen according to His purpose, which makes the redeemed worship and cry, *Glory!* (v. 9). There is nothing like the power of God. God is sovereign over all things, and He graciously gives strength to those who trust in Him (vv. 10-11). The Lord gives peace to His people who look to Him by faith.

Do you live in awe of God? Is prayer and praise a natural part of your life? How do you think of God, and how does that impact the way you live?

***Those who pursue God by faith according to His Word
delight in His plans and live with peace.***

Leviticus 23; Psalm 30; <u>Ecclesiastes 6</u>; 2 Timothy 2

What do you really want? This is a seemingly simple question, but the answer is not the same for everyone. Some want stuff. Some want long life. Some want beauty. Some want knowledge. We all want something. If we were to get what we say and think we really want, would we be satisfied? Ecclesiastes 6 makes the point that without the true satisfaction that God alone can give, there is no peace.

The rich wise man who wrote Ecclesiastes knew a lot about a lot of things. He knew what it was to have wealth, celebrity, power, and great knowledge. What he writes would be depressing if it were not for Jesus Christ. It is wise to consider everything in light of Jesus Christ. Jesus has come to give forgiveness and peace with God. Those who have peace with God are satisfied and can learn to be content in any and every situation (Philippians 4:11).

Human beings will never be satisfied with family and long life without Jesus alive in their soul (Ecclesiastes 6:1-6). Those who work hard, long hours, but do not do so for the glory of God, will never enjoy their work. God does not allow them to (v. 2). Instead, someone who has not worked enjoys the benefit. Having a large family with children does not satisfy because there is no guarantee that the kids will give care, love, or appreciate in return.

Human beings will never be satisfied with status (vv. 7-9). Whether a person is Ivy League or GED does not matter. Everyone dies. No one can see into the future. No one can know what is coming. Without God's guidance, a person will wander the world looking for a way to be satisfied. That pursuit is simply striving after the wind. Satisfaction cannot and will not occur without Christ.

Human beings will never be satisfied with something new and better or greater (vv. 10-12). Everything is just repackaged. Sure, there may be a little more technology in the things that are and that will be, but in the end, human beings have the same need generation after generation. It is a need only God can satisfy.

Is Christ your life and hope? Do you look to Jesus to satisfy? How are you tempted with vanity?

Those who look to Jesus Christ in faith will be satisfied and will have peace.

Leviticus 24; Psalm 31; Ecclesiastes 7; <u>2 Timothy 3</u>

It really bothers me when I am bothered that someone does not meet what I feel are straightforward, basic expectations. The extent of our frustration in life is determined by how far away reality is from what we expected. In 1 Timothy 3, Paul outlines what Timothy's expectations should be in life and ministry.

The world is a broken place. Although each generation is blessed by technological advances, humanity has yet to heal the broken soul with a gadget or pill. Only God can heal a broken soul, and He does so by grace through faith in Jesus alone. Because the world is filled with evil, and because human beings are sinful by nature, circumstances are always going to have some degree of difficulty (v. 1). God's people should never be surprised that sinners sin (vv. 2-7). God's people should never be surprised that some who claim to be godly oppose the truth (v. 8). Thankfully, the folly of those who oppose God's will and way can be avoided by the redeemed.

The redeemed of God have a destined life that is driven by God's will. God has a purpose for each of His children, and He provides for their needs. Timothy was blessed to have Paul as a mentor and guide. Paul showed Timothy how to live for Christ despite the hardships life brings (vv. 10-11). Paul affirmed that living a godly life in a fallen world is tough (vv. 12-13). He also encouraged Timothy in his faith by reminding him of the blessings he had been given by God since his childhood. He had been taught the Scriptures and had been given a firm understanding of his faith in Christ (vv. 14-15).

The Scriptures are a great blessing to God's people. It is vital that every follower of Jesus has a deep and intimate knowledge of God's Word. Each of us has a different level of intelligence, but we all have the same Holy Spirit alive in us. When we take the Bible seriously and study it intently, the Bible will show us what we need to know, it will challenge us to change, and it will equip us for every good work God has planned for us (vv. 16-17). By knowing and obeying God's Word, God's people gain assurance of their salvation.

Do you have a firm grasp on reality based on what the Bible says? Are you being mentored and mentoring others? Is Scripture changing you?

Faithful saints can have peace in any circumstance.

Leviticus 25; Psalm 32; Ecclesiastes 8; 2 Timothy 4

The world is filled with trouble. There is always something wrong in us and around us. Sadly, our natural desire is to join in and add to the trouble of the world. The evil in us and around us can cripple us with fear and anguish. Thankfully, salvation is possible through Jesus Christ. Those who trust in Jesus get to live a different kind of life. The practices and principles for this life are found in Leviticus 25.

God created a day of rest for a reason (vv. 1-7). God never grows weary, but He chose to rest on the seventh day. It was not that God needed a rest, but He rested because rest is good. Human beings do grow weary. Our bodies, minds, and emotions need rest. One day a week, we must trust God in a unique way. We must trust Him enough to choose to rest. Rest is not inactivity. It is focusing on God and His truth, goodness, and grace and quieting ourselves under His sovereign care.

In the theocracy of Israel, there was to be a year of Jubilee (vv. 8-22). Lands were to be returned to the original family owners, slaves were to be freed, and the land was to lie fallow for two years. This act was meant to redeem and sustain. Those who were under the burden of bad decisions would be freed. The land could rest and be rejuvenated. Families could get back what they had lost and could start again. This points us to Jesus. He gives us back the life with God that we lost. We get a fresh start – a new life in Christ.

There was also a means provided for families to redeem the property of struggling kin (vv. 23-34). This is what Boaz did for Ruth and her mother-in-law (Ruth 3:12-13). This is what Jesus does for all who believe in Him. He redeems us!

Jesus said there would always be poor people (Mark 14:7). In Israel, the poor were to be loved and cared for (Leviticus 25:35-55). Christ calls His people to love and care for the poor. Apart from Christ, we are all poor, but He gave us His eternal riches. We are to do for others what God has done for us.

Do you trust God enough to rest one day a week? Are you redeemed in Christ? How do you care for the poor around you?

Those who rest in the Lord, obey His Word, and love
other people experience a soul-satisfying peace.

Leviticus 26; Psalm 33; Ecclesiastes 9; Titus 1

God is good, but He is also holy and powerful. He is just in all of His ways. Thankfully, He is merciful and gracious. The more we come to know the God of the Bible, the happier we are to bow in reverent awe of Him. Psalm 33 is a call to live in awe of God and an explanation of what it looks like when people do.

When we see God as He is, we cannot help but sing praise to His name (vv. 1-5). There is none like the one true God. He alone is worthy to be praised and honored with the best of our abilities. The Word of God is right. The work of God is just. Those who delight in what is pure and true will delight in God. That delight will result in gladly giving God our very best in order to honor Him.

All that there is has been made by God (vv. 6-9). He spoke the creation into existence. By His might, He sustains all things. Every atom, molecule, and galaxy is held together by Him. Making and maintaining everything does not exhaust Him. Nothing is hard for God because His power is inexhaustible. There is no problem He cannot solve, no sin He cannot forgive, and no hurt He cannot heal.

Nothing can stop God! Those who seem powerful and in control are weak and insignificant compared to God (vv. 10-17). The nations of the world come and go. Those who were once in power are forgotten. So many people had plans, and some are now making plans hoping to build something that will remain. Nothing remains except God. He is at work in the world accomplishing His purpose. His purpose stands, and what He has determined to do cannot be stopped. What He has done, is doing, and will do is right and good.

The sovereign power of God is a great comfort to those who trust in Him (vv. 18-20). All that God does, He does for His glory to accomplish what is right and best in the world. Those who fear and hope in Him are saved. By caring for His patient people, He makes the hearts of those who trust in Him glad. There is no help like the help of God. He sees and knows all things, and He sustains His people by His power. His people can count on His steadfast love and faithfulness and know that His purpose will be accomplished.

Do you believe in the power of God? Are you living in awe or fear of anything other than God? Is God your hope and provision?

Those who simply trust in God experience peace.

Leviticus 27; Psalm 34; <u>Ecclesiastes 10</u>; Titus 2

There is a right way and a wrong way. Smart people know right things. Wise people do things right. Wisdom is a great blessing to those who possess it and who put it to good use. It is a bad thing to not know the good to do. It is foolish to know the right thing to do and not do it. In Ecclesiastes 10, the blessing of wisdom is expounded. Wise people not only know the right thing to do, but they also do what is right in terms of their words, actions, and attitudes.

A little foolishness goes a long way in messing up a person's life (vv. 1-3). Wise people are free to act on what they know is best. We can know we are being foolish if we refuse to do what is best. Wisdom is able to overcome our natural foolishness, and this liberates the wise from confusion and frustration.

Wise people have a reign on their tongues and their attitudes, which keeps them from harm. Those in authority are to be respected. Wise people know to keep quiet when the person in authority over them is angry (v. 4). If they stay calm and quiet, the intensity of the situation can lessen. It is best not to cause a problem. Wise people use words well and win the favor of others. It is best not to say too much at all, as this reduces the probability of saying something that will be regretted (vv. 12-14). One of the best ways to keep words in check is by keeping a positive attitude (v. 20). Those who refuse to think negatively will protect themselves.

Wisdom brings blessing, and foolishness brings hardship. When there aren't wise people in authority, pain is the result (vv. 5-7, 16-19). Different people have different abilities. Those with leadership abilities who have learned to organize and administrate effectively make life better for everyone. Blessed people have good leaders.

Dishonesty is foolish (v. 8). People who hurt people usually end up getting hurt. It is better to be honest and to work wisely (vv. 9-11, 15). Work is a good thing when it is done the right way and for the right reasons. Those who overwork miss out on good things and often lose their way.

Are you a person whom others consider to be wise? Do you control your tongue and keep a check on your attitude? Is your life characterized by respect for authority and hard, honest work?

Those who are wise and choose what is best live with peace.

Numbers 1; Psalm 35; Ecclesiastes 11; <u>Titus 3</u>

God has an order to His creation. We humans are made to eat, sleep, and work in a regulated order. Getting into a godly rhythm of life is a blessing that requires discipline. In time, those rhythms become normal. The natural way of broken humanity creates rhythms of life that are self-consumed and destructive. The way of Jesus focuses on others and brings healing and hope. Titus 3 provides a listing of the normal ways of a Christ-centered life.

It is only by grace alone that any human being would ever be able to love others the way Jesus has loved His people. A gracious love marks a disciple of Jesus. It is a life that respects authority, seeks the good of others, and honors God (vv. 1-2). Apart from God, people will only do what is expedient and self-promoting. In Christ, people are freed from sin and selfishness (v. 3). The way of hate is natural with sin-tainted love. Every human being is made in the image of God and has been given the capacity to love. That love can easily turn to hate when what is loved is attacked. The way of Jesus is unconditional love.

God's unconditional love was revealed at the coming of Jesus. Christ came to bring salvation. That salvation came at a great price. In order to save sinners, God had to defeat humanity's greatest enemies: sin and death. Christ came, and through His life, death, and resurrection, He provided salvation. Jesus has provided the gospel for salvation, and the Holy Spirit has come to bring life to those who are dead in sin (vv. 4-7). Now all who believe are born again and are able to live a Christ-centered life.

The Christ-centered life is a hopeful, productive life. It is a life filled with good works that lead to human thriving (v. 8). It is a life that does not get bogged down in needless controversies and godless disputes (vv. 9-10). It is a life that is filled with godly friends who live on mission together for the glory of God to seek and save those who are lost. These friends live for Jesus and help each other by praying for one another and supporting each other in the work God has called each person to.

Are you living a peacemaking life? Is your salvation leading you to do good works? How is your friend network working?

Those who build their lives on living like Jesus live with peace.

Numbers 2; Psalm 36; Ecclesiastes 12; Philemon

There is a simple order to God's creation. Having established a world that could sustain human life, God made human beings in His image. People have creativity, power, and ingenuity for God's purpose. Those who use those abilities to accomplish God's will experience God's blessing. In Numbers 2, God provides a simple structure for the Israelite camp. It is vital for Christians to know the truth and the principles provided in this chapter.

The organization of the Israelite camp could appear to be an insignificant piece of cultural data that has no bearing on the Christian life. That is not true. God spoke about it, which makes it important (v. 1). God spoke to Moses and Aaron. Of all the peoples on the earth, God chose Israel, and then He spoke to that nation's leaders about how they were to be organized. God is a communicating being we can know, love, and obey.

The organization of the camp is significant. The people were to be organized by their families (v. 2a). God has made human beings to be born into families. In our broken world, family life is not always easy, but it is still the best way for human beings to live life and to create and care for life. In our age of individualism, Christians must choose to live in healthy families.

These families were to be organized around the tent of meeting and were to face this structure (v. 2b). God was made manifest through the tabernacle. God's people were to build their lives around God and to face Him. They were not to be turned away from Him. They were to look and watch for Him to direct their path on their journey to the promised land. So, too, Christians are to focus on Jesus and follow Him as He leads them to heaven.

Each tribe had a specific place and purpose in God's plan (vv. 3-34). It was through Israel that Jesus came. He came specifically through Judah, the leading tribe. This cross-formed base camp pictured the object that would one day be used to crucify God's Son. The cross is a central icon for all Christians.

Are you honoring God's design? Are you looking to Jesus to guide you? Have you been saved by the power of the cross?

Those who make God the central aspect of their lives, and then align their lives around His leadership and Word, live with peace.

Numbers 3; <u>Psalm 37</u>; Song of Songs 1; Hebrews 1

Everyone draws strength and finds hope in something or someone. The way of the world is to find strength and hope in an idol or in some fleeting natural ability. Those who trust in the Lord are often tempted to envy and seek the temporary strength of the world. Psalm 37 warns against this temptation and provides solid reasons for trusting in the Lord.

The world is evil. The natural tendency of humanity is to turn against God and to depend on the flesh or a created thing. God provides a better way. The redeemed of God will often be tempted to turn away from God and live like those who are far from Him because it seems sophisticated (vv. 1-2). God's people often do not need to be intimidated by the world, but can look with hope to God's provision.

The best way to live is under God's protective care. When the redeemed of God delight in the person of God, their strength is renewed and the desires of their hearts are satisfied (vv. 3-6). The end result is righteousness. This pleases God and our own souls.

This way of life is by faith. God's will is for the faith of His children to grow stronger day by day and year by year. Faith is strengthened by trials. God puts us in situations that require us to wait on the Lord, depend on His provision, and trust in His timing (vv. 7-24). The wicked take matters into their own hands and cause pain and suffering through their selfish acts. The righteous look to God, and He establishes their steps.

The testimony of the redeemed is powerful and consistent. Over the years, God has proven faithful to those who trust in Him and hope in His provision (vv. 25-38). It is wise to look back over the centuries and study the lives of saints to see what God has done, to see how evil was overcome, and to see how victory came by faith.

Those who live by faith will be rewarded (vv. 39-40). They will see the hand of God move. God will provide for their needs. God will be glorified in their faith. In the end, those who trust in the Lord will find Him well pleased with them.

Are you trusting in God? Is your faith getting stronger? Can you give testimony to God's faithfulness?

Those who rely on God's strength experience peace.

Numbers 4; Psalm 38; <u>Song of Songs 2</u>; Hebrews 2

One of the great blessings in life is marriage – although some may argue that it is one of life's great challenges. The truth is that marriage is both a blessing and a challenge. It is a blessing because it provides the fundamental means by which a man and a woman can experience emotional and physical union with a person of the opposite sex in a God-honoring way. It is a challenge because we are all sinners, and marriage is the union of two people who struggle with sin. The Song of Songs is a collection of love poems that speak about the romance that is to exist in marriage.

Romance is when a person is made to feel as valuable as God says they already are. Human beings are made in the image of God, and saints are bought with the blood of Jesus. The image of God and the blood of Jesus cause people to have infinite worth. A man cannot add more value to a woman, and a woman cannot add more value to a man. God has already bestowed upon men and women infinite value. What husbands can do for their wives and what wives can do for their husbands is to help them feel their value.

God made human beings to be communicative creatures. Thoughts and affections must be shared in marriage. Song of Songs 2 reminds a husband and wife to express how they feel (vv. 1-2). They are to share their hopes and aspirations for their life together (vv. 3-6). It is wise that they pursue this life in the context of accountable community (v. 7) and that they seek to experience each season of life together to the fullest (vv. 8-17).

Marriage is a picture of the gospel (Ephesians 5:22-33). Words expressed in love must be matched with deeds. Ultimately, a man needs to know that he is respected by his wife, and a wife needs to know that she is loved by her husband (Ephesians 5:33). When a man leads and cares for his wife as Christ does for the church, and when a wife follows her husband as the church follows Christ, there is a great blessing.

Do you desire to have a godly marriage? Are you doing all that you can to ensure that you have or will have a godly marriage? Is it your desire to honor God in all you do?

Those who live in a godly marriage that reveals
the grace of the gospel experience peace.

Numbers 5; Psalm 39; Song of Songs 3; <u>Hebrews 3</u>

The Bible is not humanity's word about God. The Bible is God's Word to humanity. The unity and consistency of Scripture is miraculous. The Bible is composed of sixty-six books (thirty-nine books in the Old Testament and twenty-seven books in the New Testament). It was written by approximately **thirty-five** different writers over fifteen hundred years. Yet it has one consistent, compelling storyline running all the way through. It has just one ultimate author – God. The Old Testament characters and themes point to Jesus. Hebrews 3 celebrates the glory of Jesus Christ revealed throughout Scripture.

There is a unique connection that exists among all who believe in Christ. The people in the Old Testament looked forward to the coming of the Messiah. Christians now look back to the life, death, and resurrection of Jesus. Those who share this faith in the coming of Christ/Messiah are one family or house (vv. 1-6). Moses was a part of this house, but God is the architect and builder. God's plan was prepared before the foundation of the world, and everything and everyone in the Bible, including Moses, point to Jesus.

While the Bible was written by human beings, God is the ultimate author. The Holy Spirit inspired each writer to use their language, experiences, and thought patterns to write exactly what God wanted. Those who believe are filled with the Holy Spirit and can respond in faith to what He has said. He says to rest in Jesus (vv. 7-11). Those who look to Jesus in faith can rest from their efforts of trying to save themselves. They can look to what Jesus has accomplished and by faith can receive His righteousness. This is salvation – receiving forgiveness and healing in Christ.

Salvation is by grace. It is a gift that is received by faith. Unfortunately, there are some people who know the information about the gospel but have not been transformed by the truth experientially. Those who are genuinely saved will live by faith, and over time, will become more and more like Jesus – holy. Those who are not faithful to Jesus are like those who rejected God after He rescued them from Egypt (vv. 16-19).

Do you believe that the Bible is God's Word? Have you trusted in Jesus? Are you becoming more like Him?

Those who trust in Jesus have eternal peace.

Numbers 6; Psalms 40-41; Song of Songs 4; Hebrews 4

Everyone wants to be blessed. The greatest blessing is God's blessing. The blessing of God is always a result of God's grace and mercy. That grace and mercy are to be sought. Those who live in the grace and mercy of God are given a holy standing and calling in life. Numbers 6 provides a picture of what it looks like to know and experience God's blessing in the world.

There is a difference between a Nazarite, discussed in Numbers 6, and a Nazarene. Jesus was a Nazarene because He was from Nazareth. A Nazarite was a person who chose to live a unique life separated to God for a holy purpose. Jesus Christ is pictured in the person who chose to be a Nazarite. A Nazarite was viewed as someone who was uncommonly committed to the cause of God and desired to look different and live differently than the rest of the world by committing to unusual standards (vv. 1-21). All who are disciples of Jesus are to live lives that are separated unto God. They will be lives that are different from those who live without God.

The life of a Christian is to be different from the world because it is a life built on Christ. Jesus is the High Priest of the redeemed. He is described in Hebrews 7:26 as *holy, innocent, unstained, separated from sinners, and exalted above the heavens.* Jesus is holy, and is able to make His followers holy by His grace. Having come in the flesh, Jesus empathizes and intercedes on behalf of the redeemed.

Those who have peace with God are eligible for God's blessing. As the High Priest of His redeemed saints, Jesus provides His unique blessing. The blessing of Aaron and his sons that was given to the people of Israel is a blessing that Christians can seek and receive in Christ (vv. 22-27). Those who live in Christ are blessed and kept by Jesus. They are looked upon by God with gracious love. They are watched by God, and their lives are filled with peace because they know that God is in control and loves His people. God looks out for His people every moment of every day.

Have you trusted Jesus? Are you living a holy life? Do you sense God's presence and blessing?

***Those who live in God's grace and mercy live
blessed lives filled with peace.***

Numbers 7; Psalms 42-43; Song of Songs 5; Hebrews 5

God made people to worship Him. It is a part of what it is to be a human being. Worshipping God is a gift. Even though God made human beings to worship Him, none of us naturally choose to worship God because of sin. We tend to prefer idols. Only those who have been saved by grace through faith in Christ alone have access to God. Without having their sin atoned for, people cannot approach God. Psalms 42 and 43 are psalms of lament.

God is far beyond us. The fact that we can know Him and praise Him is a miracle. Billions of people have lived and do live on our planet who have never been freed to truly worship the one true God. Those who are lost in sin cannot gain access to God to worship Him. They are enemies of God in their sin. They cannot and will not be able to praise God with a heart that is truly His. Their hearts are far from God, and their worship is of created things.

Those who are redeemed in Christ can worship God, but there are times when we may not have access to a gathered church. In those difficult days, a person who truly loves God will long for Him and will desire to be with God and His people (Psalm 42:1-4). Gathering with God's people for worship is not only an act of obedience (Hebrews 10:24-25), but it is also a sign that a person truly belongs to the family of God. True family members of God desire to gather in worship for communion, praise, prayer, and preaching.

When God's people are kept from coming to worship, it is not unusual for them to experience sadness in their souls. In those moments, the saints must preach to themselves and pray the way the psalmist did in these two psalms. God is with and for His people. No matter what the difficulties may be that a saint could encounter, those who trust in God always have hope. God is greater than anything a child of God will ever face. The child of God can call to the Father and ask for help (Psalm 43:3). God's help will always lead to His praise (v. 4).

Do you long to be with God's people in worship to bring glory and praise to God? Have you been saved by grace to worship God? Is God's glory your goal?

***Those who have access to God through faith in Christ
are able to worship God and live with peace.***

Numbers 8; Psalm 44; <u>Song of Songs 6</u>; Hebrews 6

People make life both wonderful and difficult. In life, relationships do not always turn out the way we might have wanted them to. Every human being has the capacity to dream. Many people dream of love stories and of a life filled with people they care for and who care for them. Song of Songs 6 reveals some of the frustrations that are found in loving relationships in our fallen world.

The Song of Songs is a love poem with powerful metaphors and drama. In chapter 6, the woman is searching for her love and has asked for help from friends. Her friends have heard her describe this amazing man she loves, and now they want to see him for themselves (v. 1). Human beings long for true love with a lifelong spouse. It is a glorious and wonderful thing, but it is difficult to find.

The woman knows where her beloved is. He is away at work. He is dealing with the challenges of life (v. 2). This is how life goes. It is not always a honeymoon. A man and his wife have times together and times apart. In Christ, a couple can have confidence in their relationship. This woman knew that her man was hers and that she was his (v. 3). She knew what he was doing, and she understood why.

When a couple is able to come together after being apart, it is a cause for celebration. They are to tell each other how much they love each other and how beautiful they think the other is (vv. 4-10). Words have a way of falling short, but sometimes they can reach the heart and imagination and can inspire. This man attempted to express how he saw his beloved. What might sound strange to some people can be poetry to others. Lovers have a way of speaking to each other in ways that they understand and cherish.

After being apart, loving couples get to share the challenges and frustrations they face (vv. 11-13). This woman had to handle her responsibilities and manage the expectations of others. This man wanted her all to himself. It is not possible to get everything we want or to make everyone happy. A loving couple is wise to put each other first and then to look to what the rest of the world expects.

Do you long for a loving marriage? Are you willing to set your life apart for your beloved? Can God bless your decisions?

Those who trust God can see every blessing and challenge as part of God's plan, and they can have peace.

Numbers 9; Psalm 45; Song of Songs 7; <u>Hebrews 7</u>

There has never been and never will be anyone else like Jesus. He is one of a kind. He is not only God in the flesh, but as a man who walked on this planet, He was able to be simultaneously what no others can be. He was and is the perfect king, priest, and prophet. Hebrews 7 explains the greatness and uniqueness of Jesus by comparing Him to Melchizedek and the former priesthood found in the Old Testament.

Melchizedek was a distinctive person. The people of God did not know what to think of him. The fact that he remained a point of conversation for so many centuries speaks to the power of his mystique. Abraham met him and tithed to him as God's people tithe to God (vv. 1-10). This was a reflection of Abraham's exclusive awareness of this man's calling to be a king and priest.

As the Bible story unfolds, there is not another person like Melchizedek who emerges. The rest of the people of God fall into their particular tribes and specific roles (vv. 11-14). The Levites were given the responsibility of serving the nation as priests. The tribe of Judah was promised the scepter and the honor of being those who would lead the nation as kings (Genesis 49:10). Jesus was from the line of Judah, and in particular, the line of David. He was not from the line of priests, but Jesus is the ultimate priest.

The priests were responsible to educate the people about the law and to provide the rituals and atonement ceremonies for the people of God. All of these pointed to Jesus. Jesus was not a Levite. He was a priest like that of Melchizedek (Hebrews 7:15-28). He offered a better sacrifice and leadership. His life and death have satisfied the holy demands of the law of God. Jesus is now interceding for all who believe in Him.

The salvation of Jesus is made possible by the truth of the gospel. As the ultimate prophet, Jesus is the revealed Word of God. He is the Word made flesh who shows and provides the way of salvation (John 1). There is none like Jesus!

Is Jesus your hope and salvation? Do you know who Jesus really is? Are you living in awe of Jesus?

> *Those who know Jesus will love Him and will be compelled to obey Him, and in so doing, will have peace.*

God is certainly mysterious and beyond our complete understanding, but He is not keeping His plan or purpose a secret. He is sounding an alarm to all who will listen. This alarm is calling people to walk in His way, to prepare for the challenges of life, and to be wise. In Numbers 10, God commanded Moses to have two silver trumpets constructed and used for His purpose.

The people of God were about to begin their journey. God is a God of order. He established a system of communication that enabled the mass of people to know what to do and when (vv. 1-10). Only those in proximity to God's people could hear the call, and those who responded in faith were to act in unison with God and with one another. That is how the church is to function today. Each member must be in contact with the church body to hear the call of God through the proclamation of the Word. Each member is to work with God and the other members in doing God's will.

New beginnings are often exhilarating and terrifying at the same time. Those who are where God has called them to be and who go where God calls them to go can always be confident. When God roused the people to go, they responded in faith (vv. 11-28). Each local church must be in a right relationship with God and members must walk in a right relationship with one another. This produces peace. Each member has a role and a purpose. When everyone is doing what God called and destined them to do, there is peace.

In any endeavor, wisdom is needed. Moses knew this, and he asked Hobab to come and help Israel navigate the wilderness they were about to enter (vv. 29-32). This request came with hope. That hope depended on God's presence and provision. Moses sought that presence each time the people set out and also when they became still (vv. 33-36). Those who look to the Lord are the wisest of all. God knows the way, and His plan is perfect.

Are you able to hear the call of God and respond in faith to His will? Do you serve God well by using your gifts and by living in harmony with your local church? Is your life being guided by the wisdom of other godly saints?

*Those who can hear the call of God and walk in obe-
dience to His will live with peace.*

Numbers 11; <u>Psalm 48</u>; Isaiah 1; Hebrews 9

The peace of God does not come through treaties or compromise. The peace of God comes through the mighty victory of God over His enemies. Psalm 48 pictures God as the defender and champion of His people. Through His mighty hand, victory comes and the people rejoice.

God had revealed Himself to the Israelites, and they understood who He was through His divine manifestation in the city of God (vv. 1-2, 9). God made Himself known to the people in Zion and in the temple. The people of God now know God through Jesus Christ (Hebrews 1:1-3). To know Jesus is to know God. He is God in the flesh. He is the one who was promised. God is a fortress of protection for all who trust in Him. Jesus is the only and ultimate Savior of humanity.

Psalm 48:4-8 pictures a battle that took place. The people of God were saved by the power of God. Their enemies were crushed, and they fled in panic. Jesus has defeated sin and death – the great enemies of humanity. By dying on the cross, Jesus paid the penalty for sin. By being raised from the dead, Jesus has conquered death. The evil and darkness of the world tremble before Jesus. Those who rest in Him are established forever in His grace. Nothing can separate the redeemed of God from Jesus. He is their fortress and strength that none can overcome!

Having been saved, the people thoroughly thought about what it meant for God to love them and of His righteousness (vv. 9-10). These thoughts caused the people to be glad and to rejoice (v. 11). Having been rescued, the people examined the provision of God and explained God's enduring grace and guidance to the next generation (vv. 12-14). Those who have been saved by Jesus are able to meditate on the love and righteousness of God, to live under His protective care, and to make disciples of the next generation. This is the will of God. This is where the peace of God is found.

Have you trusted in Jesus? Do you regularly marvel at His goodness toward you? Are you sharing the gospel with the next generation?

Those who trust in God's provision will wor-
ship the Lord and experience peace.

Numbers 12-13; Psalm 49; Isaiah 2; Hebrews 10

Given the choice, it would be better to be physically blind and have a vision for God's glory than to have physical sight and be blind to the reality of God's glory. Those who cannot see the greatness of God and the purity of His plan will wander in idolatry and will never be fulfilled. Isaiah 2 is part of a discourse that continues through Isaiah 5. Isaiah 2 provides a vision, a condemnation, and a call to God's people. It is a call to see what is real and true.

God has an eternal plan. This plan is explained over and over again in the Bible. The Bible is a single story in four parts: creation, fall, rescue, and restoration. Isaiah tells of the second coming of Christ (vv. 1-5). In those days, God will provide perfect justice and bring about perfect peace. Jesus will reign over all. Those who gladly submit to Him in life will enjoy His leadership in eternity. Those who reject Him now will face His judgment and will miss out on the eternal blessing of His kingdom.

Those who reject Jesus can only worship and pursue the idols of this world. The created things of this planet can be good, but they can never satisfy the longing of the eternal soul. They deceive and destroy the soul of humanity (vv. 6-21). The power, pleasure, popularity, and possessions of earth seem so great at times, but they all pass away. They cannot last. The soul, though, lasts forever. Those who put their trust in idols, in created things, are putting their hope in things that cannot provide for their eternal needs.

Human beings are eternal beings. We need an eternal hope. We need a salvation that lasts. We need a God who loves us and is beyond us. God does not want us to depend on the little that we or others can do (v. 22). God wants His image bearers to trust in what is strong and vibrant. Human beings depend on breath to live. God depends on nothing. He just is! God is self-sufficient and needs nothing, and He is willing to save all who look to Him in faith. Jesus is the object of faith who is the means of salvation.

Have you trusted Jesus Christ to forgive you and to give you eternal life? Are you living in light of Jesus' return? Do you rely on yourself or other people more than God?

> *Those who can see the majesty of God, reject the idolatry of worldliness, and trust fully in God will have eternal peace.*

Numbers 14; Psalm 50; Isaiah 3-4; <u>Hebrews 11</u>

Faith is not unusual. We all live by faith. The most important thing about a person is the object of their faith. Whatever we trust in to give our lives the meaning, direction, and redemption we desire will determine everything else about us. Our faith matters. Hebrews 11 is a call to faith in Jesus Christ.

The definition and examples of faith given by the Hebrew writer is crucial to understanding the Christian faith (vv. 1-6). The Christian faith is belief in God's loving plan and purpose. It is based on the confidence that God is the creator and rewarder of life. Abel trusted, and therefore obeyed God. Cain wanted to do his own thing and approach God and life on his own terms. Enoch lived by faith and pleased God. Pleasing God should always be the goal of God's people.

The Old Testament saints had faith in Jesus. Their faith is the same as that of the New Testament saints. The only difference is perspective. The Old Testament saints were looking forward to the coming of Jesus. The New Testament saints look back to the coming of Jesus. Both count on the second coming of Christ.

The Old Testament saints were living in light of the promises of God (vv. 7-38). The promises were to come and would be revealed in Jesus Christ. These saints had to go through trials of various kinds, but were able to endure because they had faith in God's plan. They were not looking for everything to work out perfectly in their lifetime. They were looking for the heavenly country that was to come and that would remain forever.

Those who live now and are able to look back at the life, death, and resurrection of Jesus Christ are able to enjoy the hope that comes from seeing God's promise kept (vv. 39-40). Now that Christ has come, there is a better way. Salvation is not through animals and imperfect people. Salvation is through the perfect Lamb of God, Jesus Christ. All who looked forward to Jesus, and now all who look back to Jesus, are made perfect.

Is Jesus the object of your faith? Are you confident in Christ? Do you believe in God's plan and reward?

Those who live by faith in Jesus live with eternal peace in this life and in the life to come.

Numbers 15; Psalm 51; Isaiah 5; Hebrews 12

God's love does not fail. His people fail. God's people have been incredibly blessed with His grace and provision. Despite God's goodness toward His people, His people often disobey Him. Even when God's people fail, God does not fail His people. He remains steadfast. He cares. He guides. He blesses. He expects them to grow from their mistakes and learn to trust and obey Him. In Numbers 15, God's people were coming off a big failure. God showed His faithfulness to them.

The children of Israel had refused to enter into the land of Canaan as God had commanded them to (Numbers 13:1-14:38). After realizing their mistake, they sought to go up into the land without God's blessing and in their own strength. They failed and were defeated (Numbers 14:39-45). Under this cloud of guilt and disaster, God spoke to the people through Moses. God told them they would one day enter the land, and then He gave them commands about what they were to do when they were settled in God's provision (Numbers 15:1-21). They were to honor God. Those who receive God's salvation are to honor Him with their lives and resources to the praise of God's great name.

God also explained what they were to do if they sinned unintentionally (vv. 22-29). This is a reminder to all of God's people that no matter how faithful we want to be, we will never be fully faithful in this life. We will sin. There is a difference between intentional and unintentional sin, but all sin impacts our relationship with God and others (vv. 30-31). Under the Old Covenant, a person would be put to death for committing treason by breaking the Sabbath (vv. 32-36). This sin not only hurt the person, but it discouraged everyone else. What we do impacts other people.

To help the people remember the command of God, the people were to put tassels on their garments (vv. 37-41). We all need reminders of God's love and of our responsibility to Him. It is wise to surround ourselves with sounds and sights that inspire faith.

Are you faithful to God? Is your desire to trust and obey Him? Have you been a help to other believers?

Those who believe in God's promises and live in
light of them will experience divine peace.

Numbers 16; <u>Psalms 52-54</u>; Isaiah 6; Hebrews 13

The world is not as it should be. God created all things to be in harmony. There was a time when human beings loved God and enjoyed peace with Him, peace within themselves, and peace with one another. That peace was lost because of sin. Psalms 52-54 describe the realities that are now faced because of sin.

According to the title of the psalm, David wrote Psalm 52 in response to the treachery of Doeg (1 Samuel 22). This evil man presented the kindness of faithful men to Saul as a negative, and then he killed the priests who helped David, as Saul commanded him to do. God's people will often be described in the worst light by those who do not believe, and they will often be persecuted to death. God sees. God knows. God cares. God will provide life in death and hope in hard times. God's people are to trust and thank Him (Psalm 52:8-9). Justice will be limited in this world. In the world to come, there will be perfect justice. Until Christ comes, the faithful will have to live by faith and know that God is working His perfect plan for good.

Psalm 53 tells of the natural heart of humanity. The natural inclination of human beings is to deny God's existence, which causes them to be corrupt and evil (v. 1). God is still sovereign. Despite the sin of humanity (vv. 2-5), God has a gracious plan (v. 6). His plan was and is to save a people for Himself through Jesus Christ and to return one day to restore all things.

According to the title of Psalm 54, it was written at a time when David was being pursued by Saul. It is a lament and a statement of faith. David had been anointed as king, but the kingdom had not yet come to him. During this time, he was hunted and hated (vv. 1-3). He found strength in God knowing that God was his help and was holding him up (v. 4). He knew that God was just, and he sought to honor Him (vv. 4-6). He was able to look back at the faithfulness of God and look forward with hope (v. 7). By studying God's Word and biographies of faithful Christians, all of God's people can look back and see how God has been faithful, and then they can look forward with hope.

Do you trust God? Has God been faithful to save your soul? Will you praise Him at all times?

Those who trust in the Lord will suffer, but
God is with them to give peace.

We all need help. Where we go for help and what help we think we actually need says a lot about where our faith lies. There are many who claim to believe in God but who rarely depend on Him. Some only look to God after all other resources have failed. In Isaiah 7, the faith of Ahaz is revealed and tested.

Ahaz was in a tight spot. His enemies were all around him, and his own people were terrified (vv. 1-3). Life is rarely easy. People often look at celebrities and at people with power and resources and wrongly assume that they do not have any problems. Everyone is fighting a personal battle. Those who are leaders and are responsible for other people not only fight their own battles, but they also carry the burden of supporting others who are struggling.

God sent Ahaz a message of hope through Isaiah (vv. 4-9). Ahaz had a choice. He could have faith in God and have peace, or he could reject God and live with anxiety. It all came down to faith. Would he truly have faith in God, or would he choose to have faith in himself or in some other created thing? The object of our faith is the most important thing about us. What or who we believe in determines our destiny.

God understands that we are weak creatures who need our faith to be strengthened. In His grace and for His glory, God invited Ahaz to ask for a sign (vv. 10-11). Ahaz refused (v. 12). Ahaz had already decided that he could not trust God. Despite Ahaz, God provided the promise of the coming Messiah (vv. 13-16).

Not only did God tell of His ultimate plan concerning the coming of Jesus, but God also outlined His immediate plan. Ahaz would face dire consequences for his lack of faith (vv. 17-25). Ahaz was at the crossroads of his life, and the future of Judah was in his hands. Ahaz failed to believe. His lack of faith in God and his sinful trust in other governments left him and Judah without God's protection. When we turn from God, we trust in created things that ultimately betray us.

Do you have an authentic faith in Jesus Christ? When challenged, do you turn to God first? Are you enjoying the benefits of faith or the consequences of disbelief in God?

Those who have genuine faith in God will always
depend on God and enjoy peace.

Numbers 19; Psalms 56-57; Isaiah 8:1-9:7; <u>James 2</u>

How we treat people says a great deal about the kind of people we are and the kind of God we worship. Those who see people through a worldly perspective are worldly. Those who see people from God's perspective are godly. James 2 challenges godly people to treat others with respect.

The world ranks people based on the amount of power, popularity, possessions, or pleasure they enjoy in this world. God ranks people according to the amount of love and faith they have. Christians are to honor those who serve God well and to show compassion to those who don't. When it comes time to determine places of importance, God's people are not to make decisions based on the world's standards (vv. 1-13). God's people are to be wise and give deference to those who honor God. God's people are to serve those in need of grace and mercy. The proud and worldly people of the world are to be loved, but they are not to be recognized as examples of how to live and should not be given places of prominence or leadership in the church.

The focus of God's people is to be on serving those in need. The people who are rich in the things of the world are to help those who need resources (vv. 14-17). The faith of a person who is not generous with the poor is not alive. A living faith is one that has works of righteousness (vv. 18-26). Acts of obedience do not save anyone. A person can only be saved by grace through faith in Christ alone. A person who is saved will live a life that honors God. The life that honors God is a life of righteousness. Righteous living does not earn salvation. Salvation is proven true and real through acts of justice and grace made possible by faith.

The life of a Christian does not have to be complicated. It comes down to love. Those who love God and others are keeping the entire law of God (Matthew 22:37-40). An unregenerate person cannot keep all of God's laws, but a saved soul will obey God by acts of love that honor Him and help others.

Do you treat people with dignity and respect? Does your faith work through acts of kindness? Are you truly loving?

Those who treat people lovingly based on their belief
in God and His Word experience peace.

Numbers 20; Psalms 58-59; Isaiah 9:8-10:4; James 3

Constant happiness is not possible in a broken world. There is going to be some sadness in life. Sin causes sadness. When God created the world, there was harmony. When humanity sinned, death and difficulty became the norm. In Numbers 20, we are reminded of our circumstances and the possibility for peace.

Miriam was a good person even though she was not perfect. God used her to do many important things for His kingdom, but she also blew it a few times. When she died, Moses experienced a great loss (v. 1). When a saint dies, it should always be a great loss to someone. A life lived well will always be missed when it ends.

Despite the loss, Moses had to keep going forward in faith and honor God. Like all people, leaders are often tempted to want to do things their own way, in their own power, and for their own glory. God told Moses to speak to the rock to get it to yield water, but Moses struck it instead (vv. 2-13). Because of his sin, Moses missed out on God's blessing. The Lord still used him, but Moses did not get to enter the promised land. Sin has serious consequences.

God led His people through difficult circumstances. One of the hardest things in life to suffer through is the lack of support from family and friends. Edom, a descendant of Esau, who was Jacob's brother, was family. Israel probably assumed that the Edomites would be kind to them and allow them to pass through their land. They were wrong. The Edomites refused to allow Israel passage (vv. 14-21). No matter what happens in life, God's people can always count on God to provide. We should never be surprised when people disappoint us. We must trust in God. He never fails!

In the midst of losing his sister, failing God, and being rejected by his cousins, Moses also lost his brother, Aaron (vv. 22-29). Losing Aaron was a huge loss, but God provided for His leader and His people. The Lord always has a plan. We might not like God's plan or might not think it is fair or good, but God always does what is best. Wise people always trust God and obey His commands.

Are you able to trust God during times of loss? Do you trust the Word of God and obey it – no matter what? Can you trust God to provide during times of loss?

Those who will trust the Lord will live with peace.

Numbers 21; Psalms 60-61; Isaiah 10:5-34; James 4

Life is sometimes sad and will cause us to lament. Lamenting is good for the soul. Expressing sadness to those who love and care for us is wise. No one loves us like God. In expressing honest feelings to God about our circumstances and His Word, we can gain peace. Psalms 60 and 61 are both laments and provide examples for how to process life with God in prayer.

Psalm 60 is a communal lament. As stated in the psalm's title, it is to be used for instruction. It seems that it was written at a time when God's people were under a serious threat. What these people felt, saw, and thought represents the feelings of most of God's people on any given day (vv. 1-3). In this fallen world, God's people will have difficult days and seasons. It is good to express our concerns to God in those days and know that He hears us and cares.

As we express our feelings to God, we must be wise and remember who it is to whom we are praying. God is glorious. In the day of this communal lament, the Israelites remembered what God had done for them (vv. 4-5). They remembered who God is and what He can do (vv. 6-8). In light of the truth of God's Word and the hope in their hearts, they were able to pray for help (vv. 9-12). So it is with every Bible-believing saint. All of God's children can look to God's Word and know what is true of life and of God and can pray for help.

Psalm 61 is an individual lament. It provides a model for how an individual saint is to pray when trouble comes. The prayer begins with a humble request (vv. 1-3). It is a request made in light of who God is: He is the rock, a refuge, and a strong tower. The goal of this request is to find favor with God (vv. 4-5). God's favor is given to those who trust and obey His Word.

Those who trust and obey God's Word will pray about their circumstances and for the leaders they live under (vv. 6-7). They will also pray in order to bring God glory (v. 8). God-honoring prayer will cause God to be praised and respected in our hearts. God-honoring prayer will comfort us as we seek God's favor.

Do you turn to God in troubled times and pour out your honest thoughts and feelings to Him? Are your prayers biblical? Is your heart's desire to honor God?

Those who look to God for comfort and truth gain peace.

Numbers 22; Psalms 62-63; <u>Isaiah 11-12</u>; James 5

What we see now is not what we will get in eternity. Heaven is real. Jesus is there, and He will soon return and make all things new and restore His creation. God's plan for His glory, His people, and His kingdom is bigger than this current world. Until Jesus returns, God will be at work in this world. God promised that He would come and rescue His people from sin and death. Isaiah chapters 11 and 12 provide a powerful picture of what God is going to bring about in this world and beyond this world.

God said that Satan's head would be crushed (Genesis 3:15). This Victor who would crush Satan's head would be a human being and God. This Messiah is described in Isaiah 11. Jesus is the branch that came from the stump of Jesse (Isaiah 11:1). He is not a normal king like David. He is righteous, and the Spirit of the Lord rests on Him (v. 2). Jesus acted in perfect wisdom. He is wisdom and truth revealed in human form.

Jesus was born of a virgin. As a human being, He depended upon and feared God (vv. 3-5). By Jesus taking on flesh, His divinity was constrained without ceasing to be fully present. All that He did was good. He lived a righteous, holy life. Those who live well walk in the way of Jesus.

When Christ returns, He will make all things new (Revelation 21-22). There will be a new world order, and harmony will again be restored (Isaiah 11:6-10). He will draw all of His people from every nation to gather to worship Him (vv. 11-16). All of His enemies will be destroyed, and there will be peace.

That day of peace will be filled with praise (Isaiah 12:1-2). The people will be fully and finally saved from the work of sin and death. The people will drink from the river of the water of life and will rejoice (vv. 2-6). The saved people will be happy and will celebrate the provision of God. They will give thanks to Him who has saved them, and they will remember His saving works.

Do you live believing in the second coming of Jesus so much that it impacts your way of life? Have you trusted Jesus as Savior? Are you excited about the second coming of Jesus?

God's peace is experienced by those who believe that Jesus
Christ has come to save and will come again to restore.

Numbers 23; Psalms 64-65; Isaiah 13; <u>1 Peter 1</u>

Life is a gift. To be able to think, breathe, and act on decisions is a privilege. To be spiritually alive is a supernatural gift. To be able to know God, to be filled by the Spirit, and to live in Christ is a supernatural privilege. First Peter 1 reveals how the supernatural life comes about and how it is to be lived.

The redeemed of God are exiles in the world, but they are not forgotten. Peter was writing to people who did not belong to this world but were chosen by God to live in Jesus (vv. 1-2). These Christians were living in difficult days of persecution. All of God's people will be persecuted to some extent until Jesus returns. Even though life in Christ is challenging, it is also full of grace and peace.

This supernatural life is made possible by God the Father, who sent God the Son, who now lives in His people through God the Spirit. This God, who is one God in three persons, provides a life that has a hope that is living and an inheritance that lasts forever (vv. 3-5). This life comes by faith. This faith is often tested (vv. 6-9). The tested faith of a saint is a strong faith. The strong faith of a saint is assured salvation in Jesus.

To know the salvation of Jesus is to know the purpose of creation. God made the world in harmony, but humanity's sin destroyed it. In order to heal what was broken by sin, Jesus came to redeem a people for Himself. The Old Testament prophets longed to see the day of the Messiah (vv. 10-12). Jesus' redemption was promised by the prophets. Those prophets longingly wanted to see Jesus come. Jesus came in God's perfect timing. Those who now look back to the life, death, and resurrection of Jesus look back to the unfolding of God's perfect plan.

Those who are saved are given life in Jesus in order to be holy (vv. 13-25). God's will is that His people know His Word, obey it, and become what He is – holy. Holiness is a way of life empowered by the truth of God and the Spirit of God.

Have you been born again? Is the Spirit of God changing you into the image of the Son of God for the glory of God the Father? Is your hope in Jesus Christ?

Those who are alive in Christ experience a living hope that gives eternal peace.

Numbers 24; Psalms 66-67; Isaiah 14; 1 Peter 2

Spiritual leadership is both a blessing and a burden. Those who are called by God to preach His Word are given a great responsibility. The one quality needed above all others in those who have spiritual leadership is godly character that comes from genuine faith that results in authentic love for God and people. Those without character will fall. The weight of responsibility will overwhelm them. Those without love will fail. They will work for the wrong reason. Balaam was called by God to be a spiritual leader. He failed. Numbers 24 shows how God is in control and how God can even use those who are not faithful to Him.

Balaam served God, but he did so for his own advantage. Balaam cared more about his personal wealth and honor than he did about God's kingdom and renown. The king of Moab needed a prophet of God to curse God's people. He hired Balaam to do that (Numbers 22). Balaam was clear that he could only do as God enabled, but he went along with the king of Moab, hoping to get rich.

Balaam did only what God enabled. He blessed Israel (Numbers 22-23). Balaam saw that it pleased the Lord to bless Israel (Numbers 24:1). He sought God alone and blessed the nation, as God willed (vv. 2-9). This did not please the king of Moab (v. 10). The king wanted Balaam to curse Israel, but all Balaam could do was bless them (vv. 11-13). Balaam blessed Israel and cursed all of Israel's enemies (vv. 14-24). In the process, Balaam renewed the promise of God to send Jesus, the king from Judah who would bring about God's ultimate plan of salvation (v. 17).

In the end, Balaam and the king of Moab parted ways (v. 25). When people who do not love God do not get what they want from Him, they often seek other means of accomplishing their purpose. God lets them go. Even though people falter and fail, God is faithful. His promises do not depend on human beings. People are often selfish and will continue to struggle with sin. God's promises depend on God's character. God does not fail or falter!

Do you trust God to provide for you? Are you serving God and following His purpose for you? Is your hope in humanity or in God?

Those who learn from the mistakes of Balaam and choose to live by faith with a love for God and people will always have peace.

Numbers 25; <u>Psalm 68</u>; Isaiah 15; 1 Peter 3

In a consumer-driven society, we like products that are user-friendly. We like to be in control. The gods that people create can be manipulated and used to accomplish our selfish purposes. The God of the Bible is beyond the control of people because He needs nothing. He cannot be manipulated. He has His purpose, and no one can stop Him. Psalm 68 is a celebration of who God is and what He does, and it is a call to honor Him.

God is to be praised for His greatness, and songs are to be sung about His glory (vv. 1-6). All who stand against God will be scattered. Those who stand with Him and for Him are glad to see Him honored. They sing praise to Him. His desire is for His people to find their provision and delight in His protective care.

God is to be feared. Those who stand against Him have no chance of success (vv. 7-18). God has determined to save a people for His glory. He led Israel out of the bondage of Egypt and into a pleasant land where they were cared for and where He was to be honored. God has rescued a people for Himself from sin, through Jesus. All who trust in Jesus are saved. The whole earth will honor God in the end, but only the redeemed will be blessed by Him.

God is to be celebrated (vv. 19-31). What God has done to save His people is glorious. No one could stop Him. Sin and death have now been defeated, and those who live in Christ are happy to call the one true God their God. Those who belong to Christ delight to gather with God's people and worship and adore Him.

God is to be honored (vv. 32-35). Not everyone believes, but all will one day acknowledge that He is the one true God. All the world will one day know that He alone is God, and all will praise Him. Some will praise Him out of delight, and others will praise Him out of demand. When God thunders in judgment and blesses the redeemed, He will be seen as the awesome God He is. He will be attributed the power and majesty that is His alone. He is the source of all strength and of any good that exists in the universe.

Do you know the one true God? Are you His redeemed child? Is He your hope and strength?

Those who live in awe of the one true God live with peace.

Numbers 26; Psalm 69; Isaiah 16; 1 Peter 4

None of us gets it right. We all sin, and the consequences of sin are so very awful. Sin destroys what is good and removes what is needed. Without God, people do not have a moral compass and will choose to do whatever they desire, which is evil. That evil destroys relationships. Isaiah 16 describes the outcome of what happens to people who live without God. The Assyrians were coming to destroy the people of Moab. They had rejected God, and in their pride they had fallen into disgrace. Those who trust in the Lord and are obedient to Him are blessed to have peace with God and peace in all circumstances.

Moab wanted to be able to live in sin and still gain respite and safety under the provision of God (vv. 1-5). This is often the case for cultures in the West. The people want to be able to live however they want without any negative consequences. They want to define their own morality. They reject God and His Word, but when the consequences of their actions are realized, they want to call on God and gain His favor. God will not be mocked. Nations and people who turn from God will suffer for it.

The people of Moab were arrogant, and they boasted in insolence and idleness (v. 6). Those who reject God are often proud of their sin. They march in parades, make public stands for immorality to applauding crowds, and mock those who refuse to celebrate their sin. This is the pride that leads to an individual's fall and to a nation's fall.

Moab was cursed (vv. 7-14). All that was good and could have been enjoyed was destroyed. God set the timetable for their destruction, and it came to be. They would not honor God, and they were punished for it. There is nothing worse that can happen to a person or a people than for God to turn them over to their sin (Romans 1:24-32). When a person or a people set their minds to disobey God, and God releases them to live in the revelry of their sin, the result is pain and destruction. That is what happened to Moab, and that is what will happen to all who reject Jesus.

Have you humbly given your life to Jesus? Are you obeying His Word? Do you stand for Him?

Those who trust in the Lord and are obedient to God are blessed to have peace with Him and to have peace in all circumstances.

Numbers 27; Psalms 70-71; Isaiah 17-18; 1 Peter 5

The Christian life is a strange thing when compared to the way of the world. Christians do not consider themselves strong or competent without God. Christians know they must trust in God. The world does not think that way. In 1 Peter 5, the apostle lays out what leaders, followers, and all of God's people need to do in order to have peace with God and be resilient in the faith.

The goal of the world is personal gain, but the way of Christ is personal sacrifice and generosity. Those who lead God's people must lead out of gladness, a sense of calling, and humility (vv. 1-3). The leaders of the world are often glad to lead as long as they are recognized, celebrated, and rewarded with earthly things for their efforts. Those who lead God's people serve out of gratitude for what God has done and is doing in their lives. They do not work in order to get earthly gain or renown, but the reward for their effort is found in heaven (v. 4). They serve with humility and divine strength to be examples to others (v. 5).

The way of the world produces pride, but the way of Christ creates a heart of humility. Those who depend on God are lifted up by the Almighty (v. 6). They can cast their anxieties on Jesus and live with peace (v. 7). They are very aware that the adversary is out to get them (v. 8). They resist their spiritual enemy and trust God in suffering (vv. 9-10). By trusting in God, followers of Jesus are restored, confirmed, strengthened, and established in Christ. This glorifies God, who is their saving, sovereign king (v. 11).

The way of life in Christ is certainly different and sometimes difficult. To live well in Christ, we need authentic Christian community. The apostle sent this letter by the hand of a friend to a congregation of friends (v. 12). Like all Christians, Peter needed friends who loved one another and worked to create a family of faith (vv. 13-14). A humble life in Christ produces peace. It is a life that comes through Jesus.

Are you living for Christ or for earthly things? Is your strength in God or in yourself? Do you depend on other Christians, and can they depend on you?

Those who find their hope and strength in
Jesus and His people live with peace.

<u>Numbers 28</u>; Psalm 72; Isaiah 19-20; 2 Peter 1

There is a lot that can happen in a single year. It is wise to be intentional about how we spend the time we are given. We will give an account to God for every second we have spent in His creation. In His grace and for His glory, God has helped His people be wise with their time. Numbers 28 provides a listing of the offerings the Israelites were to make in a year. These ceremonial laws no longer apply to God's people, but the principles do.

The Israelites were to offer daily offerings (vv. 1-8). These morning and evening practices helped God's people focus on God at the beginning and end of each day. Christians today are to be mindful of their daily need to commune with God. Wise followers of Jesus will begin each day by studying God's Word, meditating on the truth, and praying to God. They will do the same thing at the end of the day. Throughout the day, they will be mindful of what God has said, and they will obey Him. Setting aside time to be with God is crucial for the health of a Christian.

The Israelites were to offer Sabbath offerings (vv. 9-10). They offered twice as much on that day than on the other days. Today, Christians are to gather with other believers who are members of their local church and worship together by praising, praying, and responding to the preaching of God's Word. Gathering with the saints is not an option for disciples of Jesus. It is a great blessing.

The Israelites were to provide offerings for the New Moon festival, for the Passover, and for the other feasts (vv. 11-31). These special times provided opportunities for families and communities to gather and to give. Christians are now to celebrate special days that point to the hope they have in Jesus. They are to regularly receive the Lord's Supper together. They are to give financial gifts that go beyond their tithes. They are to remember special days that commemorate the birth of Jesus, the resurrection of Jesus, the coming of the Holy Spirit, and special times of thanksgiving for God's goodness and provision.

Are you intentionally pursuing God? Do you spend time with God each day in Bible study, meditation, and prayer? Do you gather with your family and church for special remembrances?

Those who are intentional to honor God live with peace.

Numbers 29; Psalm 73; Isaiah 21; 2 Peter 2

Perception is not always reality. As it pertains to people and their sense of peace and contentment, it might be best to say that perception is rarely reality. People who seem to have it all, but who do not have Jesus, do not have peace. Only those who are relationally right with God can have peace within and can have peace in every circumstance. Asaph provided a wonderful confession and explanation in Psalm 73. He recognized that his perception was off and that peace can only be found in God's grace.

Asaph confessed that God is good to His people (v. 1). God, at great expense to Himself, has been good to His people. Having promised to save a people for Himself, God the Father sent His Son to earth to die for the sin of the world. The Old Testament believers had to offer sacrifices for their sins yearly, which was a foreshadowing of Christ. Those of us who live on the other side of the cross and the New Testament look back in faith to what Jesus accomplished. God is good to those who have faith in Jesus and choose to trust God.

Asaph confessed that he almost stumbled because he believed that he was missing out on "the good life" (vv. 2-15). It appeared to him that the people who lived for themselves and dishonored God were enjoying the best things in life. Once he thought about it, fixed his eyes on God, and discerned the end of those who do not live by faith in Jesus, he changed his outlook (vv. 16-20). Those who live for themselves will lose everything and will be judged by a holy God.

Asaph confessed he was wrong, and he renewed his faith in the promises and plan of God (vv. 21-28). He recognized how good God is and how God had been faithful to him. Asaph realized that his heart and strength would fail, but God would never fail. All who trust in the goodness of God by faith in Christ are blessed. They seek to be near God and find that the Holy Spirit is at work in them and around them for good. This is the blessing of God: His people live and die with Him and experience eternal peace.

Is your perception of God, self, and others accurate? Are you truly seeking after God? How have you been deceived by the world? Do you need to repent and renew your faith in Jesus?

> *Those who trust God by faith in Jesus in the*
> *power of the Holy Spirit have peace.*

Numbers 30; Psalm 74; Isaiah 22; 2 Peter 3

It is easy to do, but it is very dangerous to become complacent toward God. Human beings seem to thrive spiritually when things are hard. When things are going well, most people tend to lose sight of God and fall into sin. Without a clear challenge and purpose, people often fall into habits that are sinful. Israel did this over and over again. Isaiah lamented this fact. In Isaiah 22, the prophet outlines the failure of God's people and the reason for their failure, but he honors the righteousness and rightness of God.

God's people and their place in the world was meant to be an example to the nations. They were to fulfill the plan of God and reveal what it looked like to be blessed by God. They were to be those who dwelt on Mount Zion. However, the people were no longer the example of blessedness. They were now the valley (v. 1a). They had fallen from the place where God had made them to stand. God still spoke to them through visions, but the vision was sad.

The people were an embarrassment. They were not defeated as soldiers with honor on the battlefield, but they starved to death (vv. 1b-2). Their leaders had fled, but had been captured (v. 3). We can run from God, but we cannot hide from Him. Our sin will always be found out (Numbers 32:23). Without God, the souls of people will starve, and they will die slowly and painfully. Judgment will come!

Isaiah was saddened by the state of God's people (v. 4). The right response of godly people to sin and the consequences that come with disobeying God is sadness. God's judgment is just (vv. 5-8a). When God provides healing and hope, the people of God must receive this grace by faith and then live in God's provision (vv. 8b-14). Those who will not honor God for His goodness and will not pursue His purpose will lose everything (vv. 15-25). What God gives, He can take away. All that the Lord does is for His glory. It brings God glory to care for His people and bless them with His love and protection. Only those who honor Him and love Him will be sustained in life and death by His grace.

Do you take God for granted? Are you becoming complacent in your walk with God? Are you becoming apathetic toward Him? Is your life honoring Jesus, or have you become comfortable with sin?

Those who seek God in every season of life live with peace.

Numbers 31; Psalms 75-76; Isaiah 23; 1 John 1

Living every day with the confidence that Jesus Christ has purchased our sin debt, has been raised from the dead, and is now living in us by the power of the Holy Spirit gives us an assurance of salvation. There are liars in the world who deny the gospel truth and can cause the faithful to stumble. First John was written to affirm the faithful in Christ. First John 1 provides the fundamental truth that affirms the true biblical faith of the redeemed.

The Father sent His Son as a human being in order to save a people for Himself. It is a miracle. Jesus was here in the flesh and was seen, heard, and touched (v. 1). Jesus was not a backup plan. The Son was promised and has come, and He was attested to by the apostles.

Under the inspiration and direction of the Holy Spirit, the apostles wrote Scripture to proclaim the truth of the gospel (vv. 2-4). Proclaiming the truth provided them joy. It is a joy to know that God has kept His promise and has come to save a people for Himself to the praise of His great name.

God is pure and holy (v. 5). Those who are born again live in God's light and do not walk in darkness (v. 6). Those who have been saved by grace through faith in Christ live in the light and have fellowship with one another by the unifying power and presence of the Holy Spirit (v. 7). The saints of God live in peace with God and with one another based on the atoning work of Jesus.

Those who have been saved by grace through faith in Christ alone are given a redeemed standing with God, but they still struggle with sin (v. 8). The flesh of every saint is still contaminated with sin, and the saints must seek to kill the sin that is at work in their flesh. By confessing their sin and seeking to please God, the saints of God gain assurance of their salvation. Those who are unconcerned with their sin are likely not saved.

Have you received forgiveness for your sin through faith in Christ? Are you involved in a local church of redeemed saints? Do you fight for victory over sin every day?

Those who know that they know that they are saved live with peace.

<u>Numbers 32</u>; Psalm 77; Isaiah 24; 1 John 2

Influence is significant. Who we allow to influence us matters. How we influence other people is important. Numbers 32 tells us that the tribes of Reuben and Gad were making an important decision about where they wanted to live and why. Their decision was influenced by a practical need. Their decision would impact the entire nation of Israel. What they were doing was a big deal. How we choose to live matters.

The tribes of Reuben and Gad had been blessed with livestock. Material wealth brings with it great responsibility. The livestock these tribes owned needed nourishment. The land on the east side of the Jordan seemed perfect. They wanted to set up their lives there, and they approached Moses and the leaders of Israel with their request (vv. 1-5). They were not being selfish. They were seeking to honor God with their resources.

The problem was that God had called the entire nation to go west of the Jordan into the land of Canaan to settle. Moses chastised these two tribes for their request (vv. 6-15). Moses was correct to be concerned, but the tribes had already thought through his concerns. They knew that they needed to settle east of the Jordan, but they also knew that they needed to send their fighting men west of the Jordan with the nation to accomplish God's will (vv. 16-19). Wise people always think through their decisions and plans before they share them so they can be prepared to answer questions and concerns.

Once Moses understood the full scope of their plans, he blessed them (vv. 20-42). It is wise to receive the blessing of wise people. Wise people are able to listen to ideas objectively and consider their merit discerningly. Moses was wise to listen to the tribes of Reuben and Gad. The tribes were wise to consider how their decision would influence the rest of the nation. Through respectful dialogue and consideration, the people of God were able to maintain peace and provide a mutual blessing to one another.

Who are the people who influence you? Are you a good influence on others? Do you think through your decisions and consider how they will impact not just you, but also others?

Those who live to honor God by being good stewards will live with peace.

Numbers 33; <u>Psalm 78:1-39</u>; Isaiah 25; 1 John 3

God made people to be in families. This is one of the great blessings of God's design in creation. While we are now all born prone to sin, children do have hearts and minds that can be trained to think and feel certain ways about God. The influence of parents, siblings, extended family, and a church family is significant. In Psalm 78:1-39, Asaph provides a history of Israel. The purpose of this historical psalm is to challenge parents and other influencers to remember how God has been at work in the world in the past and to pass on God's Word to the next generation.

Children only know what they are taught. While we are all born with particular personalities, preferred learning styles, and gifts and abilities, we are only able to think based upon what we know. Each generation will pass on to the next generation what they truly believe. Each generation has a legacy. Godly parents and leaders must pass on the Word of God to the next generation (vv. 1-8). They must show the truth of how people fail when God is not first in their lives. God is gracious and good, and those who trust in Him will be blessed. Children must see and hear this truth!

This battle, when the Ephraimites turned back and did not advance as God commanded (vv. 9-10), is used as an example of what not to do. The Ephraimites forgot God's past provision (vv. 11-16). They doubted and tested God (vv. 17-20). They forced God to discipline them (vv. 21-31). Despite God's provision and discipline, they still did not humble themselves before God and honor Him as their hope and deliverer (vv. 32-33). God is gracious, and we are responsible to look to Him in faith and believe and obey Him.

God did not destroy the Ephraimites, but He would have been justified if He had (vv. 34-39). God remembered that they were fallen creatures incapable of doing good apart from grace. God is kind and compassionate. He knows we cannot save ourselves. God sent His Son to save us. Jesus has come. He is our living hope. He is the one who saves and provides for those who believe in Him.

What is your legacy? Are you worth following? Are you learning God's Word and teaching it to the next generation?

Those who know the Word of God and learn to
walk in the will of God will live with peace.

Numbers 34; Psalm 78:40-72; Isaiah 26; 1 John 4

Perspective is important. How we look at the world will determine our state of mind and emotions. Followers of Jesus Christ are blessed to be able to look into the past and see what the hand of God has done, to look forward with hope to what God has promised to do in the future, and to look around in the present and see that God is at work in the world. Isaiah 26 provides God's people perspectives on the past, present, and future.

God's people can look forward to God restoring things. One glorious day, Jesus is going to return and make all things new. When Christ returns, the people will rejoice (vv. 1-6). What they sing on that day is what can be sung now by the redeemed. The fact that God has promised it means that it will be done. The redeemed of God can rejoice now for what God will do in the future. The redeemed of God can celebrate God's power to protect, God's peace that is given to those who focus on Him, God's justice that will make all things right, and God's plan to bring worldwide peace.

God's people can rest now in His daily provision (vv. 7-12). The people of God can walk on level paths because the way of God is good. The people of God can trust in God's provision and live with a holy desire to experience Him in their daily lives. The people of God can live with His blessed peace every second of the day. The Lord is always providing for His people.

God's people can look back at God's provision (vv. 13-18). There were days when God's people were not faithful. No one has honored and trusted God perfectly, but God has loved perfectly. His plan has stood. His will is done. He keeps His promises and sustains a remnant for His glory.

In the end, God will be glorified (vv. 19-21). The dead in Christ will be raised to everlasting bliss. The people of God can remember His faithfulness and wait for His return in peace. The Lord will keep His promises!

Can you look back and see how God has saved you and provided for you? Are you seeing God at work in your life and in the world today? Do you live in light of the return of Christ?

Those who can see the truth of what God has done,
is doing, and will do live with peace.

Numbers 35; Psalm 79; Isaiah 27; 1 John 5

Everyone loves to win. It is not only fun, but it is also fulfilling and affirming. The Christian life is a victorious life. It is a life that is firmly in the hand of God the Father by faith in God the Son and empowered by God the Spirit. Those who walk by faith in the gospel of God overcome sin, stand on the promises and power of God, and live with eternal confidence. In 1 John 5, the saints of God are encouraged with the hope of God's victory.

The world offers behavior-modification training, but only God can change a heart. Those who choose to love God by the power of the Holy Spirit are able to overcome sin (vv. 1-5). Those who believe in Jesus know that they have sinned. They know that Jesus has died for their sin and has been raised to live in them. By loving Jesus, the people of God overcome temptation and honor the One who has saved them. It is liberating to live in obedience to God.

The faith of the redeemed stands on solid ground. Christianity is not based on an ideology or philosophy. Christianity is based upon a person who is God and man. Jesus Christ has proven His humanity and divinity (vv. 6-12). God entered space and time, and the true identity of Jesus was revealed at His baptism, at His death, and by the coming of the Holy Spirit. Those who believe in Jesus have eternal life. Jesus is a sure foundation.

The sure foundation of eternal life in Jesus Christ provides the motivation and delight to live for God. Those who are confident in their salvation not only live to honor God, but they also seek His help in prayer (vv. 13-15). Because Jesus has done so much to save them, God's people have assurance that He will hear their prayers and answer them according to His purpose.

Sin that leads to death is sin that has not been repented of or purchased by the blood of Jesus. Those who reject the grace of Jesus live and die in sin (vv. 16-17). Those who repent of sin are able to honor God and live with peace in Jesus (v. 18). Those who trust in Jesus are victorious. The redeemed do not have to depend on idols or created things (vv. 19-21). Christ is our victory!

Are you free in Christ? Is your life a testimony to His power? Have you repented of sin and trusted Jesus?

Those who look to Jesus for salvation live a life filled with peace.

Obedience is not optional for the people of God. Obedience is a hallmark of an authentic relationship with God. Those who know Jesus will love Jesus. To know Him as He truly is inspires awe and authentic love. Those who love Jesus will obey Him. This obedience comes from the heart. God demands obedience from His people that is based on love. In Numbers 36, the people of God were given directives about marriage and land ownership that may have gone against their natural desires, but they chose to obey.

The daughters of Zelophehad of the tribe of the people of Joseph were in danger of giving up their land rights to another tribe (vv. 1-4). This was not the will of God. In order to avoid the loss of their tribal territory, God commanded these women to marry men within their own tribe. By doing this, the land would remain within the tribe, which was the will of God. Christian women are to marry Christian men. God's will is that His people remain in Him and pass on their faith to the next generation.

It appears that the women wanted to marry outside of their tribe, but they chose to obey God's Word (vv. 5-12). Fallen human beings have desires that are contrary to the will of God. Those who have been saved by grace must choose to trust and obey God. It is in trusting and obeying God that God's people experience the provision of His peace.

The only way God's people can know God's will and way of life is to know God's Word. God gave His Word to Moses, and Moses gave God's Word to the people (v. 13). The people of God are blessed to have the Word of God. The Word of God guides God's people and gives them peace.

The last word of the book of Numbers is "Jericho." This pointed to the victory that God was about to provide for the people. They had no idea what God had planned for them. They did not need to know. All they needed to do was trust and obey. That is all any of God's people need to do. God has the plan! We can trust Him. When we trust Him and obey Him, we find Him faithful.

Are you living in obedience to God? Is your confidence in God's plan? Do you know God's Word so you can be guided by it?

Those who know, love, and obey God live with peace.

Deuteronomy 1; <u>Psalms 81-82</u>; Isaiah 29; 3 John

Everyone has to trust something or someone. God has given humanity good reasons to trust Him. He has made and sustains the universe. He has revealed Himself to us through His Word and deeds. Psalms 81 and 82 call God's people to remember what God has done, what He can do, and who He is.

God calls His people to worship Him (Psalm 81:1-3). Human beings are creatures made to worship. We are going to worship something. We will either worship the one true God or we will worship a created thing. God commands us to worship Him because of what He has done (vv. 4-10). God delivered Israel from the bondage of Egypt. God delivers all who believe in Jesus from the bondage of sin. God is worthy to be trusted and worshipped.

The Israelites would not worship God (vv. 11-12). Sadly, this is also often the case with Christians. Rather than pursue God by gathering with a local church on Sunday, growing in their faith each day through prayer and the study of God's Word, and impacting other people with the hope of Jesus, many Christians skip church and live to serve their own desires.

God promised that He would care for Israel if they would turn to Him and trust Him alone (vv. 13-16). God promised to provide for His people. When they were faithful, they were blessed. When they were unfaithful, they were cursed. The entire book of Hebrews tells us that Jesus gives a better hope and a stronger promise. Those who rely on God in the name of Jesus in the power of the Holy Spirit have peace with God, and they see God do great things.

God stands over all creatures. When He assembles the human authorities and the demonic, fallen angels who pretend to be gods, He overshadows them in His glory (Psalm 82:1). He chastised them for their injustice (v. 2). He commanded them to be kind (vv. 3-4). He acknowledged the needs of hurting humanity (v. 5). He reprimanded those in authority (vv. 6-7). The hope of the world is the coming of Jesus (v. 8). *Come, Lord Jesus!*

Do you love, honor, and obey God? Is Jesus the object of your faith and worship? Are you living justly and righteously?

> ***Those who trust in the God of the Bible and seek to know***
> ***Him, love Him, and obey Him live with peace.***

Deuteronomy 2; Psalms 83-84; <u>Isaiah 30</u>; Jude

Everything in the world has flaws. There are no flaws in God. He is consistently perfect in who He is and in all He does. However, how He deals with people differs. Being a holy and just God, He demands obedience. Being a gracious and merciful God, He saves sinners from the eternal consequences of their sin and transforms them into saints. Isaiah 30 provides a picture of who God is in His justice, holiness, and grace.

The children of Israel were in a tight spot. The Assyrians were coming to destroy them. Rather than depend on God, Israel looked to Egypt for help. This was not God's plan (vv. 1-7). God's people will always have trials of various kinds. The world is not as it should be. One glorious day, Jesus will return and make all things new. Until that time, God's people will struggle against sin and will face difficult circumstances. These circumstances are never a surprise to God. He has a plan for His people and will provide – if His people will look to Him in faith.

Human beings are made in the image of God. Having sinned, people are no longer capable of being holy on their own. Rather than living as God designed them to be, human beings sin. Rather than being holy, as God is holy, people trust in their carnal desires and live lives of corruption and evil (vv. 8-14). God invites humanity to trust in Him. Instead of living by faith in God, the natural inclination of people is to run from God and pursue their own results (vv. 15-17). This makes them foolish.

God is gracious. He does not abandon humanity. God has chosen to come and to save a people for Himself, giving them new life with a new path (vv. 18-29). This path leads to God's blessings. Those who depend on God rather than on their sinful desires for direction will enjoy God's favor. They will sing songs of celebration. They will be warmed with love. They will be saved. Those who reject God will end up like the Assyrians (vv. 30-33). The wrath of God will consume them in terror.

Do you know God and fear Him? Have you perceived His holiness and power? Are you saved in Christ?

Those who repent of their sin and believe in the grace of God received by faith in Jesus Christ will live with eternal peace.

Deuteronomy 3; Psalm 85; Isaiah 31; <u>Revelation 1</u>

The world is broken, but God is in our midst to save. He will one day restore all things and make them what they were intended to be. The book of Revelation uncovers God's ultimate plan for the world. This truth was applicable in the day John wrote it, and it is needed in every generation to understand what is happening and what will happen. Revelation 1 reveals who Jesus is, what God's people are to Him, and why Christians can always live with confidence in God's plan.

Jesus has defeated sin and death and is now leading His church as He reigns in heaven. He is the ultimate ruler and is accomplishing His will on earth through world events and leaders. He is coming again and will judge the world. He is the beginning and end of all things. There is none like Him. He is worthy to be trusted, worshipped, and obeyed.

The church is made up of the beloved servants of Jesus who serve Him (vv. 5b-6). Jesus has saved His people to make them into a kingdom of priests to serve in His kingdom. By dying for the sins of His people and giving them new life, Jesus transforms sinners into saints and makes them useful for His eternal purpose.

The apostle John was used by God to reveal His plan to the Christians of His day and to all the saints who would come to saving faith (vv. 9-11). The seven churches listed are like all churches that have ever been and ever will be. They will struggle and will need the correction of Jesus that comes through His Word.

The peace of the church in general, and of every local church, is that Jesus is with them (vv. 12-20). He stands among His people to prosper His purpose and to use each church to do His will. Those who know God and His plans are eternally blessed. God does not change. His plans stand. Those who stand with Jesus in the redemption He gives are truly blessed.

Do you trust, love, and obey Jesus? Are you living out your role in the world? Is your local church standing with Jesus?

No matter what may happen in the world or in a person's life, those who trust, love, and obey Jesus live with peace.

Deuteronomy 4; Psalms 86-87; Isaiah 32; Revelation 2

We all make decisions, big and small ones, every day. God's will is not a secret. While the Bible does not tell us what we are to do in every decision we make, it does tell us how to live. Deuteronomy 4 is a transitional chapter in this last sermon of Moses. Deuteronomy 1-3 was meant to inspire the people to go into the land God promised. Israel was about to enter Canaan. Moses was preparing them by giving them final instructions.

God had uniquely blessed Israel. Israel was to obey God and become a nation that honored God. They were to stand out among the nations as wise and blessed (vv. 1-14). The Word of God was to be heard, taught, and remembered by God's people. Future generations were to be instructed with this Word and were to obey it.

The temptation for Israel is the temptation that all Christians must face: idolatry (vv. 15-31). Human beings are made to worship. If we do not worship God, then we will worship idols. God warns against idolatry. Those who refuse to trust in God will suffer for it. If we will repent of idolatry and trust in Jesus, we will enjoy God's forgiveness and find new life in God's merciful covenant of grace.

There is only one God (vv. 32-40). The Lord has revealed Himself through His Word and His intervention in earthly events. God proved Himself to be real and trustworthy. He later entered human form and died for sinners. He is the only means of salvation and the only way to everlasting life. Jesus gives meaning to life.

Bad things will happen in this world. People will kill other people, but not always on purpose. God provided a place where someone who killed another person unintentionally could find safety (vv. 41-43). God is a God of justice. He knows that life is dangerous and that people will make mistakes. He gives grace and help.

God has not abandoned His creation. He has given His law, and His law stands (vv. 44-49). Those who obey God gain assurance of salvation. They act wisely. They are blessed.

Do you know the God of the Bible? Do you know His Word and live in obedience to Him? Do you love and worship Him by grace through faith in Jesus Christ?

Those who know God and obey His Word live with peace.

Deuteronomy 5; <u>Psalm 88</u>; Isaiah 33; Revelation 3

Life does not always go the way we want it to. It does not always go according to God's original design. In our fallen world, there is not always a happy ending. Sometimes the happy ending does not come until we see God face to face in heaven. What we can always know is that no matter what we must endure, God has a plan for it. God loves us and is doing what is best. If we knew what God knew, we would agree with His decision to allow us to suffer. Psalm 88 is not a happy psalm. It does not offer a happy ending to the writer. Those of us who are blessed to read it on this side of the cross can see the sacrifice of Jesus in it.

The psalmist felt completely alone and in danger of dying (vv. 1-9). This was a person who was struggling. The wrath of God felt very real and overwhelming to him. It appears that death was probable. This person's friends had left and had sought out their own best interests. This is what happened to Jesus. On the night He was taken captive, Jesus was betrayed by Judas. When the soldiers came to arrest Him, the disciples fled. On the cross, Jesus experienced the wrath of God.

The psalmist had questions about God's plan (vv. 10-12). What was happening did not seem to make sense to him. This person seemed to want to be a source of praise to God, but in this situation, the writer believed there was no way to honor God. When Jesus was hours away from dying, He prayed for God to take the cup of suffering away from Him. He was willing to drink it, but He asked God to intervene and provide. Jesus had questions, but He received no answers. He was led like a lamb to the slaughter (Isaiah 53:7).

The psalmist had no hope (vv. 13-18). There was no answer from God. Friends would not help. The writer was alone. Jesus died alone on the cross. While some of His followers came to watch, none could comfort Him. God had placed the curse of sin on Him, and there was nothing anyone could do. Grace is expensive. Jesus did what only Jesus could do. He redeemed us.

Are you grateful for Jesus? Do you honor His sacrifice? Can you trust Him with your life?

Those who can look to Jesus and trust God's love, purpose, and power in every circumstance will always live with peace.

Deuteronomy 6; Psalm 89; Isaiah 34; Revelation 4

God is a very good God, but He is very dangerous. He is holy and just and will not tolerate sin. Human beings are sinners. We are sinful from birth. Children do not have to be taught to lie, throw fits, or be selfish. That all comes naturally – but that is the problem. *God is a consuming fire* (Hebrews 12:29). Fire brings warmth and a great blessing, but it can also kill you. God offers warm love, and by His grace and for His glory He provides His blessings, but His wrath destroys what is sinful. Isaiah 34 tells of the wrath of God.

The nations referred to in Isaiah 34 lived as enemies of God and would face utter devastation (vv. 1-7). In the Old Testament, God provided specific animals to be atoning sacrifices for the sins of people. These animals were substitutes. They died in the place of the people for their sin. This reconciled people to God. Without this reconciliation, people were left to face God on their own. Those who will not receive the reconciliation that comes through the Lamb of God, Jesus Christ, who died for the sins of the world, will be alienated from God and will receive His just punishment.

The land the people loved would be completely decimated along with the people themselves (vv. 8-17). The wrath of God would be unlike anything these nations had ever seen. Their populations would be completely destroyed, and the land that they worked, loved, and depended on would become a wasteland. God would utterly abandon the people. This is God's judgment.

The abandonment of God is one of the great curses of the Almighty. In God's judgment, sinners are cast out. The souls of the condemned will be together, but in their selfishness, they will love no one. They will become completely isolated in their hate and egotism. In that darkness for billions of years, they will be filled with rage and will be frustrated that no one knows them or cares. They will be in a pit of despair.

Have you trusted Jesus for forgiveness? Do you have peace with God? Does God know you, and do you know God and find your identity and purpose in Him?

Those who trust in Jesus and have been made saints of God by grace through faith will live and die in a right relationship with the Holy One in eternal peace.

Deuteronomy 7; Psalm 90; Isaiah 35; <u>Revelation 5</u>

Who are we supposed to call on when things are broken and messed up? God made everything out of nothing for His glory. He placed the earth under the authority of humanity, but we messed it up. Revelation 5 reveals the authority, majesty, and sovereignty of Jesus to oversee and restore the universe. He is worthy!

The world is looking for someone to fix this mess we are in. The world is not as it should be. We should love our Maker. We should love each other. We should love and be thankful for who God made us to be. Sadly, though, we often don't! We are a broken race in a sinful world. But, God still has a plan for us. He knows what to do. He is worthy to do it!

God the Father holds the world in His hand like a scroll. It is the deed to reality. We are looking for someone who can take that scroll and make our sick and dirty world healthy and clean again (vv. 1-2). No creature on earth or in heaven can take the scroll. Only the one who is God can take it up. He is worthy! Jesus is worthy to take up the scroll (vv. 3-4).

Jesus has purchased His church with His death, and He now reigns in His resurrection (vv. 5-10). Humans are sick, sinful creatures who naturally do what is evil and perverse. Despite our treason and moral filthiness, God loves us. God loves us so much that He sent His Son to redeem us. Jesus has come! He came to live a holy life we can take credit for. He came to give His life to pay for our sin. He came to defeat death so we could live. Having lived a holy life, having died an atoning death, and having won an eternal victory over death, Jesus is now reigning over a nation of people who serve as priests. Those who trust in Jesus are made right with God and are given the privilege of serving Him. He is worthy to be served!

Those who are in heaven worship and adore Him who was slain (vv. 11-14). These great angels are in awe of Him. They serve and celebrate Him. They look to Him to restore what has been broken by sin and to regain the glory that is due His name. They delight to see Him honored. He is worthy!

Do you trust in Jesus? Is He your Lord? Are you living in light of His return?

***Those who look to Jesus to rule their lives and
restore the world live with peace.***

Deuteronomy 8; Psalm 91; Isaiah 36; Revelation 6

We are forgetful creatures. Given the fact that we have to exist in space and time and that we have a natural inclination to disobey God, it is not surprising that human beings forget God and deny Him the glory due His name. Deuteronomy 8 is a call to remember the greatness and goodness of God.

The Israelites had been on quite a journey (vv. 1-5). The Lord heard their groaning in bondage in Egypt. He sent His savior, Moses, to rescue them. Under the guiding hand of God, Moses led them through difficult days. The Lord was present with them. God provided for them. That is what God does for His people. That is what God is doing for every disciple of Jesus now. He has rescued us from sin. He is now with us on our journey to heaven. He is providing for our needs according to His purpose.

The Israelites were given laws to obey (vv. 6-9). These laws blessed them when they kept them. God's laws are good. The Israelites lived under the theocratic law, the ceremonial law, and the moral law of God. Christians today no longer live under the theocracy of Israel or temple worship. We are moral beings made in the image of God and are to keep God's moral law. Those who obey the law of God by the power of the Holy Spirit are blessed.

The Israelites were blessed and were likely to fall into pride (vv. 10-18). They would soon be given the desires of their hearts. They would have wealth and resources. Their tendency would be to forget God, trust in themselves, and become arrogant. This is the temptation of all divinely blessed people. Those who have been saved must never forget the one who saved them.

The Israelites were threatened with punishment if they would forget God and turn from Him (vv. 19-20). God knew they would fall away from Him. In His grace and for His glory, He warned them of their peril. Those who claim to be Christ's will be tempted and will often fall into sin. The wise will repent and will look to Jesus to restore their souls. The unwise will wallow in sin and will suffer for it.

Do you stay focused on God's goodness to you? Are you obeying Him? Do you need to repent and recommit to Jesus?

Those who can look back and remember what God has done in the world, in their hearts, and in their lives will live with peace.

Deuteronomy 9; <u>Psalms 92-93</u>; Isaiah 37; Revelation 7

So many things are constantly clamoring for our attention. Nothing is more important than our relationship with God. The God of the Bible is real. He has revealed Himself in creation and in His Word. Those who know the one true God will be transformed into the image of His Son, Jesus (Romans 8:29). Psalms 92 and 93 reveal who God is and what happens to the faithful and the faithless.

Those who know the God of the Bible are commanded and compelled by His majesty and glory to sing praise to Him in the morning, in the evening, and in every moment in between (Psalm 92:1-3). Singing praise to God is natural for those who have been saved by grace through faith in Christ alone. God is worthy to be praised and has made us to praise Him. Our praise matters to God.

Songs of praise impact us because they help us remember who God is, who we are, and what the world is (vv. 4-15). The righteous will flourish. Through the life-giving work of the Holy Spirit, those who walk with God will have healthy souls filled with love. Sinners will be tossed about with every desire, living empty and fearful lives. The things the unrighteous depend on for meaning will pass away. The souls of human beings are eternal. The soul of every person on the planet can only be sustained and made whole by the eternal, almighty grace of God.

The God of the Bible is not some weak, old man looking for a compliment. The God of the Bible is mighty and majestic. He is strong and eternally self-satisfied (Psalm 93:1-2). God does not change. He is immutable. The seas of the world are breathtaking and seemingly endless, but in truth, they are limited. Their waves have limits, as do their depths. God is greater than the seas of the earth, and He reigns over them in power (vv. 3-4). What God has said and determined will not be altered. The Word of God reveals the will of God (v. 5). God wills that His image bearers are to be holy. Those who believe God to be holy and receive the holiness that comes through faith in Christ will live forever with God.

Are you in awe of God? Do you find meaning in Him? Is He your peace?

Those who believe in Jesus live lives that are full and meaningful, and there is a deep, abiding peace in their souls.

Deuteronomy 10; Psalm 94; Isaiah 38; Revelation 8-9

It can sometimes feel as if life is out of control and that God is incompetent. However, God knows what is best. He allows us to go through difficult days in order to set our eyes on Him so we will see the world and this life for what it is. This world is broken and will not last. The Lord and His grace and love last forever. In Isaiah 38, the story of Hezekiah's healing is told. Hezekiah learned the limits of life, the kindness of God, and the goodness of godly counsel.

Hezekiah was a good king. He sought the Lord. God was pleased with his life and leadership. When Hezekiah became sick and was about to die, he called out to God for healing (vv. 1-3). God heard his prayer and answered him. God always hears and answers His people. Sometimes "no" is the answer. In this instance, God granted the request and sent Isaiah with a miraculous sign (vv. 4-8). God really is good. He always does what is best. He provides for His purpose in the lives of His people. His purpose is pure.

After he was healed, Hezekiah penned a statement of testimony (vv. 9-20). God had been kind to Hezekiah. In His kindness, God revealed to Hezekiah the brevity of life and the immensity of the love and grace of God. Hezekiah was able to look back on the bitterness of life he had tasted and see God's hand in it (v. 17). God works through our suffering and pain. It may not seem fair or wanted at the time, but God knows what He is doing. God uses difficulties to train us in righteousness and to help others to see God's goodness and grace. Jesus did not want the pain of the cross, and He sought another way – but He trusted and obeyed. This is what all of God's wise children do. They trust and obey God.

Isaiah instructed those who were caring for the king to apply figs to the boil for healing (v. 21). God uses medicine and miracles to provide healing for His people. Hezekiah sought affirmation of the will of God (v. 22). This was not a lack of faith, but proof of faith. God is at work in the world, and wise saints are looking for Him.

Do you look to God and trust Him in hard times? Has God brought you through trials? Are you looking to see how God is at work in the world?

Those who trust in the Lord will go through difficult days,
but God is working a plan and will provide peace.

Deuteronomy 11; Psalms 95-96; Isaiah 39; <u>Revelation 10</u>

There is much more going on in the world than what our five natural senses can detect. There is a very real spiritual battle raging for the souls of men and women all over the planet. Human beings made in the image of God have great value to God, which makes them the primary target of the evil that stands in opposition to Him. Revelation 10 provides insight into the mystery and majesty of God. This truth gives peace to all who believe in Jesus.

There are certain things that are just not clear in Scripture (v. 1). Who is this mighty messenger coming from heaven? What does it mean that he is wrapped in a cloud? Why a rainbow, a face like the sun, and legs like fire? The imagery has provided many opinions. What can be known for certain is that this one from heaven comes with power and purpose. God is on the move in the world, and there is no limit to His greatness and glory.

Not only is the appearance of the messenger a mystery, but the message is a secret (vv. 2-4). John was not allowed to write down the thunderous proclamation. There is majesty in the mystery. God reveals what is needed for the saints to live by faith. The message of God that was given by the prophets and apostles is coming true, and the will of God is being done (vv. 5-7). This is good news to the citizens of heaven, but the children of darkness are in danger.

It is clear what will ultimately happen to those who stand against God. They will be sentenced to eternal damnation. This is taught throughout the Bible. What will happen in time and space is not clear. Those who stand in opposition to God will have to endure great suffering. The scroll that was given to John and that he consumed was sweet to him, but it made his stomach hurt (vv. 8-10). This is what the Word does to the redeemed. It is sweet to us because it is true. It is also upsetting because of the wrath of God that will be revealed. God's judgment is coming against the world (v. 11). The redeemed will endure to the glory of God.

Do you believe in God? Are you confident in your eternal standing with the Almighty through faith in Christ? Are you ready to swallow the truth no matter how it makes you feel?

Those who rely on the power of God and seek to accomplish the plan of God live with peace.

The life of a Christian is significantly different from the life of someone who has not experienced the rebirth and filling of the Holy Spirit, the forgiveness of Jesus, and the adoption of the Father. Those who have been saved by grace live a redeemed life. In Deuteronomy 12, the people of Israel were commanded to live like the saved people they were. What God commanded of them is the same that He commands of the disciples of Jesus today.

Disciples of Jesus Christ are made holy by faith, and then they spend the rest of their lives overcoming sin. This activity is called progressive sanctification. Over time, God's children become more and more like their Father. This takes work. The Israelites were commanded to destroy all the false gods and idols in the land they were about to possess (vv. 1-27). The nation of Israel was to worship God alone and live in a uniquely Hebrew way. Christians are to worship God and live in a manner worthy of Jesus.

Not only are God's people to avoid certain sinful patterns of life and remove their influence from their lives, but they are also to trust and obey God out of a deep love (v. 28). It is not enough that God's people stop doing certain things, but it is also imperative that God's people do what He commands and obey out of love and awe of God.

Idolatry is not new. The world will always entice people to reject the real God and to accept an unworthy substitute. That is what idolatry is. It is making a god out of something God made. Idolatry is easy because it makes the ego and flesh of humanity feel good. Typically, God's people do not fall into complete secularism or paganism. Most fall into syncretism, adding elements of idolatry to genuine faith. This is what God commands His people not to do (vv. 29-31). Syncretism and idolatry can only be overcome by those who are willing to be careful to do all that God has commanded. Choosing to trust and obey God leads to a life that is blessed and is full of God's goodness.

Are you overcoming sin? Do you truly trust and obey God out of a sense of awe and love for Him? Or, have you allowed idolatry and syncretism to seep into your life?

Those who live as the redeemed of God by grace through faith in Jesus Christ live with the peace of God.

Deuteronomy 13-14; Psalms 99-101; Isaiah 41; Rev 12:1-6

Every person on the planet is unique. God loves each of us and has a plan for each of our lives. There is nothing more important about a person than what that person believes about God. A low view of God leads to a disparaging view of humanity, creation, morality, and justice. A high view of God leads to a respectful view of humanity, creation, morality, and justice. Psalms 99-101 present God as the great king that He is.

The Lord God is ruler over heaven and earth, and He is to be revered with awe (Psalm 99:1). Trembling in His sight is an appropriate response. He is over all the people and exalted in His greatness (v. 2). There is none who control Him. He is in control of all things, and thankfully, He is holy and loves justice (vv. 3-5). What a terrible world this would be if God were hateful and unjust! God revealed His glory in the past when He rescued Israel from Egypt (vv. 6-9). He is the same God today. The right response to Him is to give Him praise and glory.

Praise and glory is what God demands (Psalm 100). He is not some concept, ideology, or man-made deity. He is God. He is all-powerful. He is glorious. Those who know Him by His grace are commanded to enter into His presence and worship Him. The gift to be able to worship God rightly is a great blessing.

This blessing is made possible by God's sovereign grace. This grace comes to us through Jesus Christ. He is God in the flesh. He is the great king who perfectly does the works told of in Psalm 101. It is Jesus who honors the Father perfectly with praise (v. 1), who thinks of God's ways perfectly (v. 2), who will not seek what is worthless and who hates sin (v. 3), and who has no perversity in His heart (v. 4). It is Jesus who lived a holy life and will one day establish justice perfectly (vv. 5-8). It is wise to submit to Jesus in faith and to choose to love and obey Him. He is the King above all kings, and soon He will judge the living and the dead.

Do you know the God of the Bible? Do you honor Him? Are you living your life under the authority and grace of Jesus?

Those who know God for who He really is, as He has revealed Himself in His holy Word, will love God and obey Him and will live with Him and for Him in peace.

Jesus is one of the most controversial figures to ever walk this earth. There is none like Him. He is the kind Savior of the world. He came in humility, was raised in majesty, and will return in glory to establish His kingdom forever and ever. Isaiah 42 describes the ministry, the destiny, and the divinity of Jesus. He is the Messiah, the promised leader chosen to save God's people for Himself for all of eternity. He is the servant of God the Father and is blessed with the Holy Spirit (v. 1). This verse is used in Matthew 12:18-20 to explain that Jesus is God's chosen servant who had come to fulfill the promises of God. He is gentle, yet strong in His healing (vv. 2-4). Those who trust in Jesus trust in the only true Savior who loves them and cares for them.

The mission of Jesus is a worldwide movement that will bring healing and light to the world (vv. 5-9). King Jesus will call people to a righteous life that sets them free from the power and punishment of sin. This mission will be undertaken with great passion and force (vv. 10-17). There is a deep desire in God to save a people for Himself to bring glory to His good name. People are being deceived and are living for and exalting things that are unworthy of their life and love. Christ was sent by the Father to heal and lead the blind into His way of life.

God chose Israel to be His servant and to be a blessing to the nations, but they failed. Rather than honor and trust the Lord, Israel chose to pursue the pleasures of this broken world. They became deaf and blind to the goodness and greatness of God (vv. 18-25). The Lord had given them His law and proof of His love, but they turned away, and the wrath of God was poured out on them. The New Testament church is in constant danger of making the same mistake. Having been given the entirety of Scripture, the power of the Holy Spirit, and a new life that is imperishable, undefiled, and unfading, the church is still made up of imperfect people who can be deceived. The only hope is fidelity to the Word of God.

Have you trusted in the saving work of Jesus Christ for salvation? Are you joining God in His mission in the world? Do you hold to God's Word as your ultimate authority for truth?

All who look to Jesus will be saved and will enjoy eternal peace.

Deuteronomy 16; Psalm 103; Isaiah 43; <u>Revelation 13</u>

God is dangerous, but kind and good. God is great in power and mighty in grace and kindness. His holiness is unbearable to those who refuse to walk in His ways and receive His eternal salvation. Because of His holiness, there is a great battle between Him and evil. Revelation 13 reveals the evil that comes against God and the right response of the redeemed to these wicked enemies.

Since the fall of humanity, the large populations of people on the planet have struggled to govern themselves. For millennia, governments have come and gone. Particular nations are mentioned in the Word of God, such as Babylon, the Medes and Persians, Greece, and Rome. These government systems are reflective of all man-made governments. They have waged war against God, they are currently waging war against God, and they will continue to wage war against God (vv. 1-10). These evil systems will come and go. Those who do not worship God will have to look for something to worship. Many will choose a government system that they prefer and will choose to trust in it rather than in God.

Human beings live by faith in something. If they don't put their faith in government or in Jesus, people will typically choose a religious leader or a religion that appears powerful. There have been, there are, and there will be false religions empowered by demonic forces that will draw people away from God (vv. 11-18). These false religions will seem safe and admirable, but they cannot provide for the need we have to be made right with God. These false religions will draw people away from God and leave them in their sin. These beastly religions will be anthropocentric – human focused.

The redeemed of God will suffer, but we must keep our eyes and our hope on Jesus. We must overcome the temptation to trust in government and false religions. Jesus is the only hope of humanity. Those who believe in Him must endure in faithfulness (v. 10). Though it will be costly in life (v. 17), those who sacrifice and remain faithful will be blessed in eternity with God in heaven.

Do you trust and worship Christ alone for salvation? Have you repented and believed in Jesus? Can you discern the shortcomings of governments and false religions?

Those who remain loyal to God by faith will
live and die with eternal peace.

Deuteronomy 17; Psalm 104; Isaiah 44; Revelation 14

God's Word is perfect. It is useful to define what is right and best for all things pertaining to life and faith. In the Old Testament, there are three types of laws that were to be kept: moral, ceremonial, and theocratic. The moral law is what is true for all people at all times, and it commands what is best for human thriving. The ceremonial law pertained to the way in which the sacrificial system and priesthood associated with the tabernacle and temple was to function. The theocratic law pertained specifically to the nation of Israel and its unique national identity. Deuteronomy 17 speaks to all three. Jesus has fulfilled all three types of laws.

God is worthy of our best. He alone is worthy to be worshipped. To bring any offering to God that was not the very best dishonored God (v. 1). This did not just speak to the condition of the person's heart who brought the offering, but that person would influence other people's approach to God. Those who worshipped other gods were to be dealt with severely (vv. 2-7). This severe punishment was out of respect for who God is and was to protect others who might be tempted to turn away from God. God's people are called to trust Jesus and love and worship Him above all else.

People are sinful. Even those who have been made righteous by grace still struggle with sin in their flesh. Given the propensity for people to sin, God gave instructions regarding how people could deal with different temptations that were bound to come (vv. 8-13). The priests were to provide insight. Having been trusted with the responsibility to teach the law to the people and to offer sacrifices for the sin of the people, they had wisdom to offer. Jesus Christ is the ultimate wisdom. His disciples can look to Him for direction.

The kings who would rule the Israelites would be influential (vv. 14-20). In light of a king's influence, God set standards for who could be king and what they were to do. Jesus is the ultimate king. Those who live under His reign live under the perfect leader.

Are you living under the grace and leadership of Jesus? Is He your Savior? Do you look to Him in decision-making for your life and faith?

Those who look to Jesus and live under His
grace and authority live with peace.

Deuteronomy 18; Psalm 105; Isaiah 45; Revelation 15

Being thankful and being sure are two great blessings. Those who know God have every reason to be grateful and confident in life and death. The Lord is good to provide for the needs of those who believe. Those who believe experience the power of God. Psalm 105 is a song of gratitude that celebrates God's provision.

There are three things that every redeemed person of God will always do: give thanks, call on God's name, and make His deeds known among the peoples (v. 1). God is good to save. He is good to provide for and prevail through His people. There is thankfulness in the heart of every person who depends on God. We can happily and heartily call on God's name. Knowing that Jesus is our mediator frees us to come with confidence to God in prayer. In this confidence and to the praise of God's great name, we share the hope we have both with the redeemed and with those who are far from God.

When we are grateful, prayerful, and evangelistic, we cannot help but sing praise to our God as we glory in Him, seek Him, and remember His power and provision (vv. 2-6). Songs help us recall events and ideas. When we sing the deeds of God, we honor Him and bless our own souls. It is not only right to praise God for who He is and what He has done, but it is also good for us.

What we praise God for says as much about us as it does about God. The God of the Bible is a promise-making and promise-keeping God. He does not need humanity, but He has chosen to make a covenant with a people of His choosing (vv. 7-11). He did not choose us because we are great, but because He is a great God with a great plan and purpose (vv. 12-15). He allows us to go through trials and challenges for His glory and for our good. In redemption, He shows His love for us and power to us. We learn who He is and gain reason to give Him glory (vv. 16-42). He saves us and provides for us to show the world His goodness and might (vv. 43-45). By grace, sinners become obedient saints who honor the Lord.

Are you grateful to God for the way He has worked in your life and in the world? Do you sing His praises? Can you point back to ways He has provided for your life and salvation?

Those who live under the banner of the most high God live under the ultimate source of peace and enjoy His peace.

We are all hoping in something. We each woke up today to pursue a purpose that is based upon what we hope will happen in our lives. What we hope will happen is what drives our decisions. What we hope in is the most important thing about us. It determines if we live in peace. In Isaiah 46, God told people to hope in Him. God was clear about what created things cannot do, and also about what He can do and why.

The strange thing about all world religions (other than Christianity) is that the burden to save is placed on the believers (vv. 1-2). Idols have to be cared for. Rules must justify and reward. False religions cause worshippers to have to bear guilt, shame, and responsibility. Jesus provides a different way. He carries the burdens of His disciples (vv. 3-4). Even when we are old and cannot do anything for God, He carries us. The truth is that we cannot do anything for God. He does not need anything. We can serve Him in love with faith and can glorify Him, but He does not need us to.

Human beings are creative creatures who keep making their own gods and pursuing ideologies that they produce (vv. 5-7). Nothing humans come up with ever provides what the human soul needs. In the end, people without Jesus in their lives are left in worse condition after their devotion to their religion. God alone is God (vv. 8-11). All others are fakes. He has proven true in the past. His Word has been accomplished. His purpose cannot be stopped. Those who trust in Him and follow His ways will live in peace knowing they are a part of God's eternal plan that will not fail.

While the religions and idols of the world lead human beings away from what they need, Jesus leads people to what is needed most – righteousness (vv. 12-14). Those who are made righteous by grace through faith in Christ alone are freed from their past, have confidence in their present, and have hope for their future. When people know that their lives are being lived under the grace of God for the glory of God, they experience peace.

Are you trusting in Christ or in some made-up religion? Do you delight in the greatness of God? Have you received righteousness by faith in Christ alone?

Those who look to God for hope live with peace.

Deuteronomy 20; Psalm 107; Isaiah 47; <u>Revelation 17</u>

God is loving, kind, gracious, and good. He is also just, and He will one day judge everyone. God is *holy, holy, holy* (Isaiah 6:3). He will not tolerate sin in His presence. When Jesus comes to rule the world, all sin, along with those who were not loyal and faithful to Him, will be overcome and destroyed. His plan for His enemies and saints cannot be stopped. Revelation 17 describes the enemies of God and the power of God to vanquish them.

Babylon is symbolic of organized evil in the world. God uses Babylon to discipline His people. In the book of Revelation, God uses Babylon to reveal the hearts of humanity. Babylon is pictured as a prostitute that offers people the desires of their flesh (vv. 1-5). This evil is described as an evil woman who deceives the leaders of the world and causes people to fall into grievous sin. This evil will soon be overcome by the holiness and power of God.

This evil hates Christians and makes martyrs of them (v. 6). She is quite a spectacle, but should not be admired. She represents all government systems and people of power who oppose God (v. 7). The beast, or power, that she rides on is not eternal. It is a created thing. The beast had not yet come in fullness at the time of John's writing. This evil is from hell. Those who are not saved will marvel at its power (v. 8). The redeemed must be wise. The redeemed must never put their trust in human systems (vv. 9-13). God alone is to be trusted. The government systems, created by human beings, will trust in the evil that is to come.

This evil will make war on Jesus and His people (v. 14). This occurred with Rome, but it has continued to happen and will be the way of things until Christ returns in His glory. This evil will be corrupt and will cause chaos and pain on the planet. This is all according to the will of God (vv. 15-18). God will allow evil to run its course, and all who side against God will be revealed. Their true allegiance will be obvious. They will be judged and tormented with evil forever.

Do you trust in Christ alone? Can you see how God, for His good purposes, has allowed evil to be at work in the world? Are you confident in God's provision?

***Those who live under the reign and rule of God by
grace through faith in Jesus have peace.***

Deuteronomy 21; Psalms 108-109; Isaiah 48; Revelation 18

The world is a very complicated place. Given the capacity of human beings to think and figure out problems, it would seem that life would get easier with the advance of human capabilities regarding technology. The sad fact is that human beings often use their mental capacity for harm rather than for good. Deuteronomy 21 speaks to the human condition and also points to the grace of God.

Since the fall of humanity, human beings have been murderous creatures (vv. 1-9). God knows who has done what, and He will bring justice to each person according to their actions, just as He did with Cain. Human justice is far more limited. Murderers sometimes get away with their crimes under human-controlled systems. Under the theocratic and ceremonial law of Israel, God made provisions for the limitations of human justice so that the people of Israel could live with clear consciences when their systems failed.

God also made provisions for our desires (vv. 10-14). The Israelites were to be a pure race, but God knew that the men would find captives alluring. He made provisions for such a situation. The demands of God provided for a respectful, God-honoring union.

Inheritance rights can get tricky. God directed the Israelites as to how they were to divide the property of the deceased (vv. 15-17). This would keep conflict from erupting and would provide consistency when people's hearts might tempt them to be unwise and unfair.

Given the nature of human beings, it is not surprising that even the best of parents may have unruly children. God gave strict and harsh directives for unruly, disrespectful sons (vv. 18-21). These directives were protective for society and were meant to create a sense of fear so young men would remain respectful.

God's command for the death penalty is stark, and how it is used in the New Testament to speak to what Jesus has done for us is inspiring (vv. 22-23). The cost of sin is death. Jesus died for us as a substitutionary atonement. God's grace is expensive.

Do you love and obey God? Are you honoring Him with your decisions and way of life? Have you received the costly grace of Jesus and now trust Him as your personal Savior?

Those who trust in the Word of God and
receive His grace live with peace.

Deuteronomy 22; <u>Psalms 110-111</u>; Isaiah 49; Revelation 19

It is sometimes hard to believe, but there really is an eternal plan that is being worked out in the world. God is in control and is able to do what He promised. It all hinges on Jesus, the Messiah. He is the ultimate king and the hope of the world. Psalms 110 and 111 point to the great promises and provision of God.

Jesus is the Lord. He has been given the seat of honor in heaven (Psalm 110:1). In the days of David, the people knew that God had anointed David to serve Israel. They also knew the promise of God. There would be a king like him, but one better than him who would accomplish God's eternal purpose to save a people for Himself. He would make a new heaven and earth. The promised king is Jesus. He is the Messiah. He is the promise!

God raised up David and blessed him (vv. 2-7). The blessing being celebrated here is bigger than David. The one who is being pointed to is not only a king, but is also a priest after the order of Melchizedek (v. 4). Jesus Christ is the ultimate prophet, priest, and king. He came bringing good news of the coming of His eternal salvation in His kingdom. He provided atonement for sin, and He now serves as the high priest of heaven. His kingdom will never end. He is the great king we all need and long for to oversee our individual lives and the entire world.

Those who know God's promise and have experienced the provision of God have every reason to praise Him (Psalm 111:1). The works of the Lord are to be studied. By seeing what God has done, we gain insight into God's plan and His love for us (v. 2). He is a righteous God (v. 3). In His mercy, He caused the Bible to be written so that His wondrous works can be remembered (v. 4). His works have brought salvation (vv. 5-9). Those who fear Him are wise and do what is best (v. 10). God has chosen to love us, and in His love, He has made an eternal covenant so that those who believe in Jesus are eternally blessed by Him.

Do you know Jesus as your Savior? Is your heart filled with love for Him and your mouth filled with praise to Him? Are you living wisely?

> *Those who look to Jesus by faith and trust in God's sovereign plan to bless and provide for His people have peace.*

Deuteronomy 23; Psalms 112-113; Isaiah 50; Revelation 20

The God of the Bible is a very serious God. We live in a very serious world with very serious consequences. The world we live in is not the world God created. The world God created was perfect. The world we live in is broken. Isaiah 50 points to the cause of the brokenness of the world, reminds us that God is great, and celebrates the grace of Jesus.

The world is broken because of sin. God made us creatures who can make choices. The human race chose to side with the snake in the garden of Eden. That choice had serious consequences. Humanity is now born at odds with God. That broken relationship with God splinters our identity and makes relationships with others difficult. God desires a right relationship with us, but like the exiles, many people reject God's covenant of grace (v. 1). Sin has consequences. Choosing sin over God will lead to pain and suffering.

God has the power to save. His *hand is not shortened* (Isaiah 59:1). He knows what to do, and He has done everything needed to restore a person's relationship with Him – but each person must make the choice to trust in Jesus (vv. 2-3). God is all-powerful. Saving a sinner, although costly, is not difficult for God.

Salvation is costly because sin is horrendous. God sent His Son to die to pay for our sin. This was God's plan, and it is what Isaiah prophesied (vv. 5-11). Jesus came speaking the words of life that God gave to Him. Jesus did not act on His own. He is a member of the Trinity, and as the Son, He chose to honor the Father and do and say everything that the Father commanded. Jesus not only came with a call to repentance, but He suffered for sin. The Son of God was beaten and crucified. The Father and the Holy Spirit helped Him with the encouragement of the angels, Moses, and Elijah. Jesus is the light of the world (John 8:12). Those who choose to live by the light of their own design will live and die forever in a tormented state.

Do you believe in the God of the Bible in all of His glory and grace? Are you trusting in the power of God to save you? Is Jesus Christ your Savior and Lord?

Those who take God seriously and seek to walk in
His glorious life will live and die with peace.

Deuteronomy 24; Psalms 114-115; Isaiah 51; <u>Revelation 21</u>

The world is not as it should be, but it soon will be. God has promised that He will come and make all things new. The restoration is the end of the ultimate reality, which is revealed in the Bible. The Bible contains a single story in four parts: creation, fall, rescue, and restoration. Revelation 21 describes the restoration that God will bring.

The heaven and earth that exist today will pass away, and there will be no more chaos (v. 1). When Christ returns, the dead in Christ will be raised, and earth and heaven will become one. Under the eternal, righteous authority of Jesus, the world will exist in eternal peace.

What makes heaven so heavenly is the presence of God. He will bring His redeemed people to be with Him, and He will be with them forever (vv. 2-3). In this new reality, there will be no more pain or death (v. 4). Things will be the way God designed them to be in the beginning. This promise of God will be kept, and those who know, love, and obey Jesus will experience all of what God has promised to those who have been faithful to Him (vv. 5-8). It will be a wonderful time of rejoicing, and it will never end!

This perfect place is provided by the perfect God, and it is there that He will receive His perfected people (vv. 9-27). Only those whose names are written in the Lamb's Book of Life will be allowed into this heaven. Those whose names are written in His book are those who have been born again. They received, through faith alone, God's grace earned by Jesus Christ. The deeds of the faithful are righteous because God works in His people through the Holy Spirit. Those who abide in Jesus produce the life of Jesus, which pleases God. Jesus will be celebrated in His eternal presence forever and ever. God is all we need. He will be all we have, and those who believe will live in peace with Him forever.

Are you a disciple of Jesus? Do you live in light of Christ's coming? How is God's holiness being lived out by you? Is God's presence your hope and desire?

Those who rejoice in the coming restoration of God look forward to eternal life with God in complete peace.

<u>Deuteronomy 25</u>; Psalm 116; Isaiah 52; Revelation 22

We are a weird, wild race. Human beings are both hostile and loving creatures. We are hostile because we are born in sin and exist in a broken world. We are loving because we are made in the image of God and are loved by Him. Our love is tainted by our hostility, which leads to conflict and suffering. If we did not love, we would not care about other people. Because we love, we care about others and seek their protection and good. We sometimes seek the protection and good of those we love with destructive force. Destruction is not God's will. Deuteronomy 25 speaks truthfully about the real-life situations of humanity.

There will be conflict in this world. In those moments, when harm is caused, justice must be done (vv. 1-4). The person who has acted wrongly must be punished. Justice is good for society. It helps the criminal deal with guilt. It provides the victim with some satisfaction. It provides a warning to others. Human beings are God's image bearers and have eternal value. They are to be respected and honored. Just as animals are to receive benefit for their labor, so every human being is to be given the opportunity to gain resources and benefit from their labor.

In this life, death will come. Under the Levitical system, brothers were to care for the widow of their sibling (vv. 5-10). This rule had many good purposes. It provided the means for the family name to go forward under the same bloodline. It provided women with children who would grow up and provide for them. It provided men with a spouse. Family is a gift of God and should be honored, pursued, and protected in society.

God provided laws intended to promote morality among the people of Israel (vv. 11-19). Given humanity's natural tendency to sin, people will be tempted to provide for their families and loved ones in unjust ways. God blesses honesty. He also blesses wisdom. Those who attack God's people and seek to work against God's will must not be trusted. The enemies of God must be resisted and their influence removed from God's people.

Do you respect human beings? Are you encouraging families to thrive? Is your decision-making wise?

Those who seek to honor God will live with peace.

Deuteronomy 26; Psalms 117-118; Isaiah 53; Matthew 1

The ability to say "Thank you!" and to have someone to thank is a blessing. Those who show gratitude to the Lord and honor Him for His love and kindness are healthier and happier people. Life is hard. The world is broken. On our own, we are lost. But, God has not abandoned us. God has chosen to give us grace. In the grace of Jesus, we can know God. Psalms 117 and 118 are praises given by those who understand, have experienced, and celebrate God's grace.

God has an eternal plan for the world. While He chose Abraham and his descendants to bring the hope of salvation into the world, He did not limit His grace to them. Psalm 117 celebrates the goodness of God to all of the world. All of the world is invited to praise God for who He is. All of the world is invited to know, love, and obey Jesus. The faithful must get the message to them. The gospel is only good news to the world if the message gets to them before they die and face judgment.

The faithful are able to let the world know who God is and what He has done because of what the Bible says and because of the experiences they have had by God's grace. Every person on the planet, whether they are an Israelite, a priest, or a gentile, is encouraged to praise the Lord (Psalm 118:1-4). This is a practical response to the God whose steadfast love endures forever.

That steadfast love is experienced by grace through faith in Christ alone. Every person who looks to Jesus from the distress of their sinful condition will find redemption and hope (vv. 5-27). Every saint who is saved will be among the billions who have believed and who praise the Lord (vv. 28-29). All believers can claim God as their God. Each believer is one who has believed in *the stone that the builders rejected* (Psalm 118:22) – Jesus Christ. He is the one who frees us from the curse of sin and enables us to live in a right relationship with God. It is Jesus who causes the redeemed to be grateful. It is to Jesus that the redeemed give their thanks.

Do you praise God for His steadfast goodness? Is Jesus Christ your Savior and Lord? Are you sharing your hope in Jesus?

> *Those who know God's grace love Jesus Christ and*
> *live in peace by the power of the Holy Spirit.*

Deuteronomy 27:1-28:19; Psalm 119:1-24; <u>Isaiah 54</u>; Matthew 2

God has chosen to bless the world through a people redeemed by His grace. God chose Abraham (Genesis 12) and the Israelites (Deuteronomy 7:7-8) to be His operatives in the world. God did not choose them because of their moral, intellectual, and physical strength, but God chose them because it was His plan and purpose. Unfortunately, those blessed people did not bless the world. God's plan to bless the world and save a people for Himself from every tribe, tongue, and nation did not end because the Jews failed. Isaiah 54 reveals the plan of God and how Jesus fulfills God's will.

When the Israelites were exiled to Babylon, it appeared that God's plan would fail. However, God's plans never fail. In light of the greatness and power of God, the people of the exile were told to prepare to be the blessing to the world that God promised they would be (vv. 1-8). God's people must not fall into the temptation of allowing their circumstances to define what they believe to be true. Instead, the people of God must look to the Bible and allow God's Word to define what is true and real.

God's Word does not fail. What God says will always come to pass. God's promise that a great flood like that in the days of Noah would never occur again has stood (Genesis 9:11), and so also, God's steadfast love will never fail (Isaiah 54:9-10). God's love is not dependent upon the actions of people, but upon God's faithfulness. We change, but God does not change. He is always faithful.

The foundation of God's plan is set, and nothing can stop Him (vv. 11-17). The will of the Lord has been done, is being done, and will be done. Those who trust in Jesus have no reason to fear. There will be difficult days, but no weapon formed against God's plan will prosper. God's plan is to redeem a people for Himself who will love Him and serve Him forever. None deserve this privilege. God saves by grace alone. Those who believe in Jesus are granted a place of prestige in His family that they could never earn.

Do you know and believe God's Word? How has God been faithful to His plan in your life? Are you being faithful to God?

Those who trust in Jesus will walk in His ways, trust in
His provision, and experience His eternal peace.

Deuteronomy 28:20-68; Psalm 119:25-48; Isaiah 55; <u>Matthew 3</u>

God knows what He is doing. He is not surprised by what you are facing in your life right now. Don't panic, and don't be discouraged. Focus on what He has commanded you to do, and be sure to obey. Matthew 3 tells the story of the coming and ministry of John the Baptist and the baptism of Jesus Christ. Before Christ began His ministry in the world, God sent John the Baptist out to spread the good news that Jesus was coming. When Jesus came, He honored God and fulfilled the law. The work of John the Baptist and Jesus Christ were promised in the Old Testament.

John the Baptist lived an unusual life, but he accomplished a great purpose (vv. 1-12). John's birth and the events surrounding it were miraculous (Luke 1). When John began to preach, he fulfilled the prophecy of Isaiah concerning his life. This ministry was a sacred duty. The way he dressed and the food he ate was intentional. It would have created a connection in the minds of the people between John and Elijah. John was the last of the prophets who proclaimed the coming of the Messiah. The message of John was both terrifying and hopeful. For those who would not repent of their sin and believe in the Messiah, it was scary. For those who repented and believed, the message was hopeful.

When Jesus came forth to begin His ministry, the first thing He did was to be baptized (Matthew 3:13-17). He did this out of obedience to God. It is right to be baptized and make a public profession of our faith. Jesus did. All who follow Jesus are to be baptized to announce their new life in Him. Jesus was already God's Son. His baptism did not make Him God's Son. The baptism of Jesus was the means by which His identity was revealed. In that moment, the Father, the Spirit, and the Son were recognizable, and the triune persons of the God who is one were revealed. Those who are born again are already saved before they are baptized. Their baptism announces their identity.

Have you repented and believed in Jesus? Have you obeyed God by being baptized? Does your life announce and honor God's grace?

Those who believe the promises of God and
obey His directives live with peace.

Deuteronomy 29; Psalm 119:49-72; Isaiah 56; Matthew 4

Christianity is not like other religions. Other religions depend on the self-will of human beings. It is natural to trust in ourselves and to use God as a crutch. To trust in Jesus and live as His disciple is supernatural. In Deuteronomy 29, Moses laid out for Israel what it means to be the people of God. The people of God know God, love God, obey God, and trust God in all things.

Moses was concluding his sermon. It was time to lay out a strong challenge. The people were in Moab. The covenant Moses was calling them to now was consistent with the one made at Horeb (v. 1). He called them to believe what they had seen and to know God for who He is: the Almighty. He rescued the people from the Egyptians with signs and wonders (vv. 2-3). They knew that what had happened was miraculous. Today, those who are saved through faith in Christ can look back to the life, death, and resurrection of Jesus and know that God provided for salvation.

The Israelites did not seem to have a true love for God. They needed a supernatural work to transform their affections and cause them to delight in the Lord (v. 4). It is one thing to have head knowledge of God, and another thing to have heart knowledge of God. To truly love God, we must experience new life by the power of the Holy Spirit. Today, those who walk with God are those who have been born again (John 3:1-18).

The Lord had provided for His people (Deuteronomy 29:5-8). It only made sense that the people would now obey Him (vv. 9-28). What God expected of the people was doable. He expected them to honor and obey Him. Those who belong to Christ are expected to trust and obey Jesus.

When it comes to faith, trust is crucial. There are certain things about God that we cannot understand, but what we can know, we are to do (v. 29). God is mysterious, but knowable. Those who know Jesus are to love and obey Him. What cannot be understood is to be accepted by faith.

Do you know the one true God? Does your heart completely belong to Jesus? Are you trusting and obeying God in the power of the Holy Spirit to the praise of Jesus' name?

Those who walk by faith in the power of God live with peace.

Deuteronomy 30; <u>Psalm 119:73-96</u>; Isaiah 57; Matthew 5

The Bible is the Word of God given to humanity by God. It was given that we might understand who God is, who we are, and what it is we must do in order to live healthy, God-honoring lives. Psalm 119 is a celebration of the law of God. In verses 73-96, the call of Jesus, the command of God, and the comfort of the Holy Spirit are revealed and are discernable to those who believe.

The thoughts of the psalmist provide insight into the heart of any who trust in the Lord (vv. 73-80). What God has done for all who believe in Him is significant. There is a beautiful blessing bestowed on those who believe. This blessing is to be like Christ. These words could easily have been spoken by Jesus to the apostles concerning His calling and purpose. God made Him and enabled Him to grow in His understanding (Luke 2:52). Evil men put Him to death, but He was raised, and all who turn to Him will be saved – just as Peter proclaimed at Pentecost (Acts 2).

Those who are blessed to know the Word of God are to obey it with hope (Psalm 119:81-88). The redeemed of God long for ultimate salvation in the final restoration, and they look for the return of Jesus. During this life, disciples of Jesus will suffer. The world, the flesh, and the devil will constantly seek to cause the faithful to fall. The wise saints of God are to pray for God's protection and provision. They are to look to God in faith. His steadfast love will sustain them and provide them with a testimony of faith.

When the Holy Spirit came, as promised by Jesus (John 14-16), He provided help in understanding the plans and purposes of God. It is God's will that His children bring glory to Him by overcoming pain and sorrow. Job was able to glorify God, and the Lord used His testimony to strengthen the church. God's people are to be comforted by the ministry of the Holy Spirit, who enables believers to remember God's Word and to draw comfort in His eternal salvation (Psalm 119:89-86).

Have you heeded the call of Jesus to come and follow Him? Is it your delight to obey God's Word? Does the Holy Spirit comfort you with God's Word?

Those who believe in Jesus and walk in His ways
by the power of the Spirit live with peace.

Deuteronomy 31; Psalm 119:97-120; Isaiah 58; Matthew 6

God wants us to approach Him with a genuine heart. He is not interested in inauthentic worship. Good deeds have no value when we do them for our own personal gain. God deserves the glory. God delights in those who acknowledge their "creatureliness" and delight in His "otherliness." God is not like His creation. He is above it. Isaiah 58 calls people to recognize their selfishness, seek God's gloriousness, and find peace in giving Him praise.

God is gracious to call preachers who proclaim God's will and show people the error of their ways (v. 1). Many people are confounded by God. They believe they are doing the right things and expect God to do what they want Him to do because of their religious efforts. That is not how God works (vv. 2-5). God is looking for people who take Him seriously and choose to join Him in taking love to the world (vv. 6-7). It is when people happily and heartily obey God and choose to be a blessing to others that the Lord's pleasure is revealed and His blessings flow (vv. 8-11).

One of the great indicators that God is being honored rightly and His blessings are flowing in a person's life or in a church is that God's Word is being kept and His people are pursuing His purposes at great sacrifice to themselves (v. 12). The generation that chooses to honor God will take up His Word and make it their banner and standard. They will create a culture in which future generations are trained and are made free to find God's grace that is available through Jesus Christ by the power of the Holy Spirit.

Those who have experienced the grace of Jesus will be satisfied and will delight to rest on the Lord's Day and celebrate God's great grace through the gathering of the saints for worship (vv. 13-14). This experience will be intentional. God will be honored and praised. His name will be lifted high. His people will know His truth, feel His goodness, and do His will. Authentic followers of Jesus do not have to fake spirituality and do not feel the need to try to manipulate God. They rest in grace and obey Jesus with love.

Is your faith authentic? Do you delight to serve and sacrifice for God? Do you intentionally keep the Lord's Day?

Those who seek God with their whole heart and honor
Him with their life will enjoy God's peace.

Deuteronomy 32; Psalm 119:121-144; Isaiah 59; <u>Matthew 7</u>

Wisdom is the source of all godly living. Although not all of God's people are intelligent, all of them can be wise. Wisdom is the ability to do the right thing at the right time in the right way. Matthew 7 is the conclusion of the greatest sermon ever preached. In this section, Jesus points to the fundamentals for making wise decisions and what happens when we do.

Those who are wise do not waste their resources on judging other people, but have a discernment about them that keeps them from falling into relationships that are not healthy or helpful (vv. 1-6). God's people know they are not perfect. Realizing their own capacity for error helps them be self-aware and non-judgmental toward other people. At the same time, they choose not to associate with just anyone. They protect their time and keep people whom the Bible describes as dogs and pigs from cluttering their lives.

Those who are wise spend a good deal of time in prayer. They know God is good and powerful, and they look to Him to meet their needs (vv. 7-11). Prayer is not only good for the soul, but it also accomplishes God's will and reveals the true faith of a saint.

Those who are wise treat people the way they want others to treat them. The "Golden Rule" is one of the most famous sayings of Jesus (v. 12). It truly is relational gold and blesses everyone.

Those who are wise pursue God's way according to God's Word, which produces righteousness (vv. 13-23). The narrow way of Jesus is not easy, and the world often scoffs at it; but those who walk in it produce the fruit of righteousness, which gives an assurance of faith. Godly people live with the confidence that Jesus will recognize them on the day of judgment.

Those who are wise build their lives on the truth of God's Word (vv. 24-27). Life is filled with storms and surprises. Those who are righteous never need to fear dark and difficult days. Because Jesus is their foundation and hope, they can withstand anything. They have hope in Christ and in His authoritative teaching (vv. 28-29). The Sermon on the Mount is the greatest sermon ever preached.

Are you being wise? Are you walking the narrow way? Is your life being built on Jesus and His Word?

Those who walk in wisdom live with peace.

Deuteronomy 33-34; Psalm 119:145-176; Isaiah 60; Matthew 8

God does not change. What we experience in life and how we perceive reality does not change what is true. The reality is that God is great and mighty, humanity is under a curse, and God has a plan for us. Deuteronomy 33 declares the greatness of God and His sovereign care over His people. Deuteronomy 34 reveals the seriousness of sin as well as the grace and mercy of God.

Deuteronomy 33 begins and ends with Moses touting the provision and power of God. The Lord saved His people out of Egypt by raising up Moses to rescue them (vv. 1-5). Moses was only the vessel God used to transmit His truth. God is sovereign. He is the ruler of His people. He guided Israel into His will. He did this because of His love. He chose to care for His chosen people and provide for their needs (vv. 26-29). God helped them and enabled them to experience victory. It was they who did the work of traveling and fighting, but it was God who won the victory.

The middle section of Deuteronomy 33 celebrates the providence of God in fulfilling His promises to the tribes of Israel (vv. 6-25). The only tribe not listed is Simeon, which had been absorbed into Judah. God had a purpose for each tribe, and He guided them to a specific place and purpose. This is true for every child of God. In Christ, every saint has a place and purpose with God.

Deuteronomy 34 celebrates the grace and kindness of God and reveals the serious consequences of sin. Moses was allowed to see the land, but he was not permitted to enter into it because of his sin. He was the best of the best, and yet he still sinned. All people sin and fall short of the glory of God (Romans 3:23). Thankfully, God gives grace and makes heaven our home. This world provides the journey to God. All who walk with God will struggle, but in the end will be blessed. Moses' life was a struggle, but He knew God and was blessed. There is nothing more important for a person than to know and love God by faith in Jesus Christ. He alone gives life and peace.

Do you trust in the power of God to provide for your path in life? Is God glorified by you and celebrated in your heart daily? Are you confident that heaven is your home?

*Those who recognize the superiority of God and seek
to do His will in His way will find peace.*

Joshua 1; Psalms 120-122; Isaiah 61; Matthew 9

Worship is important. The way a person prepares for and approaches a time of worship will often determine how that person will participate in worship. Christian worship is the sacred activity of meeting with the most important Being in existence. Worship is an engagement with God. Psalms 120-122 begin the "Songs of Ascents." It is believed that these songs were sung by worshippers who made their way to Jerusalem to gather with God's people to give praise to God.

Psalm 120 is a lament. One of the great blessings of being a child of God is that the Father knows us better than we know ourselves. Life is hard. It can feel overwhelming. It is a spiritual battle. God's people should never be surprised about the emotional fatigue that comes from being in a broken world. It is a blessing to be able to seek God's face. It is a blessing to be able to acknowledge our disappointments and find refuge in His presence.

Psalm 121 is a confession of the sovereign care of God. Those who gather to worship God have great reasons to bring Him praise. He is the ultimate help to all who know Him and seek Him. God never sleeps. He keeps His focus, and His eyes are on His beloved saints. He protects His people and provides times of respite under His sovereign care. He is the deliverer of those who call on His name and who look to Him for wisdom so they can make wise choices. Wisdom keeps the saints from evil. God watches over the beginning and the end of each of our days and every second in between. Nothing gets to us that has not first gone through Him.

Psalm 122 is a celebration of the power of God. The people who were under the old covenant would go to a holy place and find security from the evil of the world. Under the new covenant, the saints of God now come to their resurrected Savior, Jesus Christ. He is peace. He is the light of the world, and darkness cannot dwell where He is. The redeemed of God are to gather together to be voices of encouragement to one another and voices of praise to their God.

Do you worship weekly with God's people? How do you prepare to worship? Is your heart hungry for Christ?

Those who celebrate God rightly, after preparing appropriately to meet with Him, honor His holy name and have peace.

Jesus has come and is coming again! The kingdom of God came with the coming of Jesus. Jesus is the ultimate king who came as the suffering servant promised in Isaiah 53. Jesus came to do what only a man who is God could do. He came to bring healing and new life, love and restoration, and the gift of eternal protection and provision. Isaiah 62 promises all that Jesus has brought in the past, is bringing now, and will one day bring.

Every person is born with a sin nature. Our sin separates us from God. God is holy, and no sin can dwell with Him. Our relationship with God had to be restored by Him. He had to heal that relationship, and that is what Jesus did (vv. 1-4). Now all who believe in Jesus have a righteous standing with God. Those who repent of sin and believe in the gospel are no longer under the curse of God. They draw near to God and are received by Him. This is new life. It is the best life.

Life with God is a life filled with love. The Lord loves us with a passionate and persistent love (v. 5). He does not love us occasionally or only when we think we are worth loving. God loves us at all times. He has restored us to Himself and has given us a holy standing so that He can bless us with His love.

God will never let us go, for we are His chosen and loved people. He will never abandon those for whom He has sacrificed so much in order to save (vv. 6-12). The holy people of God are not only forgiven, but they are also covered in the holiness of God. This holiness not only protects them from God's wrath, but also protects them from the darkness of the world. The darkness flees from the light. Those who walk in the light with Jesus stand secure in Christ, and He provides for them. Nothing happens without His permission. Every blessing has a purpose. Every trial, thorn, challenge, and temptation comes according to God's plan and for His glory. The kingdom will bring harmony again, but until that day, the saints stand secure in Christ.

Is your relationship with God restored so that you have a holy standing before Him? Are you living a holy life that makes the darkness flee? Do you trust in the completed work of Christ for salvation and in His loving care for daily provision?

Those who trust in Jesus gain His blessings and live with peace.

Joshua 3; Psalms 126-128; Isaiah 63; <u>Matthew 11</u>

God is without beginning or end. He transcends space and time. He sustains it all by His might. We can get a hint of how glorious and great God is, but we can never completely grasp how wonderful He really is. He is the Creator. We are the creation. He is infinite. We are finite. Matthew 11 points to the blessing of knowing Jesus and living for Him.

John the Baptist did not understand Jesus. John had done what he was commanded and born to do, but life did not turn out the way he thought it would. Jesus did not turn out the way John thought He would. In prison and about to die, John questioned if Jesus was the Christ (vv. 1-3). Jesus affirmed that He was the Christ, and He praised John for his life and work (vv. 4-14). God does not expect us to understand everything. He expects us to live by faith.

The world did not and does not understand God. No matter what God does or allows, whether good or bad, the world doubts Him and shuns Him (vv. 15-24). God rewards faith. John acted in faith. He did what God commanded, and he suffered for it. He will be rewarded in Jesus' coming kingdom. Some of the leading cities in Jesus' day saw Him do miracles, but they did not believe. Judgment will come to them because of their lack of repentance and faith. Those who believe in Jesus and choose to love and obey Him will receive His reward. Life without Jesus is empty and cursed.

The world offers leisure, but Jesus offers rest (vv. 25-30). Following Jesus is not complicated, but it is challenging. A godly life is filled with discipline and devotion, but there is deep enjoyment in it. The way of the world is frustrating. The way of the flesh leads to pride and confusion. We were made for God. Those who walk humbly in His ways discover what they were made to do and be. His yoke is easy and light. It is a yoke that demands effort, but there is delight in Jesus' yoke. Those who lean into the way of God find rest for their souls forever.

Do you trust God? Are you living in obedience to God's Word? Is your life under the authority and blessing of Jesus, or are you trusting in something or someone else?

> *Those who simply trust, love, and obey Jesus will live with peace, even when they don't fully understand Him.*

God does not need anything, but He graciously allows weak, treasonous creatures who have sinned against Him to serve Him. God calls sinners to be born again into new life in Christ. The Lord works through these new creations – those who receive the eternal life of Christ. Joshua 4 is an example of how God works through His people. God provides direction, and the people provide service. God is honored, and the people are blessed.

Joshua was Moses' protégé. The Lord had raised Joshua up to lead the people into Canaan and to conquer the land. Along the way, God led Joshua to have the people set up a monument of stones as a place of remembrance (vv. 1-5). Everyone did their jobs. Joshua proclaimed the command of God and appointed a man from each tribe to take a stone from the river. Each man obeyed. It is vital that leaders obey God and command people to do His will. It is vital that God's people obey God's commands.

These stones would be a reminder to the people and a teaching tool for future generations (vv. 6-10). Children would later ask about those stones, and their leaders would tell them of God's grace. Hopefully they would feel awe and gratitude toward God. The people had walked on dry ground through the river by faith. God provides experiences where faith is required. These moments are to be remembered and shared in order to encourage faith.

Once the people had crossed the river and the stones had been set in place, God's will was done (vv. 11-24). The people were where they needed to be. Joshua was esteemed, as he had to be in order to do what was needed. God was where He deserves to be. He was positioned to be known by all the earth. God is to be respected. We are to be in awe of Him. Respect for God is a result of His grace. He graciously condescended to rescue a people for His purpose and to be known. God needs nothing, but He graciously allows people to know Him and join Him in His work.

Are you living in obedience to God? Is God's will being done in your life because of your faith in Him? Do you truly know the God of the Bible?

Those who trust and obey God get to join Him in His
work and experience peace in the process.

Joshua 5; <u>Psalms 132-134</u>; Isaiah 65; Matthew 13

Jesus is the Good Shepherd. He came looking for His sheep. He did not abandon us. God chose to enter into His own creation. The plan was formed in eternity. It was, is, and will be lived out in reality. Psalms 132-134 are a celebration of the promises and outcomes of God's grace.

Psalm 132 is a reminder that God promised that He would provide the Savior of the world through the line of David. David was a righteous man who had a passion for God's glory (vv. 1-5). He influenced people to pursue God (vv. 6-7). His life pictured the Christ who would come and establish God's eternal kingdom (vv. 8-18). While God certainly blessed David and the people he led, David and those who followed him were not capable of establishing what God promised. Only a man who is God could do what God promised. God did it! Jesus came and overcame sin and death, and He will one day return and make all things new.

Psalm 133 is a reminder of what happens when God's people have peace with God. Those who have peace with God can have peace with one another. Because God has forgiven His saints so much, His saints can forgive others for anything and everything. Relationships filled with forgiveness are life-giving and provide nourishment for the soul. God pours down His grace, and His people pour it out into one another's lives.

Psalm 134 is a reminder of what the redeemed of God do – they worship God. This psalm is the last of the songs of ascents and was probably used for the beginning or ending of a festival. It commands worship (vv. 1-2) and points to the blessing that comes to those who make God the object of their worship (v. 3). When we look to God to give life meaning and hope, we are truly blessed. All other things that can be worshipped are idols and are limited in what they can offer. God gives the best things in life. He is eternal, and His blessings are eternal.

Do you believe in Jesus? Are your relationships filled with forgiveness? Is God the delight of your life?

Those who live in the salvation of Jesus are at peace with the saints of God and can celebrate the glory of God. In Jesus, they live with peace.

God cannot be manipulated. God cannot be presumed upon. Every dealing with God by humanity is a response. The response that a person gives to God's majesty, holiness, goodness, grace, and mercy will determine everything about a person's life and eternity. Isaiah 66 reveals the greatness of God and the right response of a righteous person to Him.

God is bigger than the tools He offers for saving faith. In the Old Testament, the people gained access to God through the temple (vv. 1-4). God is not impressed with religious activity. God looks to and cares about the condition of a person's heart. It is a sin to approach God without respect and awe. Those who truly believe in the greatness of God and refuse to trust in idols or in the strength of humanity will be hated by those who do trust in idols or in humanity (vv. 5-6). God's offer of grace is exclusive. Those who want to worship God in their own way or choose to worship another god or idol will despise those who hold to the truth claims of Scripture and the unilateral conditions given by God in order to enter into His covenant of grace.

God promised to bring eternal life and salvation through the Messiah. The life and blessing He brings come miraculously (vv. 7-14). Salvation in Christ is a glorious thing offered by a glorious God. He alone can provide what the soul longs for. This salvation is forgiving and life-giving. There is nothing like it.

The redeemed of God are blessed with hope in this life, but they are also given an even greater hope for the life that is to come (vv. 15-24). While the new heavens and the new earth will be glorious, hell will be horrendous. There will be suffering forever in hell. Both heaven and hell reveal the glory of God. God is just. He is holy. Only those who have been justified by the blood of Jesus can enter into His presence and experience His life. Those who live and die separated from God by sin will be judged justly. To finite creatures, this judgment seems unjust. It is not unjust. It is fair. It is right.

Do you truly love God, or are you just going through religious motions? Are your heart and mind filled with awe of God? Are you confident in your eternal hope in Christ?

> *Those who honor God and live to glorify Him*
> *now and forevermore live with peace.*

Joshua 7; Psalms 137-138; Jeremiah 1; <u>Matthew 15</u>

The best intentions of people are tainted with sin. Religious people often want to be helpful and provide boundaries for human thriving, but unfortunately, people tend to think more highly of their own ideas than they do of the Word of God. God is looking for people to live by faith. In Matthew 15, Jesus challenged the thinking of the religious leaders and taught how He wants His disciples to live.

It is easy to be critical of religious institutions, but in reality, most of them begin with good intentions. People are a mess. Left to themselves, human beings cause harm. To deal with the ramifications of sin, religious leaders often create rules intended to help. Jesus was challenged by the religious leaders of His day because He and His disciples did not keep the religious traditions they lived by (vv. 1-2). Jesus pointed out that the religious leaders had not kept God's law (vv. 3-9). Jesus taught that what defiles a person is not what is on the outside, but what comes from the inside (vv. 10-20). The heart matters most to God. Traditions and religious rituals provide nothing unless they help people love God more by faith. Traditions have a tendency to produce pride or despair.

It is not religious traditions that God blesses, but faith in Jesus. The Canaanite woman who approached Jesus truly believed in Him, and although she was not of the house of Israel, Jesus chose to heal her daughter (vv. 21-28). God honors faith! Those who believe in Jesus and trust in Him gain God's favor. Many people sought and received the healing of Jesus (vv. 29-31). Healing does not come to those who deserve it, but to those God chooses and who have the faith to truly believe in God's power and love.

When the crowds were hungry, Jesus wanted to feed them, but the disciples doubted (vv. 32-34). Jesus provided a miracle, and all were fed – with plenty left over (vv. 35-39). It was His will. God's will cannot be stopped. God is not limited by circumstances.

Do you have a heart for God, or are you just religious? Is your faith in Jesus real and strong? Are you able to trust God's will and His power to accomplish His plan for you?

> *Those who choose to follow Christ no matter what will*
> *experience the kind of peace only God can give.*

No one lives as a perfect disciple of Jesus. Although saints are made holy by the blood of Jesus and are given a righteous standing before God, they still struggle with the desires of the flesh and the temptations of the world. God is gracious, and His will is perfect. Even when God's people fail, God is faithful. The events of Joshua 8 took place right after the people had experienced a huge failure. They probably had a lot of doubts about themselves and their standing with God. The Lord led them to experience a victory where they had previously failed. This chapter teaches crucial truths. The Lord is gracious. God's people must be wise. Having a firm, confident sense of a solid, undoubtable standing with God is a must.

Because of sin and pride, Israel had failed to defeat Ai. Having dealt with their sin and having sought God's favor, the Lord called them to continue fulfilling their purpose in His plan. They were to take the city of Ai (Joshua 8:1-2). The Lord knew they would be discouraged, so He encouraged them. The Lord knew they would need assurances, so He gave them a clear plan. Joshua communicated God's plan, and the people accomplished what God told them to do (vv. 3-29). After a failure, God's people must repent and look to the Lord. When God renews His call to accomplish His purpose, God's people must be wise and do exactly what God commands in order to gain His victory.

After a failure and a recovery, God's people need to take time to honor God and renew their commitment to Him. Joshua took time to remind the people of the covenant God had made with them (vv. 30-35). Joshua read the Bible and called the people to be faithful to God. God's people need times of covenant reminder and renewal. Those who follow Jesus get to experience this kind of renewal each time they receive the Lord's Supper. This memorial points to the grace of God and the call of Christ to trust and obey.

How have you struggled to believe and obey God? When have you had to overcome and gain a victory where there had been a failure? Have you renewed your hope in Christ recently by receiving the Lord's Supper?

***Those who trust in the grace and faithfulness of
God will live and die with God's peace.***

Joshua 9; <u>Psalms 140-141</u>; Jeremiah 3; Matthew 17

God understands exactly what we are going through. Rather than keep His distance, God became one of us. Jesus is Immanuel, God with us. He knows what it is to have pain, sorrow, and difficulties of every kind. Because Christ has come, His disciples can live in His life, love, and strength. Psalms 140 and 141 are the prayers of a suffering saint. These two chapters remind us of the challenges of life and the practical help of God's Word. David experienced dark days, but God saw him through each one.

David had a lot of enemies. In His youth, his enemies were wild creatures. As a young adult, his enemies included a giant and a great king. As an adult, his enemies were nations. As an older man, his enemy was himself. As an old man, his enemy was his family. God was good to David. When David prayed for God's provision, he prayed with great assurance (Psalm 140:1-5). His assurance came from God and His Word. David believed and trusted God as his personal, loving Savior, and he saw God deliver him time and time again from his enemies (vv. 6-8). He prayed for his enemies to fail (vv. 9-11). He trusted in God's will to provide for the lowly because he knew that God is just. Those who can look to God in faith can pray with confidence that what they are asking is God's will. God's will does not change. He delights in those who depend upon Him and who seek and desire for justice to be done in the world.

David sought God with intensity, and he believed that it pleased God for him to turn to God (Psalm 141:1-2). David knew that he could be his own worst enemy. In wisdom, David prayed that God would keep him from causing harm (vv. 3-4). David sought the help of others and looked at difficulty as a means to be transformed into a faithful man, but he did not trust in people (vv. 5-7). David trusted in God to be his provider (vv. 8-10). Jesus Christ is the ultimate wise king. He trusted in the Father to accomplish His purpose. Like David, God's people must learn to lean into God and seek to become more like Jesus. Following Jesus is the goal!

Do you have a powerful, consistent prayer life? Is it your tendency to trust in God alone, or to trust in other people or circumstances? Can you see how you are becoming more like Jesus?

Those who follow Jesus and trust in Him will live with peace.

Joshua 10; Psalms 142-143; Jeremiah 4; Matthew 18

God's general will is easy to understand. God's specific will requires the wisdom and leadership of the Holy Spirit. When people turn to God through faith in Jesus Christ by the power of the Holy Spirit, they are free to pursue God's specific will for their lives. Jeremiah wanted to see Judah thrive. Jeremiah 4 is a general call from God for His people to know and do His will. It provides a practical explanation of what God wants for His people, why the people should trust God, and what will happen if they don't honor God.

God wanted His people to trust in Him alone (v. 1). The people were looking to idols and false gods. Their practices were evil and detestable. The Lord wanted His people to look to Him in faith and trust in His goodness to provide for their needs. A part of idolatry and serving worldly gods is the sense of personal pleasure and power that is felt. God did not make humans to be on their own. God made people to find pleasure in His power and to serve His perfect purpose for the world.

God wanted His people to trust in Him – not only for their own sakes, but also for the sake of the nations (v. 2). God's plan was and is to save a people for Himself and for His people to be a light to the nations. God desires the nations to repent and come to Him.

In order to be what God wants and in order to accomplish His purpose, the people of God must fight and overcome sin. They must cut it off from themselves. God called the people to invest their lives in His purpose and to turn from sin (vv. 3-4a). His command came with a threat. If they would not turn to God, then they would have to face the consequences of His wrath (vv. 4b-31). When God's people languish in sin, they suffer, and the world suffers too. God's desire is to bless, but if His people refuse to trust Him, then His judgment comes, and everyone gets hurt.

Are you pursuing the will of God by the power of the Holy Spirit? Is your life a blessing to God, to you, and to the world? How have you seen God's wrath revealed against sin in your life and in the lives of others in the world?

Those who trust in the Lord by fearing Him and seeking His will are able to live in God's peace.

Joshua 11; Psalm 144; Jeremiah 5; <u>Matthew 19</u>

The way of the world produces either pride or despair. Those who get what they want become proud, while those who do not get what they want fall into despair. The way of Jesus produces humility. Those who trust Jesus will obey the Bible and enjoy the peace that comes with being faithful to God. Matthew 19 provides three unique insights into the way of Jesus. It tells us who is in charge, who can come to Jesus, and who will be excluded from His way of life.

God's plan is best! The plan God has for marriage provides what is best for a man and a woman, for children, and for society as a whole. God's plan from the beginning was for one man to be united to one woman in marriage until death parts them. God's will is not divorce (vv. 1-12). God's will is for a husband and wife to love and serve each other. Those who get married must be ready to make sacrifices. Marriage is not easy, but it is a blessing to those who honor God and do what is right and best.

Those who are most likely to do what is right and best are those who go to Jesus with a childlike faith (vv. 13-15). Jesus welcomed the children to come to Him. The disciples, like most adults, wanted to keep the weak and often unwanted children away from Jesus so they could get on with what they perceived as important. Jesus loves those who are weak and who want to come and be with Him and enjoy His love and life.

The love and acceptance of Jesus satisfies those who trust Him with childlike faith. Carnal people pursue worldly wealth. The disciples, like most people, thought the wealthy were godly. Those who pursue the wealth of this world miss the true riches. Jesus taught that heaven provides the ultimate rewards (vv. 16-30). Perspective is crucial. Those who follow Jesus Christ understand that this world is passing, but that the kingdom and its rewards are better and forever.

Is the Bible your authority? Do you have childlike faith? Is heaven your aim and reward?

***Those who choose to walk in the way of Jesus will not be in
step with the world, but will enjoy peace with God.***

The life of a follower of Jesus is one of battle. From beginning to end, the Bible speaks of the spiritual war that is taking place in creation. Thankfully, Jesus has won the victory over sin and death, but those who believe will have to conquer their flesh. Joshua 12 and 13 remind us of the victory that has been won, the battles that are ahead, and how we can live victorious in Christ.

God promised that He would lead the Israelites into Canaan, and He kept that promise. Through the leadership of Moses (vv. 1-6) and Joshua (vv. 7-24), many of the kings of the land were defeated, but not all of them. This is a picture of what Christ has done for us. God promised that He would come and defeat our enemies and provide new life for us. This life is a gift received by faith. The faith that saves is in response to God and His love. That faith grows through obedience to God's Word. God's Word calls saints to be sanctified and freed from the sin that so easily entangles.

Those who fight sin must be wise. Once the people were in the land and Joshua was old, there was still territory to be conquered (Joshua 13:1-6). God commanded Joshua to carry out the remainder of His divine plan by dividing up the land among the tribes so that each tribe could fulfill their destiny (v. 7). In Christ, believers are saved, but they must fight to overcome the flesh. They must obey God's Word and join God in the work of sanctification. The goal of God for His people is holiness. Holiness demands that God's people fight fleshly desires and overcome sin.

God's people overcome through faith. Each tribe had an appointed area to conquer and a specific purpose to serve (vv. 8-33). Some succeeded, and some failed. In Christ, each saint must overcome the temptations they face. That will require discipline. That discipline will be fueled by delight. Those who delight in Christ will discipline their lives. Those who choose to be faithful to God will rarely be comfortable, but in the end, they will receive a great reward.

Have you received new life through faith in Christ? Are you becoming more and more holy? Is it your delight to defeat sin through the discipline that faith demands?

Those who fight the good fight of faith experience peace deep in their soul.

Joshua 14-15; Psalms 146-147; Jeremiah 7; Matthew 21

God is good. The fact that He is so kind, forgiving, generous, and glorious is reason enough for Him to be praised. We have all ruined our relationship with God. God has been very good to us, but we have sinned against Him. God gives grace. *His steadfast love endures forever* (Psalm 118). Those who receive His forgiveness gain a new life and a greater reason to praise Him. Psalms 146 and 147 are filled with praises that the redeemed can offer to God.

"Hallelujah!" That is how Psalm 146 begins: *Praise the LORD!* This is a word that is found often on the lips of the redeemed. God will be praised forever by those who have been saved by God's grace through faith in Christ alone (vv. 1-2). We are tempted to put our hope in people and government systems (vv. 3-4). That is unwise, though, because they will pass away. God's steadfast love endures forever!

Those who look to God alone for help will find all that they need. He is the maker and sustainer of all things. There is no limit to His power (vv. 5-6). He provides for the weak and oppressed. He provides for those who cannot provide for themselves (vv. 7-10). No one could see their need for salvation without the grace of God. No one could gain salvation without the grace of God. No one could have eternal, living hope without the grace of God. Those who have been blessed by God cannot help but praise the Lord.

God does not need anything. He is the great giver. All those who receive His blessings praise the Lord because they want to praise Him. They praise Him because they feel His pleasure in them. God is not pleased with those who think of themselves as powerful. God is pleased with and provides for those who look to Him in faith (Psalm 147). Those who are saved by His grace and live under His sovereign care sing praises to Him. These songs of praise are filled with lyrics about God's power, provision, and grace. It is by His Word that the saints of God know who God is and understand why and how they are to praise the Lord. He is truly worthy. It is treasonous to look to any other and to offer praise that belongs to God to any other.

Do you delight in who God is and praise Him for it? Can you celebrate His provision in song with a happy heart? Does the Lord receive His due praise from you daily?

Those who know God's grace and praise Him for it have peace.

Joshua 16-17; Psalm 148; Jeremiah 8; Matthew 22

God is gracious and is willing to sympathize and help us. We have all sinned, but God will forgive us if we will repent and place our lives under Christ's authority by grace through faith. Those who refuse to submit to Christ will live under the consequences of sin. In Jeremiah 8, we see the consequences of sin. It is a life that is cursed, is lived in ignorance, and is dishonoring to God.

To remove the remains of the dead is a great insult (v. 1). This is what the enemies of God did to Israel. They placed their dead remains in front of the gods they worshipped (v. 2). What a powerful picture of what happens in death to those without a relationship with Jesus! They must rely on and remain with their false, dead gods. They would prefer death, but it does not come (v. 3). They experience the ultimate curse uttered by Isaiah: *For their worm shall not die, their fire shall not be quenched, and they shall be an abhorrence to all flesh* (Isaiah 66:24). They suffer forever. There is no hope. There is no peace – ever.

Those who are separated from God by sin live in a constant state of confusion (vv. 4-17). They think they are wise in what they know, but what they know makes them deaf to their Maker. While the animals of the world live according to their design, human beings reject God's way and pursue the way of death. God calls to them, but they will not listen.

The result of a life that rejects God's way is eternal misery. Jeremiah saw what would become of the rebellious Israelites, and he wept (vv. 18-22). There comes a point of no return. There is a point at which human hearts become so hard that God gives the people over to their sin completely. The healing ointment of grace is removed. The people perish. God, being holy and just, will call each person to give an account for their lives. In the last judgment, everyone will kneel before God and honor Him, but those lost in sin will be lost forever.

Do you know and love Jesus? Have you placed your life under His gracious leadership? Is heaven your hope?

*Those who choose to trust in Christ find that God
leads them to a life filled with peace.*

Joshua 18-19; Psalms 149-150; Jeremiah 9; <u>Matthew 23</u>

God longs for a real relationship with His image bearers. Having made us in His image so that we could choose to love and be with Him in the most genuine way, God desires for people to truly love Him with the love that He has given to us. We have all committed spiritual adultery. Only those who have been given a new heart can truly and rightly love God. Religious activity cannot produce the heart needed to love God. If anything, religion can cause more harm than good. In Matthew 24, Jesus points out the limitations and destructiveness of institutional religion.

Jesus was not against the law of God or the truth that Moses and the prophets provided in Scripture. He told the people to respect their religious leaders, but to look beyond them (vv. 1-11). Human beings cannot be a God-substitute. Many people reject God, resulting in great harm to themselves and others. Jesus is the true teacher. He came to serve. Those who represent God are to serve out of love for God and are to pursue the purpose of God, which is always to promote and produce love for God and others.

Jesus laid out some serious criticism on the Pharisees. He pointed out their many flaws (vv. 12-36). The Pharisees, like all people, wanted good things, but their wrong view of God led to evil practices. They thought too much of themselves and too little of God. Their traditions and values did not honor God. Rather than serve with humble and sincere hearts, they pursued God for their own purposes. They used God and people to satisfy their flesh.

This led them to do the unthinkable. They killed the very people whom God had sent to help them (vv. 37-39). They soon would kill the Word made flesh, the Son of God. These leaders were standing in the presence of the Almighty, but did not recognize Him. When we can live without God's presence and not be bothered, or if we can be in God's presence and not be moved, there is something seriously wrong with us. Jesus came to save. All who look to Him for what He has promised, for what He has done, and for what He can do will live well.

Do you have a personal, loving relationship with Jesus? Are you serving God? How has your love for God grown recently?

Those who love God by grace live with eternal peace.

It is so frustrating to be going somewhere, but not know how to get to the destination. God is the provider and guide for all who believe in Him. Being God, He knows all things and works all things according to His good purpose. Having made human beings to need to be defined by something beyond ourselves, God came to give us new life. Having made us for Himself, God came so that we could know Him and love Him. Chapters 20 and 21 of the book of Joshua celebrate the goodness and faithfulness of God.

The world is not as it should be. In our broken world where sin occurs and suffering is never far off, God has provided grace. Joshua 20:1-48 tells that God provided a place of refuge for those who inadvertently killed someone. God is just, and He demands that the lives of His image bearers are to be valued and honored. The law of God demanded that the life of the killer must be taken. The cost of murder is death. Those who inadvertently killed were to go to a city of refuge where they would be saved. So it is in Christ Jesus. All who come to Him find refuge from the punishment of sin.

Joshua was given the inheritance of His choosing (vv. 49-51). God rewards His faithful servants. Although the Levites were a tribe of Israel and were faithful, they were not given a homeland. Instead, they were to serve as a sacrifice unto God. Rather than have their own homeland, they were to dwell in the lands of the other tribes (Joshua 21:1-42). They served as reminders to the people of the goodness of God. The people were to care for the Levites as the Levites served them in their calling to the Lord.

All that God did was according to His promises. He said He would provide His chosen people with land, and He provided (vv. 43-45). All who trust in Jesus will find that the world is broken, but that God is good and provides peace to those who honor and obey Him. All of God's words come to pass. The faithful must remain true to God and trust in His perfect plan. There will always be challenges and trials, but these are allowed for God's purpose.

Do you truly trust God? Have you received salvation for your soul in Jesus Christ? Are the promises of God dear to your soul?

Those who walk in the way of faith in Jesus will enjoy
God's provisions and promises and will gain peace.

Joshua 22; <u>Acts 2</u>; Jeremiah 11; Matthew 25

There are many great things to enjoy in life, but the greatest blessing is Jesus. He is the greatest blessing because He meets our greatest needs and provides for our greatest desires, which include relationships, truth, and purpose. In Acts 2, God fulfilled His promise to send His abiding presence, the Holy Spirit, into the world. This was the dawning of a new era. His coming changed the world!

When the day of Pentecost came, the disciples were all together in one place praying and waiting for God to show up (v. 1). Prayer is hard, but it is effective. It is a beautiful, powerful thing when God's people gather together in prayer.

The coming of the Holy Spirit was exhilarating! All kinds of crazy stuff started happening (vv. 2-4). People are often impressed with the manifestations of the Spirit, and they miss the person who is the Holy Spirit. The blessing is not primarily in the activity of the Spirit, but in His life that comes by grace through faith in Jesus.

The result of the coming of the Holy Spirit was a reversal of the Tower of Babel (Genesis 11). The people of different languages and tribes were unified under the truth of the gospel as many responded in faith to Peter's sermon (Acts 2:5-41). These people were not saved because they were morally superior to others or more intelligent, but they were saved by grace through faith in Christ, as the Holy Spirit empowered them. By grace, the Holy Spirit gives faith in rebirth.

The result of this miracle of God was the formation of the church in Jerusalem, which became the model for the church in our world today (vv. 42-47). What these saints enjoyed together is what God wants for His people in every generation. It is what everyone wants: truth, care, relationships built on God's love, and the opportunity to be a blessing. What they experienced is basically what any of us can have if we are willing to walk in the Holy Spirit with the love of Jesus.

Do you have real faith in Jesus? Is the Holy Spirit working in and through your life? Are you experiencing the blessing of being a member of God's church?

Those who live in the Holy Spirit experience peace and the best things in life.

Joshua 23; Acts 3; <u>Jeremiah 12</u>; Matthew 26

Everyone lives by faith. The object of our faith determines everything about how we experience life and death. Everyone struggles in our broken world. It may appear that some people have it easier than others. Maybe some do, but we all face pain and problems. What or who we hope in will determine the kind of peace we have. Jeremiah looked to God. We see in Jeremiah 12 that the prophet looked to God with confidence in who God is, but had questions about his world. The Lord responded to him with love and truth.

Jeremiah's world made no sense to him. He knew that God was good, but he still complained to God about what appeared to be injustice from his perspective (v. 1). Jeremiah knew that God was righteous. What he could not understand was how God could be so good and let the world be so bad. We can never understand the full dimensions of God's grace, plans, and patience. God always does what is best. We must pray and trust that God is doing what is best. The Lord is at work and will bring justice to all.

Jeremiah wanted instant justice (vv. 2-4). We all do. We want people who do evil to be held responsible so the rest of the world can be freed from their influence. Like the cross, God uses what is evil for His purpose to redeem and provide for His eternal plans.

Like Jeremiah, we must all learn to live by faith in God and not look to our circumstances for hope. God made it clear to Jeremiah that he was just seeing the beginnings of hardship and deceit (vv. 5-6). The worst was yet to come. The Lord clarified His purpose. He would provide justice to Israel and to all nations (vv. 7-17). This is the way of God. He is not slow in keeping His promises. He knows what He is doing. There is grace in His timeline. There is opportunity for those who are spiritually dead to be born again. God has saved, is saving, and will save a people for Himself. Those who will not repent and trust Jesus will suffer for it. God is in control, and all people are responsible for their decisions. In the end, justice will come and God will be glorified.

Do you trust God? Is your faith growing? Are you being patient in your trials and challenges?

Those who live by faith in Christ and hope in Him have
lasting peace that does not diminish over time.

Joshua 24; Acts 4; Jeremiah 13; <u>Matthew 27</u>

From the fall in the garden of Eden up to our current day, human beings have wanted to be their own gods. Those who rock the religious boat with exclusive claims about Jesus Christ will not be received well in a world that wants human beings rather than God to be the sovereign. The desire to yield to nothing except self is strong. In Matthew 27, the slippery slope of humanism's end is revealed and the plan of God in Christ is justified.

The religious leaders of Jesus' day could not tolerate Him, so they labored to have Him killed (vv. 1-2). His so-called disciple and friend, Judas, could not abide by His way of strength in weakness, so Judas turned against Jesus. Seeking his own financial gain at the cost of faith in Jesus led him to suicide (vv. 3-10). Pilate wanted nothing to do with Jesus. He came up with a scheme to free Him, but the religious leaders would not have it. In the end, Pilate chose political expediency over Jesus (vv. 11-26). Each of these men wanted power, but they ultimately gained damnation.

The crowds, the soldiers, and the unbelieving convicts got in step with the ideology of the day and rejected Jesus (vv. 27-44). This is typical. Those who are wise must look beyond what the elites dictate and instead discover the truth of God. Cultures naturally reject the one true God. He is too powerful for their tastes.

The mystery of the gospel is too much for an unredeemed, sinful mind. The vicarious death of Jesus was promised on the day of the fall. Jesus, God's Son, took on sin and experienced God's rejection in order to free people from the power and punishment of sin. Jesus provides salvation for all who believe in Him through His death and burial (vv. 45-61). His tomb was protected by soldiers because His claim that He would be resurrected was no secret (vv. 62-66). What we do with Jesus, who promised to die as the atoning sacrifice for sin and be raised on the third day, determines everything about our life and death.

Do you want to be your own god? Are you following the way of the world? Have you chosen to be countercultural and believe in Jesus?

Only those who embrace Jesus as the Christ and the Bible as His Word will gladly yield to Him and gain His peace.

Judges 1; Acts 5; Jeremiah 14; Matthew 28

Doing what God demands is never easy. We should not be surprised by how hard it is to obey God. It is important to realize that we were never intended to do God's work on our own. We are meant to depend on God and live in His strength. The problem is we do not naturally want to rely on God and His people. Our world celebrates those who stand on their own. On the other hand, God rewards those who trust in Him and who get and give help. Judges 1 reminds us that we need God and His people in order to accomplish God's will.

Israel had been given a good plan, and God had promised that they would be able to do it with His help. The people were to conquer the land God had promised to them. In faith, they prayed and asked God to provide the leaders they needed in order to do the work (v. 1). God provided Judah (v. 2). The Lord has a plan for His purpose. His plan always requires leadership. There has only ever been one perfect leader – Jesus Christ. All others are limited and will need the help of other godly leaders to accomplish God's will.

Seeing the need for assistance, Judah asked Simeon to go with him. In return for Simeon's help, Judah agreed to assist Simeon in conquering their allotted land (v. 3). God gave them success (vv. 4-20). It takes humility to seek help, and it takes faith to serve others. God blesses humble faith. It makes us wise, and it pleases God to see His children serving Him together.

Not everyone was as successful. The people of Benjamin did not do so well (v. 21), but the house of Joseph did okay with help from a traitor (vv. 22-26). The tribes of Manasseh, Ephraim, Zebulun, Asher, Naphtali, and Dan were not successful (vv. 27-36). Joseph was able to help Dan, but not because they asked. Only the tribes that sought help and gave help to others were successful. This is a lesson to all of God's people. It is wise to pursue God's plan with other believers who can offset our weaknesses and maximize our strengths. God made us to depend on Him and His church.

Do you have a clear picture of God's kingdom purpose? Are you willing to get help from and give help to others? How have you been a help to others and received help from others in the past?

Those who are willing to do God's will and seek the help of
God and His people will thrive and live with peace.

Judges 2; <u>Acts 6</u>; Jeremiah 15; Mark 1

It is easy to look back to the era of the apostles as recorded in the books of Acts and assume that it was easier for them back then. That would be a huge mistake. Yes, most of them had heard Jesus preach, had seen Him die and be raised, and had experienced the coming of the Holy Spirit at Pentecost, but those blessings did not offset the fact that they were still wrestling with sin in a broken world. Acts 6 helps us understand the challenge of being the church in a broken world and the importance of standing strong in the gospel.

Racism is nothing new. It existed in the early church. People who come from different cultures often struggle to connect and properly care for those outside of their immediate community of color or class. The early church was made up of Hellenists (Greek-speaking Jews who were not born and raised in Israel) and Hebrews (the Hebrews primarily spoke Aramaic, were from Israel, and were members of a Hebrew-speaking synagogue). The Hellenists believed they were being overlooked and not properly cared for (v. 1). Whether this was intentional or not is not known. The twelve apostles summoned the church, and godly men were selected who could serve the needs of the church without partiality (vv. 3-5). These deacons were commissioned by the apostles (v. 6). Unifying around a common cause in the name of Christ is the most effective way to overcome racism in any generation.

Although Christ had been raised, there were still many who stood in opposition to this fact because they wanted to hold on to their positions of power. They opposed one of the deacons, Stephen, who was doing miracles (vv. 7-9). It is amazing how pride keeps people from eternal salvation. The opposition couldn't withstand his wisdom in the Spirit. They had him falsely accused and arrested (vv. 10-14). This is often the strategy of the damned. But Stephen had peace (v. 15). Peace is experienced by those who live in obedience to God by walking in the hope of the gospel.

Are you helping create unity, or are you causing division among believers? Is your hope in the gospel of God? Are you willing to suffer for the sake of Christ?

Those who know Jesus will serve in His name and will share the hope of the gospel – and in the process, they will gain peace.

Judges 3; Acts 7; <u>Jeremiah 16</u>; Mark 2

God is sometimes very scary. There is nothing that He needs, and He cannot be controlled. The universe and all that has been made belongs to Him. What He commands is right and good. Those who do not want to love and trust Him are His enemies. It is a terrifying thing to be the enemy of God. Jeremiah 16 explains what happens to God's enemies.

The enemies of God lose everything that matters to them (vv. 1-9). God designed human beings to have families, but God told Jeremiah not to have one. The explanation Jeremiah was given was that considering the loss that would be coming to the land of Israel, not having a family would be better for him. God went on to tell Jeremiah not to go to funerals and to be aware that there would be an end to happy celebrations such as weddings. The cause of this loss was God's removal of His steadfast love and mercy from the people. When this grace is gone, there is no hope. Those who will not repent and believe the gospel are left in their sin and have no real, lasting hope.

The worst thing that can ever happen to a person or a people is for God to abandon them to sin (Romans 1:24-32). Once God gives up on people, they are forced to rely on the idols they trusted in rather than on God (Jeremiah 16:10-13). None of those idols help. None of those idols have the power to comfort or save. None of those idols can satisfy the human soul. Those who trust in idols suffer loss in this life now and eternally in death.

For His glory and eternal purpose, God always has a people who are faithful to Him whom He shows His grace to. The Lord promised to bring people back from exile (vv. 14-21). This remnant would be fished out and hunted in order to be returned to the land so that God's promise could be fulfilled. God promised through His prophets that Jesus would come and bring salvation to the world. Nothing could stop God's plan. Nothing can stop God! God's eternal plan for His kingdom has come, and what is not yet done will be done.

Do you trust in Jesus or in idols? Have you abandoned God? Is your current trajectory toward heaven or toward hell?

Those who happily live to know, love, and obey Jesus have a Savior who will never fail and who will always provide peace.

Judges 4; Acts 8; Jeremiah 17; <u>Mark 3</u>

There is no greater privilege in life than to be called a child of God by grace through faith in Christ alone. At great expense to Himself, God has bought His people and freed them from the power and punishment of sin. To be a disciple of Jesus Christ is to experience healing, to be counted among the eternally blessed, and to be part of God's family. Mark 3 reminds the children of God of the honor that is theirs to be called Christians.

To be a Christian is to be a person who has been healed and made alive by the Spirit of God. The religious leaders in Jesus' day offered what they had. They had their laws and their sanctimonious rules. These things kept people in bondage. Jesus brought healing (vv. 1-5). Jesus worked in line with the law and the will of God. The religious leaders hated Him for it, and along with the legal authorities, they sought to kill Jesus (v. 6).

Those who believed in the miracles followed Jesus. There were great crowds that believed in His power (vv. 7-12). Jesus healed many, and thousands sought to see Him do it – but not all truly loved Him and followed Him. Jesus had eleven men who not only believed that He had power, but they also believed that He was the Messiah, and they were His true disciples (vv. 13-19). His own town and family did not believe He was God (vv. 20-21).

Some said that He did miracles by evil power (vv. 22-27). Jesus explained the gospel, and He warned that those who would not yield to the Holy Spirit, but who instead rejected His conviction and sinned against Him, would never be forgiven (vv. 28-30). Those who repent and believe the gospel are born again (John 3:1-18). The new life that Jesus gives provides access to God in a unique way. Christians are not just an organization of people in subcultures called churches. Christians are the family of Jesus (Mark 3:31-35). They are free to call on the Father in the name of the Son by the power of the Holy Spirit, knowing that God hears them, loves them, and is working His plan in their lives. What a blessing!

Do you have a personal relationship with Jesus? How is Jesus changing your life? Are you a member of God's family?

Those who know and love Jesus are given a special kind
of life and a way of life that produces eternal peace.

The world is filled with consultants, and billions of dollars are spent every year on self-help books and seminars. It is our natural tendency to want a quick, easy solution to our life challenges. Life does not usually work that way. The best things in life often come through struggle and pain. Like the birth of a baby, there is great labor that brings forth life and joy. Judges 5 is the song of Deborah. God used Deborah's wisdom, faith, and influence to inspire victory. Her song provides insight into how God's people can overcome challenges and accomplish God's plan, which produces peace.

The first thing that must happen in order for us to accomplish God's plan for our lives is that we must offer ourselves willingly to the Lord (vv. 2, 9). We cannot fix what is broken inside of us or in our world, but God can. If my car is broken, I need to get it into the hands of a person who knows how to fix it. Informed faith is required. I must go to a person whom I believe can fix it, and then I must willingly offer it to the repair person. In the same way, we must believe that God can restore us, and we must offer ourselves to Him by faith.

We must celebrate who God is and what He has done (vv. 10-11), and we must partner with those who are willing to walk by faith (vv. 12-15a). There will be people who will disappoint us and will not stand with us (vv. 15b-18). Having a clear vision and confidence in God's power provides the strength to go forward no matter what. The victory comes by God's power.

Be prepared to be surprised and to happily recognize the contributions others make. Give honor where it is due. Deborah celebrated Jael (vv. 19-30). She then prayed for God to vanquish His enemies (v. 31). The prayer of the faithful will always be for God's glory and praise. It is crucial that we pray, and that as we pray, we speak to God's glory, always keeping that as our focus and goal. God gives His blessing of peace to those who live to bring Him honor and glory.

Do you trust God to provide for your needs? Can you look back and see how God has been faithful to do great things? Who are the people whom you depend on who depend on you?

Those who willingly offer themselves to God, those who celebrate God, and those who partner with the faithful live with peace.

Judges 6; Acts 10; Jeremiah 19; Mark 5

Strange things happen. In those odd moments, it is easy to think like a pagan or a secularist rather than like a Christian. There is no such thing as coincidence. There is only providence. God is engaged in His creation accomplishing His eternal purpose for His glory. Acts 10 tells the story of people being impacted by God's direct, supernatural involvement in their lives.

Cornelius was a successful Roman soldier with resources and influence (v. 1). He also feared God and had a genuine love for people that was revealed in his generosity (v. 2). As a man of prayer, he was comfortable and familiar with talking to God. It was probably very startling to have God communicate directly with him through an angel (vv. 3-6). He responded in faith to God's command (vv. 7-8). When God speaks, it is wise to listen and obey. Cornelius did.

The next day, Peter was praying, and the Lord spoke to him (vv. 9-16). The Lord told Peter three times to eat what he had been taught was unclean. While Peter was trying to figure out what to do, Cornelius' men showed up. Given what he had just heard from God, Peter went with them (vv. 17-23). Going to the home of a gentile was also something he had been taught not to do. Peter obeyed and preached the gospel (vv. 24-43). This needs to be the response of God's people. We should always obey and look for ways to spread the gospel of God to the perishing. Rather than focusing on what we think God wants for us, we need to be focused on what God wants to do with us. He has already blessed us eternally.

Having done what he could do, Peter saw what only God could do and had intended to do. The Holy Spirit fell on those who heard the gospel (vv. 44-46). This is how God brings salvation. Christians share their hope, and the Holy Spirit gives new life. These new believers were then baptized to make a public profession and identification with Jesus (vv. 47-48). Everyone who is born again is commanded to be baptized to celebrate the fact that their old life is dead. They are washed clean and raised to new life.

Do you see events as providential or accidental? How has God shown up in special ways in your life? Have you been baptized?

Those who discern the hand of God in their life and in the world gain an eternal perspective that provides great peace.

It is a mistake to assume that the easy way in life is God's open door for us to walk through. When discerning the will of God, we must not simply look at what we want, but we must always consider what God wants. God always wants us to be true to Him and to His Word. This is not always easy to do. In Jeremiah 20, the prophet reveals the hardship that can come with being faithful to God, and he gives insight into the emotional battle that often takes place in the heart of a person who walks with Jesus.

As children, we learn to seek the applause and approval of those in authority. Honoring those who have the power to bless and provide for us is smart. Sometimes God will call us to do what is not appreciated or applauded by people. Jeremiah was called to prophesy the downfall of Jerusalem. He was beaten for doing what God called him to do (vv. 1-2). For Christians, gaining applause is not always good, and being beaten is not always bad.

The consequence for standing against God is severe. Jeremiah prophesied about the horrible judgment that awaited Pashhur, the man who beat him (vv. 3-6). Sooner or later in life, and certainly in death, God brings judgment against His enemies. The consequences Pashhur faced point to the suffering that comes to all who refuse to honor God by faith in Christ. There is loss, shame, and hopelessness. The pain does not end.

Although Jeremiah was faithful, he was not comfortable. He felt deceived by God because of the pain he had to endure (vv. 7-8). He was compelled to preach God's Word, but obedience comes at a cost (vv. 9-10). Even in his frustration and doubts, he had peace. He knew that God stood with him (vv. 11-13), but there were still days when he wished he had never been born (vv. 14-18). Like Christ, the faithful may have to suffer for God's purpose. Jesus was holy, He was full of love, and He was merciful and compassionate – but He suffered and was crucified in doing God's will.

Are you willing to obey God and speak His Word no matter what? Would you be willing to shed blood for your faith? Can you trust God to do what is right, even when it does not feel right to you?

> *Walking with God will require sacrifice, but a child of God who obeys the Lord can always have peace.*

Judges 8; Acts 12; Jeremiah 21; <u>Mark 7</u>

As people, we are often concerned with appearances. Not only do we celebrate others who are physically attractive and want to be physically attractive ourselves, but we also want to appear to be successful, happy, and trustworthy. God looks beyond appearances to the heart. In Mark 7, God deals with people and reveals what matters most – love.

The religious leaders of Jesus' day were very concerned about their man-made rules. They had rules for almost everything. The rules were a way for the religious leaders to have power and to control people. The disciples were once eating with dirty hands in front of the Pharisees. That triggered these leaders because the disciples were not following their traditions they held so dear (vv. 1-5). Jesus set the record straight and made it clear that what matters to God is what comes out of the heart (vv. 6, 14-23). He rightly accused the leaders of hypocrisy (vv. 7-13). God cares much more about love than He does about man's own traditions.

Jesus then went into hiding, but a gentile woman found Him and asked Him to heal her daughter. Jesus refused on the grounds that the will of God was for Him to work first with the Jews, as God had promised. Jesus was not being mean. He was being responsible to His calling and purpose as ordained by the Father. This mom did not give up, but pleaded and reasoned with Jesus; the Lord relented and healed her (vv. 24-30). Jesus revealed the heart of God. The heart of God is to heal. Rules and procedures are not bad, but what matters most is love. Jesus loved her and healed her daughter, even though it went against His overall plan and policy.

When Jesus got back to Galilee, a man was brought to Him to be healed. Jesus took him aside, healed him in private, and told the man to tell no one (vv. 31-37). This was an act of compassion, not communication, by Jesus. Jesus was not looking to reveal His power. Many of His miracles were done in order to communicate His divinity. Jesus healed this man out of love from His heart.

Are you more concerned with your appearance than you should be? Do you have a heart for God and people?

***Those who live with healthy hearts that seek to
love and honor God live with peace.***

We must be very careful how we think about ourselves and other people. Each of us is easily tempted to think that our selfish actions are benevolent and helpful. While owning property and responsibly providing for ourselves and our families are good things, we can become greedy and convince ourselves that our greed is wise stewardship. When sin takes root, it produces fruit and easily multiplies. Those with charisma and strength are capable of convincing themselves and others that their evil intentions are good. When that happens, sin multiplies. In Judges 9, we see what happens when a gifted person falls into sin. His impact is awful, and his treachery multiplies.

Abimelech was an angry young man. His father was a respected warrior, but his mom was just a female servant (v. 18). Others probably often reminded him of his lineage. He wanted power, and he was willing to hurt others to get it. He murdered seventy of his brothers, except Jotham, who escaped (vv. 1-6). Abimelech had convinced himself and his nearest relatives that his leadership was needed and that the other sons of Gideon must be removed. It is amazing what we can allow ourselves to do and the kinds of people we can support when it suits us.

Jotham provided a powerful fable (vv. 7-21). He spoke from Mount Gerizim, where Israel had pronounced the blessings of God. The sin of Abimelech and the people would have consequences. Sin always causes brokenness, pain, and suffering. It multiplies.

The sin of one person often results in sins committed by others. When people see someone prosper in their selfishness, they often sin as well. Abimelech's sin resulted in pride, treachery, and violence in others (vv. 22-57). So many people were mercilessly killed, and others became killers. That is what sin does. It destroys and inspires destruction.

Do you know how you are tempted to sin? Are you afraid of what your sin will do to you and inspire others to do? Have you repented of sin and turned to Jesus?

Those who see their sin for what it is and repent and believe in Jesus will gain forgiveness and enjoy peace.

Judges 10; <u>Acts 14</u>; Jeremiah 23; Mark 9

Being sensibly cautious and using common sense may sometimes be contrary to what God wants us to do. God has called millions of people to be martyrs. Every year, thousands of men and women leave their homeland to live on foreign soil to take the gospel to the ends of the earth. Business leaders often give up their wealth and opportunity in order to enter the ministry. This may not make sense to the world, but it makes perfect sense to heaven. In Acts 14, Paul and Barnabas show what faith demands.

Faith demands that we proclaim the bold claims of the gospel no matter how others may respond. While Paul and Barnabas were preaching in Iconium, divisions between those who believed and those who rejected the gospel became cantankerous (vv. 1-5). The gospel is divisive. Those who preach it will make both friends and enemies. In light of the danger, Paul and Barnabas fled (v. 6). This was not a lack of faith. Faith does not demand that we always live in danger. There is a time for safety.

Faith demands that we refuse to rob God of praise and glory. Paul healed a man, and it caused the inhabitants of Lystra to think that he and Barnabas were gods (vv. 7-13). Rather than enjoy the benefits of their newfound celebrity status, they sought to bring clarity and to point to the goodness and power of God (vv. 14-18). They were barely able to restrain the crowd. People often prefer false gods and celebrities to the true God because they cannot manipulate and control God the way they can the others.

Faith demands sacrifice and an unfaltering dedication to the mission of God. The people of Lystra were deceived by the enemies of Paul and Barnabas, and they stoned Paul (v. 19). He did not die. Instead, he got up and finished his mission (vv. 20-25). After completing the work they were called to do, Paul and Barnabas headed home and gave a report of praise for how God had used them to take the gospel to the gentiles. They were not mad and did not complain. They praised God.

Are you willing to live by faith no matter what? Will you serve God no matter what? Are you grateful no matter what?

> *Those who are willing to go against their natural inclinations and choose to serve God will live and die with peace.*

Perception is not always reality. What we think is preferable, and even what we might think is God's blessing, may really be a curse. God alone knows what is best. It is important that we learn to look beyond circumstances and seek to know the true will of God. It is better to be in difficult places while in the will of God than to be in places that are comfortable, but outside of the will of God. The prophet Jeremiah was given a vision in Jeremiah 24. The interpretation of that vision is important and provides perspective to us.

Many prophets had warned Judah that God was going to allow Babylon to come and bring God's judgment against them. When Nebuchadnezzar finally did it, he wiped out the real leadership of the land (v. 1a). The only people remaining in Jerusalem were those whom Nebuchadnezzar did not consider a threat or a help to his nation. While it may have appeared to some that God had spared certain people for His high and holy purpose, that was just not the case. The reality was that they were not wanted.

After the country had been left in shambles, God gave Jeremiah a strange vision and a powerful explanation (vv. 1b-10). The prophet was shown a basket of figs. One basket contained all really good figs, and the second had bad figs. God explained that those who were sent into exile were the good figs. He was going to bless them and use them. The bad figs represented those who remained in the land. They would be cursed and decimated.

Looking at the situation in that moment, a lot of people probably thought just the opposite. Many probably assumed that the ones God was blessing and would bless were left in the land of promise. Their perception was not reality.

Those who were forced to leave were very sad. They were taunted by their captors and were forced to live in a place with customs and practices contrary to their former way of life. They probably thought they were cursed. Their perception was not reality.

Have you ever been in a circumstance when it seemed that you were out of the will of God, while in fact, you were where God wanted you to be? What does it mean to be blessed by God?

Those who are blessed by God and chosen to be His people can have peace in any circumstance.

Judges 12; Acts 16; Jeremiah 25; <u>Mark 11</u>

We should never be surprised that we do not have God completely figured out. He is, after all, God. He knows all things. He is all-powerful. He does what is best. He is perfect in every way. We cannot always see the hand of God, but we can see the effects of His hand at work. God's will is not always clear to us, but we can look back and see how faithful and good He has been in the past. In Mark 11, Jesus was doing and saying things that were confusing to some people, but there was a plan and a purpose for it all.

Almost five hundred years before the birth of Jesus, His triumphal entry into Jerusalem to launch Holy Week was prophesied in Zechariah 9:9. God's plan was carried out with secrecy. Jesus sent two disciples to a man with a coded message about needing his colt (vv. 1-7). Jesus' entrance into Jerusalem was a spectacle. He did not come in on a warhorse. He came in on a colt. This was probably confusing to those who were laying their cloaks and palm branches down in front of Him and calling for salvation (vv. 8-10). He did not come into the city as a conqueror. He checked out the temple and headed to Bethany (v. 11). Were the disciples confused?

The next day, Jesus cursed a fig tree (vv. 12-14) and cleared out the temple (vv. 15-19). He didn't explain about His actions in the temple, but He did explain about the fig tree and the power of faith and prayer (vv. 20-26). Did the disciples understand, or were they made more confused? This was an amazing insight that was being offered to them. There is no record that they asked any questions, but with those amazing statements, it is not hard to imagine that they would find it difficult to know what to ask first.

Later that week, they headed back into the city. The religious leaders tried to engage Him, but Jesus turned the tables on them and asked them a question they could not answer (vv. 27-33). Why wouldn't Jesus just tell them who He was?

We don't know what Jesus thought or what the disciples did or did not know, but we do know that God had a plan that was at work.

Do you trust God? Have you seen the effects of His hand in your life? Is Jesus free to lead you as He sees fit?

***Those who trust in God to have the right plan and the power
and goodness to execute it the right way have peace.***

Humanity has been looking and continues to look for someone who can fix what is broken in the world. We all know that the world is not as it should be. We are all frustrated with the suffering and pain that fills our existence on this amazing planet. Most people do not know that God promised to send a man who would crush evil and bring healing to humanity. God did what He promised. Some do not know that Jesus has come. They are still looking for a savior. Many are confused. Judges 13 tells the beginning of a story of a hero who came to save, but could not do what Jesus did.

When Jesus was about to be born, an angel appeared to Mary, and later to Joseph, to tell them they would be the parents of the promised Savior of the world. When Christ came, the people of God were living under the tyranny of the Romans. A similar thing happened when Samson was about to be born. The people of God were in bad shape, living under the tyranny of the Philistines (v. 1). An angel appeared to Manoah, Samson's mom, and alerted her to the special child she would give birth to and telling her how she was to raise him. She went and told her husband the good news (vv. 2-7). The good news of God should always be shared.

Manoah responded in faith and prayed (v. 8), just as Mary did. God sent a miraculous message to Manoah and her husband (vv. 9-14), just as God sent miraculous messages to Mary and Joseph. Manoah and her husband responded in faith by making a sacrifice and worshipping God for the grace and goodness He had shown them (vv. 15-23). Mary and Joseph also made sacrifices in faith. God's will always requires faith and sacrifices.

Manoah gave birth to a son, just as God promised. The Lord blessed him, and the Spirit began to stir in him (vv. 24-25). Jesus was born to Mary, and He, too, was blessed. Samson ultimately failed, but Jesus succeeded in bringing salvation to all who believe. The Old Testament is filled with hints about humanity's Savior and God's eternal plan.

Have you repented and believed the gospel? Can you see the promises of God in the Bible?

The Bible points to the promise of God in Christ, and all who look to Jesus will be saved and will experience peace.

Judges 14; Acts 18; Jeremiah 27; Mark 13

A favorite saying among some Christians is "When God closes a door, He opens a window." The idea is that God is always providing a way, even if it is not the way we would have preferred. One of the greatest obstacles to growth in the life of a believer is the believer, and one of the greatest obstacles to growth in a church is the church. We often get in God's way. In Acts 18, we see God opening a number of windows.

Having left Athens, the city of learning, Paul headed for Corinth, the city of sin (v. 1). At that time, Corinth had almost two hundred thousand inhabitants. The temple of Aphrodite overlooked the city and filled it with sexual sin. Paul planted a church there with Priscilla and Aquila using his normal process (vv. 2-4). Once Silas and Timothy showed up, Paul was able to give more time to the work of the gospel, which created opposition (vv. 5-9). This was nothing new for Paul. Paul was not one to give up, so he just went next door and kept serving. He used the window God opened. Jesus encouraged him in a vision, and he ended up staying six months (vv. 10-11). We must never give up. We must always seek the new way God is providing for us.

Paul and the leaders of the church faced increased persecution, and Sosthenes, a new leader and the ruler of the synagogue where Paul preached, was beaten by the Jewish leaders (vv. 12-17). God often allows His people to suffer, but their suffering is not wasted. The faith of a suffering saint is power. Their faith is difficult to ignore. It is often an open window for unbelievers.

Having established the church in Corinth, Paul moved on to other cities to strengthen the disciples (vv. 18-23). He never gave up. In the meantime, God raised up Apollos to lead. He was blessed to be trained by Priscilla and Aquila (vv. 24-28). When God closes the door of one person's ministry, He often opens a window for another leader to be raised up and serve. We must trust God's plan and take advantage of what and who He sends.

Have you seen God close doors in your life and open new windows of opportunity? Is your faith strong enough to endure suffering? Do you trust that God has a plan for you and for your life?

Those who trust Jesus and follow His leadership live with peace.

It is not easy to say hard things that people do not want to hear. Telling people what they want to hear is easy. If we have to choose between telling the truth that people may not like, or telling a lie that people want to hear, we must tell the truth. The truth may hurt, but a lie can kill. As told in Jeremiah 28, the prophets Hananiah and Jeremiah each made a decision about how they would handle the truth. One experienced life, and the other experienced death.

Jeremiah and Hananiah were from the same tribe. Being prophets from the same tribe, they probably knew each other pretty well (v. 1). When Hananiah claimed to speak on behalf of the Lord, yet said what was not true, Jeremiah called him out on it. Jeremiah wanted what Hananiah said would happen to happen. It was a good thing, but Jeremiah knew that it was not true (vv. 2-8). Hananiah said that which was contrary to what Jeremiah had prophesied. Speaking lies to people in the name of God is a sin with serious consequences.

In response, Jeremiah pointed out that the only way to know if a prophet was from God and was telling the truth was if what he said would happen actually happened (v. 9). So far, what Jeremiah had said would happen had happened. Hananiah got so mad that he broke Jeremiah's sermon illustration, a yoke on his neck, and claimed that the Lord would do the same with Nebuchadnezzar's yoke on Israel (vv. 10-11). At some point, God had Jeremiah tell Hananiah that he was wrong and that the Lord was going to take Hananiah's life that year because of the lie (vv. 12-16). The fact is that we must never let the fear of what other people may think or do keep us from telling the truth.

Jeremiah proved to be right. Hananiah died that year (v. 17). The cost of sin is death (Romans 6:23). The gift of life is given to all who repent and believe in Jesus. We all must choose either to lie or to stand for the truth in Jesus Christ. It is better to stand with Jesus and be rejected by the world than to lie and be judged by Jesus.

Do you trust in Jesus to forgive you of your sin and give you eternal life? Are you willing to speak the truth in love, even if it offends people? Do you fear God more than you fear other people?

Those who tell the truth and claim Christ for their Savior
will live an honest life with peace in their hearts.

Judges 16; Acts 20; Jeremiah 29; <u>Mark 15</u>

Determining between right and wrong is not nearly as difficult as we sometimes make it out to be. Fear is often what makes a choice difficult. We worry
about what people will do or think. Choosing what is right might cause loss
or pain. Faced with social pressure, we will be tempted to do what is wrong.
Doing what is wrong might be commanded or applauded, but it is still crucial that we do the right thing. Mark 15 tells about a lot of choices people
made. Some choices were right, but many were wrong. Our choices matter.

Pilate did not believe that Jesus had done anything wrong, but he killed
Jesus anyway (vv. 1-14). He was afraid of what the crowd might say about
him or do to him (v. 15). We all have a tendency to claim we are victims of
circumstance, but our choices are our own.

The soldiers abused, mocked, and then crucified Jesus (vv. 16-20). On the
day of their death, when these soldiers met Jesus face to face, they probably
made the excuse that they were simply following orders. We all want to blame
someone else for our sin, but no one can sin for us. We choose it ourselves.

Simon of Cyrene carried the cross of Jesus (vv. 21-22). Would he have
done that if he had not been forced to do so? I wonder if I would have. Would
you have helped Jesus that day?

Jesus could have come off the cross and killed every person there who
had harmed Him and mocked Him (vv. 23-30). What they said was true:
He could not save others and also save Himself (v. 31). They reviled Him
as He chose to die and suffer to pay for the sin of all who would believe in
Him (v. 32). Before He died, He took on the sin of the world, and God the
Father poured out His divine, eternal wrath on Jesus (vv. 33-34). The people
did not understand what Jesus was saying or why the temple curtain was
torn (vv. 35-38). Many still don't.

The centurion claimed that Jesus was the Son of God (v. 39). Jesus' mom
and friends mourned Him and buried Him in public (vv. 40-47). That
marked them as His followers and probably cost them in life, but blessed
them for eternity. Honoring Jesus will often lead to difficulties in life, but
there will be great blessings in death.

Have you chosen to follow Jesus? Do you choose to obey Him? Will you
be rewarded or condemned by God at death?

Choosing to obey God is hard, but it leads to peace.

It is so easy to convince ourselves that we are not as sinful as the Bible says we are. It is so easy to deny the authority of Scripture and to affirm ourselves based on our own sinful standard. It is no wonder that the modern heretics can convince us that God wants us to be rich and happy at all costs. It is no wonder that we buy their books and watch their broadcasts. They tell us the lies we want to believe, and they make God out to be our servant. Judges 17 shows what happens when people reject the God of the Bible.

Without the authority of Scripture, there is no conviction of sin or clarity concerning how to live. Micah was a thief who stole from his own mother (v. 1). Out of fear for himself from the curse she uttered, and not out of godly conviction, he confessed what he had done (v. 2). Out of happiness to have her money back, she claimed to dedicate a portion to the Lord, but that is not what she actually did. She actually created an idol (vv. 3-5). It is so sad that so many people give money to religious charlatans, thinking they are honoring God, when in fact they are helping to build idols.

Without the authority of Scripture, people do whatever they want (v. 6). There was no king in Israel. There were no prophets. The judges would come and go. Without a leader to point them to God, people turned their backs on Him and chose to do what pleased their flesh. It is so sad that so many people are on their way to hell, yet feel completely fine.

Without the authority of Scripture, what is evil can appear to be good. Micah found a Levite and employed him (vv. 7-13). Levites were given the responsibility to care for God's people. Obtaining a Levite for the face of his cult positioned Micah to have greater authority and the probability that more people would come to his idol and pay money for blessing. Like modern heretics, Micah and this Levite robbed money from God's people and glory from God by making their idol the means of hope in life.

Is the Bible the authoritative truth of your life? Can you discern religious charlatans from true biblical leaders? Are you happy to know and obey God's Word?

Those who submit to the authority of Scripture can know the truth and be set free to believe in Jesus and gain peace.

Judges 18; <u>Acts 22</u>; Jeremiah 32; Psalms 1-2

To say that something has been watered down is to say that it is not as strong or potent. In order to dilute the alcohol content of wine, people would water it down. In every century, there have been leaders in the church who believed that the best way to create a unified, strong church was to water down the truth so that everyone could accept it and feel comfortable with it. That is not what Paul did. In Acts 22, the apostle shared the truth of his convictions and faced the wrath of religious and secular leaders.

Like Jesus, Paul was arrested in Jerusalem for a crime he did not commit. Before being taken to the jail, he was allowed to speak to the hostile Hebrews who had sought to harm him (vv. 1-2). Paul explained who he was. He explained his upbringing, his former hatred of the church, and how Jesus had changed his life (vv. 3-20). The people seemed okay with his story, even the supernatural parts of it, but what they could not stand was his admission that he had been called by God to minister to the gentiles (v. 21). It is sad how prevalent racism is in every generation.

Not knowing what else to do, the officer in charge of his arrest sought to bring Paul into the jail to examine and flog him (vv. 22-24). Paul pointed out his legal status as a Roman citizen, which kept him from being flogged (vv. 25-28). This scared the tribune and his fellow officers because what they had done in binding him was illegal. It is wise for Christians to use the law of the land to help create safety for themselves so they can spread the gospel.

The next day, the tribune brought Paul and those who had sought his arrest together to get to the bottom of the matter (v. 30). Paul was not willing to water down the truth. In every instance, Paul spoke the truth. He did not concern himself with how people felt about it. He was committed to being honest and revealing what Christ Jesus had done in his life.

Have you ever been tempted to water down the truth of what the Bible says so that it is not as offensive? Are you willing to speak the truth in love? How does standing for the truth create difficulty for you?

The Word of God is true, and those who truthfully speak what
it says and tell how it has changed their life have peace.

It can sometimes seem as if God has forgotten us and that we are shut in by our pain and problems. While we may very well be placed in positions where we feel stuck, God is never far off. He is always at work bringing about His eternal purpose. This world is filled with difficulty, but God knows what He is doing. We can trust Him. Jeremiah had a hard life, but God spoke to Him and through Him. Jeremiah 33 is an example of that.

While Jeremiah was stuck in the prison of a city on the cusp of destruction, God showed up and gave him a message of hope (vv. 1-13). Our world is so broken and our lives are so shut in by sin, shame, and confusion that it can seem impossible for God to bless us. God's greatest blessings for His people have often come during their most difficult and dark days.

The ultimate blessing and goal of God is the righteous reign of Jesus Christ. We cannot help but process the world through the limited lens of our perspective. The wise saints study God's Word and learn to see life through the revealed will of God. God promised to send Jesus, who would rule as the mighty king of heaven, serve as the high priest of heaven, and proclaim the truth of God as the prophet of promise (vv. 14-22). Jesus has come! The promise of God has been kept! There is more to come!

Until Christ returns with His new heaven and new earth, the saints of God must learn to trust God's plan. His plan involves all those who have been saved by grace through faith in Christ alone. The principles and promises of God's Word apply to all who have been born again. God's kingdom has come and is coming again (vv. 23-26). Because God rules over all things and sustains them by His might, He can do what seems impossible. God's children can hold to His promises and live with peace.

Are you able to get past your feelings and circumstances to see life through God's Word? Have you experienced the saving power of Jesus? Is your heart filled with hope because of God's goodness, or are you downcast because of cares that will pass away?

Those who can see life through the lens of the Bible will rejoice
in God's promises and provision and will experience peace.

Judges 20; Acts 24; Jeremiah 34; <u>Psalms 5-6</u>

With God, we never have to fake how we feel. He knows. He understands. He cares. There will always be the temptation to doubt God's love and goodwill toward us. This world is broken, and there are evils in us and all around us, but we do not need to fear. We can rejoice in God. Psalms 5 and 6 remind the redeemed of who God is and why we can rest in peace under His care.

I love King David. I look forward to getting to heaven and hearing him sing praise to God and tell how God had been faithful to him. David's psalms have helped me tremendously. Psalm 5 has often lifted me up and reminded me of who God is and what I must do in order to thrive in the chaos of life. I must pray (vv. 1-3). I must believe that God loves me and wants to do good to me (vv. 4-8). I must see myself and other human beings for what we are – deceived creatures in need of saving (vv. 9-10). I must take refuge in God and not trust in idols to save me (vv. 11-12). The Lord God is a shield of protection against the lies of this world that I often believe.

As we look to the Lord and hide in the shelter of His love and power, we can talk freely with God about how we feel. David had been blessed with many great gifts. He was a warrior, an artist, a handsome man, and a gifted leader. God promised Him an eternal kingdom. However, this did not keep David from having to go through hardship and difficult times. As children of God, we are all gifted and loved. Each one of us has a special place in the heart of God and in the world. In order to find peace in the midst of life's storms, we must speak honestly to God as David did and hold tight to the promises God has given (Psalm 6). A single prayer can feel like a roller coaster. If we are being honest, that is how life goes. One minute we are at the pinnacle of praise, trusting in God's sovereign grace, and in the next breath we are overwhelmed by the evil in us and all around us and are frustrated and scared. In every moment, we can trust in God's goodness. He is good!

Do you have a personal relationship with God? Has God seen you through difficult days? Can you trust in His promises today and hold tight to the hope He gives in Jesus?

***Those who are willing to get real with God and seek to see
how great a God He is will find peace in life's storms.***

Judges 21; Acts 25; Jeremiah 35; Psalms 7-8

Never say never. None of us have any idea of what we are capable of if we get pushed to an extreme. Human beings are selfish creatures with a strong desire to survive. When survival is at stake, we can be reduced to animal behaviors. This is clearly seen in Judges 21. This last chapter of this sad book presents what happens when a society abandons God. Thankfully, there is still good news. Despite our sin, God is willing to forgive.

The Benjaminites had been slaughtered by the rest of the Israelite tribes. There were only six hundred men left. No women or children remained. In their passion to exact justice, the other tribes had vowed not to give their daughters in marriage to the Benjaminites. It later dawned on them that this would mean that the Benjaminites would be eradicated and Israel would lose an entire tribe (vv. 1-8). Justice is a good thing, but vengeance needs to be left to God. God alone has the moral compass to provide the proper punishment. Human beings tend toward extremes.

Given their situation and wanting to save the tribe of Benjamin, a horrible, cruel, brutal idea was suggested. We often justify that which would typically be considered inconceivable if it brings about the end we believe is right. Thinking that the end justifies the means has led to some of the most atrocious actions imaginable. Israel decided to kill people, steal their virgins, and then kidnap other virgins to provide a wife for each man (vv. 9-24). It is easy to judge them, but we need to be careful, for we have the capacity to think what they thought and do what they did.

The book of Judges ends with a thought that had shown up a few times previously in that book. There was no leader, and everyone did whatever they wanted (v. 25). A person, family, or society that turns away from God will soon destroy itself. God help us! We are never more than a single generation away from being a godless society.

Are you aware of how sinful you are and of how sinful you could be? Does it scare you to think about what evil you could do or that could be done to you and your family without godly restraint? Are you growing closer or further from God and His will?

Those who know the Bible and follow the leadership of Jesus will live lives of love and experience God's peace as a blessing.

Ruth 1; <u>Acts 26</u>; Jeremiah 36, 45; Psalm 9

God has the power to change a life for good. Every person who has been born again from death to life and has been changed from a sinner to a saint by the power of the gospel has a testimony. A testimony is a personal story of what God has done and is doing in the life of a believer. All stories of gospel transformation are miraculous. This makes testimonies an important method for helping others understand the gospel. The apostle Paul had an amazing testimony. In Acts 26, we read how Paul shared his story and expected his hearers to be saved.

Paul was not in an ideal situation. He had been wrongly accused by the Jews and was in the process of being sent to the emperor of Rome. The government officials needed to give the emperor an explanation as to why Paul was being sent to him. They created an inquisition, which provided Paul with a great opportunity to share his hope (vv. 1-3). We may find ourselves in situations we do not want to be in, but we can always trust that God has us where He wants us. We must be ready and faithful to share the gospel.

Paul explained his Jewish upbringing and that he had persecuted the church (vv. 4-11). He was clearly not naturally inclined to trust in Jesus. None of us are. Faith in Christ comes about by the intervention of God. Jesus met Paul on that road to Damascus and transformed his life (vv. 12-23). While not everyone may have an encounter like Paul's, all who are saved can tell of a time when they chose to repent and turn to Jesus by faith.

Paul's questioners thought he was crazy, but Paul made it clear that what he was saying was completely true and believable (vv. 24-25). He challenged them to repent and believe right then and there (vv. 26-29). It is crucial that we not only share our story, but that we also invite people to repent and believe the gospel.

Paul's questioners walked away (vv. 30-32). Not everyone will believe. Our responsibility is to share. God's part is to save and transform lives.

Do you have a faith testimony? Are you sharing the gospel? Have you made a disciple of Jesus?

Those who have repented and believed the gospel have a testimony to share that explains why they have peace.

Who we respect and listen to will have a huge impact on how we live our lives, and will also communicate to others what kind of people we are. How we respond to difficult circumstances and good opportunities also says a lot about the kind of people we are. Zedekiah was not wise. He did not listen to Jeremiah the prophet, and he did not take advantage of opportunities to walk with God. Jeremiah 37 provides an example of how not to live.

Zedekiah did not listen to God's word spoken to him through the prophet Jeremiah (vv. 1-2). Instead, he chose to listen to people who would tell him what he wanted to hear. The Chaldeans were about to take his kingdom down, so he sent representatives to ask Jeremiah to pray for them (vv. 3-5). He did not want to obey God's commands or even hear what God had to say, but Zedekiah did want God's protection and provision.

God provided a reprieve for Israel. The Egyptians came out to fight, and they drew the Chaldeans away. God spoke to Jeremiah and explained that the Egyptians would back down and the Chaldeans would return (vv. 6-10). Zedekiah did not take advantage of this information and this valuable time. He did not repent and seek God. He continued to reject God. A wise person takes advantage of quiet moments to pursue God and gain greater faith.

During the reprieve, Jeremiah went to check on his business in the land of Benjamin, but he was stopped and arrested. He was wrongfully accused of treason and was imprisoned (vv. 11-16). Zedekiah was afraid to look weak, so he spoke with Jeremiah in private and provided for Jeremiah's needs (vv. 17-21). Despite the offense and harm caused to him, Jeremiah spoke the truth to the king. This news should have resulted in Zedekiah's repentance, but he refused to trust in God. He rejected the truth. He chose to listen to those who were not wise or godly. His foolishness led to his downfall and the destruction of Jerusalem.

Whom do you honor and listen to for direction in life? Have your taken advantage of God-given opportunities, or have you squandered them? Do you truly want God, or do you just want His blessings?

Those who honor godly people and choose to live their lives to know and honor God have peace.

Ruth 3-4; Acts 28; Jeremiah 38; <u>Psalms 11-12</u>

One of the sad conclusions that has become a standard of belief in the hearts and minds of some Christians is that God never expects us to suffer or be in harm's way. This kind of belief allows believers to abandon their responsibilities and limit their liability to God. The Bible shows that God's will is often done through the suffering of saints. Psalms 11 and 12 provide axioms for how God's people are to live in our broken world.

God's people must not surrender to their fears. We will often be an object of disdain by those who deny the reality of divinity. Like David, those who trust in God must not flee (Psalm 11:1-3). Yes, we may be attacked, as David was in Saul's courts. Yes, we may see the moral foundations of decency crumble without the authority of Scripture, just as David saw Israel falling apart under Saul once God and Samuel had abandoned him. Though the world hates us and society becomes unstable in sin, the saints can take refuge in God and know that He has a plan.

God's plan is to strengthen His people through the tests and trials that come with being hated by a religiously ignorant and intolerant society (vv. 4-5a). God will ultimately judge sinners (vv. 5b-6), but He will delight in His people who will see His face. This is the source of our confidence in Christ. Our peace does not come because life is comfortable, but because Christ is returning to save us.

Until Christ returns, there will be difficult days. It will seem that there are no more righteous saints left (Psalm 12:1). The world will be filled with liars (vv. 2-4). Thankfully, the plight of the poor will move the hand of God to intervene (v. 5). God will keep His promises, and those who trust in Him will find peace, even as vileness is exalted by society (vv. 6-8). Even though the world around us collapses into moral chaos, God's people can anchor themselves in God's Word and hold on to His promises. Our circumstances will not always be good, but our God always is.

Have you been tempted to give up on people and just hide with your faith? Can you trust God to provide for you? Are you looking forward to the return of Jesus and living in light of it?

Those who know the promises of God that are found in Scripture and trust in those promises will live with peace, even as darkness prevails.

1 Samuel 1; Romans 1; Jeremiah 39; Psalms 13-14

We have no idea how God is pulling the strings that are people's lives into a beautiful tapestry that forms the picture of His eternal plan. We are each to pray and pursue God's purpose, and as we do, God uses our lives to cross and connect with others. The end result is a miracle. First Samuel 1 tells the story of the birth of Samuel. His life was a gift to his praying mother, but his life also blessed the sinful nation of Israel and our broken world.

While God was providing a family for Boaz and Ruth that would produce David and even the Messiah, Jesus Christ, God was inspiring a barren woman named Hannah to pray for a child whom she would dedicate to God (1 Samuel 1:1-11). This is how God works. Things happen or don't happen in life that make us sad. People come along and say and do things that break our hearts. All of this pain moves us to pray. The prayers we pray are heard by God, and in His grace and for His glory, He answers.

While Hannah was praying, Eli the priest saw her and thought she was drunk (vv. 12-14). Hannah clarified her motive, and Eli blessed her (vv. 15-18). There is great peace in knowing that our lives are free from shame and that others can affirm our prayers.

God answered Hannah's prayer (vv. 19-20). She had a son whom she named Samuel. She weaned him and gave him to God (vv. 21-27). He was cared for by Eli in God's presence (v. 28). It was there that Samuel would learn to pray and hear the voice of God. It was there that the Lord would establish his ministry. It was there that God would begin to lead the nation through a man who would remind them of the Son of Man who was coming to save the world from sin. Samuel would later anoint David as king. Jesus would later come through the line of David. Salvation came through the life of two heartbroken, praying women – Hannah and Ruth. They did not know each other, but God knew them and used them for His purpose.

How is God leading you to pray? Do you have faith that God can work in your life for His eternal purpose? Can you look back and see how God has brought people and events to be a part of your story for His eternal purpose?

Those who trust in God will go through hardship, but God will use them and provide peace to them for His glory.

1 Samuel 2; Romans 2; Jeremiah 40; Psalms 15-16

Everyone knows how to pretend. For fun as children, we all pretended to be someone we weren't. This ability is given by God to allow us to imagine what He can do in our lives for His glory. In our sin, we have learned to use this ability to fool ourselves and other people. We like to think of ourselves and to present ourselves in the best light. God calls us to be real and to be transformed into Christ's likeness by grace. Romans 12 is a warning to all who would feign religiosity. By grace, we can be like Jesus – good.

The church at Rome was struggling. When Paul wrote to them, the Jews were returning to the city and the church. Emperor Claudius had forced the Jews to leave (Acts 18:2). They were now coming back to a church that had been led by gentiles for years. The church had changed, but God had not. Paul wrote to them to help the church be mindful of the will of God. God wants His people to be good (Romans 2:1-11). He does not want people to pretend to be good. He does not want people to be judgmental. He wants all people to know their sinful inclination and the righteous judgment of God, and He desires all people to receive His grace and be transformed.

The transformation of the life saved by grace through faith in Christ alone is supernatural. While we can all change aspects of our behavior, none of us can change our hearts. God changes hearts. God's law reveals what is right and best. Those who know the law by training and those who know it by conscience are all responsible to obey it. Any who break the law will be judged by God. Any who break the law will deal with the consequences that naturally come in life (vv. 12-16). It is not enough to have the outward appearance of being a law keeper. God demands that we seek the praise of God and not of people (vv. 17-29). To please God and receive His eternal reward, we must repent of sin, and we must love and desire to obey Him from the heart. In obeying God, we find God's blessing. In God's blessing, there is life and peace.

Do you know and obey Jesus? Are you more concerned with what people think than with what God thinks? Are you a genuine disciple of Jesus who lives for Him because you love Him?

> *Authentic disciples of Jesus are joyful and not judgmental, and they gladly obey God and have peace.*

1 Samuel 3; Romans 3; Jeremiah 41; Psalm 17

Doing the right thing the wrong way produces negative results, causing harm to ourselves and others. We are not nearly as smart as we think we are. Our perceptions are not as accurate as they need to be. How we see ourselves and others is not as pure as we might think. We have tainted motives and ideas. We are sinful creatures living in a confusing world. It is a wonder that anything good is produced in human societies. Jeremiah 41 reminds us that the best of intentions can lead us to do awful things that cause great harm, even though we want to do good.

Jerusalem had been destroyed by the Babylonians, and Gedaliah was appointed by the foreign conquerors to oversee what remained of Judah. Ishmael was of the royal family – probably a descendant of David. He did not want a foreign puppet overseeing God's people, so he deceived Gedaliah and killed him and many others (vv. 1-10). Ishmael wanted the line of David to rule. This was what God promised. What Ishmael did not perceive was that God was pruning Israel and preparing the world for the coming of Jesus. Ishmael was not wise. He did not honor God. His passion led him to cause pain and destruction.

Decisions always have ripple effects. When people are killed, those who love them will often rise up to seek justice. In a broken world, justice without a good legal system can and often will become reckless. Ishmael knew this. When Johanan and his men came to put things right, Ishmael fled (vv. 11-16). Thinking that the Chaldeans would respond in anger and cause more destruction, Johanan led the people to Bethlehem to prepare to flee to Egypt (vv. 17-18). There were no good options. If they stayed in Jerusalem, the Chaldeans might have come and killed them all. This is what happens in a world without wise leadership. Decisions are shortsighted and cause more problems.

When making decisions, do you look at what you want in the moment, or can you think of the greater good? Have you seen people cause harm with selfish decisions? How can you make wise decisions in a broken world that benefit you and your community?

Those who look to Jesus and make decisions that honor Him
will have peace, even when the world is falling apart.

1 Samuel 4; Romans 4; Jeremiah 42; <u>Psalm 18</u>

One day, all of God's people will be in heaven celebrating all that God is and all that He has done. There will be stories of God's gracious, miraculous interventions. All of the stories will be to the praise of God. The great thing about being a Christian is that we do not have to wait to give God praise for His provision. We can proclaim what God has done for us and celebrate God today. Psalm 18 is a psalm of celebration. David wrote it to give praise to God for how the Lord had delivered him from all of his enemies.

David began by proclaiming his love for God and for what God was to him. The Lord was David's strength (v. 1). God was David's rock, fortress, deliverer, refuge, shield, salvation, and stronghold (vv. 1-3). God had been so good to David. God chose David to be king, and then allowed him to be trained through several life challenges. God always trains those He calls.

The challenges that David faced were intense. He was in danger of dying many times (vv. 4-5). He cried out to God (v. 6), and God responded in terrifying ways (vv. 7-15). Nothing can stop God. There is no end to His power. What might seem to be an impossible situation to us is nothing to God. Because God is so big and mighty, nothing is a big problem to Him.

When David was stuck, God stepped in (vv. 16-19). Having walked faithfully with God, David was able to trust in God's promises – and God kept His Word (vv. 20-30). There is no God except the God of the Bible, and He blessed David's life with grace and mercy (vv. 31-48). David knew it was God who saved him, and he gave God all of the glory.

David praised God by singing to Him and by telling of His great goodness (vv. 49-50). The people of God are to sing. We are to lift up our voices in praise. The people of God are to preach. We are to proclaim who God is and what He can do. Everyone needs God's help. We must tell the world how God helps us.

Do you have stories of how God has provided for you? Are you lifting up your voice in praise to God? Who can you help to know the goodness and power of God?

Those who live by faith will experience the salvation of God, and in their praise and proclamation, they will enjoy God's peace.

God is so kind to relate to His image bearers the way He does. He loves humanity so much that He came to be one of us to take our punishment for the sins we committed. To see how much God loves us and how serious sin is, all we have to do is look at the cross. The cross tells us how precious people are to God and how costly sin is. It is a mistake to forget God's love or His holiness. It is a mistake to treat God as something less than the Almighty. First Samuel chapters 5 and 6 remind us of God's love and holiness.

Before Christ came, God showed His love by choosing to save His people. Under the leadership of Moses, the people built the ark of God. It represented God to the people. When the Philistines captured it, they did not know how to honor God properly, and they paid for it dearly (1 Samuel 5). God is holy. We cannot approach Him on our own terms. We must approach Him in the way He demands. Unfortunately, the Philistines did not know God. They did not know to honor Him. Their lack of information did not change the reality of God's holiness. His justice was poured out on them.

The Philistines could not make God fit into their world, so they removed His presence from their land (1 Samuel 6:1-2). Their diviners had the sense to honor God (vv. 3-13). The Lord was gracious and allowed their efforts to remove the ark of God from their land. Sadly, the people who should have known to honor God rightly did not. Yes, they offered sacrifices and had the Levites handle the ark itself, but some of the people dishonored God's presence (vv. 14-19). In a panic response, they sent the ark away (vv. 20-21). They could have repented in fear, and in awe of God they could have been blessed to house and hold up the ark of God as holy. It is a great honor to know God and experience His presence. In His love, He pours out blessings on those who love Him. In His justice, He curses those who dishonor Him. He is a holy God. He is a loving God. He is to be loved and honored.

Do you have both great love for God and fear of God? Are you willing to change your life in order to be blessed by God? What changes do you need to make in your life to honor God?

Those who believe that God is loving and who fear Him because He is holy can experience God's presence and live in peace.

1 Samuel 7-8; <u>Romans 6</u>; Jeremiah 44; Psalms 20-21

We all make decisions, and our decisions impact us. God made us with the capacity to think and choose. Those choices are in bondage to our desires. While we may deny our desires for a season, in time, we do what we desire. The most effective way to live a life of good decision-making is to desire what is good. By nature, we love sin. Thankfully, Jesus changes what we desire. Romans 6 reminds us why it is a privilege of grace to be a Christian and why being a Christian is liberating.

Experiencing true, saving faith is a result of a complete life change. Those who are saved are given new life. We die to our old way of life and begin a new life that is identified with Jesus (vv. 1-4). The new life that Jesus gives is unlike anything we could produce as human beings. It is supernatural. It is transformational. It comes at a great price.

In order to experience the new life God gives in Christ, we have to die to our old life (vv. 5-11). Becoming a Christian is not simply adding Jesus to who we are and what we have. Becoming a Christian is making Jesus the source and purpose of the life we live. Because we died to sin by grace, we can now live for God by grace (vv. 12-14). Every good thing that comes to us in life comes by grace. Salvation from the power of sin is the ultimate gift of God.

Grace does not give us the freedom to sin. Grace gives us the freedom to obey God (v. 15). Christians are liberated to live holy lives because they have happily become slaves of righteousness (vv. 16-19). We can now choose not to sin (vv. 20-22). We used to only be able to sin. In Christ, we are now saved by grace, which sanctifies us and produces in us eternal life.

This grace is expensive. It cost Jesus His life (v. 23). It also costs us our old life. Jesus died to pay the penalty for our sin. Death is the wage of sin. Eternal life is the gift that comes by receiving the new life Jesus paid for and now gives. In order to receive that gift, we have to die to our old life of sin.

Have you given up your old life without Jesus to begin a new life in Jesus? Are you sinning less? How has your life changed since you received new life in Jesus?

Those who receive new life in Christ live with peace.

1 Samuel 9; Romans 7; Jeremiah 46; Psalm 22

It is easy to get so caught up in our lives and issues that we miss the broader story that is unfolding in the world. Each day, millions of Christians get up and read their Bibles and pray. Most of us are looking for strength and provision for only ourself and our loved ones. If there is a glance to the broader issues of the day, it is only a glance. If there is concern, it is typically only because the events may impact our fortunes or plans. Jeremiah 46 tells of the downfall of Egypt. This great empire lost its place as a perennial power in the world. God was working His promised plan.

God is concerned about the nations (v. 1). Every person on the planet is made in the image of God. Every Egyptian and Babylonian who fought in that battle was judged by God at death. Their lives mattered to God. Every person matters to God so much that He sent His Son to die for our sins. The dignity God has given to all people is a gift. We are to love and honor all people.

Nothing lasts forever in this world. Ecclesiastes 3 speaks to the changes in life. There is a time for every activity under heaven. Egypt experienced a time of greatness. They also experienced a time of defeat (Jeremiah 46:2-12). The arrival of Babylon on the scene changed everything. For a season, Babylon became the new world power (vv. 13-26). They would one day fall. That is the way of the world. Nations rise and fall, but the will of God is done. God always accomplishes His promised plan.

God had placed Israel in captivity in Babylon in order to save the Israelites and provide for His promised plan (vv. 27-28). Yes, God was punishing Israel for their sin. He was also placing them in a place of protection. In time, God would release the Israelites from their captivity in Babylon and send them back to the land of Israel. Once there, they would establish their nation and lay the foundation for the coming of Jesus Christ. Their captivity, the conquering of Egypt, and the rise of Babylon was all according to God's promised plan. God's kingdom was coming, has now come, and is coming.

Are you concerned for the souls of all people? Do you pray for God's work in the world? Is your concern for God's kingdom?

Those who seek to perceive and pursue God's will in the world
will find peace by trusting God to keep His promised plan.

1 Samuel 10; Romans 8; Jeremiah 47; <u>Psalms 23-24</u>

There are two aspects to every relationship. There is a coming toward and a receiving in. To relate to someone, we must be willing to engage them. There must be a willingness to see them and recognize their presence in relation to us. We must also receive their presence and allow them to interact with us. This is what God does with us. Psalms 23 and 24 reveal how God engages His people and who is allowed to interact with Him.

Psalm 23 is one of the most famous chapters in the Bible. Portions of it are seen in various places in people's homes and offices and on their property. This psalm speaks to the way God engages His people. We are His sheep, and He is our shepherd. He seeks us out and cares for us (vv. 1-3). He knows what we need, and He knows when we need it. He provides what is best. Even though we face challenges, we do not need to fear because God is with us and for us (v. 4). Life, under the authority and direction of God, is a blessed life (vv. 5-6). It is not a problem-free life, but it is full of love and care. It ends in God's presence, where we will dwell with Him forever.

Psalm 24 humbles us and reminds us who God is and how we are able to relate to Him. Entering into God's eternal presence begins by entering into a relationship with Him in this life. This happens by grace through faith in Christ alone when we repent of our sin and believe the gospel. We are received by God as His own. He does not need us. He is God. He is the maker and owner of all things (vv. 1-2). God does not need anything from us, but we need Him. By grace, we gain a new, holy life with clean hands and a pure heart that worships Christ alone (vv. 3-4). This holy life is blessed by God (vv. 5-6). The righteousness of Christ is the greatest blessing we receive. Having been given Christ's merit, we can enter into the holy gates of heaven. Jesus entered there first, having made the way possible for us through His death and resurrection. I imagine heaven erupted with shouts calling for the gates to open when Jesus was raised and went to His eternal home (vv. 7-10). All who trust in Jesus will be admitted there too.

Is the Lord Jesus your shepherd? Have you repented and believed in Jesus? Is heaven your eternal home?

Those who have a relationship with Jesus have eternal peace.

1 Samuel 11; Romans 9; Jeremiah 48; Psalm 25

We are in a spiritual battle. It is crucial to know what our enemy is desiring to do. If we can know our enemy's desired end, we can know how to fight. The enemy of God wants to embarrass God and rob Him of glory. The devil wants to be praised and honored. To gain his desire, the devil seeks to defeat God's people and force them to submit to sin. We must fight against that. First Samuel 11 helps us understand the battle we are in and shows us how we can defeat the devil.

The Ammonites are like the devil. Both were defeated, but both refused to give up. The Ammonites had been defeated years before this attack on Jabesh-gilead (v. 1). The devil was defeated at the cross and at the empty tomb of Jesus. Jabesh-gilead was willing to give in and give up to the Ammonites and make a treaty. Some of God's people are willing to give in to the devil. The Ammonites did not care about Jabesh-gilead. They wanted to embarrass Israel. They demanded to be able to gouge out the right eyes of the people of Jabesh-gilead (v. 2). The devil wants to embarrass God by humiliating His people, which robs God of praise and glory.

Jabesh-gilead asked for time to seek the help of Israel, and their request was granted because they thought it would humiliate Israel (v. 3). When the people of Israel heard the news, they wept (v. 4). When Saul heard the news, the Holy Spirit moved him, and he led the people to victory over the Ammonites (vv. 5-11). That is how God works. He raises up a leader to overcome the devil. The people are moved by the Spirit to follow the leader and fight. Victory is by the Spirit.

After the battle was won, some Israelites wanted to kill those who had not supported Saul as king (v. 12), but Saul would not allow it (v. 13). Instead, the people gathered and crowned him as king (vv. 14-15). When the church is blessed, the people must not condemn and attack each other. Instead, the church is to gather and celebrate Jesus as king. We are to honor and praise Jesus.

Do you understand the goal of the devil? How are you fighting against the devil's schemes? Are you gathering with the church every week to celebrate Jesus and give Him praise and glory?

Those who fight against the goal of the devil and live to bring glory to Jesus through holy, faithful living have peace.

1 Samuel 12; <u>Romans 10</u>; Jeremiah 49; Psalms 26-27

The world is full of bad news, but God has good news. It is the best news. It is life-changing, soul-satisfying, heart-moving, mind-blowing, hand-clapping, amazing news. The world tells us that we are accidents who are going to die and become dirt. God tells us that we are masterpieces made to live and love forever. Romans 10 helps us understand God's good news and how important it is for us to spread it in our world.

Paul was a Jew. He loved the Jewish people. It broke his heart that many of them were without hope in the world. It was his desire and prayer that the Jews would be saved (v. 1). He knew they had a zeal for God, but no real experience of God's righteousness (vv. 2-4). The law was a taskmaster whom they could never please or satisfy (v. 5). God is holy and just, and His law is perfect, but He is more than a rule maker. He is the lover of our soul. He is the giver of life. He gives us new life by faith (vv. 6-8). The world needs to hear this news.

More than that, the world needs to know how to respond to this news. We need to tell them to confess and believe that Jesus is Lord (vv. 9-11). Anyone can confess and believe. Salvation is not just for the smart, religious types. Salvation is for everyone who is willing to call on the name of Jesus (vv. 12-13). People need to know who Jesus is, what He has done, and what He can and will do.

If we do not tell them this truth, they will not be able to believe (v. 14). We must preach to them. We are all proclaimers of the truth, no matter what our title or job is in the world. We are to help send people to take God's good news nearby, as well as to all the nations of the world (vv. 15-17). We must get the word out.

When we do, we will find that God is at work. God tells the good news throughout all of the Bible (vv. 18-19). The Bible is true. God calls all people to believe His truth. Those who know His truth are responsible to believe it. All who believe are able to believe because God has sought them and enabled them (vv. 20-21). Have you confessed and believed Jesus to be your Savior? Are you telling others the good news of God? Are you helping send others to share the message far and wide?

Those who receive God's good news have eternal peace.

1 Samuel 13; Romans 11; <u>Jeremiah 50</u>; Psalms 28-29

God is mysterious, and He works in mysterious ways. He does not force Himself upon us. He gently nudges us and encourages us to seek Him. God made us to know Him. We are empty until we find satisfaction in Jesus. The Lord uses circumstances to reveal Himself. We do not see the hand of God, but we see the results. Those results must be recognized and responded to with faith. Jeremiah 50 is a powerful prophecy. God announced His plans. The faithful responded in faith.

Babylon was a tool in the hand of God. While the leaders and people convinced themselves and the world that their might was a result of their vigor and intelligence, God's people knew better. They knew that God was using them. That is what God said He was doing. Chaldea was not God's love. Israel was God's love. God promised to rescue Israel and destroy Israel's captor (vv. 1-3, 9-13, 29-56). God never stops loving His people or pursuing His plan.

God's plan was to bring the Messiah into the world through the nation of Israel. Although the people of Israel were not led well by their shepherds, God was able to care for them. The people repented with weeping (vv. 4-8). God was gracious to them. He took up their cause and brought peace on earth through Jesus Christ (vv. 33-34). This was and is God's plan. Peace comes through the victory of Jesus.

Just as the Lord used Babylon to discipline Israel, He used the Persians and Medes to destroy Babylon. They were instructed what to do (vv. 14-16, 21-27). This would not take place for a long time, but God's Word can be trusted. He is the Lord. For those who live by faith and not by sight, the world makes sense. God is accomplishing a great rescue of His people and creation.

The Lord is at work. Just as He was clear about what He was about to do to Babylon and then did it, so He has been clear about what He is doing in the world now and what He will do – and He will do it! The people saw the effects of the hand of God. Today we can see the effects of God's hand. The faithful must respond.

Do you see the effects of God's hand at work? Are you responding in faith? Is your hope in Christ's promised return?

Those who look for God's hand at work in the world and respond in faith to what they see live with peace in their hearts.

1 Samuel 14; Romans 12; Jeremiah 51; <u>Psalm 30</u>

It is amazing how quickly life can change. One minute we are having the time of our lives, and the next minute we are in the emergency room awaiting the results of an X-ray. One day we love our job, but things change and it becomes a real bummer. Life changes, but God does not. He sees us through every change. In Psalm 30, David went from celebratory to scared. In either state, David looked to God and gave praise to His holy name.

David was often in a tight spot. Emotionally, he struggled at times in the pit of despair. Over and over, God lifted him up and kept his enemies from rejoicing over his difficulty (v. 1). He found renewal in God's provision (v. 2). The Lord saved his life (v. 3). Whether this is emotional or actual, as with David, we all need God's help. God is wise. He knows how to care for us.

There is always a reason to praise God. His holiness is reason enough (v. 4). There is nothing impure about God, and He is worthy to be praised for that. No one else is holy like God. His holiness demands justice, but His holy wrath is satisfied with His grace, and He shows His favor to the repentant (v. 5a). His grace overcomes our sin, which gives us joy that is new each morning (v. 5b).

Like a teenager with a caring parent, we don't always think we need God's help – but we do (v. 6). Without God, everything falls apart. Without God, there is no hope (v. 7). Knowing that we have a loving Father who hears us when we pray and cares for us when we hurt gives us peace. We can cry out to God and reason with Him (vv. 8-10). Like a parent with a grateful child, God loves to hear us speak of how we need Him.

God's people can always look back and celebrate God's faithfulness. We can remember what He has done for us and what He has done for others. When we see God provide, we are glad (v. 11). Our satisfaction in God brings Him great glory. Angry, frustrated followers do not bring God glory. When we glorify God because of the happiness we have in God, He is greatly honored.

What ups and downs have you been through lately? Have you turned to God for help, or have you tried to figure life out on your own? How has God been faithful to you and others in the past?

Those who look to God in every season of life enjoy His peace.

1 Samuel 15; Romans 13; Jeremiah 52; Psalm 31

Fear is not a bad thing. Fear in a fallen world will lead us to make wise decisions. What we fear matters. If we fear people more than we fear the Lord, then we are fearing a bad thing. If we fear the Lord more than we fear anything else, we will make wise decisions that honor God and result in God's blessings. First Samuel 15 shows what can happen when we fear people more than we fear God.

When we fear people more than we fear God, we will only do as much of what God commands us to do as people want us to do. The Israelites wanted to defeat their enemies, but they did not want to give up the opportunity to make a few bucks (vv. 1-25). Saul knew what God expected him to do, but he was more afraid of people than he was of God. Living to please people leads to a miserable life. People are never satisfied. Living to please God is such a joy. He delights in our faithfulness and sacrifice.

When we fear people more than we fear God, we miss out on relationships and opportunities that only God can give. Samuel continued in his path with God, but Saul was not on that path. That path with all of its blessings and opportunities was removed from Saul (vv. 26-31). Rather than continue with Samuel and serve God as king, Saul was forced to continue with the people who did not honor or obey God and serve as their king. Serving people's desires leads to misery. Serving God's desires produces peace.

When we fear people more than we fear God, God replaces us with someone else, and we miss out on the joy of doing God's will. Saul was supposed to put Agag to death, but because he would not, Samuel had to do it (vv. 32-33). Saul missed out on fulfilling God's calling on his life. Saul grieved God, and God replaced him with David (vv. 34-35). Saul spent his life isolated from Samuel, and he never had peace in his own mind or home. This is what happens to those who miss their divine calling and choose to please people instead of God. They never have peace.

Do you truly fear dishonoring God more than anything else? Have you ever disobeyed God out of fear of people? How did that go? When are you most tempted to fear people more than God?

Those who fear God more than anything else live with peace.

1 Samuel 16; Romans 14; Lamentations 1; Psalm 32

The church is one of the few recognized organizations in the world that truly exists to serve those outside of it. The same is true of every individual Christian. We do not live to serve ourselves. We live to serve Jesus. Jesus came to serve and to give His life for others, and we are to do the same. There would be a tremendous outpouring of love in our churches and throughout the churches of the world if Christians could get this right. Romans 14 reminds us of our calling to serve Jesus and love people in practical ways.

One of the most practical ways we can love others is by not being argumentative over opinions (vv. 1-13). There are as many opinions as there are people in the world. If we are going to require people to agree with us on everything before we love and associate with them, we will live miserable, isolated lives. We are to look to the commands of Christ and obey Him. He is our Master. We are to have convictions about what the Bible teaches. We are to be faithful to obey those commands and to live and die pleasing Jesus to the best of our ability. That will produce glory to God, peace in our hearts, and service to others. Pleasing Jesus will often require that we choose not to please ourselves. There is joy in pleasing Jesus.

When there are disagreements, we must be very careful to speak to the issue and be honest without being judgmental of other people (vv. 13-23). Being honest and truthful is a cornerstone of the Christian life. God does not want us to lie or ignore what we believe to be right and true. God does not want us to think less of others simply because they do not agree with our stance or opinion on issues. A wise and helpful Christian is able to discern the difference between opinions on issues and core beliefs of the faith. It is imperative that believers seek peace with one another. Peace is a hallmark of life with God. Being a peacemaker proves who we are. Jesus said, *Blessed are the peacemakers, for they shall be called sons of God* (Matthew 5:9).

Do you seek to serve or to be served? Are you able to love those who don't agree with your opinions? Is peacemaking a central part of your identity and purpose?

> *Those who humbly serve others and choose to be peace-makers will produce and enjoy peace.*

1 Samuel 17; Romans 15; <u>Lamentations 2</u>; Psalm 33

The human experience in our broken world is difficult. The world God created was in harmony. God was honored. God's image bearers had peace with Him and with all created things. This is not the way of the world now. Human beings love sin. Sin creates pain and suffering. These are dark times. Lamentations 2 is a painful chapter that speaks to what Israel went through in their exile. Their exile is like our exile from God's paradise.

Human beings are under a curse. Because we were made to be the caretakers of God's creation, the whole world is under God's judgment (vv. 1-10). There is nothing we can do to fix our relationship with God. There is nothing we can do to fix the world. God is just. What is happening in the world is because of our choices. We all choose to sin, and the consequence of sin is misery.

No one wants to think about how bad things are. We want to pretend we are okay. We want to be told we are okay. The human race is not okay. God said it would be like this. He warned us, but we ignored Him and we ignored the conscience He gave us, and now we are stuck in our sin and pain (vv. 11-19). The demons rejoice in our suffering, and God is robbed of glory. Those made in His image are living like animals, but were made to live like angels.

There is still hope. God has not abandoned us. We can turn to Him. We can pray (vv. 20-22). The fact that we can pray tells us that we can connect with God. We can turn from our wicked ways and be healed. This is the gospel, the good news of God. God said of Israel, *If my people who are called by my name humble themselves, and pray and seek my face and turn from their wicked ways, then I will hear from heaven and will forgive their sin and heal their land* (2 Chronicles 7:14). Jesus said, *Repent and believe in the gospel* (Mark 1:15). God is gracious. If we will turn from sin and believe that Jesus died to pay for our sin and has been raised to give new life, then we will be saved.

Do you believe that the world is broken and is in need of restoration? Do you believe that human beings are in need of salvation? Do you believe that Jesus has come to save sinners and give new life?

Those who are willing to see the world and their sin for what it is and are willing to turn to Jesus in faith will be saved and filled with peace.

1 Samuel 18; Romans 16; Lamentations 3; <u>Psalm 34</u>

God is not only holy, but He is also good. To say that God is holy is to say that He is perfect. To say that God is good is to say that He is kind. Because He is holy, everything God does is right and perfect. Because God is good, His actions are compassionate. What a great God we can worship and love! Everything He does is perfect. His kindness is without flaw. Psalm 34 speaks about the goodness of God and the ability of His people to be beneficiaries of His grace.

It is truly possible to bless the Lord at all times, to boast in His provision, and to call others to join in celebrating His great name (vv. 1-3). While our circumstances are not always what we want them to be, God is always everything we need. When we are able to seek Him because of His grace, we pray and are delivered from our fears, knowing that He has both the will and the power to provide for us (vv. 4-6). Those who have tasted the goodness of the Lord know what it is to take refuge in God's sovereign care (v. 7). To trust Him is to fear Him (vv. 9-10). It is wise to fear God. He is all-powerful and holy, and we are sinful. Knowing who He is humbles us and inspires us to go to Him by faith in Christ. We do not approach Him based on our merits. We go to God through Jesus, who makes us worthy to approach God.

The life of a saint is not complicated. Those who fear the Lord are happy to hear and obey God's Word, which leads them to turn away from evil and do good (vv. 11-14). Those who do good never need to fear life's circumstances. We can always seek God's peace and know God's peace. We know God hates evil because it destroys the beauty He has made. The Lord is glad to save His people and restore the beauty of His image in human beings. He hears the cries of the redeemed and provides for their needs (vv. 15-18). We will have struggles in life, but God will deliver us (vv. 19-20). Looking to Jesus in faith frees us from condemnation (v. 21). Believing in Jesus saves us from sin and death (v. 22). All of these blessings come by grace and are enjoyed through faith in Jesus.

Do you fear the Lord? Have you been saved from sin and strengthened in life through faith? Are you confident in God's willingness and ability to sustain you and provide for your needs?

Those who trust in God's goodness live with peace.

1 Samuel 19; 1 Corinthians 1; Lamentations 4; Psalm 35

Relationships are gifts from God. It is crucial that we stay humble and allow the people God has placed in our lives to do the work that is needed to sustain us. Living in isolation leads to failure. God has provided different kinds of relationships to bless our lives and meet our needs. Those relationships must be sustained and strengthened with peace. First Samuel 19 shows how important it is to have healthy relationships with friends, family, and spiritual mentors who can counsel us and help us through life.

Friends are a crucial aspect of spiritual, physical, and emotional health. We do not need a lot of friends. A few will do. Each relationship must be prioritized and protected. David had several key friends in his life. His best friend was Jonathan, Saul's son. When Saul wanted to kill David, Jonathan stepped in and discouraged his father from pursuing his deadly plan (vv. 1-7). We all need faithful friends.

Even with Jonathan's help, David's life was still endangered by Saul because of Saul's great jealousy. David was a help to Saul in battle, and he sought to soothe Saul's troubled mind with music. Saul still tried to kill David (vv. 8-10). David's wife, who was Saul's daughter, had to step in to save David (vv. 11-17). Clearly, David had built a strong bond with her so that she cared more about helping David than she cared about pleasing her father.

Having escaped with his life, David went to his spiritual mentor, Samuel (v. 18). Under Samuel's spiritual care, David was protected by the supernatural power of God (vv. 19-24). Spiritual mentors are crucial in life. They provide words of encouragement, as well as power through their prayers. God's mighty hand was with Samuel, and through Samuel's presence, God provided for David. When we come to saving faith in Jesus and are born again, we are filled with the Holy Spirit. The Holy Spirit often leads us through mentors and provides for us through their faith.

Do you have great godly friends, faithful family members, and spiritually strong mentors? How can you strengthen those relationships? Has God provided for you through them before?

Those who trust in God and build strong relationships with key people are able to maintain peace while going through challenges.

1 Samuel 20; <u>1 Corinthians 2</u>; Lamentations 5; Psalm 36

The world likes to think of the church as being just another human organization or institution. Without a clear perception of who God is and what He has revealed about Himself in the Bible, there is not much the world can know of the truth. When we are born again, we come to understand reality in a way that those who are not Christians cannot fathom. First Corinthians 2 reveals the unique knowledge of those who are Spirit-filled.

The apostle Paul was called by God in a miraculous way (Acts 9). God made it clear to Paul that he was to be a missionary to the gentiles. This hardcore Jew became a servant of the people he had been raised to despise. This happened by the power of God. Leaving the comforts of Israel, Paul went to cities like Corinth, and he preached Christ crucified with fear and trembling (1 Corinthians 2:1-3). There was not much about his presentation that was remarkable except for the fact that the Spirit of God was at work (vv. 4-5). Lives were changed by the message Paul preached.

Paul's message was a unique wisdom that God had determined to reveal before the foundation of time (vv. 6-7). This message is the hope found in Jesus Christ. The religious rulers of Israel did not understand this message. If they had, they would not have crucified Jesus (v. 8). In their ignorance, they turned away from the gift of God. They missed the Messiah, and they murdered Him.

Paul and all who believe are beneficiaries of the promises of God in Christ Jesus (v. 9). These promises are perceived as the Holy Spirit enables (v. 10). The promises are delivered by the power of the Spirit of God and received by the Spirit's enabling (vv. 11-13). Those who are dead to God are only alive physically. They cannot accept or understand the things of God because the things of God can only be discerned by those who have been born again by the Spirit (vv. 14-15). Those who have been born again have the mind of Christ. To think, feel, and live like Jesus is a gift of grace made possible by the gospel of Jesus Christ.

Have you been born again? How has the Spirit of God been at work in your life to give you an understanding of God's Word? Do the promises of God fill you with hope in all circumstances?

Those who are Spirit-filled know the truth that gives peace.

1 Samuel 21-22; 1 Corinthians 3; <u>Ezekiel 1</u>; Psalm 37

Strangely, the worst of times are often the best of times spiritually. In moments of great distress, God's children are more apt to look to heaven for help. God loves His children. Although He disciplines us, His steadfast love never ceases. God is always accomplishing His purpose. Ezekiel 1 helps us remember the kindness, greatness, and sovereign care of God.

Ezekiel seems to be pointing to his age in this unique introduction (vv. 1-3). He speaks in the first person and then in the third person. When God deals with us, it often seems surreal. Although it is God dealing with us, the experience is so powerful that it almost seems to be happening to someone else. It almost feels unreal. Ezekiel knew where he was and how old he was when God spoke to Him. It was a bad time for the Jews, but God showed up and made it glorious. Every Christian has a unique story with special moments with God.

This young prophet saw something strange. It was the coming of God (vv. 4-28a). What does God look like? No one knows. It is apparently impossible to explain. God gave odd appearances that represented His Being to Ezekiel. What we can know is that God is mighty. He has a plan and a system to what He is doing. By His might and for His glory, God is engaging in our world to accomplish what He has promised. There is no stopping God. His wisdom is too deep. His power is too great. His love is too strong. His plan is too perfect. God cannot be stopped.

Ezekiel's response is consistent with what others did in the Bible. He fell on his face before God (v. 28b). Submission to God out of recognition of His glory is the only right response for a finite human who sees God. Awe is the appropriate response to God every single day. God is at work in the world. He is spreading His love with sovereign care. He is kind and mighty!

Have you experienced special times with God? Do you gladly bow to the greatness of God and seek to walk in His ways? When you think of God, what images come to your mind? Do you perceive God as awesome and knowable?

Those who understand the might and goodness of God happily bow before Him in faith and live with peace.

1 Samuel 23; 1 Corinthians 4; Ezekiel 2; <u>Psalm 38</u>

God knows that we are not perfect. That is why Jesus came and died. Through the death and resurrection of Jesus, believers are free from the wrath of God. Those who repent and believe receive the grace of God because Jesus took our place and received the justice of God on the cross. Although saved and secure for all of eternity, believers still struggle with sin in this life. We sin, but we grieve over it. Psalm 38 is the cry of David over his sin, and it reveals how those who are right with God feel about their sin.

David sinned and there were consequences for his sin, but he was not without hope. He cried out to God because he knew that God would hear him and help (v. 1). God is gracious to us. He knows what it is to be tempted. He understands the challenges we face. When we turn to the Lord, we find healing and hope because He loves us and cares for us.

God often wounds us to help us. Like a surgeon with a scalpel, the Lord digs into us to deal with the disease of sin in our flesh (v. 2). David felt the pain of His sin in his heart, mind, and body (vv. 3-10, 13-14). Guilt is overwhelming. Believers in Jesus are made righteous, and sin disturbs every aspect of our existence.

Sin also impacts our relationships (vv. 11-12, 19-20). David's friends pulled away from him, and his enemies drew near. Sadly, there are situations when sin scares saints, and rather than stand together, we scatter. When we scatter and are alone, the enemies of God step in and slander us and seek to destroy us with shame.

The good news is that God never leaves us or forsakes us. The Lord is good to His redeemed people. David looked to God and prayed (vv. 15-16). He recognized his guilt, confessed his sin, and pursued the Lord to find peace (vv. 17-18, 21-22). The promise of God stands: *If we confess our sins, he is faithful and just to forgive us our sins and to cleanse us from all unrighteousness* (1 John 1:9). We are saved by grace and are free to come to God in prayer through Christ. He hears us and helps us.

Are you struggling with a particular sin? Do you have siblings in Christ who can help you with prayer and accountability? Are you talking with Jesus and seeking His help and strength to overcome sin with His love and grace?

Those who look to God for grace overcome sin and enjoy peace.

Don't force it! That wise counsel is often given to strong-willed people who wrongly think that all they need to do is push harder to fix their problems in life. Unfortunately, when someone is a hammer, every situation looks like a nail. Sometimes the best thing we can do is wait on the Lord. In 1 Samuel 24, David was tempted to take matters into his own hands and force an issue, but he chose the better way that honored God and provided peace.

King Saul had wanted to kill David for a long time. When Saul heard that David was in the wilderness of Engedi, Saul went there with a large force to hunt David down and kill him (v. 1). While on the hunt, Saul found a cave to use to relieve himself. What Saul did not know was that David and his men were hiding in that cave (vv. 2-3). David was encouraged by his men and very easily could have killed Saul, but David refused. Instead, he cut off a portion of Saul's robe and compelled his men not to kill Saul (vv. 4-7). Even cutting off Saul's robe caused David to feel guilty. David knew that God had called him to be king, but for the time being, Saul was king. He knew that God had anointed Saul to be king, and that made Saul untouchable.

After Saul had finished his business in the cave, David called out to him to show him that he could have easily killed him, and he explained that it was not his intention to do so (vv. 8-14). David called on God for justice and deliverance from Saul (v. 15). This humbled Saul, who repented and admitted that one day David would be the king of Israel (vv. 16-20). He asked that David would be gracious and not kill his family, which was the normal practice for a new king (v. 21). David gladly swore that he would not kill Saul's family after he became king. Saul then left, and David and his men went to a safe place. The end result was peace. David could have taken matters into his own hands, but he trusted God and chose the better way of faith and God's timing.

Have you ever been tempted to take matters into your own hands rather than trust God? How would you have handled the situation with Saul in that cave if you had been David? Do you truly trust God to provide for His plan for your life?

Those who trust in the Lord experience peace with God.

1 Samuel 25; <u>1 Corinthians 6</u>; Ezekiel 4; Psalms 40-41

Being a child of God who is saved by grace in Christ alone results in many wonderful blessings. We are blessed to be a part of God's eternal family, and we have significant responsibilities. We are blessed to be given a new life. We are blessed to be the dwelling place of God. Paul speaks about these blessings in 1 Corinthians 6.

Corinth was a town with some problems. Paul ministered there for quite a while, and he had several occasions of correspondence with the church. The city was filled with prostitutes, businesses, religions, and Roman government. The Christians struggled to embody their new life in Christ. The things of the world kept creeping back into their lives and the church. One issue was lawsuits (vv. 1-8). Paul made it clear that the saints would one day judge angels for their service. In light of that fact, Paul concluded that the church could settle their own disputes. They did not need to go, and should not go, to secular officials to handle their grievances against one another.

The people of the church were also to live holy lives. Sure, they were once like the rest of the people in the city, but Jesus changed all of that. Those who live unholy lives will never be citizens of heaven. Only those who are born again and live in a personal relationship with Jesus through faith can live with God forever (vv. 9-11). Faith in Christ results in a significant life change.

In Christ, there are many freedoms, but God calls us to what is best. What is best is to give our lives to the Lord and be the kind of people He made us to be (vv. 12-13). In Corinth, the believers were surrounded by sexual perversion. It is no wonder that so many struggled with sexual sin, but this was no excuse for their sin. The redeemed of God are members of Christ who will one day be raised to reign with Jesus forever (vv. 14-17). Those who have been made alive in Christ are now temples of the Holy Spirit and have been purchased by the blood of Jesus (vv. 18-19). God owns the redeemed, who are to glorify Him with their bodies. They are to live holy lives that serve God. This gives peace.

Have you been given new life in Christ? Are you living your life faithfully to Jesus as a part of a local church? Do you live to serve and honor Christ, or are you being deceived by sin?

Those who live to obey Christ experience peace.

1 Samuel 26; 1 Corinthians 7; <u>Ezekiel 5</u>; Psalms 42-43

Life always has a context. That context has an influence on the way we experience God and live our lives. We are always impacted by the physical world, the spiritual world, and our private emotional world. These three perceptions are always pressing on us and driving our thoughts and actions. How we perceive God is crucial. In Ezekiel 5, the prophet is explaining God's will through an action sermon. He did something that explained God's plan.

God was about to do something fearful. The Israelites were about to experience the wrath of God for their sin. Not everyone shared the same level of guilt. Not everyone was as bad as the worst of sinners, but the evil of many impacted the lives of all. God was about to bring a sword – an army of judgment – against Israel, and the people would be balanced out in thirds and face calamities that had never been seen and would not be seen again (v. 1). God has the power, the right, and the understanding to bring judgment. No human being influenced by sin can fully understand the perfect will of God or His perfect actions. The righteous must simply live by faith and trust God's plan.

God's plan was to divide the people into thirds to bring His unique judgment (vv. 2-17a). A third of the people of Jerusalem would die of pestilence. A third would die by the siege of Babylon. A third would be scattered, but not the entirety of them. Some would receive God's special care. There would be a remnant who would be saved to return to Jerusalem and rebuild so that God's eternal plan to bring Jesus to save the world could take place.

As bad as things can get in the world, the hope of the saints is that God is in control. What God has said, He will do (v. 17b). The Lord has spoken. He promised that Jesus would come to pay for sin and be raised from the dead. That happened. Jesus promised that He would build His church in all the world. That is happening. He promised that He would come again and make all things new. He will. The best thing we can do is trust God's plan, live by faith, and honor Jesus.

Do you trust that God has a perfect plan? Can you suffer with hope? Are the promises of God your strength and peace?

Those who can perceive God's sovereign hand at work in
the activity of the world can rest in peace at all times.

1 Samuel 27; 1 Corinthians 8; Ezekiel 6; <u>Psalm 44</u>

Westernized people are encouraged to be individualistic and to use systems and structures to their personal advantage. The church is commanded to do the opposite. God's people are told to see themselves as a part of God's work in the world and to connect their lives with others to accomplish His purpose. Living in the first person plural (we) can be challenging, but it is a blessing. Psalm 44 reveals the blessing of being a member of God's family.

As God's family, we have a strong faith heritage (vv. 1-3). The people of God can look back and see how God provided in the past. God does not change. He is always holy, loving, and sovereign. God's people have been saved by God over and over again. He will always be faithful to His people.

As God's family, we each honor Jesus as our God and as the ruler of our lives. We trust Him to provide for us all (vv. 4-8). Thankfully, God has defeated our greatest enemies – sin and death. We could not save ourselves. God has saved us by grace, and we can now live in the peace that comes by God's grace.

As God's family, we face hardship together (vv. 9-22). There is always a faithful remnant within the realm of God's kingdom. Sometimes God's people get off course and need to be corrected to gain direction. Sometimes God's people get complacent and need a challenge to gain passion. Sometimes God's people get proud and need a trial to grow their faith. These are often difficult times. God's people can get overwhelmed and will often be tempted to doubt God's love. In those moments, the people must rally together and seek God's face in prayer and repentance.

As God's family, we can always go to the Lord in prayer, knowing that He hears us and will care for us (vv. 23-26). God has given us the Bible. In the Bible, there are promises that God's people can hold to. These promises give God's children the boldness to approach Him and to ask Him to act according to His Word, which reveals His will. It is crucial that God's people know His Word.

Are you serving faithfully in a local church? Do you connect with other believers? Can you pray God's promises?

Those who live in God's family by faith live with peace.

1 Samuel 28; 1 Corinthians 9; Ezekiel 7; Psalm 44

In a secular society, the supernatural is nothing more than a fairy tale or a fool's pursuit. Our modern or postmodern minds seem to have no sense of the spiritual realities of creation, but that has not always been the case. There have been times when the dark and light spiritual realities were far more apprehensible. One of those seasons when spiritual realities were perceived more readily is described in 1 Samuel 28.

It was a dangerous moment in the life of Israel. Saul was king. The Philistines were preparing to attack, and David seemed to be on their side (vv. 1-2). Samuel the prophet had died, and there appeared to be no way of gaining spiritual insight from godless or godly sources (vv. 3-6). When enemies are on the hunt, when leadership is divided, and when there is no answer from heaven, the people of God are in serious danger.

God refused to speak to Saul, so Saul took another approach. He found a medium, someone who could speak with the dead. His people found a woman at Endor who could serve Saul's purpose (vv. 7-11). Many contemporary readers find it difficult to believe that this woman actually raised up Samuel from the dead (vv. 12-15). Some people struggle with this because they don't believe in God. Those who believe in God struggle with this because this account does not seem to match the teaching of the New Testament concerning the afterlife. Before Jesus was raised, all who died entered Sheol. The redeemed entered paradise, and lost sinners entered Hades in Sheol. Today when saints die, they immediately enter the Lord's presence.

Samuel told Saul what God had already promised. Saul was going to be cut off from being king (vv. 16-20). This crushed Saul (vv. 21-25). It is interesting that Saul was not overwhelmed because he was talking to a man who had died, for he was more concerned with human matters. Like the rich man's brothers in Jesus' story, many people refuse to look to God, even if a dead man is raised and eternity is revealed (Luke 16:19-31).

Do you believe in God? Is heaven in your eternal future? Are you more concerned with earthly things than eternal things?

Those who have eyes that can see the spiritual reality of life
and look to Jesus for salvation live and die in peace.

1 Samuel 29-30; 1 Corinthians 10; Ezekiel 8; Psalms 46-47

We all have our reasons for what we do. There are many decisions that we make out of habit, but those decisions are built on choices of the past. Whatever we choose has a motive. God calls us to be motivated to honor Christ in all we do. In 1 Corinthians 10, we are commanded to choose what is best.

All who are saved are made righteous by faith in Christ. Those who were saved before the coming of Jesus were saved by looking forward to the coming of the Messiah. Those who were and are saved after the coming of Christ were and are saved by looking back to the life, death, and resurrection of Jesus. The Israelites who were rescued out of Egypt lived by faith. They trusted the Word of God, were baptized in the waters of the sea, and ate the manna. They drank of the hope of Christ (vv. 1-5). Not all were faithful, and many missed the blessing of the promises of God.

They are a reminder to us to be faithful to God so that we do not miss out on the blessings that come through faithful obedience (vv. 6-11). Temptation comes to everyone, but we do not have to sin (vv. 12-13). If we humbly recognize our tendency toward sin and choose the way of escape that God provides, we will overcome.

Victory in Christ demands that we retreat from idolatry (v. 14). Idolatry is hoping in and finding our identity in anything other than Christ. We must choose. We will either be identified with Christ and worship Him alone, or we will fall into idolatry (vv. 15-22). One leads to God's blessing, and the other leads to a curse. Trusting in Christ alone and honoring Him as the ruler of our lives leads to His blessing.

One of the great challenges is choosing between what is good and what is best. There are many things we can freely do as Christians that are not beneficial or best. It is always best to do all that we do for the glory of God (vv. 23-33). If we seek to honor God rather than satisfy ourselves, we will obey God in all things and be effective witnesses to those who are far from God. Our goal must be to be like Jesus and serve others rather than to serve ourselves.

Is Jesus Christ and His love and hope the foundation of your identity? Do you daily acknowledge your capacity to sin and reject idolatry? Are you seeking to serve others so they can know Jesus?

Those who live under Jesus and for Jesus live with peace.

1 Samuel 31; 1 Corinthians 11; Ezekiel 9; Psalm 49

One of the great frustrations often uttered by the psalmists, the prophets, and different believers in every age is the seeming unwillingness of God to act in the world and bring justice. When He does, there is a dissimilar reaction. People do not want God to bring holy justice. It is as if we want something in between – just enough justice so we feel comfortable and safe. God's justice is holy. It is precise. It is ultimate. It is terrifying. Ezekiel 9 reveals God's wrath against sinners and His grace toward saints.

God promised to bring His wrath against His people because of how they had dishonored His name in the temple and in the world (Ezekiel 8:18). To accomplish His purpose, God sent six angels to execute His judgment (Ezekiel 9:1-2). It is important to note that they were carrying weapons. In chapter 10, judgment comes by fire. When God judges His people, He does it with precision, one person at a time. Each soul takes responsibility for their own sin, and the punishment is exact. God does not miss a thing. He knows our hearts and minds, and He takes note of our every deed.

There was a seventh angel present who was responsible for placing a mark on the saints who were faithful to God and safe from the wrath of God (vv. 3-4). The righteous are safe from God's wrath. Those who look to Jesus by faith are covered in His righteousness and are saved. There is no other means by which a person can be saved than by faith in Christ alone.

The judgment of God is without mercy (vv. 5-11). The angels of God will wield their power and perform their tasks perfectly. Those who have denied God and are liable for their sin will face terror that is unimaginable. The prayers of the saints are profitable now, but once judgment has come, it is final. God will save a remnant. He always does. Sinners will suffer, and the angels will give an account to God for their responsibility. This reality should terrify sinners and lead them to repent and receive grace, and then should inspire them to share their hope in the gospel so others can be saved.

Do you fear God's judgment? Have you come to understand the real wrath of God? Are you living in light of the coming judgment of God on every person on the planet?

Those who love God in Christ can be confident and at peace.

2 Samuel 1; 1 Corinthians 12; Ezekiel 10; <u>Psalm 49</u>

Jesus told the story of the rich man and Lazarus in Luke 16:19-31. In the story, the rich man, who had good things in life, is sentenced to Hades, while Lazarus was sent to be with Abraham in paradise. The Bible teaches that the soul of humanity is immortal. While our bodies turn to dust, our souls enter into eternity at death. We enter either eternal suffering or peace. The saints are reminded of the reality of the eternal outcome of life in Psalm 49.

The psalmist announces his intention to provide teaching to the world in a song (vv. 1-4). The teaching is a "proverb," which in Hebrew culture had a dark, foreboding sense to the truth being taught artistically. The world needs to know the reality of heaven and hell. The world needs to see that what each person does in the world will determine what happens to them in eternity. The eternal reality of God and the immortality of our soul is meant to inspire devotion to God and love for other people.

The writer of Psalm 49 is confident to the point of almost being cocky. He relates what he understands about the coming judgment of those who seem to have everything this world can provide (vv. 5-14). Those with resources and power will not be able to take their advantages into the afterlife. All they have will be passed on to another. Their legacy on earth may be one of admiration, but before God, they will be doomed.

This is not the case of the redeemed of God (v. 15). The writer of the psalm is sure of his salvation and of his standing with God. There is complete confidence that he will be saved and vindicated. His soul will be ransomed. This is what Jesus came to do. The Father promised that He would send His Son, who would pay for the sin of all who believe, and purchase our inequities, giving us a right standing with God. The redeemed will be vindicated by the judgment of God against those who placed their hope and identity in their earthly wealth (vv. 16-20). Soon, all that is will pass away. Jesus will create a new heaven and a new earth and will reign forever over His people with peace.

Are you confident in your personal relationship with Jesus? Do you believe our souls are eternal? Is your identity and eternal hope found in earthly, passing things or in Jesus?

Those who trust in Jesus will spend eternity in peace.

2 Samuel 2; 1 Corinthians 13; Ezekiel 11; Psalm 50

Human beings are intelligent creatures, but we often use our knowledge for a destructive end. The book of Proverbs says, *There is a way that seems right to a man, but its end is the way of death* (Proverbs 14:12; 16:25). God's way is the way of life, but only a few choose that narrow way (Matthew 7:13-14). The way of God is revealed by His Word. Those who follow after God will align under His leadership and will battle against the plans of those who are in opposition to God's will. In 2 Samuel 2, we see what happens when the plans of people stand against the plans of God.

It was no secret that David was to be king over Israel. King Saul and his son had even acknowledged this. At their deaths, David was led by God to live in Hebron and was recognized there as the rightful king of Israel (vv. 1-4). In his love and wisdom, David sought to honor Jabesh-gilead because they had buried Saul and Jonathan. David invited these honorable people to be blessed under his leadership (vv. 5-7). Jesus has come, and all who will align under His leadership will be blessed. Jesus invites us to follow Him.

Abner, the commander who had overseen Saul's army, had other plans. He recognized Saul's son as king, and all except the tribe of Judah were loyal to him (vv. 8-11). This was not God's will, but Abner wanted power. Saul's son was just a puppet. Abner wanted to maintain his position and possessions. People will usually do what is in their best interest. It is wise to look at people's motives in order to understand their actions.

Those who will not follow God's will and way are always in conflict with God's faithful people. Abner's men fought against David's loyal officers. The battle was not decisive and did not end the war, but it revealed who had the advantage. David's men had far fewer losses and maintained a strong geographical position (vv. 12-32). Truth wins in the end. It is always best to stand with God and His will. God's people experience losses, but they will win in the end.

Are you standing with Jesus? Do you fight for truth? Are you safe in the strong, enduring will of God?

Those who stand with Jesus, the ultimate king, will fight many battles, but they will always know that they are standing with the One who is God's anointed, and they will have peace as they stand with Jesus.

2 Samuel 3; <u>1 Corinthians 14</u>; Ezekiel 12; Psalm 51

Why we do something is as important as what we do. If we do the right thing, but without love, we will not have peace. The Holy Spirit will not be pleased. He will convict us of our wrong-heartedness. It is best to do the right thing with the right motive. In 1 Corinthians 14, the apostle Paul challenged the church to experience worship the right way with the right heart.

Everything that is done in the worship gathering of a local church is to be done to the glory of God for the encouragement of the church (vv. 1-19). Paul was concerned that the people were getting too caught up in the spiritual gift of tongues. His desire and encouragement was for the people to speak in a language that all of the church could understand so everyone would benefit. The worship gathering of a church needs to be clear and needs to use simple language and practices that everyone can understand.

The worship gatherings must not only be of use to those who believe, but must also be of use to those who do not believe (vv. 20-25). The worship of a family of faith is a wonderful way to introduce the doctrines of grace to someone who does not yet believe in Jesus. It is by grace that we are saved. When the church gathers, language and practices need to be used that enable those outside of the faith to be able to grasp the goodness of God in giving His Son to pay for our sin. The Holy Spirit can transform lives with that truth!

The worship gatherings do not have to be dumbed down in any way. Children of God need to be immature in the ways of sin, but mature in the knowledge of God (v. 20). Saints grow in knowledge through the preaching and teaching of God's Word. Every local church needs to have biblical doctrines preached to them. These doctrines need to be taught in orderly ways. The worship gatherings themselves need to function in orderly ways so that everyone can understand (vv. 26-40). Worship needs to be done with the right motive – to serve – and in the right way – orderly.

Is your worship pleasing to God? Can you explain your faith in simple terms? Are nonbelievers welcomed in your church?

Those who worship rightly serve God with peace.

2 Samuel 4-5; 1 Corinthians 15; Ezekiel 13; Psalms 52-54

A half-truth can sometimes be more dangerous that a complete lie. A complete lie is more identifiable because it is in stark contrast to the truth. A half-truth is clothed in attractive garb. The enemies of God have been ruthless in their attacks on the truth since the beginning. Even the snake in the garden hid its lie in a general truth. God's people must be on their guard against the enemies of God. Ezekiel 13 testifies to the anger God has for those who pronounce half-truths in order to deceive His people.

Those who know the truth must be careful to protect it and to speak God's truth without partiality (vv. 1-2). The message of the faithful is simple: *Hear the word of the Lord!* God has been faithful to reveal truth. It can be seen in creation and read in the divine revelation of Scripture. Because all of God's children are ambassadors of Jesus, each one must stand for the truth and defend the integrity of what God has said.

Those who proclaim half-truths must be called out. This is not only for the good of those who would be deceived by lies, but it is also good for the deceivers themselves in the hope that they will repent of their lying ways and stand on the truth of Scripture. Half-truths do not provide a strong foundation or a hearty defense against evil (vv. 3-9). Deceivers often desire to tell people what they want to hear rather than what is true so they can gain influential power (vv. 10-21). Power does not only manipulate the masses, but it also pollutes and deceives the people who seek it and have it.

God deals harshly with false prophets because they grieve and dishearten the faithful and encourage the wicked (vv. 22-23). God's will is to fill the earth with His presence. Jesus is full of grace and truth. Grace and truth liberate sinners. Grace and truth give us hope and healing. Grace and truth produce peace in the soul of every saint who repents and believes the gospel. Without truth, grace appears unnecessary. Without grace, no one can be saved.

Do you have a firm handle on the truth of the Bible? Are you able to identify false teachers who proclaim confusing half-truths? How can you defend your soul against the attacks of the enemy who seeks to confuse and confound you?

Those who know the truth and stand with Jesus have peace.

2 Samuel 6; 1 Corinthians 16; Ezekiel 14; <u>Psalm 55</u>

The greatest threat to a group of friends, a church, or a nation is the enemy within. When the enemy is on the outside looking in and is recognizable, the battle is easy from a physical, mental, and emotional perspective. When the enemy is from within our trusted ranks, life gets tough. Paul warned the Ephesian elders to watch out for the wolves within the flock (Acts 20:28-30). In Psalm 55, David shares the personal experience of having to deal with the consequences of a friend who became his enemy.

The experience was a blessing in that it caused David to cry out to God and draw closer to his Lord (vv. 1-3). God is all-present and knows all things, but we are not always mindful of Him. God delights to be the focus of His people, and He will often allow relational difficulties to draw us to Himself.

The experience was terrifying to David because of the danger to his body (vv. 4-8) and to his reputation (vv. 9-11). Enemies often want to do more than cause physical pain. They often want to create a negative view of us so others reject us and refuse to give us any support.

This experience was emotionally difficult for David (vv. 12-14). This enemy was a friend who had been a part of David's inner circle. They had spent time together in God's house and had sought to be a source of help to one another. Now this enemy was against him, and David was so hurt that he wanted the person to die (v. 15).

Like Jesus, David sought the help of God to find strength and hope in his hurt (vv. 16-23). In the garden of Gethsemane, Jesus cried out to God and asked for help. Judas had betrayed Him. The religious leaders were coming for Him. His disciples would soon abandon Him. For our sake, God would forsake Him. Jesus knows what it is to be hurt by those He loves. However, Jesus gave grace. He commands us to follow His example. Forgiveness is not just a gift we give to others. It is a gift we give to ourselves. It is liberating.

Have you been hurt by those you trusted? Are you being a faithful friend by seeking the good of those who trust you? Is there anyone you need to forgive?

> *Those betrayed by loved ones can look to Jesus for the*
> *strength to give forgiveness and gain peace.*

2 Samuel 7; 2 Corinthians 1; Ezekiel 15; Psalms 56-57

Ambition is not a bad thing when it is holy. The human heart is selfish and sinful. Left to ourselves, we will seek what we want at the expense of our conscience and the well-being of others. Holy ambition seeks to honor God and fulfill our destiny. God is so powerful that He has a plan for every person on the planet. In 2 Samuel 7, we see David's holy ambition and God's sovereign grace guide David to fulfill his destiny.

David was destined to be king of Israel. That did not just happen. God called David and led him on his journey, but David had to pray, fight, and make a million decisions. God's plan and David's faithful obedience placed David in a position of power and peace (v. 1). In the end, all of God's people will arrive in heaven, their eternal home. Their enemies will be vanquished. They will be with God. There will be perfect peace.

Until that time, we must keep our eyes on God and seek to bring Him glory. David desired to glorify God by building the temple, but that was not God's plan (vv. 2-11). God's will was for David to establish a firm foundation on which God would build a house. David wanted to build God a house, but instead, God built David a house. This was a family line that would lead to Jesus Christ (vv. 12-17). Jesus is the one who will reign forever and ever. He is the eternal king of heaven.

What an honor was bestowed on David! It was by grace that God chose him, saved him, and established his family line. Yes, David worked hard and was faithful, but God provided the blessing. David was far from perfect. He sinned, but he repented and believed, and God blessed him. The only right response to this was gratitude. David was grateful (vv. 18-29). Those with holy ambition who gain success are not proud. They are grateful to God for His great grace and divine destiny.

Do you believe that God has a great plan for your life? Is your ambition a holy ambition? Can you speak clearly of God's calling on your life? Are you grateful to God for the grace that saves and guides God's people through this life and on to heaven?

Those who seek to honor God with their lives and fulfill their divine destiny experience peace.

2 Samuel 8-9; 2 Corinthians 2; Ezekiel 16; Psalms 58-59

God's plan is rarely a straight line that avoids obstacles and difficulties. The path on which God leads most of His people is jagged and filled with loops. We always go forward, but we often find ourselves in strange and surprising places. There is a peace in the journey knowing that God is guiding us. We do not have peace because our lives are easy, but because God is in our lives. The apostle Paul did not have an easy life, and in 2 Corinthians 2 we gain insight into how hard life can be and how good God is.

Paul and the church at Corinth had an up-and-down relationship. They drove Paul crazy. They were saved and secure in Christ, but they were unwise and often walked in the way of the flesh. Paul was sometimes harsh with them, but he was always loving toward them (vv. 1-4). Christians are going to experience conflict. That is just part of life. By God's grace and for His glory, Christians are called to be and are capable of being peacemakers. That is one of the primary responsibilities of each believer.

The church plays a vital role in the peacemaking process. When a saint sins, the church must step in with discipline and seek to restore the one who fell. The church at Corinth had done that, and now it was time for the man to be restored (vv. 5-8). There is a time to discipline and a time to restore. Satan would like to have us always fighting, but we are aware of his schemes (vv. 9-11). Restoring saints out of sin is tough. There are a lot of steps forward and backward. The church must be faithful to obey God's Word and to do His work with love.

That was Paul's desire. He wanted to be where God wanted him to be. He was blessed with friends who helped him. Doors would open and close, but through it all, Paul kept his eyes on Jesus and celebrated His great grace (vv. 12-17). Like Paul, we are ambassadors of King Jesus. We are not peddlers of human ideologies. We are in God's grand procession of saints who glorify God and announce that His kingdom has come.

Are you being faithful to your calling? Is your church making peace? Have you seen saints fall and be restored by the church? Are you willing to be used by God in whatever way He wants?

Those who trust and obey God live with peace.

2 Samuel 10; 2 Corinthians 3; Ezekiel 17; Psalms 60-61

The Bible is not a fairy tale about a distant land and people that never existed. God gave His Word through real people who lived in the real world. The Lord spoke to them and through them. We now read the Scriptures and are blessed with all sixty-six books. Each book is part of the one story that tells about God's great love and eternal plan. Ezekiel 17 reveals God's plan as it was explained at a real time in the past to help us understand the future.

The chapter begins with a riddle and a parable meant to help Israel understand their reality (v. 1). The story is about an eagle that planted a vine that was unfaithful (vv. 2-10). This is not a popular story. Most Christians do not know it. It is a sad story. It explains what happened to faithless Israel. It does not inspire. There are no cute sayings that would be fun to have on a coffee cup or calendar. Parts of God's Word are hard. The Bible is fully true, and the sad truth is that Israel was not faithful to God.

Israel was displaced by Babylon, but Babylon was not a horrible leader. It was the eagle that planted the vine, Israel, so that Israel could be restored in God's grace (vv. 11-12). Rather than trust God's Word and yield to God's will, Israel sought the help of Egypt (vv. 13-17). Egypt failed to help, and Israel fell into greater ruin (vv. 18-21). It is always best to trust and obey God, especially when we do not agree with Him. He is the Lord!

Despite Israel's hard-heartedness and sin, God did not completely reject the nation. His promise was to work through her to bless the world. God promised to take the faithful remnant of Israel and plant that nation and make it into His blessing to the world (vv. 22-24). From the foundation of the world, it had been God's plan to give the Messiah through Israel. Jesus has come. He is the mighty God who takes away the sin of the world. Through Him, all who believe will be saved. There will be people from every tribe and tongue who are saved (Revelation 5:9). Nothing can stop God's will.

Do you believe that the Bible is God's Word to humanity explaining God's work in the world? Are you a faithful saint who obeys God? Are you looking forward to the return of Christ?

Those who know the promises of God and choose to
trust and obey God's commands live with peace.

2 Samuel 11; 2 Corinthians 4; Ezekiel 18; <u>Psalms 62-63</u>

We should never be surprised by the hurtful actions of people. What should surprise us is when people act kindly. The world is broken, and we are all trying to navigate the personal and worldwide cultural challenges that continue to come up. In a world filled with hurting, scared people, a lot of hurtful decisions get made. In Psalms 62 and 63, we learn how to perceive the threats of broken people and how to respond to them in God-honoring ways.

David was not a perfect man, but he was a good man. God called him to be king, and although that was a great honor, it brought with it a great deal of strife. When his son Absalom sought to usurp David's power and become king, several wise men and valiant warriors sided with Absalom against David. Rather than be angry with God about the situation, David honored God and reaffirmed his faith in God's place in his life (Psalm 62:1-8). By looking at God, David was able to see the true condition of his enemies (vv. 9-10). Compared to God, everyone and everything else is small and finite. God is infinite! David was confident in God's wisdom and providence (vv. 11-12). God is powerful and provides steadfast love and provision to those who trust and obey Him.

God's provision comes in the times and quantities He deems best. Just because God is able to provide all of our wants does not mean that He will. There will be times in our journey through this broken world that we will feel weak and overwhelmed (Psalm 63:1). David felt that way at times, but he was able to rouse his hope by remembering God's power, glory, and steadfast love (vv. 2-8). He was able to celebrate God's goodness, even though he was facing terrible circumstances (vv. 9-10). David sustained his confidence in God's promises. David knew that his enemies could not keep God from doing what He had planned. The enemies of David would be vanquished because of God's sovereign care of His servant. David knew that, and so he rejoiced (v. 11). When things are bad, God is greatly glorified when His children continue to rejoice in Him.

Do you know that Jesus is your Savior? Are you confident in God's power and plan? Do God's promises and power give you peace in this world?

Those who rely on God and obey Him live with peace.

2 Samuel 12; 2 Corinthians 5; Ezekiel 19; Psalms 64-65

Life has its ups and downs. We all know that. There are going to be good days and bad days. It is difficult when we get hit with really bad days all at once with only a few good days mixed in. That is a roller-coaster ride that can debilitate the strongest of people. In 2 Samuel 12, we see that David is having some rough days mixed in with some good days. It is helpful to us to see that he survived them.

David was selfish and stupid. Even though he was a man after God's own heart, he was still a man. He was at the wrong place at the wrong time without anyone to keep him accountable. He committed adultery and murder. He thought he had gotten away with it, but God loves us too much to keep us from the consequences that teach us the lessons we need to learn. Nathan the prophet showed great courage and set King David straight (vv. 1-12). David's response was admirable. He confessed and accepted the penalty for his sin (vv. 13-23). He sought the Lord and prayed for a miracle, but God refused his request; David felt the consequence of his sin. It could have been debilitating, but it wasn't.

Rather than get angry with God or wallow in self-pity, which are both results of pride and ingratitude toward God, David chose to be a man of God. He righted his relationship with Bathsheba, and God provided them with a son, Solomon (v. 24). They named him Solomon, but God called him Jedidiah because the Lord loved him (v. 25). This was God being gracious.

The goodness of God continued to shine on David. Although David had delegated the fighting to Joab, it was crucial for him to be visible from time to time so that the army and the people would know that they were fighting for their king who was blessed by God (vv. 26-31). God is good to raise up leaders who need and receive His grace. Their lives help us remember how vulnerable to sin we all are and how gracious God is to all who believe. God is faithful in both the good times and the bad.

Have you lived through difficult days that were a result of your sin? How has God been faithful to you, even when you were not faithful to Him? Can you give God praise for the grace that He has shown you in the past that gives you peace for the future?

Those who trust God have peace in both the ups and downs of life.

2 Samuel 13; <u>2 Corinthians 6</u>; Ezekiel 20; Psalms 66-67

When a person becomes a follower of Jesus, many wonderful things happen. There is life where there once was death. There is peace where there once was hostility. There is hope where there once was frustration. The redeemed of God become a part of God's life, and God's life becomes the source of their own. In 2 Corinthians 6, followers of Jesus are given an explanation of what it means to live in unity with God and His people.

As ambassadors for Christ, God's children are working with God (v. 1). We are a part of God's family business. It is vital that God's children allow the gospel to have its full effect. When it does, we not only listen to the Lord and receive His help, but we also call others to believe (v. 2). One of the critical aspects of being of good use to God the Father's eternal business is to avoid making it hard for others to believe in Him (v. 3). We must be able to commend ourselves to them in Christ in every way (v. 4). Paul provided a list of ways God had miraculously worked in His life (vv. 5-10). The transforming power of the gospel is one of the most striking evidences of the gospel to a doubting world. Like Paul, we must share our lives freely with others and allow our hearts to be opened so they can see God's love in us (vv. 11-13).

That love is to be visible in how we love one another. Jesus said that the world would know we are His disciples by how we love one another (John 13:35). God's people are different in so many wonderful ways, but they are the same in a very specific way. The one thing that all of God's children share is God's holiness gained by grace through faith in Jesus Christ. God's people are pictured as the temple of God (2 Corinthians 6:14-18). While believers can disagree on many things and have different opinions and expressions of the faith, they cannot be divided on the gospel itself. The gospel is what gives light and life to all who believe. Unity under Christ makes God's family business strong.

Are you serving in God the Father's family business? Do you allow people far from God to see the light and love of God that lives in you? Are you united with the church under the lordship of Jesus Christ by the shared belief in the gospel?

Those who serve faithfully in God's family business have peace.

2 Samuel 14; 2 Corinthians 7; Ezekiel 21; Psalm 68

Everything about God is amazing. He is truly glorious in His personhood and in His activity in His creation. There is not anything that He does not know. All His decisions are right. He is gracious and desires to bless, but He will bring His holy judgment against His enemies. Ezekiel 21 reveals how God deals with His enemies, and it also points to Jesus, who makes us friends of God.

The Israelites had run out of time. God had been very patient with them. He had sent prophets to call them back to faithfulness. Warnings had been given. Nothing had worked. The people had turned away from God and were not coming back to Him. In light of their rejection, God raised up His sword, Babylon (vv. 1-7). Babylon was not acting on its own accord. The actions of the nation were wielded by the hand of God.

The plan of attack was not haphazard. The sword was prepared. It was sharpened and polished (vv. 8-17). The army was aligned and directed to go to Jerusalem and slaughter the inhabitants because of their sin (vv. 18-26). The Lord's work is not random. God works in every detail to accomplish His eternal purpose. His desire is to give grace, but when He is rejected, the result is catastrophic and complete. God does not miss a thing. He knows exactly the right thing to do. Sadly, some who suffered were righteous. When a culture conforms to sin, harm comes to all who are part of that culture.

The Lord would ruin Israel, but His plan to bring the Messiah through them into the world would be accomplished (v. 27). This might be the most amazing thing about God: He is able to accomplish His perfect plan through people who are far from perfect. His grace is eternal and unyielding.

Judgment begins with the house of God, but it does not end there. All who reject God, as the Ammonites did, will suffer (vv. 28-32). God's judgment is perfect. No one is spared. Everyone will have to give an account for their life. Thankfully, grace is found in Jesus.

Do you fear the judgment of God? In what ways have you seen God bring judgment to the world? Have you decided to follow Jesus and become a friend of God?

Those who follow Jesus and obey Him out of love live with peace.

2 Samuel 15; 2 Corinthians 8; Ezekiel 22; <u>Psalm 69</u>

Bad days are bound to come. It is so important to have empathy for those who are struggling. When we have a bad day or enter a season of pain and suffering, we need to know that God cares about us and that He wants us to draw strength and hope from Him. Other people, institutions, and all created things do not have the capacity to sustain us. We are broken human beings. Only God can heal us. Psalm 69 gives us permission to speak of our hurts and shows us how to go to God for help.

David was hurting (vv. 1-4). We can never know what another person is going through. It is crucial to always be kind to everyone for God's sake. David, like all people, needed compassion. We are living like Jesus when we choose to love hurting people.

If we are only going to care for people who are deserving, we will never help anyone. No one is perfect (v. 5). David's hope was in God, which was part of the reason he was suffering (vv. 6-12). David was a sinful man who truly loved God. He was suffering both for his sin and for his love. In reality, human beings are loving, imperfect creatures who need to give and receive love.

David looked to God for help (vv. 13-18). We must always go to God first and seek to know Him and His will for our lives. People will fail us to some extent. Some will cause harm on purpose (vv. 19-21). It is hard to come to terms with the fact that there are just some people in the world who are not going to like us. They may even hate us. The right thing to do is to trust God with them (vv. 22-28). We don't have the wisdom to always know what is just. Our knowledge is limited. We can trust God to do what is best.

Trusting God means that we share our hurt with Him (v. 29). It also means that we praise Him no matter what (vv. 30-32). God always hears His people and understands their needs (v. 33). By faith, God's people are to worship Him and to trust Him to provide (vv. 34-36). God gives steadfast love and applies perfect wisdom. Rather than depending on ourselves or getting mad at others, the wise way to live is to simply trust God and focus on His goodness.

Whom do you know who needs compassion right now? How has God been good to you? Is God truly your refuge and strength?

Those who trust the Lord in times of pain live with peace.

2 Samuel 16; 2 Corinthians 9; Ezekiel 23; Psalms 70-71

Motives are powerful and important. Why we do the things we do will often determine how much energy and consistency we put into our actions. God knows our hearts and measures our motives. Doing the right thing for the right reason provides a clear conscience and strong motivation to the heart. We all have motives. It is important to know what they are and why we have them. In 2 Samuel 16, men are making decisions based on their motives.

Ziba was a servant of King David. When David was fleeing Jerusalem to get away from his son Absalom, Ziba brought him resources for the journey (vv. 1-2). It was a very kind gesture. He had been assigned by David to care for Mephibosheth, the son of David's best friend, Jonathan, who had died (2 Samuel 9:9-11). This appeared to have been retribution for how Ziba had spoken despairingly of Mephibosheth. When Ziba brought the supplies, David asked where Mephibosheth was, and Ziba said he was back in Jerusalem celebrating (2 Samuel 16:3). David then gave Mephibosheth's property to Ziba (v. 4). This was clearly Ziba's goal. His motive was to help himself by helping David. When we serve God to help ourselves, we are not serving God. We are serving ourselves and our own interests.

When Shimei came out cursing David, David did not have him stopped (vv. 5-11). David hoped that God would see this disgrace and give David grace (vv. 12-14). David's motive was not to save Shimei's life, but to bless himself and the people with him. David sought to gain God's favor by rousing God's jealousy. God is jealous for His people because they represent His name.

Hushai remained in Jerusalem to serve Absalom (vv. 15-19). Unlike Ahithophel, Hushai was not out for Absalom's best interest (vv. 20-23). Hushai was there to spy on Absalom and get information to David and to confuse Absalom and give David an advantage. Absalom's arrogance led him to believe that Hushai was serving himself by serving Absalom. That was a mistake.

Can you measure your motives? Are you able to discern the motives of other people? Do you truly want to serve God and others out of love, or are you doing what you do to get stuff for yourself?

Those with pure motives live with peace.

2 Samuel 17; 2 Corinthians 10; Ezekiel 24; Psalm 72

There is a difference between being confident and being arrogant. The confident Christian has a firm handle on Jesus and knows that Jesus never lets go of His redeemed saints. Different situations demand different responses. In 1 Thessalonians 5:14, Paul told a group of new believers to *admonish the idle, encourage the fainthearted, help the weak, be patient with them all*. Paul put his own words in practice when he wrote 2 Corinthians 10 to a church that was struggling to follow Paul's leadership.

Paul was about to go and visit them, and he did not want to have to be bold with them. He wanted to instruct them with compassion and teach them to overcome the evil that was fighting against them (vv. 1-6). Paul was a spiritually gifted man and a very smart man. God had trained him to overcome the forces of darkness and the arguments against the faith. He loved these Corinthian Christians and wanted to help them. Some thought that he was arrogant in his letters and weak in his presentation. Paul was just trying to help them remain faithful to God. That should be every Christian leader's goal.

There appeared to be a group that was stirring up trouble and trying to undermine Paul's authority. Paul called not only the leaders into question, but also those who were following those leaders (vv. 7-12). If there was anyone who could measure up to other people, it was Paul. This was a man who had been through spiritual warfare that few others had been through. His goal was not to promote himself, but to promote Christ. That, too, should be every Christian leader's goal.

There was no denying Paul's love for this church and his right to claim authority and influence over them. He and his companions had left their homeland to take the gospel of Jesus to them so they could be saved (vv. 13-16). Paul was proud of what God had done in that church. He gladly boasted in what the Lord had done. He was confident that the Lord was pleased with him and that Jesus would commend him for his service (vv. 17-18). Paul wanted to see this church thrive. That is every Christian leader's goal.

Are you confident in Christ and able to handle personal attacks? Can you discern how to minister to different people with different needs? Do you support your spiritual leaders?

Those who are confident in Christ live with peace.

2 Samuel 18; 2 Corinthians 11; Ezekiel 25; Psalm 73

Why does it matter that God judged Ammon, Moab, Seir, Edom, and Philistia? Most of us do not even know where these places are. These places and people are listed because God wants us to know what He does with His enemies. The Bible tells of God's redemptive plan. Within that plan are many twists and turns that help the disciples of Jesus in every generation understand who God is and how we are to respond to Him by faith. In Ezekiel 25, God reveals His love, His power, and His plans for His people and the world.

God has an eternal, steadfast love for His people. Even when He is disciplining them, He loves them. This love causes Him to discipline them. If God did not love them, He would allow them to wallow in sin and suffer loss. God gives all people the common grace of conscience, family, and government. These all act to restrain us so that we will not destroy ourselves. God gives the redeemed the right to be members of His eternal family. God is jealous for His children. When He disciplines them, He does not appreciate His enemies mocking them.

God's love compels Him to defend His people who represent His name in the world. By His might and for His glory, God sustains His people and overcomes His enemies. These nations listed in Ezekiel 25 had no respect for God or His people. God revealed His power first by promising what He would do to them, and then by accomplishing His plan. There is a reason we do not talk regularly about these nations. God crushed them in His power.

He was not completely reactionary in His dealings with these enemy nations. God's plan from the beginning was to raise up Israel in order to release the gospel of Jesus Christ through them. This plan cannot be stopped. Those enemy nations were a threat to the plan of God. God poured out His wrath on them. God will judge all nations and people. We each will have to give an account for our own lives. Those who have hidden themselves in Christ by repenting and believing the gospel will be saved.

Have you come to saving faith in Jesus? Is it your desire to honor God? How do you bless God's people and help His plan?

Those who are under the protective care of God live with peace.

2 Samuel 19; 2 Corinthians 12; Ezekiel 26; <u>Psalm 74</u>

God saves us to transform us into people who live like Jesus. The difference God makes in the lives of His people brings Him glory. Willpower can only get us so far. The power of the gospel can produce eternal peace. This is the blessing that comes to all who repent and believe the gospel. The growth into Christlikeness is a process. Psalm 74 reveals the process that produces peace.

It begins with an understanding of our sinfulness. Before we can look to God for salvation, we must stop looking to ourselves or to anything else. When we trust in what we can do or in what any created thing can do in order to try to find peace, we cause ourselves and others pain. Rejecting God is a sin. Sin always leads to brokenness (vv. 1-11). Sin comes in and destroys every good thing in our lives. It robs us of a relationship with God. It devours our love for others. It leaves us ravaged and dirty. Sin is costly.

Jesus came to pay the cost for our sin. God could have abandoned us in our sin, but because He chose before the foundation of the world to establish His covenant of grace, we can be saved (vv. 12-17). By the power of Jesus, anyone who repents and believes the gospel can be saved. Jesus overcame sin on the cross and defeated death in His resurrection. The great beast of the pit of hell has been overcome, and all who turn to Jesus are freed to walk in the light of the gospel of God. The journey begins with faith.

Walking in this light leads to a great blessing. The peace of every saint is not found in our strength to hold on to God, but in God's strength to hold on to us (vv. 18-23). Our enemies are great, but our God is greater. The devil cannot have our souls, but that does not keep him from trying to dissuade us from a life of obedience. The hounds of hell howl at the heels of the disciples of Jesus, but as we humbly turn to God in prayer, we find peace. God will not give up on us. He will defend His cause. His cause is His glory. His glory is revealed in our transformed lives.

Do you have a personal relationship with God through faith in Jesus? Have you repented of self-sufficiency? Are you choosing to live by the power of the gospel of Jesus Christ?

Those who repent of sin and look to Jesus for salvation will be transformed and will glorify God with their lives of peace.

Hurt feelings are hard to get over. God calls us to forgive. To forgive does not mean to forget. Memories remain, which makes the forgiveness that is given very expensive to the one who forgives. Forgiveness always has a cost. To forgive is to pay the debt of another and to not hold the offense against them. If we do not forgive, the cost is conflict. Conflict has a ripple effect that impacts those closest to us. The cost of keeping hurt feelings is revealed in 2 Samuel 20.

Israel and Judah were united under David, but there were long-kept divisions that still existed. Judah was fully faithful to David, but there were people from the other tribes who heartlessly followed David out of convenience. When given the opportunity, Sheba, a Benjaminite, called Israel to follow him instead of David (vv. 1-3). Amasa was in charge of David's army, although he had sided earlier with Absalom's rebellion against David. David ordered him to gather the army and quench the revolt, but Amasa did not obey the order (vv. 4-5). Leaders must always face reality concerning the loyalty of others. Naivety is never a friend.

David wisely looked to a loyal leader, Abishai. He rallied the troops with his brother Joab, who killed Amasa (vv. 6-13). The soldiers were confused by this act. Division among leaders at home or in any organization will always destroy momentum.

Once the army had cornered Sheba and his band of revolutionaries, a wise woman intervened and had him killed, which allowed the bloodshed to stop (vv. 14-22). Wisdom will produce peace when it is guided by the right motive.

Second Samuel 20 ends with loyal leaders positioned in their proper places (vv. 23-26). Good leaders are not only able to inspire, but they are also able to provide organizational systems with strong, faithful leaders over specific areas of work. Those who would lead their home, team, or any organization well will make peacemaking a primary function, truth a primary pursuit, and loyalty a primary value.

Are you being realistic in your evaluation of the people in your life? Do you harbor hard feelings that need to be released through forgiveness? Is your life being led well?

Those who minimize conflict can pursue and often find peace.

2 Samuel 21; Galatians 1; Ezekiel 28; Psalm 77

We hate feeling that our life and future is out of our control. We want to feel that we are providing for ourselves. There is a certain pride and sense of accomplishment that comes from that. Part of that is good. God made us to be responsible creatures made in His image. The bad part about our desire to be in control is that we are sinful and cannot save our own souls. Only God can do that. Galatians 1 speaks about God's work that saves sinners and tells why we must believe the gospel and grow in it.

The apostle Paul was a faithful minister of the gospel who was used by God to spread the hope of Jesus to the world. He was able to make many disciples in Galatia, a region of present-day Turkey. Paul loved these people and wanted them to experience God's grace and peace, which can only come from God through faith in Jesus Christ (vv. 1-5).

Paul was disappointed that these saints were turning away from the God-honoring gospel that they had so happily received (v. 6). What they were believing was not true, and Paul made it clear that they needed to reject anyone who taught that there was any other way to God except through Jesus Christ (vv. 7-9). There is no other way to be saved. Jesus Christ is God. He lived a holy life and died to pay for our sin. He was raised three days later. Jesus has defeated the punishment and power of sin in order to save believers.

It appears that the people had been told that they could not trust Paul. Paul made it clear that he was not doing "man's work," but was doing what God had called him to do (vv. 10-17). While on the road to Damascus, Paul was called by God through a supernatural encounter with the risen Christ (Acts 9). When Jesus spoke to him, He made it clear that Paul was to be a witness to the gentiles. It was not until several years after this encounter that Paul made his way to Jerusalem to speak to James (Galatians 1:18-24). Paul glorified Christ with his life and teaching. He was an inspiration to the early church. Paul, once an enemy of God's people, had become a leader in God's gospel movement throughout the world.

Do you trust Jesus to save you? Are you holding to the gospel for your hope? Is your faith an inspiration to other believers?

Those who trust in Christ alone for salvation have eternal peace.

2 Samuel 22; Galatians 2; <u>Ezekiel 29</u>; Psalm 78:1-39

It is always best to be for who and what God is for, and to be against who and what God is against. The Lord is always right and always does what is best. As holy, God is blameless. As good, God is kind. As just, God is right. The one true God can be trusted, and wise people follow Him and delight to join in praying for and pursuing His will. God has not hidden His will. He may allow treachery, but in the end, He will judge all sinners just as He did with Egypt. In Ezekiel 29, the will of God is on display.

Egypt had arrogantly set itself up as a god. The Lord promised judgment for Egypt's pride and deception. There is only one true God, and the people of God, Israel, had been deceived into trusting Egypt for salvation. That is what false gods do. They rob God of glory and deceive the people. God called their leader a monster and determined to destroy him and the nation for their deceit (vv. 1-12). The enemies of God always seek to rob God of glory and to deceive people.

Although God is righteous in His judgments, He is also gracious. He promised that after forty years He would allow the Egyptians to once again establish their kingdom. Egypt would be too weak to claim to be a god and deceive the people (vv. 13-16). God does not delight in destroying. He is the maker and sustainer of life, and He would rather bless than curse.

What is so amazing about God is that He is in complete control, but human beings are completely responsible for their own actions. God led the Babylonians to gain power (vv. 17-18). The Babylonians chose to attack, but it was God who provided the victory and benefited them with Egyptian resources (vv. 19-20). This is a great mystery we cannot understand. We can know, however, that God is in control and that we are each responsible for our own actions.

God has provided Jesus, the Savior of the world, but we each must choose to repent and believe in Him. Jesus is the Messiah. He is the horn that would spring up for Israel (v. 21). He is the promised one who would heal people of sin. This is what Jesus does. He frees us from the power and punishment of sin.

Do you trust God? Are you serving His purpose? Have you seen Him provide for His purpose in your life?

Those who join God in accomplishing His will live with peace.

2 Samuel 23; Galatians 3; Ezekiel 30; Psalm 78:40-72

It is difficult not to take people and opportunities for granted. We are forgetful creatures. Assuming that we deserve what we have is our natural way of thinking. What we have is a gift. God made us, and He provides the earth we stand on and the sky we sleep under, but we often forget Him. Psalm 78:40-72 addresses the problem of human ingratitude and our inclination to take God for granted, as well as telling us where that neglect leads.

Israel was nothing. They were a wandering people who came from an insignificant shepherd. All that Israel became was because of the will of God. The Israelites forgot that. When we forget God, we forget His salvation by grace, just as Israel did (vv. 40-51). Once the punishment of sin is removed and heaven is promised, God's people often forget the supernatural grace that made that happen. This is a huge mistake because it minimizes the power of God and His place in our lives, and it leads us to think we deserve grace.

God not only saved Israel, but He also led them through the desert to their promised home (vv. 52-53). Salvation in Christ is just the beginning. It is the first step in a journey of becoming more and more like Jesus. Through many trials and challenges, God leads His people through His plan. God's plan gives us peace.

Once the Israelites were in the land, God overcame the enemies in the land that the Israelites were to possess (vv. 54-55). When we are saved, we not only gain the freedom from the punishment of sin, but we are enabled to defeat the power of sin. In the flesh, we will always battle sin. The Spirit of God helps us and empowers us to kill the sin that so easily entangles us so that we can live free in Christ.

Israel did not live free. Instead, they fell into the sin of idolatry and trusted in the gods of this world (vv. 56-58). Their sin led to their captivity in Babylon (vv. 59-66). However, God's plan was not undone, for God chose Judah to bring about His plans. Judah gave birth to David, and Jesus came through the line of David. This is the power of God. His plan never fails. We fail God, but God is too powerful to be stopped.

Have you been saved by the grace of God? Are you walking in righteousness? Is your life fulfilling God's plan?

Those who remember God and His grace live with peace.

2 Samuel 24; Galatians 4; Ezekiel 31; Psalm 79

God is in control. That does not mean that He makes the decisions for each person. We all have to choose what we will do and why. This is true of both human beings and angels. Some angels decided they did not want to serve God, and they turned against Him. Those angels became demons who now and forevermore serve under Satan. They each made a choice. Choices have consequences. In 2 Samuel 24, we are reminded of the complexity of God's will and the importance of every decision we make.

David knew God and loved God, but he still sinned against God. The problem with humanity is that we were made in God's image. That gives us power. That power has been corrupted by sin. Those who are saved by grace through faith in Christ alone are given new life, but are still tempted to sin. God allows it. David was allowed by God to be tempted to sin (v. 1). Temptations and trials are allowed by God so we can overcome and gain affirmation of our salvation. When we sin, we struggle and then turn to Christ. When we reject sin, we do so by turning to Christ. In either decision, we honor God because we turn to Him.

David sinned by taking the census. He was discouraged from doing it, but he did it anyway (vv. 2-9). After he had sinned, he was convicted of his sin and sought the Lord's forgiveness (v. 10). God is gracious to forgive. He is also gracious to teach us to avoid sin by allowing us to feel the consequences of our decisions. David felt the consequences of his sin (vv. 11-16). Remember – our sin will not only impact us, but it will also impact those whom we love.

David begged God to relent (v. 17). God provided the means for salvation. David was to build an altar and make a sacrifice for sin (vv. 18-25). God received the sacrifice, and the plague was averted. We were plagued by sin. Jesus came and made the ultimate sacrifice for our sin. The plague has been averted, and we can now walk in God's favor. This is the grace and power of God. He forgives. He gives new life. He provides.

Are your choices wise and righteous, or are they unwise and sinful? What consequences for sin have you faced? Have you sought forgiveness in Christ?

Those who choose to trust Christ live with peace.

1 Kings 1; Galatians 5; Ezekiel 32; Psalm 80

How we begin a journey will have a significant impact on the outcome of the journey, but it is not the deciding factor. Every step along the way matters. How we begin our walk with God is crucial. If it is based on grace by faith through Christ alone, our journey will have a happy ending. The first step of faith in Christ must be followed by other steps that are empowered by the Holy Spirit. In Galatians 5, followers of Jesus are encouraged to walk in the freedom that grace gives by the power of the Holy Spirit.

When the Bible speaks of freedom, it is not encouraging a lack of restraint. Freedom in Christ provides the liberty needed to live a life that is purposed by God. The Galatian church had been deceived into believing that they were made right and remained right with God by keeping the ceremonial law of the Old Testament (vv. 1-15). Paul made it abundantly clear that Jesus saves His people by grace. This grace sets us free from dependence upon ourselves and enables us to live completely dependent upon God.

The liberating dependence of God is made possible by the power of the Holy Spirit (vv. 16-24). The Holy Spirit came – just as Jesus promised He would (John 14-16). Those who repent and believe the gospel gain new life by the power of the Holy Spirit. The Spirit produces the fruit of His life in the lives of all who live in Christ. This fruit is a great blessing to the believer and to the world. What a wonderful world it will be when Christ returns and all the inhabitants of the world are only producing the fruit of the Spirit, and there will no longer be sin and death!

God is on the move, and He is moving His people along on their individual journeys. We are to *keep in step with the Spirit*, who is guiding us into God's will (Galatians 5:25). When we keep in step with the Spirit, we are able to enjoy the benefits of God's power at work in and through our lives. It is an incredible blessing to know that we are exactly where God wants us to be. It is an incredible blessing to have the Holy Spirit work in and through us.

Are you trusting completely in the atoning work of Jesus and His resurrection power for salvation? Is the Holy Spirit producing His fruit in your life? How is your journey to heaven going?

Those who journey with Jesus in the Spirit have peace.

Honesty is absolutely the best policy. Unfortunately, many of God's children have the eternal, unchanging truth in their grasp, but rarely share it. Spreading the truth of the hope of the gospel to make disciples is one of the primary purposes of God's people. Very few Christians are open and honest about their faith. Of those who tell what they know of God, only a small portion have obeyed the Great Commission of Matthew 28:19-20 and made a disciple whom they baptized and taught to observe God's commandments. In Ezekiel 33, God tells of His expectations for His people, His desire for humanity, and His righteous justice.

Just as Ezekiel was made a watchman by God, so every Christian saved by grace through faith in Christ alone has been given the responsibility to speak to the threat of sin and death and announce the trouble that humanity is in (vv. 1-9). We have all sinned. The world is filled with brokenness, but there is life and healing in Christ. Those who have experienced the life-changing power of Jesus are responsible to tell others about the seriousness of sin and the goodness of God that can save them.

God does not delight in seeing humanity suffer under the curse of sin and death. In His grace and for His glory, God has come to redeem us. Jesus has come to bring new life. Many who know of the way of Jesus have rejected Him. They are like Israel who rejected God (vv. 10-20). They will be judged and condemned for all of eternity. We are born as adversaries of God, but those who choose to repent and follow Jesus gain new, eternal life.

Giving life and forgiveness is the desire and delight of God. He does not want people to drink the cup of wrath He has prepared for all who sin, but God will bring justice – and all who live and die in sin will drink that awful cup (vv. 21-33). They will suffer forever. Those who had access to the gospel will suffer the worst. They will remember the messages they heard of God's grace and will remember how they rejected God's Word. For all of eternity, they will suffer and know that they could have been saved.

Are you making disciples of Jesus? Do you have God's heart for sinners? Is your life truly under the grace of Jesus?

Those who live to serve Jesus experience eternal peace.

OCTOBER 1
1 Kings 3; Ephesians 1; Ezekiel 34; <u>Psalms 83-84</u>

Perspective is crucial. If we lose a sense of divine, eternal perspective, we will easily be overwhelmed by life's trials and challenges. We will easily be tempted and fall into sin. Disciples of Jesus must be wise and look at every circumstance and season of life with the belief that God is in control and that He loves us. Psalm 83 and 84 are extremely helpful in giving God's people a proper biblical perspective.

It is not difficult to get overwhelmed in this world. God has strong enemies who hate Him. Because they hate God, they hate us. We are made in God's image. We are dearly loved by God. There is nothing that the forces of darkness love more than to see God's people turn away from Him and fear them. Like Asaph, we can often name the enemies we are facing and speak to their motives (Psalm 83:1-8). As God's people, we have strong weapons: the Bible, the church, and the Spirit. The Bible tells us how great God is and how much He loves us. The church provides love, compassion, and encouragement in our time of need. The Spirit guides us in truth. By keeping our minds on the Bible, being strengthened by the church, and being instructed by the Spirit, we can remember how God has been faithful in the past (vv. 9-18). We can honor God in our trials and bring glory to His name.

When we glorify God, our hearts will be turned toward heaven, from where our help comes and from where our hope is found. Heaven is our home and is the place we desire to be (Psalm 84). It is liberating to be reminded of the eternal bliss that awaits those who are found in Christ. We would rather be there than anywhere else.

When that is our true perspective, we do not mourn loss, face difficulties, or suffer without hope. We know that God is our protector and sustainer in this life. He protects and provides for His sheep. Knowing what we need and having a plan to provide, God is at work. That is what gives us peace. Our peace is in knowing that God is in control.

Do you believe that God is in control? Are you confident that God has a plan for everything you face? Have you set your heart on heaven and decided it is better to be there than anywhere else?

Those with an eternal perspective in Christ live with peace.

1 Kings 4-5; Ephesians 2; Ezekiel 35; Psalm 85

Most of us know what to do in bad times. We just hang on and do what we have to do to get through. Few people know what to do with good times. Good times are those moments in life when we are not harnessed with hardship and are free to make the choices we want with our time, money, and energy. How we use the resource of freedom tells us who we are, what we value, and what we are living for and why. First Kings 4 and 5 show that King Solomon started out with good choices.

Solomon had been in a precarious position. His brother, Adonijah, tried to take power. His reign would have positioned Solomon in a weaker position – and may have even cost him his life. Instead, Solomon became king, and through divine wisdom, he established his authority over the kingdom of Israel. This put him in a situation in which he had control of vast resources. One of the first things he did was to establish the leaders who would serve him (1 Kings 4:1-19). It is important to wisely choose the people we allow to speak into our lives and who speak for us to the rest of the world, for this has a significant impact on the lives we build. God's people must be wise and build friendships and trusted relationships with godly, effective people.

Determining a budget and calendar is crucial for success. Early in his reign, Solomon established how he would gain and spend money, and he also determined what he would give his time to (vv. 20-34). How we spend our money and time reveals what is truly important to us. God's people are called to live for Jesus, and that is to be reflected in our bank accounts and our schedules.

God calls His children to live for something bigger and better than themselves. Solomon was blessed to build the temple where God manifested His presence. This took intentionality (1 Kings 5). Those who serve God well and build His church in the world must be extremely intentional and disciplined with their resources. God is gracious to allow us to be a part of His plan. God's plan is eternal, and it brings hope and healing. What an honor to join Him!

How are you spending your money and time? Are you investing in relationships and activities that honor God? Is your goal to build God's kingdom, or are you living for less?

Those who discipline their lives to serve God live with peace.

1 Kings 6; Ephesians 3; Ezekiel 36; Psalm 86

What in the world is God doing? When we make that question about us specifically, it is not unusual for us to experience confusion. God has plans that are bigger than we are, and it is sometimes hard to understand our part in God's plan. When we make that question about God, it is not difficult to discern the hand of God. Ephesians 3 reveals the mystery of the will of God in the world and how we are to live and respond to God's greatness.

God is making known His eternal plan through the people whom He has saved and will save by His grace (vv. 1-9). God created the world with a plan. He gave humanity the capacity to choose, and we chose sin. He knew we would. In His grace and for His glory, God determined to enter into His creation to redeem sinners and transform us into saints. This plan was a mystery to many. The pre-Christ people had promises and prophesies to rely on for faith, but today those who have trusted Christ know the truth. Jesus has come and has brought redemption for humanity.

Because Christ has come in power and for His glory, the redeemed of God have a relationship with Him and a responsibility to reveal what He has done and is doing in the world (vv. 10-13). Those who believe are not only witnesses to a dying world, but they are partakers of a blessedness that grows in us (vv. 14-19). The coming of the Holy Spirit and the presence of Christ in us is a reality that is to grow in us all of our days. With all the saints, we are to become more and more like Jesus. We are to pray for one another toward this end. We are to expect and anticipate the love of God to become more real and manifest to us day by day.

This will lead to us praising God. When we discern who God is and what in the world He is doing, we will give Him the glory and honor that is due His name. We will praise Him because He is able to do more than we can possibly think or imagine, as His power works in us (v. 20). As His people, we will praise Him together and join in the eternal worship of all His saints (v. 21). What a blessing to be God's people!

Do you understand what in the world God is doing? Are you joining God in His work? Is His praise on your heart and lips?

Those who know what in the world God is doing live with peace.

God has the power to take what is dead and bring it to life. He did this with Jesus. Jesus was dead in the tomb, but God raised Him from the dead. What is impossible for a human being or any creature to do is possible for God. He is all-powerful. Thankfully, He is all-wise, kind, and loving. That means we can trust Him in how He chooses to use His power. God loves to heal and restore His creation. In Ezekiel 37, the power and goodness of God are on display in His promise to heal and restore His people.

Ezekiel was both a prophet and a priest. As a prophet, he had a unique relationship with God. God spoke directly to and through Him. As a priest, he had a unique perspective on humanity. He saw people at their worst and at their best. He was not naive. Ezekiel understood the power of God and the limitations of people. When God placed him in a valley of very dry bones and asked him if those bones could live, Ezekiel's answer was a non-response (vv. 1-3). As he looked around him, it was not difficult for him to deny the practicality of the situation. These people were dead.

God's command for him to preach to the dead was strange, but as usual, God had a plan (vv. 4-6). We may not always understand or agree with God's plans, but we can always trust Him. We can know that God has reasons for everything He does and allows. Our job is not to question God, but to trust and obey God.

Ezekiel obeyed God, and He saw the power of God revealed as he received the promise of God (vv. 7-14). God was about to reunite Israel and provide the promised Messiah who would lead the people forever (vv. 15-28). This was God's plan from the beginning. He chose Abraham, then Judah, and then David to be the line through which Jesus would come. God would do what only He could do. He would take what was dead and bring it to life. This is what God did with Jesus, and this is what God is doing in the world now. He is taking dead, divided people and giving them new life by the power of the Holy Spirit to live under the leadership of Jesus. The church is a miracle of God!

Have you been born again from sin and death? Are you willing to trust and obey God no matter what He commands?

Those who believe God and obey Him experience peace.

OCTOBER 5

1 Kings 8; Ephesians 5; Ezekiel 38; <u>Psalm 89</u>

Our perception and personal experience do not provide the final word on reality. We can only taste and see a small part of the eternal goodness of God. Our lives matter. God cares about every single person made in His image. He loves us. He desires to be in a right relationship with every person on the planet, but He won't bless sin. Those who are forgiven of sin and made righteous by grace are truly blessed and gain what only God can give – new life. Psalm 89 honors the greatness of God and points to the life Jesus gives.

Grace is possible through Jesus alone. He is the promised one who came and fulfilled the Old Testament prophecies. We sing praise to His name and pray in His name (vv. 1-2). Jesus created a new covenant in His blood, just as God said He would (vv. 3-4). Christ has come, and all who believe in Him praise His name and proclaim the goodness of His steadfast love.

Jesus is all-powerful. He is praised in the heavens and adored by the angels (v. 5). Nothing compares to Him (vv. 6-8). He rules over all creation with justice (vv. 9-16). Jesus is the ruler of His people, and they are exalted and cared for by Him (vv. 17-18). Not only did Jesus pay for sin and overcome death, but He is now ruling in heaven and bringing about God's eternal decrees. He will soon return and make all things new. He is Lord over all!

God's plan cannot be stopped. Having promised the Messiah from the beginning and having confirmed that the plan would be fulfilled through the line of David, God has saved and will save a people for Himself and bring them safely to heaven (vv. 19-37). Sometimes it might seem as if God has abandoned us (vv. 38-45). In those difficult times, the redeemed are free to call out to God and seek His face based on the promises He has made (vv. 46-51). God delights to care for His children and to hear them pray His Word. Through prayer, the Lord is exalted by His people and we are truly blessed. In that blessed state of peace, the redeemed of God bless the Lord (v. 52). It is a blessing of praise that will last forever.

Have you trusted in Jesus to be your Savior and the leader of your life? Do you delight to praise God for His greatness and goodness to you? Are you confident in God's power?

Those who look to Jesus in faith live with peace.

The world is a very harsh place, but it was not meant to be this way. God placed humanity in a garden that we were to care for. Had we done our job, the world would be filled with the beauty of that garden, and billions of image bearers all under the authority of God would be blessed. Instead, we live in a broken world. We do have hope. God is gracious. We must choose to follow God or face consequences. In 1 Kings 9, Solomon shows us the way of the world, along with blessings we can gain and mistakes to avoid.

Solomon obeyed God and built the temple for the Lord. The Lord spoke to Solomon and commanded him to be faithful to God and to train Israel and future kings to be faithful (vv. 1-5). The blessings that God gives to those who trust and obey Him are wonderful, but the curse for disobedience is awful (vv. 6-9). God will not bless sin. He is not afraid to remove His manifest presence from places and people who reject Him. Those who live without the presence of God are dead to God and are without hope in the world. They have no hope in the kingdom that is to come.

Solomon was a wise man, but he made mistakes. He was seemingly not careful to give sufficient honor to those who were good to him (vv. 10-14). Hiram was not pleased with the cities that Solomon had given to him. It is crucial that God's people be fair and just in their dealings, and also to be thankful for what we receive.

There are winners and losers in our broken world. Because of God's blessing and their obedience to God, the children of Israel were winners and the foreigners and enemies of God were not. Solomon had the foreigners provide forced labor so that the Israelites were freed from doing that work (vv. 15-23).

Although Solomon was wise, he set himself up for failure by marrying Pharaoh's daughter (v. 24). Yes, he continued to worship God and build a wealthy nation (vv. 25-28), but marrying a non-believer set him and future generations up for disaster. God's people must obey God and worship Him alone.

Has God blessed you to know, love, and obey Him? Are you acting justly in the world? Will future generations be blessed by the example of faithfulness to God that you have set?

Those who obey God in all aspects of life live with peace.

OCTOBER 7
1 Kings 10; Philippians 1; Ezekiel 40; Psalm 91

The life God designed for humanity is certainly individualistic, but is best suited for community. We each must make decisions about what we believe and how we live. These decisions impact us and those we love. In Christ, our individual lives are blessed to be in a communion of saints whom God calls us to journey with to heaven. Philippians 1 reminds us of the impact of our individual decisions and the need for a church family.

The church at Philippi was an important church for many reasons. A portion of God's Word was sent to the early church at Philippi, a letter that now serves us all. The letter to the church at Philippi is a blessing to all believers. It calls us to live in Christ as saints who are given grace and peace from God our Father and Jesus, the Son of God (vv. 1-2).

Every saint is called by God to inspire joy in others (vv. 3-5) and to grow in Christ (vv. 6-11). Life is hard. There are plenty of means provided by the world, our flesh, and the devil to keep us discouraged. Each saint is responsible to live a life that encourages other believers as they examine our growth and see the real difference that the risen Christ makes in us.

What helps others is not as much when they see us thrive in times of ease, but when they see us thrive in hardship. Paul was in prison, but he was encouraged to know that his imprisonment was God's will (vv. 12-14). While the enemies of God may be stimulated to stir up trouble when they see us suffer, the saints are challenged to be bold (vv. 15-18). The boldness of Paul and his perspective on suffering give all saints reason to rejoice, just as Paul did (vv. 19-30). When we are happy in Jesus, it is because we are standing firm in the gospel with others who believe. Our faithful stance as individuals and as local churches makes clear the ultimate destruction that is to come to the enemies of God and the sure victory that is ahead for all who follow Jesus.

Are you living a faithful life in Christ? Do other believers draw strength from your life? How are you growing in Christ?

Those who choose to live for Jesus and make it their goal to be a help and a source of hope to others have peace in their soul.

1 Kings 11; Philippians 2; Ezekiel 41; Psalms 92-93

Humility and gratitude are two of the most crucial elements in the life of a disciple of Jesus. When we realize how holy and awesome God is and how sinful and weak we are, it becomes overwhelming to think of how God loves us and is gracious toward us. When we experience God's love and grace, we cannot help but be humble and grateful. Philippians 2 is a wonderful source of truth that helps followers of Jesus to be humble and grateful.

Jesus existed before there was time and space. He is holy and perfect in every way. He loves us. In obedience to the Father, Jesus became one of us to rescue us from sin and death. What He did is inspiring to those who believe. He unifies us by His works (vv. 1-11). In His love and grace, Jesus came and sacrificed Himself to save us. He did not look to His own interests, but He chose to provide salvation for us. He humbled Himself to serve us. When God's people follow Christ's example by humbling themselves to serve the greater good, God is honored, the gospel is shared, and the world is made a little bit better.

It is an honor to be able to live a life of sacrifice in the name of and for the glory of Jesus. Those who know the greatness of God through the grace of Jesus are thankful for the life they get to live in Christ. He lives in and through us and enables us to gain assurance of our salvation (vv. 12-18). We can live each day knowing that when we are judged, we will be admitted into God's heaven to celebrate with all of the saints what God has done. This future makes us glad and causes us to rejoice with thanksgiving.

When we live humbly and gratefully in Christ, we will make what the world thinks are great sacrifices, but it will not seem so to us. Like Timothy and Epaphroditus, we will simply do what we are called and gifted to do, even if it costs us our lives (vv. 19-30). Our lives are means by which we show our love and delight in Jesus. What is called sacrifice is simply love and devotion being lived out for the glory and honor of King Jesus. Those who trust in Jesus give all they can, knowing that heaven is the reward.

Are you humbled by Jesus? Do you live a grateful existence? Is it easy for you to sacrifice for the Lord's sake?

Those who give all they are for the glory of God have peace.

1 Kings 12; Philippians 3; Ezekiel 42; <u>Psalm 94</u>

Self-preservation and self-promotion guided by the flesh and human insecurity lead to injustice and frustration. Societies that are cursed with dishonest, selfish leaders are filled with angry populations that do not trust authorities or those who promote them. The citizens often end up calling for revolutions that can lead to destruction. Psalm 94 is the prayer of a frustrated person who wants to see God rise up and remove unjust rulers.

Jesus is the perfect leader. He came to serve. The power He had was used to care for the hurting and to provide cures for the ills of society. Those in leadership at the time of the writing of Psalm 94 provided leadership that was the opposite of what Jesus provides. They were proud and not humble (vv. 1-4). They caused harm (v. 5). They killed the most vulnerable (v. 6). They thought they would not get caught (v. 7). Left to ourselves, we can become monsters and do the most heinous acts.

Thankfully, God is in control. He knows what evil is up to, and He has a plan to overcome it (vv. 8-11). God's desire is not to destroy, but to disciple. The Lord is willing to forgive. Wise people will look to the heart of God and receive divine discipline as an act of gracious correction (vv. 12-15). The Lord is just, and it is wise to pursue justice for all rather than personal gain at the expense of others.

It can sometimes appear that the Lord is not in control. It can sometimes appear that the Lord does not care and that He is going to allow the wicked to overcome. That is what it looked like on the day that Jesus died on the cross. In reality, the Lord is at work. He will rescue His people and provide justice (vv. 16-23). There is nothing that can stop God! He is the Almighty! What He plans to do will be done. The faithful can always be certain that the evil of the world has a limit. That limitation is determined by God. God uses evil to accomplish His good purpose. It is hard to discern God's hand. When we are hurting and are in need of help, God often seems distant and unconcerned. However, God knows, God cares, and God provides.

Are you part of the problem of injustice in the world? How can you join God in helping the hurting? Have you seen God provide for His plan through your pain before?

Those who rely on God and act justly live with peace.

1 Kings 13; Philippians 4; Ezekiel 43; Psalms 95-96

We have a tendency to serve God and others to the extent that it pleases us, but not to the full extent that we could serve. We are half-hearted creatures in our sin-tarnished flesh. What we could do is rarely done to the fullest extent because we don't have the heart for God or a truth-based, biblical mindset. The experience of a man of God in 1 Kings 13 reminds us of the importance of doing exactly and only what God commands us to do.

Jeroboam was being religiously devout, but he was not being faithful to God. God sent a godly man to call out Jeroboam's sin and to call down a curse and a promise (vv. 1-3). The promise that Josiah would come and serve God and that the altar would be used to bring death to evil priests and would be crushed into ashes was incredibly detailed. To those who believe the Word of God, it is not surprising that everything happened just as the man of God said.

When Jeroboam tried to arrest the man of God, his arm shriveled. This humbled the king and led him to ask the man of God to pray to the man's God on the king's behalf. Grace was given according to the prayer of the righteous (vv. 4-6). The prayer of the righteous is powerful. Seeking to gain an ally, Jeroboam invited the man to dine with him, but the man of God refused (vv. 7-10). God's people need nothing except God's provision for His plan.

The man of God was faithful, but not fully. He was easily persuaded to turn away from God's command (vv. 11-32). We must always discern what is true based upon God's Word, and never based upon our feelings or the words of other people. God's Word is true and trustworthy. It is to be fully obeyed. Partial obedience will lead to total destruction. God demands complete submission.

Just as the man of God returned to the land God had commanded him to leave, Jeroboam returned to his sin (vv. 33-34). A single experience of divine intervention does not make someone a disciple. True disciples remain faithful to God to the end. A life that is faithful to God demands obedience and singular dedication.

Are you fully obeying God? Can you discern what is true based on the Bible? Is your devotion to Jesus real and permanent?

Those who serve God with a willing heart to the fullest extent of their ability will live and die in peace.

1 Kings 14; <u>Colossians 1</u>; Ezekiel 44; Psalms 97-98

The world wants pleasant, inclusive, and nonobtrusive religion. God offers none of that. The gospel of God speaks of humanity's sin and the necessity of a blood-bought salvation. That salvation is exclusive. It is in Christ alone. In Christ, believers of Jesus have their entire identity and activity in life altered. Colossians 1 spells out the fundamentals of the gospel and what is required of those who are saved by Jesus.

Jesus gives us a unique calling to pursue and a church family to serve (vv. 1-2). Paul was an apostle. This was his calling given to him by God. He did not choose it. God chose it for him. Paul was writing to a church family. Every redeemed saint is a member of the universal church, but is called to be a faithful member of a local church. Those who are members of a local church family have grace and peace from God our Father.

Jesus requires His saints to live by faith in love with hope and to pray faithfully for God's people (vv. 3-14). The gospel is the object of our faith, the inspiration for our love, and the reason for our hope. We hear of it through God's people, and we pray for those who know the truth to bear fruit and grow in the knowledge of the new life we are given. The Christian life is filled with light because Jesus delivers us from darkness.

Jesus is the image of the invisible God (vv. 15-23). He is God manifested in flesh. He created and now sustains all things. Through Him, there is reconciliation between sinners and God. Jesus took the punishment of sinners so that the just requirements of God are fully satisfied. Those who live and continue in the faith will become more and more holy until the day we enter into heaven and find eternal rest in God's presence.

Jesus is at work through His people (vv. 24-29). Like Paul, every saint has a unique way of living out the general calling that God gives all of His people. We are all to pursue Christ and help as many people as possible to know and love Him. That happens as God's Word is preached and the hope of glory is experienced.

Are you a believer in the exclusive claims of Jesus Christ? Are you praying for God's work? Are you becoming more like Jesus?

Those who know Jesus know and experience peace.

1 Kings 15; Colossians 2; <u>Ezekiel 45</u>; Psalms 99-101

How we read the Bible will determine our understanding of reality. God's Word was given to an original audience in a particular place that was facing unique challenges. The Bible is to be understood in light of its original readers, and also in light of the rest of God's revealed truth. We must never try to make the Bible say what we want it to mean. The Bible is God's Word to all people, and it reveals what is true. Ezekiel 45 provides a powerful picture of the world that is to come.

The original readers would have found great comfort in this promise of God. They were in exile and were looking for the coming Messiah who would revitalize their nation and rule in a powerful way so that they could have peace and blessings. There would be order to society. The ordering of the land let the people know that God had a plan (vv. 1-6). God's plan is being accomplished now. His kingdom is coming and will bring order and peace.

The prince who was to come would establish the order and peace the people longed for through justice and strength (vv. 7-8). He would be sovereign and would gain honor and prestige. When Christ came, He instituted a new order through the church. The world now is being impacted by the hope of Jesus. One day, Jesus will rule over all, and peace will reign everywhere forever.

The peace that Jesus will bring is pictured in the peace the people longed for in the land they would return to after the exile was over (vv. 9-25). Those who were in exile longed for a new life, and now we who are in exile long for the world that will come when Christ returns. It will be a world filled with justice. Each person will happily serve God in holy reverence of Jesus. The Prince of Peace will provide structures that celebrate the salvation of God so people can live in a constant state of worship. Jesus will be at the center of this new world. He will reign with perfection and will restore His created order. *Come, Lord Jesus!*

Do you long for the second coming of Christ? Are you living faithfully under His leadership now and seeking to expand His kingdom in our broken world? Is Jesus the center of your life and the reason you have hope?

Those who live for and look to the return of Jesus have peace.

1 Kings 16; Colossians 3; Ezekiel 46; <u>Psalm 102</u>

Jesus said, *I have said these things to you, that in me you may have peace. In the world you will have tribulation. But take heart; I have overcome the world* (John 16:33). God gives peace to all who abide in His grace. His peace is not circumstantial. It is a peace that lives within those who trust and obey Him. We are going to struggle in this life. That is a promise of God. It is a promise that is easy to believe. The good news for the redeemed of Christ is that we can live with peace in any circumstance. In Psalm 102, we read the prayer of an afflicted child of God, and we learn how we are to think, pray, and pursue God's peace in tough times.

Most people believe that the writer was in exile. Some think that the prophet Daniel wrote this psalm, but we don't know for sure. Regardless of who the writer is, we can all understand that this person was in pain. He was praying in distress (vv. 1-2). When we suffer, our first thought needs to be to pray. It is wise to think about who God is and to talk to Him about our life in light of how powerful He is and how needy we are (vv. 3-17).

We are to pray not only for ourselves, but also for those who will come after us (vv. 18-22). Every generation will have to deal with problems. The problems are different, but also very similar. The cause may be different, but the feelings are the same. God is the same. The peace that comes from God is the same. God looks down from heaven and hears the groans of His people. He cares for us and helps us to worship Him with praise.

This praise comes from a desire to honor God no matter what. The pursuit of a saint is the same in all circumstances: trust and obey God. The writer of the psalm understood that his situation might not change. He also understood that God is sovereign and everlasting. His prayer is practical and is based on the promises of God (vv. 23-28). Every generation will come and go, but God will remain. The Lord provides for His people. God's people must trust and obey. It is under the care of the Almighty that we dwell securely in peace.

Have you gone through seasons of suffering and found God faithful? Do you trust in God's plan and power? What gives you peace in the midst of life's storms?

Those who trust in Jesus and abide in His promises have peace.

1 Kings 17; Colossians 4; Ezekiel 47; Psalm 103

God is full of surprises. Just when we think we have Him and life figured out, He shows us what we do not and could not know on our own – and everything changes. This is the experience of the saints of God. We do what we know to do based on the Word of God. We obey to the best of our ability. God graciously guides us and shows His kindness to us through others. It is a blessed life to walk with God. It is a life of peace. It is a life that requires faith. In 1 Kings 17, we see something of the way of God and the blessings He brings to those who walk by faith.

Elijah had obeyed God and brought the message of God's divine justice on the land (v. 1). This would have put him in danger of King Ahab. God intervened. The Lord spoke and commanded Elijah to go to the middle of nowhere to be taken care of through miraculous means (vv. 2-6). God always provides for His people when they follow His plans. After a while, the provision was removed and another step of faith was needed (v. 7). God's people must never put their trust in God's provision, but must trust and obey the Provider.

The next step for Elijah was a trip to Zarephath, where God had culti- vated a widow's heart to live sacrificially by faith (vv. 8-12). By faith, Elijah commanded her to provide for him, and he promised her that in the process, God would provide for her and her son as well (vv. 13-16). By obeying, this widow learned that God is faithful and provides for His plans for His people.

She and Elijah probably thought they had God and life figured out and that there would be no more need for faith – but that is not the way of God. He always allows trials of various kinds in order to strengthen the faith of His people. God allowed her son to die. She thought it was divine justice for her previous sin (vv. 17-18). Elijah lived by faith and asked God for a miracle. The boy was raised, and through this experience, the woman learned that her past sin was pardoned (vv. 19-24). She gained peace through faith. This is the way of God.

How has God required you to live by faith? Did you grow in your under- standing of God and His grace in the process? What kind of sacrifices do you need to make by faith to honor God?

***Those who walk by faith experience God's grace
and provision, which gives them peace.***

1 Kings 18; 1 Thessalonians 1; Ezekiel 48; Psalm 104

Good, godly friends are a true treasure to every disciple of Jesus. God has made us to be creatures who connect with other people in meaningful relationships. The hallmark of every Christian friendship is love bound in truth, expressed in encouragement, and exercised in a godly lifestyle. The apostle Paul, writing one of his first letters that would become a book of the Bible, encouraged his friends. In 1 Thessalonians 1, we see the love that Christian friends get to experience with one another.

These friends were bound by the shared truth they held to. God had revealed His love in Jesus Christ to the Thessalonians through Paul's preaching (v. 1). The truth that Paul brought to them was life-changing. Paul, Silvanus, and Timothy had ventured to their city by the will of God. They preached about the grace that God gives through His Son. This grace has the power to give peace to all who receive it.

This grace was troublesome to the Jews of that city, and they persecuted Paul and caused him to have to leave. Although Paul left physically, he never forgot the Christians there. He loved them and wrote to encourage them (vv. 2-5). Paul remembered them in his prayers. Their faith was working and was leading them to be laborers of love with steadfast hope in the Lord. The Holy Spirit had moved on them in power, and they became followers of Jesus. Paul encouraged them to know that their standing in Christ was real.

This standing became a lifestyle. Paul taught them how to live, and these friends now shared a lifestyle that honored God. It was a way of life that others could model their lives after (vv. 6-9). When God's children turn from idols and choose to walk in obedience to Christ, the world notices. Testimonies of faithfulness inspire others to live lives that honor God and bless others.

Do you have a strong circle of friends? Is encouragement a central aspect of those friendships? Has your godly lifestyle been used to inspire others to believe and remain steadfast in their personal devotion to Jesus?

Those with godly friendships in God's grace live with peace.

1 Kings 19; 1 Thessalonians 2; <u>Daniel 1</u>; Psalm 105

We should never be surprised at dramatic changes that happen in our world and lives. This world is broken and is far from what God made it to be. There will always be changes in our world of sin and darkness. Some will be good, but many will be harsh. During times of change, God's people have a sure anchor that will not move. Jesus will not fail. Daniel 1 presents a challenging set of circumstances for a few of God's people and provides insight into how all of God's people can be sustained in times of change.

When darkness is on the move and Christians find themselves in a godless culture, it is important to remember who we are in Christ. Israel had been taken into captivity, but Daniel, Hananiah, Mishael, and Azariah each had a godly name to remind them who they were (vv. 1-7). The name *Daniel* means "God is my judge." *Hananiah* means "God has favored." *Mishael* means "Who is as God is?" *Azariah* means "God has helped." These young men had been provided with a godly heritage for the pagan world in which they would live. Those who are taught to know, love, and obey Jesus and who carry the name of "Christian" are blessed.

These four men refused to defile themselves and were provided with the favor of the steward who was responsible for them (vv. 8-16). These four ended up being more healthy than all the other youths. A godly lifestyle will always produce health physically, mentally, emotionally, and spiritually.

These young men did not feel sorry for themselves. Instead of focusing on what they did not like about their new life, they sought to make the most of their opportunity. They leaned into their assignments and were successful (vv. 17-21). God's people can look past their feelings and fears and stay focused on the Lord. When we live to honor God and use our natural abilities and spiritual gifts to their fullest potential, we won't have time to feel sorry for ourselves. We will be too busy fulfilling God's plan.

Are you living up to your name that all redeemed saints are given – Christian? Do you have others who are seeking the Lord with you? How have you seen God provide for you in difficult days and use your abilities to enable you to thrive?

Those who hold on to Jesus in every circumstance live with peace.

1 Kings 20; 1 Thessalonians 3; Daniel 2; <u>Psalm 106</u>

Praise is a natural function of human existence. All people in all places in every generation have been prone to praise. Not only do we give praise, but we also seek the blessing of receiving praise that comes with a life that is obedient to God. Giving praise to God is the best thing a person can do. He is worthy of our praise. Psalm 106 gives an outline as to why all of God's people are to praise Him.

We are to praise God because of who He is to us (vv. 1-5). He is good to us, and His love for us will never fail. He has done great things that no creature can do. He is God. As God, He has established order in His creation. We call it justice. When families and societies observe God's law and do what is righteous, there is a great blessing. All who know God long to see that blessing. It is a blessing that enables people to fulfill their created purpose and, in the process, provide for their needs to God's glory.

We are to praise God because of what He has done for us (vv. 6-46). Like Israel, all of God's people have sinned and fallen short of God's right expectation of us – yet God has not abandoned us. Just as God rescued Israel from the bondage of the Egyptians through miraculous means, so God has rescued the followers of Jesus who look to the miraculous grace of Christ. In Jesus, all who believe in Him are given freedom from the power and punishment of sin. God's grace is sufficient to see us through the difficulties of life. His provision is reason for praise!

We are to praise God because we can go to Him in prayer and seek His divine provision (vv. 47-48). *Help!* That is one of the best prayers any of us can pray to God. Our cry for help is a cry to be saved from a lost life and to be gathered to God with all of His people. We are like sheep, and we need the Good Shepherd to rally us and guide us to the path that leads to the blessed hope of God. This blessed hope is the goal of God's people. All who hear this prayer and seek God's salvation say, "Amen!" We agree that God alone is our peace and is the everlasting God we need in life and in death.

Do you delight to praise God? Is your life one that God can bless and praise? Are you living as a member of a local church and sharing in the journey toward heaven with them?

Those who praise the Lord rightly live with peace.

1 Kings 21; 1 Thessalonians 4; Daniel 3; Psalm 107

The world is filled with injustice and violence. God sees it all and loves us still. There is a natural inclination in all of us to sin. We do not all act on our desires to sin, but the desires are there. When we do sin, God is faithful and just to forgive us if we humble ourselves, repent, and seek His grace. First Kings 21 tells us that Ahab sinned, but found favor with God by humbling himself.

The events related to Naboth's vineyard are sad, but they are not uncommon in this world (vv. 1-16). A person with very little power has something of great value. Those with power want it and seek to obtain it. When they cannot get it through just means, they pursue sinful tactics. Rather than live with the peace that comes as a result of mutual respect and honor, human beings create conflict and chaos by pursuing selfish, sinful desires.

God sees this sin and brings judgment (vv. 17-24). God's judgment is not always swift. The Lord is patient. He will often provide time and opportunity for repentance. Those who repent and seek forgiveness in Christ gain peace with God and help produce peace in the world. Those who refuse to repent will face judgment. Judgment was promised to Ahab and his wife. Judgment comes to all in the end.

Ahab believed the words of Elijah and was humbled by them (vv. 25-29). Ahab was a very evil and idolatrous man. He did not have much regard for God, but when he heard of the judgment he would experience, he humbled himself. This kept the promised calamity from happening to him. He did not repent. He did not return the land to Naboth's family. There was no change. God demands that we not only humble ourselves, but also that we repent. To repent is to stop doing what is wrong and to do what is right. Ahab did not do what was right, and his sinful behavior led to God's judgment in his son's lifetime. There is always a cost to sin. God has paid for our sin through the death of Jesus. All who look to Him will be saved, will have peace with God, and will be a blessing.

What sin do you need to repent of and, by grace, gain peace with God? Are there negative consequences in your life that are a result of sin? Have you trusted in Christ to gain forgiveness?

Those who humbly repent of sin have peace with God.

1 Kings 22; 1 Thessalonians 5; Daniel 4; Psalms 108-109

There is great peace in knowing that what was, is, and will be is planned by God. Every person who repents and believes the gospel is saved, and salvation brings with it more blessings than a person can count. It will take all of eternity to praise God for all of His goodness and for the good He has done. Writing to the church at Thessalonica, the apostle Paul speaks about the goodness of God and His blessings that belong to His children (1 Thessalonians 5).

As children of God, the redeemed of God do not need to concern themselves with when Christ will come and what the circumstances surrounding His second coming will be (vv. 1-11). Jesus is going to come like a thief in the night. No one can know the precise moment. What we can do is live lives that honor Him so that when He does come, we are ready. We don't have to be hypocrites and fake it until we make it. We can make our way through life in the hope of the gospel and experience peace day by day.

As children of God, we belong to a family that is structured to bring healing and hope to those who believe. God provides leaders who are called according to His purpose. We are to live under them and at peace with one another (vv. 12-13). Living in peace takes place when we serve people according to their needs. We each have different needs depending on our personal challenges. Sometimes we need to be admonished, sometimes encouraged, and sometimes helped, but we always need to have patience with each other (v. 14). We are to always be kind to one another and to pray all of the time with gratitude toward God (vv. 15-18). We are to honor the Spirit and love the Word of God (vv. 19-21). This is how the family of God is able to thrive.

As children of God, we are to abstain from evil (v. 22), be sanctified (v. 23), and trust God to accomplish His purpose for and through His family (vv. 24-28). Living the life of a child of God is not complicated, and it produces peace in the process. This glorifies God by revealing His goodness and the good He does.

How has God been good to you? Are you living as a faithful child of God? In what ways can you better serve your siblings in Christ and be served by them?

Children of God enjoy the peace of God.

2 Kings 1; 2 Thessalonians 1; <u>Daniel 5</u>; Psalms 110-111

What does it mean to fear the Lord? Fear has a very negative connotation in our therapeutic age and in our emotionally driven world. In the Bible, the fear of God is a positive thing. It is respect and honor that is bestowed on God in the heart of a person so that decisions are always based out of respect for God. There are often negative consequences when fear of God is missing. The fall of the king of Babylon as recorded in Daniel 5 inspires us to fear the Lord.

King Belshazzar was surrounded by a thousand subjects who were seeking to bolster his success. To impress them, he called for the holy vessels of God's temple to be used for their drinks. They used those holy vessels to praise their idols (vv. 1-4). This is what happens when human beings don't know God. They become prideful and dependent on created things for hope.

God showed up to the party. He wrote an encrypted message that only Daniel was able to discern (vv. 5-28). The message was clear that the king and his country would soon fall to the Medes and Persians. There is always a consequence for rejecting God. Life without God is chaotic. The world is filled with ups and downs. Those who walk with Jesus are able to trust in God to work His plan. Those who live their lives without God are trapped in a cycle of ups and downs that frustrate and confound.

To celebrate Daniel's achievement, the king gave Daniel a reward that he had already requested to be given to someone else (v. 29). That night, the prophecy of Belshazzar's fall came to be. Darius became the new ruler (vv. 30-31). This is the way of the world. Those in power often become proud, and then at some point they fall. It may be by failure, or it may be at the end of life when death takes everything they had. This is the sad reality of all who live without God. They ultimately lose everything for all of eternity. Only those who know God and fear Him live and die with peace.

Do you have a healthy fear of God? What characteristics have you noticed in those who do not fear God? How can you grow in your fear of God?

Those who fear God live with peace.

2 Kings 2; 2 Thessalonians 2; Daniel 6; <u>Psalms 112-113</u>

Psalm 1 speaks of the blessed man and what he is like. In Matthew 5, Jesus speaks of the person who is blessed and what that person receives. Psalm 112 gives another overview of the blessed life and why it is to be pursued. This life is only possible because of the God from whom all blessings flow. Psalm 113 explains that the name of God is a blessed name because God is a blessed being and blesses those who look to Him by faith.

While some of the blessings of Psalm 112 are capable of being experienced in this life, there are some that will be fulfilled in the final restoration at the second coming of Christ. Those who are blessed fear the Lord and delight in His judgments (v. 1). In our broken world with infrequent justice, there is great peace in knowing that God is the ultimate judge and brings holy, perfect judgments in life and death. The blessed are generous with the poor (vv. 5, 9). Blessed people are *not afraid of bad news* because they know that the Lord works all things for the ultimate good (v. 7). The wicked people of the world hate the righteous because while they cannot keep what they lived for, the blessed do (v. 10).

The blessed look forward to the coming of Jesus. They will receive a reward that does not perish (v. 10). They will be remembered forever (v. 6). Their reward will last forever, along with Christ's righteousness received by faith (v. 3). They and everyone whom they have helped to know the Lord will reign with Jesus forever (v. 2). When Christ returns, there will be eternal joy!

This blessed life is possible because of the greatness of God, who is worthy to be praised forever (Psalm 113:1-2). From beginning to end, Jesus is worthy of our praise (v. 3). He is above all and unlike all (vv. 4-6). He is good to those who seek His reward (vv. 7-8). He gives a home to those who are barren, and He gives them the joy of His eternal family (v. 9). Every saint of God is able to serve the Lord and bring the light and life of Jesus to others. All is done by the saints to the praise of God. He alone is worthy!

Are you living the blessed life found in Christ alone? What blessings are you missing? Is God the one you live to praise?

> ***Those who live a life that is blessed by God to the praise***
> ***of the name of God have everlasting peace.***

God will often allow difficulties to arise in order to draw us close to Him. God is at work in every circumstance in life. He has a plan for everything that happens – from national calamities that make the news to personal decisions that are made in the privacy of a heart. God knows. God sees. God is at work. In 2 Kings 3, God drew three kings together and forced them to seek wisdom from a prophet and victory through God's hands.

Jehoram was not a godly man, but he was not as evil as his parents (vv. 1-3). When Moab rebelled against him, he asked Jehoshaphat, the king of Judah, to help him. Because Edom was under Judean rule, they also went with Judah to help Israel (vv. 4-8). These three kings did not consult the Lord, and they lost their way in a wilderness where there was no water (vv. 9-10). Godly people who are wise will always seek the Lord before taking any significant action. Without God, we lose our way – and destruction is inevitable.

Elisha was nearby and was sought out for counsel (vv. 11-12). Elisha mocked Jehoram for his idolatry, but he was willing to serve them because of the faith of Jehoshaphat (vv. 13-17). Miraculous provision was promised along with victory. This was said to be a small thing to God (v. 18). Everything is small to God. We often struggle and wonder if God can help. There is no limit to God's power. We must learn to trust Him and obey.

Elisha promised victory and commanded the armies to ruin the land of Moab (v. 19). God provided what was promised through the prophet (vv. 20-26). In the last moments of the battle, the king of Moab sacrificed his son to his false god and the Moabite soldiers began to fight fiercely, causing Israel and those with them to withdraw (v. 27). How strange that they would fear these Moabites who were clearly defeated! God's people must be careful to not be intimidated by those of this world. This requires faith. Faith will always result in obedience to Jesus. Each day of our lives, we choose either faith in God or fear of the world. Choose faith!

Do you look to God before making serious decisions? Whom do you turn to for godly counsel? Are you walking by faith in God, or are you living in fear of worldly people and circumstances?

Those who trust and obey God live with peace.

2 Kings 4; <u>1 Timothy 1</u>; Daniel 8; Psalm 116

There is an art to mentoring well. It is a harmonic symphony of truth, affection, and structure that forms a relationship with the purpose of making one person like another. This happens all the time in families, teams, and in industry. When it happens in the church in the power of the Holy Spirit, the result is miraculous. In 1 Timothy 1, Paul's mentoring skills are on display.

Timothy was Paul's spiritual child (vv. 1-2), though Paul had not led Timothy to Christ. Paul met Timothy while in Derbe and Lystra. Timothy was a third generation believer after his mother, Eunice, and grandmother, Lois. His father was a Greek. Before taking him on his second missionary journey, Paul circumcised him (Acts 16:1-3). The foundation of their connection was Jesus Christ. There was a lot of trust in their relationship.

Timothy was responsible for the church at Ephesus. There was a lot of work to be done in order for that congregation to become a thriving, autonomous body of believers. The greatest challenge to any congregation is doctrinal purity. Paul commanded Timothy to see to it that this congregation was being taught the truth about the gospel so that a sincere faith would be produced (1 Timothy 1:3-5). As is often the case, there were teachers causing confusion and division. Paul explained what Timothy was to teach (vv. 6-11). It is the gospel that sustains the faith of a person and a church.

Paul did not pretend to be something he wasn't. He was honest with Timothy about what he once was. Paul praised God for the mercy he had received in Christ Jesus (vv. 12-17). All mature believers take their sin very seriously. It often seems as if we are the worst of sinners. All sin is bad, but the weight of our own is the worst. Paul's testimony rings true for many believers.

Paul affirmed Timothy's calling and reminded him of what had been said about him in the past to encourage him to engage in his work with confidence (vv. 18-19). Paul reminded him of those who had failed and had been turned over to Satan (v. 20). God gives us positive and negative examples from which to learn.

Who has mentored you in Christ? What did they teach you? Are you living out the faith Christ has called you to?

Those who are mentored in love are blessed with confident peace.

2 Kings 5; 1 Timothy 2; <u>Daniel 9</u>; Psalms 117-118

Effective prayer is always based upon the Bible. If we are to pray rightly, we must pray according to the Word of God. The Bible is God's revealed truth to humanity. It is by the Word of God that we understand the way and will of God. We are to walk in God's way and pray for God's will to be done. Daniel knew the Bible. He prayed for God's will. God responded to his prayer. Daniel 9 provides believers with the peace to know that God hears His people and responds to those who pray according to His Word.

Daniel had been reading the Bible. More specifically, he had been reading the book of Jeremiah. Through his study, Daniel was able to discern that God was about to act on behalf of His people because the seventy years of punishment were almost over (vv. 1-2). With these facts in mind, Daniel prayed a prayer of repentance (vv. 3-15). He used the books of Moses to guide his prayer. He acknowledged Israel's sin, and then he asked for forgiveness (vv. 16-19). This repentance was sought to bring God glory. Supplications are presented rightly when they are for God's glory.

The Lord heard Daniel's prayer, and Gabriel was dispatched to give Daniel an answer (vv. 20-22). Gabriel told him that the Lord had responded at the beginning of his pleas for mercy (v. 23). The Lord knows the information that is on our heart. It is good for us to outline the facts and tell the Lord what we know. God already knows, but He delights to hear His children speak to Him because He loves them. Gabriel made it clear that Daniel was loved by God. The greatest comfort of the redeemed is to know that they are loved by God Almighty and that He hears their prayers.

Gabriel explained God's plan for the future. This information was consistent with the rest of Scripture (vv. 24-27). While there is disagreement on the meaning of the weeks and timeframe, it is clear that Jesus was coming as promised. He would atone for inequity. The world would continue to suffer, but God's will would be done. We can know that Christ has come and that God's will is being done according to His Word. We are to pray for His will to be done.

Are you praying God's Word? How has God answered your prayers? Do you trust in God's faithfulness?

Those who pray God's Word live with peace.

OCTOBER 25
2 Kings 6; 1 Timothy 3; Daniel 10; <u>Psalm 119:1-24</u>

God gives a great blessing to those who walk in His way in obedience to His Word. That is why the Bible is so precious to the saints. It provides instruction in God's ways and is the source of all truth. By knowing the Bible and obeying it happily, the saints of God do the Lord's bidding and find peace for their souls. Psalm 119:1-24 tells of the blessing of God that comes from obedience to His Word and explains how to maximize the Bible's effect.

The Bible consistently draws distinctions. In Genesis, there is a distinction revealed between light and darkness, between Abel and Cain, and between those who sought the Lord, like Noah, and those who did not. There are those who are blessed by God and those who are not (vv. 1-3). Those who are blessed have a specific way of life. It is a life ordered around the instruction of Scripture. Saints desire this instruction and pursue it, and they praise the Lord for giving it to them (vv. 4-8). There is much benefit in studying and praying the Scriptures. Fruitful Christians are proof.

The means of acquiring the blessing of the Bible are clear. A young man can keep his way pure by guarding it with God's Word (v. 9). It takes passion to maintain steadfast devotion to the Scriptures (v. 10). The best thing to do is to memorize it and to seek to be instructed and to instruct others in it (vv. 11-14). Meditating on God's Word gives focus and a delight for God that is not easily forgotten (vv. 15-16). The "blessed man" is one who meditates on God's Word day and night (Psalm 1).

Bible study is not meant to be a completely human endeavor. Without the help of God, no one can expect to see the fruit of happy obedience. Those who desire to be blessed must pray for God's blessing (Psalm 119:17-23). When the Holy Spirit is at work in our lives, there will be consistent changes. We all wrestle with sin. Victory over sin comes by the Word and the Spirit. The more we overcome sin, the more we delight in the testimonies of God that serve to counsel and correct us (v. 24). We must be willing to do the work of Bible study, prayer, meditation, and obedience.

Do you have a Bible study and memorization plan? Are you being blessed? What changes in your life are you praying for?

Those who know and obey the Bible live with peace.

2 Kings 7; 1 Timothy 4; Daniel 11; Psalm 119:25-48

There are times in life when it may appear that there is no hope. It may be because of sinful decisions, natural disasters, or just the way our broken world goes sometimes. No matter what is happening in the world, there is always a way forward with God for those who love Him and follow Him. God has made great promises to His people in the Bible. God keeps His Word. In 2 Kings 7, a promise was made by God through His prophet. The fulfillment of that promise was doubted, but it came to be.

We should never doubt God. We have every reason to doubt ourselves, other people, and human-based systems, but there is no reason to doubt God. When God speaks, what He says gets done. No matter how long it may take or no matter what pieces must fall into place, there is nothing God cannot do. God said that the people under siege would eat within a day, but the captain doubted (vv. 1-2). His doubt cost him his life. There is no hope in disbelief. Those who are blessed to believe are saved, but those who reject the promise and grace of Jesus are cursed.

It was not hard for God to scare off the Syrian army (vv. 3-8). Nothing is hard for God. He can kill and heal as He chooses. He can change the weather. He can bring about calamity or calm. Nothing is too hard for God. No weapon formed against Him can prosper. No lie can be sustained against His truth. He is the Almighty, and He is worthy of our trust.

The lepers who found the blessing of God did not keep it to themselves. They had found salvation. Unlike many in the church today, they did not keep it a secret (v. 9). The king and others wondered about their testimony, but when their good tidings were found to be true, all who could do so rushed out to receive God's blessing (vv. 10-16). The man who had doubted God did indeed hear and see that God's miracle had been done, but he was crushed and killed by the crowds (vv. 17-20). God's promise was kept. The day of judgment will catch many by surprise. Don't miss God's blessing. Trust in Jesus now and receive the promise of eternal life.

Have you trusted in Jesus? Are you confident in the promises of God? Do you live by faith or by sight?

Those who trust in God's provision live with peace.

2 Kings 8; 1 Timothy 5; Daniel 12; Psalm 119:49-72

Families are funny. They are all so different. In their own special way, every family has strengths, weaknesses, and weirdness. The same is true of local-church families. Each one is unique. Families are fundamental to the social order God designed. Church families provide community for every redeemed saint. In 1 Timothy 5, the apostle Paul instructed Timothy to lead his church to function like a family and to challenge everyone within the church to fulfill their roles in their personal families.

How we relate to one another determines the culture that gets created. Timothy was told to treat people according to their age and gender (vv. 1-2). He was told to care for widows in a special way, but to expect a widow's children and grandchildren to look after her (vv. 3-8). When the church honors one another and treats one another with love, a culture of care is created. Every local church is to have a culture of care that is based on love for Christ and one another. Love will always result in kindness and compassion.

It is important for every member of a church to take reasonable responsibility for themselves and their families. Leaders must demand this (vv. 9-16). When people are allowed to let other people do what they could and should do for themselves, laziness and frustration set in. It is best for each person who can work and carry on household responsibilities to do so and to look after those who cannot. Deciding who can and cannot requires wisdom.

Elders who oversee the church and guide in the decision-making of the church must be wise. Their wisdom will yield a proper respect that enables them to provide proper care and supervision of the church (vv. 17-19). Those elders who persist in sin must be rebuked publicly to make clear to all what God demands of leaders and those who follow them (vv. 20-25). A church with godly leaders will be a great blessing. They will model what it looks like to live a healthy life that honors God.

Are you a faithful member of a local church family? How are you involved in taking care of those who are vulnerable and in need? How are you contributing to a healthy church culture?

Those who serve others with love promote a culture of peace.

2 Kings 9; 1 Timothy 6; <u>Hosea 1</u>; Psalm 119:73-96

God wants the very best for His people. He loves us. There is nothing greater or better than God. For God to want the best for us is for God to want us to have Him. This is God's desire. It is not that God needs us. God is satisfied and whole in Himself as Father, Son, and Holy Spirit. He is worshipped by the angels of heaven. He does not need our love or praise, but He wants them because He made us for Himself. He wants us to be what He made us to be: happy, holy people who love Him. Hosea 1 provides a powerful picture of God's love and the brokenness of humanity. God help us! Without God, there is no peace.

God called Hosea to be a prophet during a time of great prosperity (v. 1). Prosperity can be both a blessing and a curse. It can produce pride and the false notion that we do not need God. God called Hosea to do something very strange. He was to marry a prostitute and have children with her (vv. 2-3). This marriage and these children were living examples of the relationship that Israel had with God at that time. God is like the prophet. He is honorable and desirous for good. Israel was like Gomer. She was unfaithful. Their children are the result of their union. Because Israel is unfaithful, there will be punishment and no mercy, and the people will be abandoned by God (vv. 4-9). When God is rejected in favor of sin, there will be negative consequences and suffering.

God's plan for redemption does not change (v. 10). The Lord will always have a remnant. There will always be those who know and worship the God of the Bible. Those who love Jesus and come under His headship will be gathered together (v. 11). This is the promise of God. This promise was fulfilled in the coming of Christ and in the birth of the church. There is now on earth a people who are God's people (1 Peter 2:9-10). They will be a scattered people who go into all the earth and proclaim the good news of God and the salvation that is found in Jesus Christ.

Are you a member of God's redeemed people? Do you desire to honor God and pursue His purpose and plan in the world? With whom are you sharing the gospel and praying for their salvation?

***God has an eternal plan to bless those who love and obey
Jesus, and He will give His faithful remnant eternal peace.***

2 Kings 10-11; 2 Timothy 1; Hosea 2; <u>Psalm 119:97-120</u>

There are a lot of smart people in the world, but there are not many who are wise. Wisdom requires information and an understanding of facts, but it is more than that. Wisdom is the capacity to know what is true and to do what is best. In Psalm 119:97-120, the psalmist praises God for the ability to live wisely because of the work of the Word.

What we love will influence how we live. Those who love the law the way the psalmist did will meditate on it all of the time (v. 97). A biblical way of thinking is the foundation of wisdom. Those who are wise can overcome those who would cause them harm, as well as excelling those who teach and those who are older than they are (vv. 98-100). While others may know more, we can do what is best because our way is kept from evil and is guided by rules that are right (vv. 101-102). The blessings that come from wisdom make God's Word sweet to us and cause us to hate false ways (vv. 103-104).

This way of life is illuminated by Scripture (v. 105). The Bible helps us see where we are and helps us know where we are going. No matter what our circumstances are, we can have peace. This peace is a result of a life-style that delights in and obeys God's Word (vv. 106-112). Life is filled with challenges, trials, and thorns. The Bible speaks to every circumstance we will encounter. The Spirit, who authored the Bible, will guide us in truth (John 14-16).

A love for God's Word will lead us to hate hypocrisy in ourselves and in others (Psalm 119:113). In its truth, we will find safety and strength (vv. 114-117). In response to our biblical prayers, God will discipline us in love. God will remove the dross from our souls. God will give us discerning minds that fear the Lord and rejoice in the truth (vv. 118-120). The transformation that takes place in our lives by the Word of God comes as a fulfillment of the promise of God, and it comes in the power of the Holy Spirit and to the praise of the name of Jesus.

Are you growing wise through your daily study of the Scriptures? Is your heart moved by God and finding delight in God's Word? What changes have you seen in your life this year?

> *Those who love the Word of God will live wisely in our broken world and will experience peace in every circumstance.*

2 Kings 12; 2 Timothy 2; Hosea 3-4; Psalm 119:121-144

As long as we live in this broken world, God's children will never have perfect peace. There will always be challenges, trials, and temptations. There will be some days of victory when God is honored and we are blessed. There will be many days of defeat when we turn from God and choose to trust in ourselves. Perfection on this planet is impossible, but spiritual transformation is possible through faith in Christ by the power of the Holy Spirit. The life and challenges of Joash recorded in 2 Kings 12 give us an example of the difficulties we face and the importance of our decisions.

Joash was blessed to be one of the good kings who did what was right in the sight of God (vv. 1-2). This was a result of Joash having a good biblical teacher. One of the greatest blessings a person can have is a Bible-preaching pastor with Bible-teaching mentors. Joash had that in Jehoiada. Although Joash did well, he was not perfect. Idolatry was still present (v. 3). This is true of Christians today. While we are made righteous and blessed with many sources of sound biblical teaching and preaching, there will always be idols which can draw us away from God.

Because of Joash's love and devotion to God, he wanted to see the temple repaired (vv. 4-5). The condition of the temple reflected the condition of the spiritual life of the people. Although Jehoiada was commanded to make repairs, he refused to do so, and Joash was forced to step in and manage the process (vv. 6-16). There will often be disagreements about how money should be spent in the church. In the end, leaders must lead and the congregation must follow.

It is crucial that leaders lead with faith in God rather than depend on their own devices. Joash did not trust God. Instead, he gave up the gold and sacred gifts that belonged to God and paid off Hazael, king of Syria (vv. 17-18). Those who trust in God get to see miracles. Those who trust in their own abilities rarely do. Joash died due to a conspiracy of his servants (vv. 19-21) because he had killed Jehoiada's son (2 Chronicles 24:20-21). Faith in human efforts always leads to death and destruction.

Are you living to serve God or self? Is your hope in God's power? How have you seen good people fail and fall?

Those who trust in God live with peace.

2 Kings 13; 2 Timothy 3; Hosea 5-6; Psalm 119:145-176

God provides a blessed way of life to all who trust and obey Jesus. Life is filled with temptations to sin. Sin is any activity that is contrary to God's design and purpose. The Lord made the world in harmony, but sin entered the world through humanity. The sin of humanity has led to great suffering and pain. In Christ, there is a blessed way of life that leads to healing and peace. In 2 Timothy 3, the apostle Paul explains to Timothy the contrast between the way of life of the redeemed and the way of life of the unredeemed.

Those who live in sin without the grace and goodness of Jesus in their lives are enslaved to the desires of their flesh and the ways of the world. In *the last days*, which began when the Holy Spirit came at Pentecost (Acts 2), people who do not love Jesus will be recognized by their lifestyles and desires (2 Timothy 3:1-4). They may have an appearance of godliness in order to appear to be trustworthy, but they do not have the power of the Holy Spirit at work in their hearts and minds (v. 5). Christians are not to live as or in association with these people. They are people who oppose God's will and work in the world (vv. 6-8). They will ultimately suffer great loss both in this life and in the life to come (v. 9). The blessed life is the life that belongs to Jesus.

Those who belong to Jesus have been bought with His blood and have received His life into themselves by faith. They follow the teaching, conduct, aim, faith, patience, love, and steadfastness commanded in Scripture (v. 10). They are willing to sacrifice for the call of Christ and to honor God no matter what it might cost (vv. 11-15). Their lives are lived under the authority of Scripture that has been breathed out by the Holy Spirit through men who wrote exactly what God wanted, making the Bible God's Word (vv. 16-17). When we study the Scriptures, we should always ask four questions:

1. What does it say about God and me?
2. How should I change my behavior?
3. What good should I do?
4. How can I help others?

The Bible is given to honor God and to teach His people how to follow Jesus.

Are you a redeemed saint? How has God changed your life? Is your daily time in God's Word changing your life?

Those who know and obey God's Word live with peace.

2 Kings 14; 2 Timothy 4; Hosea 7; Psalms 120-122

God alone has our best interest in mind. The world, the flesh, and the devil could not care less about us, but left to ourselves, we go to these things to get information to make our decisions. In the garden of Eden, the devil convinced us that we could not trust God. We have believed that lie since that day. Hosea 7 shows what happens to a people who refuse to trust God and who choose to live in the way of the world, the flesh, and the devil.

The Israelites were idolaters. Idolatry is trusting in anything other than God to define us, to provide for us, or to please us. It is a form of worship. It is sinful, and it always leads to pain. The Israelites knew of God and even gave a nod toward their national, institutional religion and traditions, but they were not faithful to God. They chose to build their lives around their selfishness: they were dishonest thieves (vv. 1-2); their culture: they pleased their worldly leaders (v. 3); and their fleshly desires: they were adulterers (vv. 4-7). Rather than worship and serve the true God, they served idols and abounded in sin.

Idolatry is ignorant. Because it is sinful, it always costs us more than we wanted to pay, takes us further than we meant to go, and gives us less than it promised. God told the people that they were making fools of themselves. They were being robbed of strength (vv. 8-9), but they ignored God (v. 10). Human beings were made to be with, under, and for God. When we refuse to be what we were created for, we suffer the consequences.

Idolatry has both natural and supernatural consequences. Idolatry not only leads to negative outcomes in our lives, but it also causes God's judgment to come down on us. The Israelites looked to other nations and their idols for direction (v. 11). These nations and idols failed them. Because Israel rejected God and wasted the blessings of life, vigor, and love on worthless idols, His judgment fell on them (vv. 12-16). Once God turns people over to their sin, they can no longer gain peace (Romans 1:18-32).

Do you find your identity in Jesus? Are you turning against sin and idolatry and pursuing Jesus? Are you experiencing the blessing of God or the consequences of sin in your life?

Those who worship and serve Jesus live with eternal peace.

2 Kings 15; Titus 1; Hosea 8; <u>Psalms 123-125</u>

Small reminders and songs that can be sung that call to mind the goodness of God are great treasures. One of the blessings of being raised in church from childhood is learning songs that teach basic truths that will be helpful throughout life. Psalms 120-135 are a collection of short psalms that it is thought the people sang to encourage their faith and to gain peace. Psalms 123-125 each have a different function. Each provides God's children with reasons for having peace in any circumstance.

All of God's children are prone to sin. Although we have been forgiven of our sin and have been given the righteousness of Christ, we are still in the flesh and will battle sin until we see Jesus face to face. Until that day, we must trust in God's mercy and be quick to repent. Psalm 123 is a prayer of repentance. Those who have the faith to pursue the mercy of God will have peace with God. Nothing causes concern and unrest in the soul of a saint like ongoing sin. It is one thing to slip up and sin, but it is another thing to wallow about in sin. By grace and the work of the Holy Spirit, all of God's children can gain peace through repentance.

Gratitude is as fundamental to a Christian's life as breathing is to a human body. Those who are under the grace of God by their personal faith in Christ have an eternal number of reasons to give thanks to God. Psalm 124 is filled with gratitude. Those who can see how God has been good to them in the past will enjoy peace in the present. God has saved us from the devil, that devouring lion. Those who trust in the name of the Lord are free and grateful.

We will never be all that God desires us to be on this side of death, but we can be more like Christ today and tomorrow than we were yesterday. Psalm 125 reminds us that God is our protector and provider. Those who walk in humble obedience to God live a blessed life full of peace. God is worthy of our trust. Sin is a rejection of God and His authority. There is no blessing in that. God blesses those who are faithful to Him.

What is the sin you need to repent of? Are you truly grateful to God? Is God blessing you in your obedience to Him?

Those who hate sin and are quick to repent, are grateful to God, and trust and obey God live with peace.

2 Kings 16; Titus 2; Hosea 9; Psalms 126-128

Human beings cannot help but to live by faith. There is an inclination within us to seek and to serve something or someone greater than ourselves. Our pride and arrogance want us to believe that we are self-satisfied beings capable of standing on our own, but we know that is not true. We wake up every day looking for something to do that will make our lives meaningful and seemingly important. If we do not find our salvation and meaning in life through faith in Jesus, we will be like Ahaz and place our faith in idols and do what is evil in the sight of the Lord. In 2 Kings 16, we see the sin of Ahaz.

Ahaz was raised in a godly home, but he did not honor God as his father had done. His father, Jotham, did what was right in the sight of God, but Ahaz walked in the ways of the kings of Israel (vv. 1-3a). He went so far as to sacrifice his son to the Moabite god, Molech. This sick act was carried out by placing a living child into the arms of a beastly metallic image that had a fire within it. The children were rolled into the fire as a sacrifice. Ahaz sacrificed his son to this idol and also participated in other cult worship (v. 4). He was a lost man looking for life and meaning in all the wrong places.

When Ahaz was threatened, he did not turn to God. Instead, he turned to another pagan king (vv. 5-9). He gave the treasure that belonged to God and His people to Assyria's king. While Ahaz was meeting with this king, he saw an idolatrous altar. He liked it and had one made like it in Israel (vv. 10-19). God had ordered the placement of the altar and the process for the temple worship. Ahaz created his own and rejected God's rule in his life and nation.

The one good thing that came from his life was Hezekiah (v. 20). This is a reminder of the power and grace of God. While children typically follow the pattern of their parents, God has a way of saving people and giving new life supernaturally. Hezekiah is a reminder of the power of God to transform people.

Is Jesus the Savior of your life and your source of meaning and purpose? What are you tempted to worship in place of Jesus? Do you sacrifice your children for your worldly desires?

Those who simply trust and obey God and reject the sinful ways and idols of the world gain God's peace.

2 Kings 17; Titus 3; Hosea 10; Psalms 129-131

God constantly calls His people to remember. One of the crucial elements of worship in a local church is the Lord's Supper. In this remembrance, we celebrate our peace in Christ. As Christians, it is crucial for us to remember what we were and what we could have missed out on if the Holy Spirit had not intervened in our lives. Being judgmental of other people is not helpful to our souls or to the hearts of others. God calls us to remember His grace to us each day and to show respect to others. Titus 3 challenges disciples of Jesus to live lives that are helpful and that promote peace.

Peace is an experience and a posture of those who have repented and believed the gospel. God gives grace to those who request it. Having received God's grace, disciples of Jesus are to be good citizens in their country; they are to be peacemakers and are to be kind (vv. 1-2). Being divisive is easy. It is difficult, though, to be patient the way God has been and is with us. The more we realize and celebrate what we have been saved from, the more effective we will be in helping others know the peace of God (v. 3).

The peace of God is gained by grace through faith in Christ alone (vv. 4-7). The Holy Spirit gives new life, and in that regenerated state, a person is able to repent of sin and believe in the gospel of Jesus. The gospel changes everything!

The gospel enables saints to do good works that are helpful to others (v. 8). The gospel enables saints to avoid conversations that cause unnecessary conflict (vv. 9-11). Those who stir up contention and division must be disciplined. That discipline is for their sakes and for the sakes of all the saints – and for those in need of redemption.

One of the great blessings of being a peace-loving and peacemaking saint is that we become helpful to others. Titus was helpful to Paul. Paul trusted him (vv. 12-13). Paul called on Titus to lead others to live helpful, blessed lives (v. 14). Titus was loved and appreciated (v. 15). By being kind and caring, we can be useful saints who are helpful to the cause of Christ.

Are you a kindhearted person who is quick to make peace? Do people desire to be like you and to spend time with you? Is your lifestyle one that exhibits Christlikeness?

Those who are kind like Christ live in and promote peace.

2 Kings 18; Philemon; Hosea 11; Psalms 132-134

Gratitude leads to the best blessing that God gives. When we are grateful, we are mindful of the goodness and provision of God. That leads to an awe of God and a right understanding of who we are and who God is. When we lose our sense of the awe of God, we find something else to worship and pursue. That is where sin comes from and is what sin does. In Hosea 11, God condemns Israel for their sin and outlines the devastation that awaits all who sin.

God had been so gracious to Israel (vv. 1, 3-4). The history of the nation is filled with miracle after miracle. It was gracious how God chose Abram out of all of the people of the world and gave him and Sarah their son Isaac. It was gracious how God used sinful Jacob to become the father of the nation. It was gracious how God rescued Israel out of Egypt and provided for the people in Canaan. God's goodness and mercy had been given to them.

However, Israel rejected God (v. 2). It seems that the more God did for them, the more they turned from Him. Rather than live under the authority of God and trust in His goodness, they turned to Baal and other idols. God fed and cared for His people, but they were not appreciative. Rather than live by faith and honor God, they chose to live in the flesh and disgrace themselves.

The consequence of sin is significant (vv. 5-11). God is patient and steadfast in His love, but He is no fool. He is just and holy. There are always consequences to rejecting God. Those consequences are not always immediate, but they will come. Some of the consequences come in this life, and some come in the life to come. While faith in Jesus results in eternal life and blessings, sin results in hell and pain.

The Lord will always have a people who love and serve Him (v. 12). While Israel rejected God, Judah was still faithful. That would soon change. They, too, would ultimately reject God and would be exiled, but God would keep a remnant and fulfill His promise to Abraham through Jesus Christ (Genesis 12:1-3). The plans of God do not change. His kingdom has come, and it is coming.

Are you grateful to God? Do you trust and obey Him? Will you enter into heaven at the end of your days?

Those who live in awe of God and choose to trust and
obey Him live with eternal peace in life and death.

NOVEMBER 6

2 Kings 19; Hebrews 1; Hosea 12; <u>Psalms 135-136</u>

Life is filled with ups and downs. Followers of Jesus who are filled with the Holy Spirit have the great blessing of knowing and experiencing God with peace in every high and low. God has a plan for His people. That plan involves both easy days and hard days. God is faithful every day! Psalms 135 and 136 provide praise to God and a reminder to God's people about how we can experience peace in every kind of day while giving God praise and glory.

There are so many people on the planet who live without the peace of God. Without a knowledge of the goodness and greatness of God, they remain in their sin and die under God's wrath. The redeemed of God know how great God is and how He is able to accomplish His plans (Psalm 135:1-7). They know that God is the one who defeated Pharaoh. They know that He is the one who later even defeated sin and death through Jesus Christ. They know that He vindicates and liberates sinners and makes them saints (vv. 8-14). Those without Jesus have no lasting peace (vv. 15-18). The redeemed must celebrate Jesus and make His name known among the nations so they can repent and believe (vv. 19-21). God is worthy to be praised, but He will be robbed of praise if His people will not spread the gospel around the world. The goal of spreading the gospel is to bring God glory.

Because of who God is and what He has done, His people can give Him praise at all times (Psalm 136:1-3). God is good. He is steadfast in His love and is greater than all others. He has created and sustained the universe (vv. 4-9). He has defeated His enemies and humbled them (vv. 10-22). He has not abandoned or forgotten His people, although they have often turned away from Him (vv. 23-26). It is by grace we are saved through our faith in Christ alone. Some of these words are found in Mary's song that she sang when she found out she would give birth to Jesus (Luke 1:46-56). Mary, like all who trust and obey God, was blessed to be a part of God's eternal plan. Jesus was coming. She would be His mother. Jesus is coming again. We get to be a part of His family and to call others to know Him, love Him, and obey Him.

Are you experiencing God's peace? Is your focus and purpose in life to glorify God? Who are you helping to believe in Jesus?

Those who make Jesus known glorify God and bring peace.

We are pitiful, forgetful creatures. God is kind and gracious to us. He is patient toward us. He knows what is best for us, but we do not always remember that. We have brief lives filled with both good and grief. Through it all, God interacts with us. Through prayer, we have access to God. Through creation and His Word, God speaks to us. Hezekiah's pursuit of God and his proud mistake, recorded in 2 Kings 20, help disciples of Jesus discern how best to live.

Providence is one of God's attributes that goes beyond human capacity to fully understand. We can comprehend the reality in part, but we can never completely comprehend it. God is working in all things for an eternal purpose that brings Him glory. Each of our lives is a part of it. Unlike God, our lives have a beginning and an end. That is part of living in a fallen, sin-plagued world; yet God is good to us. He is working. God let Hezekiah know that his life was about to end (v. 1), but because of his faith and prayer, God allowed Hezekiah fifteen more years of life (vv. 2-7).

Rather than receive the blessing without doubt, Hezekiah asked for and received a sign (vv. 8-11). God did not seem displeased with this request. God demands that His people live by faith, but not blind faith. The faith taught in the Bible is built on facts and observable truth. Gaining assurance of faith is wise.

Hezekiah was not wise in the choices he made with the time God gave him. When envoys came from Babylon, Hezekiah received them and flaunted his prosperity (vv. 12-15). Because of Hezekiah's pride, Isaiah made him aware of the consequences for Hezekiah's progeny (vv. 16-18). Sadly, Hezekiah was not concerned about the lives of those who would follow him, and he died in peace, unconcerned about the future of his family and his people (vv. 19-20). We must not allow sin or sinful people to influence our lives. Pride and the sin that follows will impact us and those close to us.

Do you have steadfast faith in the goodness and plans of God? How has God answered prayer in your life and provided blessings to you and for you? Are you making decisions that will bless your life and the lives of those who will come after you?

Those who are willing to trust in God through prayer and who humbly seek His desire enjoy peace in both good times and grievous times.

2 Kings 21; <u>Hebrews 3</u>; Hosea 14; Psalm 139

Feelings are wonderful things. They provide meaning and significance to our experiences in life. If it were not for feelings, each day with all of its interactions and activities would be nothing more than events in time. Feelings make markers and define the value of the people and occasions of our lives. Although feelings are wonderful, they cannot be trusted. They cannot be the final arbiter of truth. Hebrews 3 challenges Christians to believe in Jesus and to sustain faith in Him no matter how they feel.

The Jewish people who were written to in the book of the Bible we know as Hebrews had a very strong emotional connection to Moses and the Old Testament law. When Christ came, He fulfilled all that Moses and the prophets had written (John 5:46; Luke 24:27). Those who repent and believe the gospel become holy and share in the holy calling of Christ (Hebrews 3:1). Jesus is the faithful one who fulfilled the plan of God and saved a people who have become the household of God (vv. 2-5). The household of God consists of those who have peace with God through faith in Christ.

Those who confess Christ are to be wise and faithful to Jesus. The Holy Spirit spoke in Psalm 95:7-11. He called God's people to faithfulness, but unlike Moses, the Israelites refused to trust God and obey His commands. They missed the blessing of entering into God's rest (Hebrews 3:6-11). The rest of God is the peace of God that comes to all who trust and obey Him.

All of God's people must be careful to remain faithful by sustaining their belief in Christ (vv. 12-15). Belief is a mental activity that drives our emotions. We can feel the impact of our belief, but our feelings must never define our beliefs. There will be days when we do not feel like trusting and obeying Jesus. Those feelings must be rejected and Christ must be pursued, or we, too, will miss out on God's rest (vv. 16-19). The peace of God is a gift that is received by faith in Christ and obedience to His Word. Without obedient faith, there is no peace.

Have you placed saving faith in Jesus Christ? Are you trusting and obeying Jesus? Do you have the peace that comes from resting in the finished work of Christ and in His leadership in your life?

Those who are faithful to Jesus live with peace.

For the redeemed of God, this world is as bad as it gets. For sinners separated from God, this world is as good as it gets. In this world, we will all have blessings and tragedies. The redeemed are not defined by either. The redeemed of God are defined by Christ Jesus, our Lord. When we go through difficulty (and we will), the Lord is with us. We never need to fear. We can trust that God's sovereign power and purpose are at work to accomplish what is best. The perishing have no hope beyond this world, and when this world falls (and it will), all their hope will be lost. The prophet Joel calls for the redeemed to return to God and for the unredeemed to wake up before it is too late and judgment settles on them.

We do not know much about Joel. He had a passion for God and received a message from the Lord (Joel 1:1). He told the elders of Judah to return to the Lord and to train the next generation to be faithful (vv. 2-3). There had been a locust plague (v. 4). Joel told the people to understand that God is holy and is to be feared. He calls those far from God to weep and to turn to God before it is too late (vv. 5-12). Natural calamities are nothing compared to the eternal wrath of God that is to come. When the world struggles, it is an opportunity to be reminded that God is God and that every person on the planet needs His loving care for their souls.

Joel also called the redeemed to repent and to renew their faith commitment to God (vv. 13-20). Those who have repented and believed the gospel of God are free from the punishment and power of sin. This does not mean, though, that we are not responsible for our lives. Joel calls God's people to be wise by trusting and obeying God. The Lord is not impressed with our strength and success. We are a passing wind. God honors and delights in the faith of His people. God enjoys having His children call to their heavenly Father and rely on Him to have their needs met. When God's children do not honor Him, He disciplines them. This is an act of love.

How have difficult days in life led you to turn to God? Who do you know who needs the Lord? Are you depending on yourself, or are you looking to God in faith to provide for you?

Those who delight in the Lord live and die with peace.

2 Kings 23; Hebrews 5; Joel 2; <u>Psalm 142</u>

God knows. God understands. God cares. As a man, the Lord Jesus Christ suffered. Jesus knows what it is to have family misunderstandings. Jesus knows what it is to be abandoned by friends. Jesus knows what it is to be hated. When we cry out to God in our suffering, our pain does not fall on deaf ears. God empathizes with us. Psalm 142 is a lament. It was written by a person being honest with God and seeking God's care.

God knows what is going on a lot better than we do. When we pray, we are not bringing information to God that He does not already know. We are bringing information to Him and letting Him know how it is affecting us. Prayer is a supernatural experience. It provides human beings with the opportunity to commune with God. The capacity for prayer exists within all people. Those who pray in the name of Jesus gain access to God through familial mediation. We are treated as children of God.

Crying out to God and bringing our concerns to God is good to do (vv. 1-2). It provides us with the opportunity to express what we are feeling to the one who loves us more than any other. It is best for us not just to speak of our situation, but also to speak about how we are dealing with it and with the people involved (vv. 3-4). David states clearly that He is spiritually fatigued. This kind of fatigue impacts the mind, the emotions, and the body. What made matters worse for David was that he had no sense that anyone else really cared. They probably did, but he did not feel anyone's care.

David made the wise choice. Rather than depend on himself to pull himself together or to look to other people to provide for him, David looked to God (vv. 5-7). He looked to God to hear him, help him, and to provide for his soul. Through the gospel, the saints of God have the blessing of God's supernatural presence in the Holy Spirit. We can count on Him to do for us what David requested God to do. He will lift us up and surround us with love and peace.

Can you remember times when you felt abandoned by everyone and were in a difficulty that was overwhelming? How has God been faithful to you? Is the gospel your means of peace?

Those who trust God to provide live with peace.

God is gracious and just. We can choose to receive His grace. This requires humble faith. When we repent of sin and choose to trust in the atoning sacrifice of Jesus that He made on the cross, we are saved. There is nothing we can do to save ourselves. All we can do to be saved is to trust Jesus. If we will not repent of our sin and self-dependence, we will have to stand on our own. We will be found guilty, and the eternal wrath of God will come down on us. In 2 Kings 24, we see something of what the wrath of God is like.

The wrath of God is poured out on those who are evil. The Israelites under the rule of Manasseh were evil. This treacherous king created a culture of violence and destruction in Israel (vv. 3-4). Nothing worse could be said of a person or people than that *the Lord would not pardon*. There was no redeeming hope for this nation. Each person chose to live the way they wanted, and each person was responsible for their individual actions. The combined actions of the people was such that God removed His protection from His chosen people and allowed the nearby nations to ravage Israel (vv. 1-2). The consequences of all this sin was felt by future generations (vv. 5-7). Our sin does not only impact our own lives, but it also impacts the lives of those near to us.

When God's judgment is poured out in life, the only wise choice is to humbly accept the consequences and seek mercy. God is merciful to the humble. God allowed Jehoiachin and thousands of the leading people of Israel to live (vv. 10-16). He provided Israel with some leadership (v. 17). However, those who were left in Israel still were not humble. In the midst of God's judgment, they did not seek God. They did not turn from their wicked ways. Instead, they attempted to figure out their own way through life without God (vv. 18-20). We are blind. We cannot see tomorrow. God is willing to guide us (Isaiah 42:16). God sees what is ahead and will show us the way forward if we will trust Him.

Are you willing to stop relying on yourself and completely trust in the mercy of God? Is it your desire to live in obedience to the will of God? Do you truly fear the Lord?

***Those who are humble and seek God's mercy are able
to enjoy the favor of God and His peace.***

2 Kings 25; <u>Hebrews 7</u>; Amos 1; Psalm 144

The Bible tells of the greatness and goodness of God, who sent His Son to come and save a people for His glory. The Bible reveals the sovereign power of God and His ability to accomplish His will. Throughout the Bible, God reveals His will to save His people. The Old Testament continually points to Jesus as the promised king who would come and rescue His people from sin and death. The book of Hebrews explains the connection between the Old and New Testaments. Hebrews 7 explains that Jesus is the fulfilment of what the mysterious Melchizedek and the Levitical priesthood pictured.

Melchizedek was a king and priest (v. 1). Abram tithed the spoils of his victory to him (v. 2). This *king of peace* is mysterious because nothing is known of his beginning or end. He resembles Jesus in his timelessness (v. 3). There is no person like Melchizedek in the rest of the Bible. He has a unique place in the story of God and in the redemptive plan (vv. 4-9). There is a lot that we can know and understand about God and the Bible, but there are a number of mysteries that will not be made clear until Christ returns. Until that time, we can delight in the mysteries of God and serve in the known commands and clear will of God.

While Melchizedek was blessed and the Levitical priesthood was effective in accomplishing what God determined, they could not provide the perfect ministry that Jesus did (vv. 10-28). Unlike Jesus, these men were not God. Jesus alone is able to provide the holy sacrifice necessary to provide for the salvation of God's people. Unlike the men who lived and died and ceased to sustain their ministry, Jesus is eternal. His mediation is eternal. There is no end to His power or His grace to forgive. Jesus is more than a priest and a king. He is also the prophet promised by Moses (Deuteronomy 18:15-18). He is *full of grace and truth* and is the Word of God made flesh (John 1:14). He is prophet, priest, and king.

Have you repented and believed in Jesus? Is He your source of truth, life, and leadership? Are you living each day in awe of who Jesus is and what He has done for you?

> ***Those who know Jesus as prophet, priest, and king and choose to live under His grace experience the eternal peace of God.***

1 Chronicles 1-2; Hebrews 8; <u>Amos 2</u>; Psalm 145

The devil desires to see humanity in one of two conditions. He either wants us to be full of pride or full of despair. While he certainly loves to see us suffer in despair, he also likes to see us dishonor God in our pride. Nations and societies that have resources and free time tend to fall into pride. We believe that we are competent to handle our lives on our own, so we ignore God. Proud people do not mind the idea of God and may even say they believe in Him, but they do not honor Him. They are too busy honoring themselves. The prophet Amos prophesied about proud people. In Amos 2, the prophet turned his words against Moab, Judah, and Israel.

The Moabites were the people from whom Ruth came. Their ancestry goes back to Lot (Abraham's nephew) and Lot's oldest daughter. This incestuous bond created this people who lived just east of Judah on the other side of the Dead Sea. Animosity between Israel and Moab started back in the days of Moses. They were a proud and disrespectful people (Amos 2:1-3). They had no regard for the dignity of human bodies. God's judgment would come to them by the hand of the Assyrians.

Up to this point, the Israelites, now made up of the Northern Kingdom of Israel and the Southern Kingdom of Judah, would have been happy with Amos' prophecies that cursed the gentile nations around them. When Amos spoke of the judgment of God coming against them, it must have surprised these proud people. Judah was cursed for rejecting God's law (vv. 4-5). Israel was guilty of injustice (vv. 6-7a), immorality (v. 7b), idolatry (v. 8), and forgetting the faithfulness of God (vv. 9-11).

God would bring judgment on both nations and would crush them for their sin. It may sometimes seem that God does not see our sin or the sins of the nations of the world, but He does. God knows all things and will judge all people. The only hope we have is in Jesus. Jesus took our judgment on the cross. We can receive salvation by faith in Jesus and humbly live our lives under His grace, which brings peace.

Are you saved by faith in Christ? Do you live a humbly grateful life? Is Christ honored by how you treat other people?

Those who honor God and humbly serve Jesus by loving God and other people live with God's blessing of peace.

NOVEMBER 14

1 Chronicles 3-4; Hebrews 9; Amos 3; Psalms 146-147

The God of the Bible has power without end. That is hard for us to comprehend. As creatures, there are limits to our strength and the strength of everything around us in creation. God is beyond creation. He is the creator and sustainer of all things by His might. In His grace and for His glory, God calls His people to rely on Him and to look to Him for provision and peace. Psalms 146 and 147 call God's people to trust Him and honor Him as their king.

Both of these chapters begin and end with the command to *Praise the Lord!* The covenant name of God, Yahweh, which is translated with all capital letters as Lord in our English Bibles, speaks to the goodness of God in allowing people to know and trust Him. This name evokes awe and peace. It evokes awe because it is God who is in control. It evokes peace because God is awesome, yet allows us to know and trust Him. It is in awe and peace that God's people rightly worship God (Psalm 146:1-2; 147:1).

In this world, we will often be tempted to rely on ourselves or on other created beings or things. People cannot be completely depended upon because they are temporal (Psalm 146:3-4). God alone can be trusted because He is willing and able to redeem and heal people from sin and make peace with them (vv. 5-9). He alone is able to be counted on to save because He is eternal (v. 10). There is no end to God. There is no end to His power to save, His love to save, or His grace to save.

When God saves, He transforms the heart of a sinner and makes that person a saint. He then gathers His people together, as He did with Jerusalem, to heal them and make them holy (Psalm 147:2-3). He does this because of His might (vv. 3-20). He is the God over creation and human affairs. Those who are willing to place their trust in the grace of God as revealed in Jesus Christ become His followers. He becomes their king. He is the great king who provides for His people and fills them with peace. This peace is not temporary. It is eternal, and it satisfies the eternal souls of the people who are willing to place their trust in Jesus.

Is God the object of your praise? Do you depend on God to provide for you? Is Jesus your king who has saved you?

Those who trust in Jesus live with eternal peace.

Our decisions have huge consequences for our lives and for the lives connected to us. Wise people never underestimate the impact that their decisions will have on the people they love. Great peace comes to those who make choices with the end in mind, and "the end" never ends with the person who is making the choice. Rather, the end involves the line of people who will be impacted by the decisions being made. The Bible makes it clear that our decisions matter, as well as being clear that God is sovereign. In 1 Chronicles 5-6, there is a listing of descendants of several of the tribes of Israel. The tribes of Reuben, Judah, and Levi provide crucial lessons in choices.

The tribe of Reuben lived under a cloud. This should have been the tribe of the eldest son with all the blessings that came from that designation. Instead, this was just another tribe that was never prominent (1 Chronicles 5:1-26). Reuben's sin against his father was never forgotten (Genesis 35:22). Sin has a way of impacting those we love. Reuben's family had to live with his legacy. Even though Reuben saved Joseph (Genesis 37), the sin he committed caused him to lose his place in the family order of blessing. The tribe of Reuben was left to be like Gad and the half-tribe of Manasseh. All were lost when Assyria attacked.

God's choice is seen in Judah's place in the world (v. 2). This tribe was selected to be the one from which the king of Israel would come. This is the tribe of Jesus, the eternal king chosen by God before the foundation of the world.

Levi never received a land inheritance, but was spread out throughout all of Israel (1 Chronicles 6). This was a result of Levi's decision to act in revenge with his brother Simeon (Genesis 34). God provided Levi with the great honor of becoming the tribe of priests who served God's people. The faithful service of Moses and Aaron paved the way for the tribe of Levi to be a well-respected and remembered people.

What decisions by your family both negatively and positively impacted your life? How has God uniquely blessed your life with things beyond your control? How can you create a godly legacy?

Those who choose to honor God enjoy the peace that comes
from providing blessings for themselves and those they love.

1 Chronicles 7-8; Hebrews 11; Amos 5; Luke 1:1-38

We all live by faith. The thing to figure out is what is the object of your faith. The Bible calls us to have faith in the God who loves us, saves us, and guides us. God the Father loved us so much that He sent us His only Son, Jesus as the atoning sacrifice for our sin. The Holy Spirit loves us so much that He gives us new life and leads us through life. The Bible gives us reasons to have faith in God. Hebrews 11 challenges believers to have faith in God and provides multiple examples of people who lived by faith.

Faith is crucial to the Christian life. Without faith in the atoning sacrifice of Jesus, we remain stuck in our sin. Those who repent and believe the gospel are able to live by faith and please God. Our faith pleases God because it acknowledges His goodness and power (vv. 1-2). God gives us reasons to have faith in Him.

One of the first examples of faith is that of Abel, who came to God on God's terms – unlike his brother Cain, who did not (v. 4). Enoch lived by faith and never died (v. 5). These men, like many others, pleased God (v. 6). They believed that God existed, and they believed that He would rightly reward those who seek Him because He is holy and just. Belief in God's existence and judgment is an act of faith.

The chapter goes on to list a number of heroes of the faith (vv. 7-38). Some have called this chapter the Bible's hall of fame. What made these people heroic was their willingness to trust and obey God no matter what it cost them. They were able to make great sacrifices and endure much suffering because their hope was in heaven and not in earthly, created things (vv. 12-16). In heaven, the saints of God will be recognized by God as His people.

Until that time, God's people will have to endure hardship and pain in this fallen world. Those who are listed in this chapter lived by faith in the promise God made concerning Jesus' first coming (vv. 39-40). Today, we who live by faith in the God of the Bible are able to look back and see that Jesus came as God promised, and we can look forward to the second coming of Jesus that God has promised.

What is the object of your faith? Are you growing in your faith? Does your faith require you to hope for heaven?

Those who live by faith experience peace in every circumstance.

1 Chronicles 9-10; Hebrews 12; <u>Amos 6</u>; Luke 1:39-80

Owning and enjoying the finer things in life is not a sin, but dishonoring God is. Those who think little of God and much of themselves are inviting disaster. God is great and glorious, but He will allow people to ignore Him for a while. God does not force Himself on anyone. He is a gentleman. The Lord reveals His greatness and offers His grace. Those who reject Him suffer great loss. The people described in Amos 6 were making a huge mistake that robbed them of true peace, and it caused them much harm.

A soldier in enemy territory will never feel completely at ease. There will always be a sense that home is distant and danger is present. God's children are not at home in this world. Those who are at ease in this world and feel secure surrounded by sin have a false peace (vv. 1-3). Although disaster can be ignored, it cannot be avoided by those who reject God's steadfast love and tender leadership. God alone gives real peace.

This real peace is experienced by those who acknowledge the real danger of sin, repent of it, and choose holiness. Sin always seems appropriate to the mind that is far from God. Even religious people can become lazy. People can sing songs of praise and still be ignorant of their sin (vv. 4-6). Judgment finds everyone, and when it does, revelry becomes misery (v. 7). Sadly, many people will be shocked at the heavenly exile of judgment that their sin so much requires.

Ignorance is no excuse for sin. God has promised to bring judgment (v. 8). The cost of sin is death, and those who refuse to repent and walk in the goodness of God are left to live by superstition (vv. 9-10). The judgment of God leaves sinners stuck in sin and incapable of understanding justice or appreciating righteousness. The souls of sinners remain rotten for eternity, and there is no peace for them (vv. 11-14). This is not God's desire for His image bearers, but He will give what is earned. Those who are wise will repent while they can and seek the mercy and grace of God. The mercy and grace of God give eternal peace to the soul.

Are you indifferent to sin and comfortable in godless places and with godless people? Do you hate sin and seek to kill it? Will your eternity be a sweet abode or a horrific dungeon?

Those who truly love God hate and reject sin and enjoy peace.

1 Chronicles 11-12; Hebrews 13; Amos 7; <u>Luke 2</u>

She is pregnant! It is a miracle every time a woman conceives a child. Unfortunately, we are so familiar with the concept of human reproduction that we often fail to recognize the absolute miracle that it is. The conception of Jesus was an even greater miracle, but familiarity with the story causes some people to lose their sense of awe of it. In Luke 2, the birth narrative and early childhood of Jesus is described. It is all amazing!

It is amazing that the Son of God was born and placed in a manger in Bethlehem (vv. 1-7). God manifested in the flesh! His mother was a young virgin. She was not powerful or popular. She had few possessions and no pleasure associated with the event. This was God's will, and Mary accepted her calling. What a miracle!

It is amazing that shepherds were the first to hear the news and see the baby who was God (vv. 8-21). Jesus came for the outsiders. Shepherds lived quiet lives out of sight. God allowed these unappreciated, poor men to be the first to see Jesus. They came and worshipped Him. What a miracle!

It is amazing that Jesus was presented at the temple, that the promise made to Simeon was kept, and that Anna was blessed to be the first evangelist (vv. 22-38). Because Jesus was a Jewish male, He had to go through the purification rituals. God had promised Simeon that he would see the Messiah. Simeon had waited and believed, and his faith was rewarded. Anna, having served God all of her adult life, was blessed to be one of the first to tell others that Jesus had come. What a miracle!

It is amazing that Jesus grew up in Nazareth very much like other Jewish boys (vv. 39-52). He visited the temple with his family, and although He stayed behind to be at His Father's house, He was just a boy. That boy grew up, and there was nothing about Him other than His wisdom and favor with God and man that set Him apart. Jesus is the Son of God, yet He experienced the hardship of being a human. What a miracle!

Do you view the birth of Jesus with awe, or have you grown comfortable with it? Are you amazed at God's providence in Christ? Are you sharing this miracle story with others?

Those who live in awe of Jesus have peace.

1 Chronicles 13-14; James 1; Amos 8; Luke 3

God is gracious, but He will not surrender His ways for our ways. The Lord is righteous in all of His ways and judgments. He does not make mistakes. That cannot be said of human beings. We are sinful by nature. Even those who have been saved by grace through faith in Christ alone are still tempted and will often be deceived. The best thing a person can do is to obey God. Obeying God leads to the blessing of peace. King David was a good man, but he was not perfect. In 1 Chronicles 13-14, we are able to see some of his mistakes and accomplishments. The good that occurred was a result of David trusting God.

David wanted to bring the ark to Jerusalem. We are not sure what his motive was. We do not read where God commanded it, and to make the decision, David looked to people (1 Chronicles 13:1-4). Popular opinion is rarely the best place to go for a spiritual decision. Decisions about the will of God must be determined through prayer and with God's Word.

When people seek to do something for God without consulting God, they often do it wrong. David and the people did not take proper precautions in transporting the ark, and Uzzah died for it (vv. 5-10). Rather than repent, David got mad (v. 11). He also became fearful of having God near him (v. 12). Rather than consult God and seek God's will, David abandoned the ark and sent it away to someone else who gained God's blessing (vv. 13-14).

David had multiple wives and children who sadly later turned on each other (1 Chronicles 14:1-7). David was successful at war. David sought God's Word when it came to war. He inquired of the Lord and did what God said (vv. 8-17). David's victories in battle established him as a leader and as one who was blessed by God. Those who humble themselves and choose to seek God and obey His Word are blessed.

Are you seeking God daily through prayer and Bible study? When have you made decisions without seeking God that led to disaster? How have you seen God guide you in decision-making?

Those who look to God for direction and directives have peace.

1 Chronicles 15; James 2; Amos 9; Luke 4

The way of the world is very difficult to abandon. We all have sinful tendencies. There is a natural loyalty in us to live the way our flesh desires and according to worldly values. Our natural inclination is to look down on poor people and to have a faith that is expressed, but not always lived. Faith in Jesus demands that we live and love like Jesus. James 2 is a wonderfully challenging chapter that helps disciples of Jesus to live and love like Him.

Jesus did not show partiality. If anything, Jesus was harder on rich people and people of power than He was on poor people. God loves poor people. He commands His followers to care for them and help them. James pointed out our natural tendency to show partiality to rich, powerful people (v. 1). He gives an example of something that would typically happen. A rich person is given attention and special care, while a poor person is neglected and disrespected (vv. 2-4). James commands God's people to care for the poor (vv. 5-7). This is the way of Christ.

The way of Christ is the way of love. The Bible commands us to love God and to love people. This royal law leads to human thriving (vv. 8-9). God gives mercy to those who trust in Him. Those who trust in Him are to honor and obey Him (vv. 10-13). Without the mercy of God, there is no peace. Those who receive mercy from God and then offer mercy to others have peace.

Rather than having a faith that is in word only, we are to have a faith that is at work in the real world (vv. 14-26). One of the worst things Christians can do is to confuse themselves and others by claiming to have faith without having acts of obedience to God. If God has indeed saved us, it is only natural that we will want to honor Him and keep His commandments. Obedience to God reveals our love for God. Obedience to God does not earn God's love. God chooses to love us by His grace and mercy. We do not deserve to know God. We know Him by faith because He has revealed Himself to us. Believers in Jesus live like Him.

Are you a believer in Jesus? Do you treat all people with respect? Does your way of life reveal your love for God and affirm that you are a person who truly believes in Jesus?

Those who live and love like Jesus experience peace.

1 Chronicles 16; James 3; Obadiah; Luke 5

God is always working to bring about His purpose. We are often caught in a moment and lack enough self-awareness to be hopeful and humble. The children of God can always be hopeful because they are the children of God. Our Father in heaven always looks after us. The children of God should always be humble because all that we have that is good comes by grace. It is wise to stay focused on God and obey His Word. Those who lack a fear of God end up like the Edomites. The prophet Obadiah, who wrote the shortest book in the Old Testament, told that God would deal with Edom, and in time would bless the house of Jacob, God's people.

Jacob and Esau were the sons of Isaac (Genesis 25-26). The sons of Jacob became the Israelites, and the sons of Esau became the Edomites. These two nations never got along. When the Babylonians crushed Judah, the Edomites rejoiced and even took advantage of the situation by taking up residence in some of the Judean villages. This lack of respect for God's chosen people incited the wrath of God against Edom (Obadiah 1:1-14). Rather than taking advantage of enemies when they are down, it is wise to seek to offer and pray for peace. It is best to show grace and to give help where we can. That is what God has done for us.

God gives hope to the humble. Israel had been divided and then had been wiped out by the Assyrians and Babylonians. There was only a remnant left, but God always has a plan for keeping His covenant promises. He will bring judgment against all who reject His rule (vv. 15-18). He will give grace to His repentant people (vv. 19-20). The Israelites would return in small numbers and struggle in the land until the coming of Jesus. When Christ came, He brought the final victory God had promised (v. 21). God's plan cannot be stopped. It may appear at times that all hope is lost and that the proud and powerful will win, but God wins in the end! Our finite perception is limited. The Word of God is true, and we need to see the world by faith through the lens of Scripture.

Do you trust God's plans for the world and for your life? Are you living with hope and humility under Jesus? Is Christ the source of your identity and peace?

Those who trust Jesus with hope and humility will live with peace.

1 Chronicles 17; James 4; Jonah 1; <u>Luke 6</u>

Christianity is more than a system of beliefs and sociological connections. The life of a Christian is a life lived by faith in the living God. It is a supernatural life. Jesus Christ lived this life perfectly. Jesus' way of life is what God designed for all people, but only the redeemed can live His way. The Christian life is a life that results in peace. In Luke 6, Jesus models how God's redeemed people are to live and what they are to pursue.

Jesus ate, healed, and prayed. He was God, but in flesh. His existence in time and space required Him to live by human limitations. He got hungry, and He and His disciples ate (vv. 1-5). They did not eat according to the rules of the rabbis, the Jewish teachers. Jesus healed people (vv. 6-11, 17-19). Again, He did it in love, but not according to the rabbinic rules. Jesus honored God, but did not honor the traditions or institutions of humanity. Jesus never sinned. He honored the Father and sought to do His will by praying and then acting. He prayed and then selected the disciples who would become His apostles (vv. 12-16). Some things are only revealed through prayer.

Life is filled with blessings and woes. The way of God is a way of disciplined sacrifice. The sacrifices God demands of His people will lead to God's blessings (vv. 20-22). The way of the world can appear appealing, but it leads to woes. Only those who have faith in Jesus will choose to make the sacrifices that lead to His blessings.

Faith in Jesus will lead His followers to act in ways that are contrary to worldly ways. The way of Christ will cause His people to love and care for their enemies (vv. 23-36). His way will keep His people from being judgmental, but not naive (vv. 37-42). The Christian life is a life that results in holiness and can stand the challenges that come in life (vv. 43-49). The fruit of a life rooted in Christ is holiness. The holiness of God is revealed in the Word of God. Obedience to God's Word results in holiness and strength.

Are you living your life under the leadership of Jesus? Is Jesus the model and goal for your life? Do those who know you well consider you to be a person at peace with God?

Those who love and live like Jesus experience peace.

1 Chronicles 18; James 5; Jonah 2; Luke 7

For a child of God, every day is a battle. This world is not our home. We are surrounded by spiritual enemies, and our flesh is a traitor. The only way to have peace in life is through war. God calls His children to battle against our ultimate enemy – sin. The life of David serves as an example for how Christians must function. David had to battle enemies and make wise choices concerning his circle of confidants. The victories and wisdom of David that are recorded in 1 Chronicles 18 serve as a model for how followers of Jesus must live.

After this is an interesting way to begin a chapter (v. 1a). It forces us to look at what came before this chapter. In 1 Chronicles 17, David heard from God that the Lord would establish a kingly line through David that would produce the Messiah. This gave David a clear understanding of his role in God's eternal plan. God has revealed His will in His Word. When we walk in God's way, the Holy Spirit reveals the specific plans God has for us. God's will is for us to be holy. In holiness, we find our destiny.

David understood that it was his destiny to clear out and conquer the land that God had promised the Israelites. Not only was David a gifted musician and a likable person, but he was also a warrior. He fought and subdued his enemies (1 Chronicles 18:1b-13). With each victory, David honored God. All the redeemed of God are to live as warriors for holiness. We are to fight against sin, and just as David dedicated the spoils of his victories to God, we are to dedicate each aspect of our lives to God. With every victory over sin, we bring glory and honor to our God and King.

David was a wise king. He was recognized as having provided justice and equality for his people (v. 14). Putting the most talented and capable people in the highest offices of the land was wise (vv. 15-17). It is wise for us to fill our lives with godly people who are talented in the things of God. An isolated child of God is a vulnerable child of God. Jesus saves us to live in His church. It is in the safety of community that we can enjoy God's peace.

Are you pursuing God's general will and unique plan for your life? Do you daily fight the good fight of faith? Whom are you helping to be faithful to God, and who is helping you?

Those who battle wisely for holiness live with peace.

1 Chronicles 19-20; <u>1 Peter 1</u>; Jonah 3; Luke 8

Christians might never have all they want in life, but in Christ they have all they need. The peace of Christ that surpasses all understanding comes from knowing who we are, what we have, and what we are to do as followers of Jesus. By grace through faith, we become God's people, and as God's people, we live holy lives. In 1 Peter 1, the apostle encourages his discouraged readers to remember their identity, gifts, and purpose in Jesus.

The letter has a powerful way of addressing the saints: *To those who are elect exiles* . . . (v. 1). This world is not the home of the redeemed. We are exiles here in this fallen world, but we have been chosen before the foundation of the world *according to the foreknowledge of God the Father* to be God's people *in the sanctification of the Spirit* and *for obedience to Jesus Christ* (v. 2). What a privilege to be identified with the Holy Trinity!

God gives His privileged people new life with a living hope and an inheritance that lasts forever (vv. 3-4). We are guarded by God (v. 5). Even though we struggle with trials, these challenges build our faith and confirm our salvation that was promised by God through the prophets (vv. 6-12). Of all the gifts God gives His people, His Word is certainly one of the greatest of them all. The Old Testament points to the coming of Christ. The Gospels explain the entrance, sacrifice, and resurrection of Jesus. The rest of the New Testament explains the plans of God to bless the world and restore all things at His coming.

The identity of the *elect exiles* and the gracious gifts of God are provided for God's glory and our transformation. God does not save us to be a better version of our fallen selves. God rescues and redeems us from sin. The goal is to make us holy as He is holy (vv. 13-21). Holiness is a result of love. When we love God, we love one another. Loving God and loving others leads to holiness (vv. 22-23). We learn of this love and of the life of Christ through the Word of God that endures (vv. 24-25). It is good news to those who receive it and live it.

Do you identify with the *elect exiles* in Christ? Are God's gifts your hope and peace? Is your life marked by holiness?

Those who live and love as Christ live with peace.

It is sometimes comical, but it is usually sad to see someone who thinks they know what is right and true end up being completely wrong. It is comical when it is a silly thing and people are able to laugh at themselves. It is a sad thing when it is a life-and-death thing and people are unwilling to see their mistakes. Thankfully, God is patient. He gives peace to the humble and corrects them with love. In Jonah 4, the prophet is out of line, and God has to correct him. Did Jonah learn his lesson? Will we learn the lesson of Jonah and honor God and His priorities.

Jonah was mad, but God did not want him to be mad (vv. 1-4). Jonah had been called by God to go up to Nineveh, but he ran away from God and went in the opposite direction (Jonah 1). The Lord was gracious to Jonah, but Jonah was not grateful enough to be gracious to the Ninevites. He did what God commanded. He preached to the Ninevites of God's coming wrath, and when the people repented, Jonah became angry. Jonah hated the Ninevites and would have preferred for them to die. Jonah thought he was right to be angry, but he was wrong.

God allowed Jonah to pout, but He brought about circumstances that would allow Jonah to see his mistake. The Lord provided a plant that comforted Jonah, but the next day God provided a worm that ate the plant. God then sent a scorching, sunny day that made Jonah miserable (vv. 5-9). Jonah wanted to die. He was very upset about the plant. God asked him about the sense of his emotional state. It was just a plant. It was just another hot day. These were trivial things. The way of our fallen world provides for both good and bad days, but they pass. Jonah wanted to die over his loss of comfort.

God questioned Jonah's values (vv. 10-11). Jonah was upset about a plant and a little discomfort, but he had no concern at all for the thousands of people and animals of Nineveh. God was concerned about the souls of His image bearers and His creation. Jonah only cared about himself. Did Jonah learn the lesson God had for him? Learning to honor human life and creation is crucial.

Are you looking at life from God's perspective? Can you admit when you are wrong? Do you value human life and God's creation properly?

Those who share God's priorities live with peace.

1 Chronicles 22; 1 Peter 3; Micah 1; Luke 10

Jesus came into the world to bring peace. By grace through faith in Christ alone, people can gain eternal peace with God. Those who gain that peace are called to share God's peace, to value God's peace, and to experience God's peace. In Luke 10, we learn what God wants His followers to do with His peace.

Jesus wants His followers to share God's peace with the world. He sent seventy-two men to go out in pairs to tell and demonstrate God's good news (vv. 1-12). They were to go with humility, but they were also to go with faith in God's power to look for those who desired God's peace. Those who received the message were saved, but those who rejected the hope of the gospel were cursed (vv. 13-16). It is a troubling thought to think of the many souls suffering in hell who heard the gospel from those missionaries sent by Jesus. They have no excuse.

Jesus wants His followers to value God's peace. When the seventy-two men returned, they were excited about the results of their labors (vv. 17-19). Jesus told them to value the fact that their names were written in heaven (v. 20). We often value the passing things of this world more than the eternal blessings of God. It is wise to be grateful for God's eternal reward rather than to be focused on temporary gains and losses. Jesus praised God and challenged the disciples to be grateful for the peace they have with God (vv. 21-24). The world is passing away. Christ is coming soon. All that truly matters is what we did out of love for God by His grace.

Jesus wants His followers to experience peace. Peace comes to those who are kind and compassionate (vv. 25-37). The Bible teaches us to do good and to be a blessing to others. That is where peace is found. It is in doing good out of love for God. But, Martha was upset because she was laboring, and Mary wasn't (vv. 38-40). Mary had chosen to sit at Jesus' feet, which was better. Martha could have served with peace and could have been happy for Mary, but she was serving out of frustration and duty. God calls us to serve with love. That is how we experience peace.

Are you sharing God's peace in the world? Do you truly value heaven's reward? Is your service for God being done with love?

Those who receive and obey Christ with love have peace.

1 Chronicles 23; 1 Peter 4; Micah 2; Luke 11

Change is hard. Even good change can cause anxiety and challenges. The one thing that is certain to happen in life is that there will be change. God explained the beauty of change, telling us that there is a time for everything under heaven (Ecclesiastes 3). Even though we all know that changes are coming and that God has a plan for each one, change is difficult. In 1 Chronicles 23, David prepared God's people for the changes that would come with his death.

David knew that he would soon die, and in wisdom he named his son, Solomon, to be his successor (v. 1). David was great at many things, but he doesn't appear to have been the greatest father. There was confusion in his family. Death and destruction had come about in his family (2 Samuel 13-19). David named Solomon as his successor (1 Kings 1). It was wise, but it was also out of necessity that David chose Solomon (1 Chronicles 23). If David's mistakes and good choice of Solomon teach us anything, it is that we must make wise choices and act on them.

After choosing Solomon to be king, David organized the Levites to serve the people (vv. 2-23). Without direction, people will do what they have always done, or they will simply do what they prefer to do. That may work out for good, but it usually doesn't. It is wise to prepare people for change and to organize them properly.

Not only must people be organized for change, but they also need to understand why change is needed. David explained that God had blessed Israel and their needs were now different. The Levites needed to provide what the people needed (vv. 24-26). This wise counsel provided clarity for the future. The Levites prepared themselves, and the nation was blessed by them (vv. 27-32). Change can be a great blessing when people understand what it is, why it is, and how it is to happen. We may not always have the benefit of understanding. In those moments, we must simply trust God and live by faith that His plan is perfect.

What changes have you gone through recently? Were you prepared? How can you best prepare for changes that are coming?

Wise people obey God in times of change and enjoy peace.

Submitting to God is tough in our fallen world as we live in our selfish flesh. It is really difficult to submit to other people whom we know are sinful and prone to be selfish like us. Despite the difficulty, God commands us to do so. There are things that can be done to make submission easier. In 1 Peter 5, we are given insight into how submitting to other people and to God can be made easier.

Submitting to servant leaders is easier than submitting to tyrannical egomaniacs. Those who are to give oversight to a local church are to do so humbly with sincerity and love. They must view their task in light of the coming of Christ (v. 1). They must serve willingly with the intention of giving more than they get (v. 2). Rather than trying to dominate people with personality, positional authority, or peer pressure, God expects overseers of His church to serve as examples of Jesus (vv. 3-4).

Christlike elders make it easier for the congregation to follow the leadership of the church. Young people often have limited perception and need to be reminded to respect the elders (v. 5), but everyone in the church is to live humbly toward one another.

That kind of humility comes easier to those who have submitted to Christ out of a clear understanding of the spiritual battle we are all facing (vv. 6-9). We can trust Jesus to empathize with us and guide us with love. He has lived on this broken planet and understands the challenges we face. He has defeated the devil with His holy life, atoning death, and resurrection from the dead. When we resist the devil, we delight our Lord. We are to resist evil, knowing that we are not alone. Not only is God with us by the Holy Spirit, but we are joined in suffering by all who call on Christ. In time, Christ will restore, confirm, strengthen, and establish us under His righteous reign of love (vv. 10-11).

When we submit to our leaders and our Lord, we develop bonds of friendship that bless our lives. Peter closed his letter by speaking of Silvanus, Mark, the church at Rome, and others (vv. 12-14). Submitted saints enjoy a blessed community of peace.

Are you living in submission to leadership? Is your leadership serving like Christ? Do you have godly friends?

Those who live in submission as God commands live with peace.

In reality, a Christian never really has a bad day. Even on our worst day, God is with us and for us. By grace through faith, we can have the same mentality as the apostle Paul had. He explained that death is a gift because it gets us to heaven, and life is a blessing because we can live as Christ (Philippians 1:21). Even in our times of affliction, there is a great reward that is promised to come (2 Corinthians 4:17). This biblical perspective is crucial for the mental and spiritual health of a Christian. Micah 4 provides a biblical perspective that produces peace in those who honor God.

Micah prophesied during a transitional period in the life of Judah. He was a contemporary of Isaiah, and he probably preached to people who could not perceive or apprehend the truth he was presenting (Isaiah 6:9). During his ministry, the Northern Kingdom fell to Assyria. Judah thrived materialistically, but suffered spiritually. Micah spoke to a prospering people about the ultimate restoration of creation under Christ and the impending doom that was coming to Jerusalem.

Micah pictured the coming of Christ that was described by the apostle John in Revelation 21-22. This will be a glorious day! There will be justice and peace on earth (Micah 4:1-8). These days will come, and they will never end. This is the hope of the redeemed that provides them with peace during difficult times. We can always know that God has a plan for us that ends in heaven.

In this life, we will suffer. The people of Judah had rejected God, and there would be significant consequences for their actions (vv. 9-13). They would soon be without leadership, without a home, and without hope. The Babylonians would soon come and destroy Jerusalem and take the people into captivity. There would be no fear of God among their enemies. Like wild animals, their enemies would devastate the land and desecrate the temple. Even those who were faithful to God would suffer. That is how life goes now. The righteous suffer along with the unrighteous.

Do you have peace about your life and future? Is heaven your hope? Are you honoring God with your life and enjoying the blessing of peace that comes to those who trust and obey God?

Those who see reality with a biblical perspective have peace.

1 Chronicles 28; 2 Peter 2; Micah 5; Luke 14

If living as an outwardly religious person is boring, but not difficult, then living as an authentic disciple of Jesus is never boring, but rarely easy. The Christian life is lived by faith in love, and that faith and love are manifested in practical ways. Living like Jesus, with Jesus, and for Jesus changes everything! In Luke 14, the unique lifestyle of an authentic disciple of Jesus is revealed.

An authentic disciple of Jesus does not live by the law, but by the Spirit (vv. 1-6). The religious leaders of Jesus' day created rules that limited people's capacity to show love and to provide acts of service. This is still the case today. Those who reject legalism and live by the Spirit are free to share and show love humbly. This humility is seen in how we care for people and in how we choose to be servants (vv. 7-11). While no one may ever recognize our acts of service, they are certainly felt. They matter. Most importantly, they matter to God. He will one day recognize those who served well.

One of the most important acts of service that any authentic follower of Jesus can render is to announce the coming of Christ. It is good news that Jesus has come and is coming again! Those who believe this good news are servants of God and are called by Him to invite others into God's eternal blessing (vv. 12-24). Unfortunately, many people are far too busy with worldly things to accept God's invitation to the great honor of knowing Him and being with Him.

Being with Jesus is not easy. It is a great blessing, but it is a blessing that comes at a great cost. All who follow Jesus will have to make significant sacrifices (vv. 25-33). Compared to the eternal bliss and blessing that is to come to those who live for Christ, the sacrifices are nothing. In this life, the sacrifices that God demands feel weighty. In reality, they are not that big of a deal, and the sacrifices keep us from becoming worldly and sinful. The Christian life is a life of great flavor that preserves the good that comes to a community and society that has access to God and His Word. Where there are authentic Christians living out their faith with love, there will be healthy people, which leads to healthy societies.

Are you an authentic disciple of Jesus? Do you gladly sacrifice and serve? Have you lost your saltiness?

Authentic disciples of Jesus live with and promote peace.

What will you be remembered for? You are somewhere in life at a certain stage in your journey. There are people who are with you now. They may be family, friends, work associates, healthcare workers, or other students. How you live today and what you choose to do will be the legacy you leave with them. What do you want your legacy of this segment of your journey to be? King David left a strong legacy at the end of his life. In 2 Chronicles 29, we get a glimpse of the legacy he left behind and how he did so.

King David looked to provide for the future of his son and his people (vv. 1-9). He recognized the inexperience of his son. Rather than berate him or attempt to drill concepts and skills into him, David chose to model leadership. He made sacrifices and called the people of Israel to willingly step up and give to God's work. Seasons of sacrificial giving are special times. These projects provide for the future and give us the opportunity to honor God. David left a legacy of a strong, lasting kingdom that was built on faith.

King David honored the Lord and exemplified his faith in front of the people (vv. 10-22a). He celebrated God and His goodness by looking to the Word of God and praying the will of God. The Lord had promised to use Israel to be a blessing. David prayed God's Word and asked for God's blessing. The people agreed with the prayer, and they celebrated God in unity. David left a legacy of authentic faith in God.

King David left a legacy of faithfulness (vv. 22b-30). After he died, the nation had a wise king, the nation was well-resourced and unified, and the nation was happily under the care of God. This is a great legacy. This was David's destiny. The Bible later said of David, *For David, after he had served the purpose of God in his own generation, fell asleep and was laid with his fathers* (Acts 13:36). David fulfilled God's purpose for his life. David left a legacy of purpose.

Are you living in such a way today that you will leave behind a godly legacy? What are the primary things for which you want to be remembered for doing, saying, and being? Who are the people you hope to influence with your godly legacy?

Those who want to leave a godly legacy by making sacrifices, living by faith, and serving others will live and die with peace.

2 Chronicles 1; 1 John 1; Micah 7; Luke 16

The greatest act of grace there has ever been was when God sent His Son to save humanity from their sin. We have all committed treason. Everyone has sinned and continues to struggle with sin, yet God forgives us through Christ. God loved us so much that Jesus was sent to save us. Many people deny this truth. The apostle John was inspired by the Holy Spirit to affirm the coming of Christ. In 1 John 1, John explains the gospel and challenges us to believe.

The epistle begins with a familiar ring. It sounds like chapter 1 of the gospel of John, which sounds like Genesis 1. This is John's testimony. Christ, who was the author of creation, was there at the beginning of time. Because He came into the world, John and many others heard Jesus speak, saw Jesus heal, and even touched Jesus after His resurrection (vv. 1-2). The coming of Jesus is good news to all who believe. John and all who believe proclaim the gospel so that others can join the fellowship with God and rejoice (vv. 3-4).

The gospel tells us that God is light (vv. 5-6). Those who know and love Jesus walk in the light as He is in the light. Those who claim to be Christians but delight in living in sin are not authentic believers. Jesus is the light of the world who has come to vanquish sin and death. He defeated sin when He died on the cross, and He defeated death with His resurrection. Because of His sacrifice, all who trust in Him are saved and are given new, eternal life (v. 7). This new, eternal life of Christ is imparted to us by grace through faith alone.

Our faith in Christ gives us a holy standing with God, but as long as we are living in this fallen world in our sin-desiring flesh, we will struggle with sin. Those who say they do not sin are fooling themselves. They do not fool God or other people. Everyone knows, as God reveals in His Word, that we all sin (v. 8). The good news is that if we confess our sin, Jesus is faithful and just to pardon us (v. 9). When we repent and seek to honor God by trusting in His grace, we affirm that He is alive in us (v. 10).

Is Christ alive in you by your personal faith? Do you share the hope you have in Jesus with others? Are you living a life of repentance and humble subjugation to God?

Those who believe the gospel of Jesus live and die with peace.

Every human being has a concept of God. It may or may not be a right concept, but everyone has an idea of what they believe about God and of what He is like. The popular version of God that seems to linger from generation to generation is that He is an impotent potentate who deserves very little consideration. The reason many people do not take Him seriously is because of their belief that He is not dangerous because He is simply loving. However, the God of the Bible is very dangerous because He is not only loving, but He is also just and holy. In Nahum 1, we get a good glimpse of what God is like and what happens to those who do not live in awe of Him.

The people of Nineveh had heard the message of God through the reluctant prophet, Jonah. When Jonah preached, they repented. A century later, Nahum preached to them (v. 1), but they disregarded his message. His message was terrifying. He presented God in His just wrath (vv. 2-6). Those who stand against God will receive punishment for their sin. He will bear down on them with all of His righteous fury. Nineveh was destroyed soon after this.

God is gracious and gives steadfast love to those He knows (v. 7). He is a strong tower to the faithful. He is good to them and sees them through their times of trouble and struggle. The adversaries of God will be utterly destroyed (v. 8). Those who plot against God and conspire to cause harm to His name and to His kingdom will be decimated (vv. 9-14). What happened to Nineveh is what will happen to all who live and die in their sin. They will be justly judged and found guilty. They will suffer forever.

Those who repent and believe the gospel will rejoice. Jerusalem rejoiced in the judgment of God against His enemies (v. 15). It is not the people who are to be hated, but the sin and the evil that is perpetrated against godliness are to be hated. In heaven, the redeemed will celebrate the victory of Christ over darkness. There will be festivities that will not end. God will be glorified, and His people will be happy to see His name vindicated and creation restored.

Do you fear God? Are you concerned about the souls of those who stand in opposition to God? Will you be among those counted as righteous on the day of God's judgment?

The righteous in Christ have eternal peace with God.

2 Chronicles 3-4; 1 John 3; Nahum 2; <u>Luke 18</u>

The Bible provides a general call to all people to come to Christ by repenting of sin and believing in the gospel. Many people think they have to be good before they can go to God. That is not true. No one is good. The only way we can become good is by going to God. We first go to Jesus and are filled with the Holy Spirit, and then He makes us good. Luke 18 helps us understand who we are and how we are to go to God.

We are to go to God in prayer with persistence (vv. 1-8). God is not bothered when we consistently go to Him. He is bothered by our lack of prayer. The Father loves to hear His children pray in the name of Jesus and He delights to answer prayers of faith.

We are to go to God in humility (vv. 9-30). One of the blessings of being raised in a godly home is that a person learns a biblical worldview. A potential negative aspect is pride. The Pharisee was arrogant. The wretched tax collector was heard by God because he came humbly to God like a child. A childlike trust honors God. When we go to God with our agenda, expecting Him to do our will, we do not honor Him. When we go to Him as our provider, He is honored and we are blessed by knowing that He really is holy and good. None of us are good. We all lack faith to some degree. The best way to know where you lack faith is to complete the following sentence: If I lost _____, I would die. Whatever you would put in the blank tells you what you are not trusting God for. God calls us to give all to Him and to trust Him.

We go to God by faith in His atoning sacrifice (vv. 31-43). Jesus was sent to die and be raised again on the third day. His death paid the penalty for our sin. All who believe in Jesus are healed from the power and punishment of sin. We are all like that blind beggar. We need Jesus to take away our spiritual blindness that was caused by sin. By His grace and for His glory, we are freed to walk in new life where we see what is true and where we are free to pursue God's will.

Are you a person of persistent prayer? Is humility a quality that others would say you have? Have you trusted in Jesus to take away your sin and give you new life in Him?

Humble saints who humbly trust God live with peace.

God describes His people as His temple (1 Corinthians 3:16). What an honor! All who repent and believe the gospel are filled with the Holy Spirit. God dwells in us and is with us. This honor comes with much responsibility. In the Old Testament, many of the kings of Israel defiled the temple by allowing unholy things to inhabit the space and allowing practices that were idolatrous. We must avoid that mistake. We must be holy! In 2 Chronicles 5:1-6:11, the temple of Solomon is dedicated, and it serves as a reminder to the redeemed to honor God.

Solomon led the people to build the temple, and he placed in it all of the dedicated articles for its service (5:1). Christians are to build their lives and to provide the tools needed to serve God. We are to build our lives on the foundation of the Word and erect a life of friends and family who love the Lord. We are to proclaim the greatness of our God and call others to repent and follow Jesus. The tools of our worship are prayer, praise, preaching, and repentance.

The temple was to be a place of worship where God would dwell and reveal His glory, goodness, and grace (vv. 2-14). God's people are to be physical reminders of God's power. The presence of God is to be manifest in our lives. There should be times of overwhelming intensity that cause us to barely be able to stand. Both sinners and saints should see the presence of God in us and be moved by His glory that is alive in us. The temple was not powerful. God is. We are not powerful. God is.

God has made promises, and He has kept them. Solomon was able to point to the promises made to David and celebrate how God kept them (6:1-11). Those who are in Christ can point to the promises given to Abraham, David, and the prophets. We are part of the fulfilled promise of God. We are part of the nations of the world who would be blessed. The redeemed of God stand as a monument to the goodness and power of God!

Are you living as a holy temple to the Lord? Do you live a life of worship that reveals the power and goodness of God in the world? Is your life a testimony to the saving power of Jesus that was promised long ago?

Those who live as holy temples of God have God's peace.

2 Chronicles 6:12-42; <u>1 John 5</u>; Habakkuk 1; Luke 20

What does it mean to be a Christian? That is a simple question, but the answer is not so simple. Strangely, many people have different definitions of what a Christian is. Some consider the answer to be based upon geography. They may live in a nation that considers Christianity its primary religion, and because they live in that place, they think of themselves as Christian. For some people, it is a sociological question. They were raised in a Christian home or attend worship gatherings at a church, and they try to be nice to others – and they believe that makes them Christians. In 1 John 5, the Bible gives a clear explanation of what a true Christian is.

A Christian is a person who has been born of God and loves Jesus (vv. 1-5). Those who are born of God love God. Because they love God, they obey God. While the temptation of the world will always be real, a person who loves and obeys God will overcome the world and its enticements.

A Christian is a person who holds to sound, biblical doctrine (vv. 6-12). Jesus was born of God. He was baptized. He died on a cross. He was raised to life. These truths are fundamental beliefs of Christianity. However, knowing that information does not make a person a Christian. The demons of hell know that information. What makes a person a Christian is the experience of that truth. Christians experience the truth, and it changes how they live. They gain a personal testimony of life in Christ.

A Christian is a person who lives in the life of Jesus (vv. 13-21). Christ is alive in us. We pray in His name. We serve in His name, seeking to draw others from sin and death. We reject sin and idols. This activity is not natural. It is a work of Christ in us by faith. It is not simply activity that mimics Jesus, but it is activity that is done in the resurrection power of Jesus to the praise of His great name. It is a life that delights to do the will and work of God. It is not a mere duty, but it is a genuine delight.

Have you been born again to obey God in love? Do you believe that Jesus is born of God and that He was sent to live and die for us? Is your life now lived in the power and presence of Jesus to accomplish God's purpose through prayer, service, and devotion to Him?

All who are born again and love God live with eternal peace.

There comes a point when a Christian just has to wait on God to see what He is going to do. God expects us to pray and to act on what we know to do, but after we have done all we can and there is nothing else for us to do, we must be patient. We must be diligent to look for the hand of God to move. Habakkuk was a prophet who was passionate about the nation of Israel. He could not fathom how God could use a godless nation to overthrow His chosen people. Habakkuk 2 is an example of a person of faith looking for God to act and do what is best.

Having prayed to God and having argued his point with the Almighty, Habakkuk had nothing else to do except to wait (v. 1). He took on the role of a watchman. A watchman would be situated on the highest point of a defensive wall to sound an alarm when a threat appeared. That was what Old Testament prophets were to do. They were to seek out the Lord and deliver His message to the people. Typically, the prophets were used to sound an alarm of concern.

In response to Habakkuk's prayer and position, the Lord answered him and had him take note of His response (vv. 2-5). God would bring about the destruction of the Babylonians, but it would not happen immediately. The Lord's judgment would come in time, and the righteous would have to live by faith. Living by faith is a constant theme in Scripture. It takes faith to trust God and experience peace in a tumultuous world.

God gave Habakkuk a taunting song that told of God's coming judgment (vv. 6-19). A woe is a divine threat. The Chaldeans (another name for the Babylonians) had acted in a way that roused the anger of God. There would be consequences for their oppression, covetousness, violence, and idolatry. Sin is a serious thing to a holy God.

The redeemed can rest in the knowledge that God is in control and is accomplishing His will (v. 20). The world is filled with opinions, but wise people remain silent before God out of respect for His glory and power. They trust God to accomplish His will.

Do you trust God? Have you done all you know to do to fulfill God's purpose? Can you wait with faith and be at peace?

Those who trust God will have peace as they wait on the Lord.

2 Chronicles 8; 3 John; Habakkuk 3; <u>Luke 22</u>

No Christian should expect life on this broken planet to be easy. If we are following in the way of Jesus, we will always face challenges. The life of Christ is a life built on truth, sustained with love, and riddled with challenges. There is not a single person who can live the Christian life perfectly, but growth is expected. In Luke 22, the way of Christ and the challenges that come with being a follower of Jesus are presented.

Jesus was feared. The religious leaders of His day were afraid that the people would follow Him and that they would lose their influence. They decided to kill Him, and they got Judas to help (vv. 1-6). Jesus was aware of what was happening, and He focused His attention on preparing His disciples for His death. He transformed the Passover meal into the Lord's Supper (vv. 7-22). What Jesus did with the bread speaks to what He does with us. He takes people like us and blesses us, breaks us, and gives us to be used for His eternal purpose. The Christian life is a life of service.

The flesh still wants to be first. Every Christian struggles to be selfless. None are perfect like Jesus. We are like the disciples who want to be recognized as the greatest (vv. 24-30). We want to be celebrated. We are like Peter (vv. 31-34). We are not aware of our weaknesses and how easily we can and will fail.

Our life is meant to be lived on mission. It would be best if we saw ourselves as missionaries and would wisely prepare ourselves as Jesus has commanded (vv. 35-38). The most important thing we can do to prepare and to serve is to pray (vv. 39-46).

The next best thing we can do is to prepare for heartache and disappointment when friends like Judas reject Christ and betray us (vv. 47-53). We must prepare for trials like those Peter faced (vv. 54-62). Like Peter, we will often fail, but as long as we are living under the gospel of Jesus, our failures will not define us. God's love and grace will. We must prepare to be hated like Jesus was (vv. 63-71). People will attack us and twist our words. They will reject us the same way they rejected Jesus. We must see this as an honor.

Do you expect life on this planet to be hard? Is it your goal to be like Jesus? Are you ready to pay the price for your faith?

Those who live like Jesus will be hated, but they will have peace.

2 Chronicles 9; Jude; Zephaniah 1; Luke 23

The Bible has a hero: Jesus. The Bible is about Jesus and His rescue mission to save a people for God. From the beginning to the end, the Bible is a story about God's great love revealed in the sacrifice and victory of His Son. All who follow Jesus as king are empowered by the Holy Spirit and enjoy God's peace. In 2 Chronicles 9, Solomon is celebrated, but his death reminds us that the king we need is Jesus.

Solomon was a wise king, and his fame had spread all over the region. People wanted to know him, do business with him, and be liked by him. Because of his great renown, the Queen of Sheba came to find out if Solomon was as great as everyone said he was (vv. 1-12). She discovered that his reputation was well-deserved. The way he thought, organized his government, and led his people impressed her. She acknowledged that Israel was blessed to have him as their leader. That is what will be said of Jesus when He returns. The world will celebrate His wisdom, power, and might.

Solomon was a wealthy king (vv. 13-28). He maximized Israel's geography and partnered with other nations. Each nation had specific resources that were desirable. Solomon distributed those items and made a fortune in the process. He displayed his wealth and was intimidating. One day the whole world will bow to Jesus. The nations will bring Him tribute, and His power will not be a facade. His true power will cause every knee to bow and every tongue to confess that He is Lord.

Solomon died a normal death (vv. 29-31). This proved that Solomon was not the Messiah. He was not the anointed one who would bring justice and peace to all of the world as the prophets promised the Messiah would do (Isaiah 9:6-7). Jesus is the king who is from everlasting to everlasting. He is the one with infinite wisdom and power. He will rule the world and bring peace on earth. Sinners will be judged, and those who have been made saints by grace through faith in Christ alone will worship Him and serve Him forever.

Is Jesus your true king and the leader of your life? Are you happy to serve Him and make His name known in the world? Do you look forward to Jesus' return to rule over all?

Those who submit to Jesus as king have God's peace.

2 Chronicles 10; <u>Revelation 1</u>; Zephaniah 2; Luke 24

Jesus is coming again! He promised that He would (John 14). What will it be like when He returns? How can the faithful prepare themselves for His return? What are God's expectations for His church in these last days? That is what the book of Revelation is about. Christ came as promised. The Holy Spirit has come as promised. The church is alive in the world and is responsible to accomplish God's will until He returns. In Revelation 1, we are reminded of our hope in who Christ is.

John begins the book by explaining what kind of book he has written and how it is to be read and understood (vv. 1-3). This special revelation was given to John to pass on to the faithful so they can know what to expect in the future. There is a promised blessing to those who read this book, understand it, and obey God. This is the blessing that comes with all of Scripture.

The letter is to seven churches. It is a special message from God to His people (vv. 4-8). The number seven is symbolic of being complete. When John says he is writing to *the seven churches*, he means he is writing to all churches. This message ultimately is for those who are saved and gather in Jesus' name. These churches are under the authority of Jesus. He has no beginning and no end. He is sovereign over the universe. He graciously rules over the kingdom of priests who are His church, and He gives us peace.

It was on a Sunday when Jesus showed up to speak to John, and what Jesus had to say and what He revealed is marvelous (vv. 9-10). The Lord showed up in glory and commanded John to produce this book of the Bible (vv. 11-16). The vision of His glory was more than John could bear, and he fell down to die – but Jesus gave him hope and lifted him up. Jesus spoke words of comfort and encouragement to him (vv. 17-20). Jesus revealed the mystery of what was to come. John was to write it all down. God has spoken through His Word, and we can know Him and obey Him by grace through faith in Christ alone by the power of the Holy Spirit.

Do you truly believe that the Bible is God's Word to humanity? Are you in awe of the resurrected Jesus? Can you imagine what it must have been like for John that day?

Those who read, understand, and obey the Bible have peace.

2 Chronicles 11-12; Revelation 2; Zephaniah 3; John 1

No matter how bad things may get in society because of sin and darkness, God's goodness remains. He stands in stark contrast to the evil of our age. God provides truth with grace, and those who trust and obey Him live with peace. Humanity has a bad habit of taking God's good things and turning them into evil tools. In Zephaniah 3, the prophet reveals the destructiveness of sin and the goodness of God in bringing blessings of peace.

God's judgment may appear to be slow in coming, but it is not. In the grand scheme of eternity, the righteous judgments of God are swift and accurate. The nations that will be brought down by God earn this disfavor (vv. 1-8). It is troubling to see so many nations reject God and fight against Him. They are deceived by their leaders who choose the things of this world rather than the things of God. Creation provides order. This order is from God. Those who reject God's good design will suffer for it.

God saves some people (vv. 9-13). Those whom He saves are transformed. While this change certainly takes place in life, it will fully and finally take place at the second coming of Christ. Under the reign of Christ in the new heavens and new earth, the earth will be filled with God's glory and the redeemed of all nations will experience peace and prosperity. Until that time, God's people must live by faith and enjoy the peace that comes through obedience to God.

God promises to make everything right again and to be in the midst of His people (vv. 14-20). Christ has come. He dwelt among us, and He was seen, touched, and heard. The victory Jesus has brought over sin and death delights the souls of the faithful. The great news is that God is not finished. What Christians now enjoy is just a taste of what is to come. Although we have peace in our souls and have the ability to make peace and live in peace with others by the power of the gospel, a day is coming when there will be peace in every aspect of reality. There will be peace in the world, in our souls, and among those who worship the Lamb.

Are you saved from the judgment of God by grace through faith in Christ alone? Is it your desire to see Christ return in holiness? Do you have peace in your life through the gospel?

Those who live by faith and obey Christ have eternal peace.

2 Chronicles 13; Revelation 3; Haggai 1; <u>John 2</u>

The difference or gap that exists between our expectations and reality determines the level of pleasant surprise or frustration we experience. We all get frustrated or pleasantly surprised from time to time because what we thought would happen did not happen. When Jesus came into the world, He pleasantly surprised some people and frustrated other people. In John 2, the reality of Jesus is revealed. Some people were not surprised, some were pleasantly surprised, and some were frustrated by what Jesus did and said.

When Jesus and His disciples were invited to that wedding in Galilee, Jesus seemed to have had no intention of performing a miracle to get that married couple and their family out of a bind (vv. 1-2). When the wine ran out, they were in an embarrassing situation. To enable them to sustain their honor in the community, Jesus' mom offered Jesus' services to them. Jesus first had to make it clear that He didn't obey people, and His mother appropriately stepped back and recognized that all authority belonged to Him (vv. 3-5). Jesus then had mercy on their need and performed a miracle by turning water into wine (vv. 6-9).

The master of the feast was pleasantly surprised (vv. 10-12). This wine was really good. Usually, people would serve the good wine first, and once people were a little tipsy, they would bring out the lower quality wine. God takes regular stuff like water and people and transforms them into something wonderful. Redeemed saints are pleasantly surprised by Jesus' grace to transform.

The religious leaders and merchants were frustrated by Jesus. He cleared out the temple and would not tolerate their disrespect for His Father's house (vv. 13-22). They expected Jesus to accept their authority to do and say as they pleased. He didn't. He frustrated them. The crowds celebrated Him, but Jesus did not entrust Himself to the crowds (vv. 23-25). People have a way of being selfish. As long as Jesus was doing miracles by healing people or providing food and wine, the people were happy. When He called them to repent and believe, they got angry. This still happens today.

Are you pleasantly surprised by God or are you frustrated by Him? Can you happily submit to the changes Jesus demands? Are you saved?

Those who simply trust Jesus and accept His will live with peace.

We all need help. Life is challenging. We are each limited creatures with strengths and weaknesses. When we face challenges of any kind, we have to choose who to seek help from. We can look to God and pursue what He provides, or we can look to created things. God is great and mighty. He is gracious and good. He is willing to help any who will humble themselves under His gracious authority. Humanity's main problem is pride, which keeps many from God. In 2 Chronicles 14-15, the humble wisdom of Asa is rewarded. His story challenges Christians to grow in their faith.

Asa knew of God's greatness and goodness. He knew the stories of Moses and Joshua. His father had experienced the provision of God. The faith of Asa was strong, and he continued in his father's footsteps and honored God (2 Chronicles 14:1-5). He was a wise steward. He fortified the cities of Judah and recognized that the blessings they enjoyed were given because the people had chosen to be faithful to the Lord (vv. 6-8). Asa's faith was strong.

God is gracious to continue to grow our faith by allowing trials of various kinds. When the Ethiopians came against Judah with one million men, Asa cried out to God for help (vv. 9-11). The Lord stepped in and defeated the Ethiopians (vv. 12-15). God does not expect us to overpower opposition. God expects us to trust and obey His Word by believing what He has promised.

Coming off that great victory, Asa revealed the authenticity of his faith. He was not proud. He knew it was God who had provided the victory. When Azariah approached him and challenged him to pursue God and take the next steps of his faith journey, Asa did all he could (2 Chronicles 15). He gathered God's people and honored God. They renewed their faith commitment and removed from their midst any who were not willing to be faithful. This takes courage and commitment. Asa was more concerned with pleasing God than with pleasing people.

Do you look to God for help? How have you seen God provide for you and for those you love? Is your desire to continue to grow your faith, even if it causes you difficulty?

Those who are willing to ask God for help as they face challenges in life will find Him faithful and will experience peace as Asa did.

2 Chronicles 16; <u>Revelation 5</u>; Zechariah 1; John 4

The world is under the dominion of darkness, but God has a plan. While the devil certainly has some sway over what happens, God is sovereign over all things. There is a plan that is unfolding. There is a story being lived out. This is the will of God. In Revelation 5, there is a dramatic scene in heaven that reveals the power of God revealed in Jesus Christ in order to accomplish God's plan.

Having just seen all of heaven bow before God in His exalted glory (Revelation 4), John's attention turned to a scroll in God's hand (Revelation 5:1). It appeared to be like the scroll given to Ezekiel (Ezekiel 2:9-3:3). Scrolls written on the front and back were typically contracts that had the details on the inside and a general summary on the outside. This scroll was completely sealed so that only the intended reader could open it.

There is only one who is worthy to unveil and implement God's eternal plan. There was no one found in the royal court of heaven or on earth who could do it, and this upset John (Revelation 4:2-4). It appeared that God's will would not be done. One of the elders made it clear that Jesus could do it (v. 5). Jesus is the promised king who was born in the tribe of Judah of the line of David. All of the promises and prophecies of the Messiah find their fulfillment in Jesus. He is worthy to be trusted, praised, and served.

Jesus is the Lamb of God who was slain to provide the ultimate and final sacrifice for sin (v. 6a). He has seven horns, which means that Jesus is all-powerful (v. 6b). He has seven eyes, which means that He knows all things (v. 6c). Jesus was able to take the scroll from the Father (v. 7). Jesus has the authority and power to accomplish all that has been promised.

When those present saw that Jesus was able to take the scroll in order to accomplish the eternal plan of God, they erupted in praise to Jesus (vv. 8-12). The praise spread from heaven to all of creation (v. 13). They celebrated the worth, power, dignity, wisdom, and blessing of Jesus. He is worthy!

Do you delight to praise Jesus for who He is, what He has done, and what He will do? Are you confident in God's plan? Is it your desire to join in the eternal praise of Jesus in heaven?

All who trust in Jesus' power and purpose live with peace.

2 Chronicles 17; Revelation 6; <u>Zechariah 2</u>; John 5

God is calling people to leave worldly ways and to enter into His grace by becoming citizens of His kingdom. The kingdoms of this world are going to fall. It makes no sense to invest our lives in things that will not last. The kingdom of God is an eternal kingdom with an eternal king. Jesus is the King of Kings and is calling all who will hear to join in His life. In Zechariah 2, the calling of Jesus is pictured in the calling of God to His exiled people.

The chapter begins with a quizzical conversation between an angel and the prophet (vv. 1-2). The angel was going to measure Jerusalem, but then another angel showed up with a message for Zechariah. Jerusalem would soon be so big that the walls of the city would not be able to contain the inhabitants (vv. 3-4). There would be a great drawing in by God. The numbers of souls inhabiting the space will be massive. This is what heaven will be like. A multitude that no one can count with blessings beyond anything that we can imagine now on this broken planet will be enjoyed.

The angel also spoke of the protection the people would have (v. 5). There would be a wall of fire, and the Lord would be in their midst. This reminds us of the garden of Eden that was protected by the cherubim and the flaming sword (Genesis 3:24). This also reminds us of the Holy Spirit, who came with fire to seal every saint until the day of judgment (Acts 2; Ephesians 1:13).

Judgment was coming to Babylon, and the people of God were to flee for their lives (Zechariah 2:6-9). Judgment is coming to our planet. All who are without the covering of Christ will be condemned. All who have found a home in Christ through faith will be saved.

This salvation will result in singing and rejoicing. Other nations will join God's kingdom and will enjoy the presence and blessing of God (vv. 10-13). This is what heaven will be. There will be a celebration of God with people from every tribe and tongue taking part. All will be in awe of God.

Have you entrusted your life to the care of Christ? Are you calling others to come to faith in Jesus? Is the second coming of Christ something you are looking forward to with hope?

Those who abide in Christ are citizens of heaven who live in peace.

2 Chronicles 18; Revelation 7; Zechariah 3; <u>John 6</u>

One of the ways God grows our faith is by testing us. He allows us to experience situations that demand something that we cannot supply. God does this so that we will learn to look to Him to provide for us and for all that is needed to do His will. In John 6, Jesus tested His disciples in order to strengthen their faith.

Having made His identity known to the religious leaders and to all who would listen, Jesus went to the other side of the Sea of Galilee. He went up on the mountain with His disciples so they could look down and see that a vast crowd had gathered. Jesus asked how they would feed all of those people (vv. 1-5). Jesus already knew what He was going to do, but he asked them to test them (v. 6). The disciples admitted their inability to provide, and they saw Jesus provide for all. After the miracle, Jesus withdrew, knowing that the people would want to make Him an earthly king (vv. 7-15).

He sent the disciples to cross the sea since night was coming. The sea became rough, but Jesus showed up walking on water, and He immediately got them to the other side (vv. 15-21). Once there, the crowds again gathered to Him, and Jesus began to preach a message that was difficult for the people to listen to (vv. 22-59). The people had come to Jesus hoping to get another meal out of Him, but they received something much better. They heard the gospel preached by Jesus, and He called them to receive Him. The people did not understand this strange calling of eating His flesh and drinking His blood. Many today do not understand the call of Jesus to die to self in order to gain life and live eternally in Christ.

Because of the difficulty of the command and the confusion in their hearts, many of those who had followed Jesus turned away from Him and stopped following Him (vv. 60-66). This often happens. Some people who only want a comfortable faith reject Jesus when the tests come to make their faith strong. When the crowd left, the twelve disciples remained. Jesus asked them if they also wanted to leave. Peter confessed Christ (vv. 67-69). Jesus acknowledged their faith, but He also spoke of Judas being of the devil. Not all who claim Christ are His.

How has your faith been tested? Are you willing to go through difficult things in order to grow? Is your faith getting stronger?

Those who have a strong, tested faith have great peace.

2 Chronicles 19-20; Revelation 8; Zechariah 4; John 7

The Lord's favor does not guarantee a problem-free life. Those who are saved by grace are sustained by grace. This grace does not remove challenges, but it provides wisdom, strength, and faith to endure and honor God. This is the goal of the redeemed – to stay faithful to God and to honor Him in all things. In 2 Chronicles 19-20, Jehoshaphat models for us what it means to be faithful to God in trials, as well as how to choose friends wisely.

Jehoshaphat was well-intentioned. When he went to help Ahab, king of Israel, his intentions were good. God had determined to judge Ahab, and Jehoshaphat should have known better than to align himself with a godless man. God was gracious in showing Jehoshaphat his error, and He guided him to be a blessing to God's people (2 Chronicles 19:1-3). In response to the grace God had given to him, Jehoshaphat called his people to be faithful (v. 4), and he appointed judges to serve the people of Judah (vv. 5-7). He also called on certain Levites to serve Jerusalem by settling disputes (vv. 8-11). God's people need wise leaders who will inspire them to live honorable lives that please the Lord.

God blessed Judah by giving them peace within their borders, but God also allowed enemies from the outside to attack. When nations came against them, Jehoshaphat called the people to fast and to gather in front of the new court he had established (2 Chronicles 20:1-4). A clear conscience never hesitates to call on God. Obedience leads to confidence so that in the day of trouble the righteous will feel free to ask God to act on their behalf. That is what the people of Judah did. They asked God to protect them as He had in the past, and they praised Him (vv. 5-21). The Lord was gracious and routed their enemies (vv. 22-28). This brought God glory. The nations around them feared God and enabled Jehoshaphat to finish his reign in peace (vv. 29-34).

Sadly, Jehoshaphat did not learn to choose his friends wisely. He entered into a contract with another godless king of Israel, which led to loss (vv. 35-37). God's people must choose godly friends and only align with children of light.

What poor choices have you made concerning friendships? How has God provided for you? Are you being wise?

Those who honor God and act wisely live with peace.

DECEMBER 18

2 Chronicles 21; Revelation 9; Zechariah 5; John 8

Before Jesus came to be born in Bethlehem, the people of God had to search the Scriptures to prepare themselves for His appearance. Now the people of God must search the Scriptures to be prepared for the second coming of Christ. The people before Christ came struggled to understand how to interpret the Scriptures rightly concerning Christ's first coming. Now we struggle to interpret the Scriptures rightly concerning the second coming of Christ. The book of Revelation is a great example. Many good, godly people disagree on how to interpret this book. Revelation 9 is one of those chapters that provides an interpretive challenge. What we do know, though, we must hold on to confidently.

We do know that there is a real devil who has been and will be given authority to cause harm (vv. 1-2). The devil is limited in power. An angel will release him. He won't release himself. His power to do harm is limited. He will not be allowed to destroy the grass and trees or those who have been marked as God's people (vv. 3-4). This attack of the devil is limited to five months (v. 5).

We do know that this will be a terrible time and that people will desire to die, but will not be able to (v. 6). There will be wars that will cause great suffering (vv. 7-10). During this time, the devil will live up to his name (v. 11). He is a destroyer. He will bring destruction and will cause God's image bearers to suffer. This is the devil's desire.

We do know that this terrible time will not be the last. There will be two more significant seasons of suffering (v. 12). The sixth trumpet will release a war that will kill one-third of the human population (vv. 13-19). This kind of devastation is hard to imagine. People of all ages will suffer.

We do know that despite this divine wrath being revealed, people will still refuse to submit to God (vv. 20-21). The heart of humanity can only be changed by the Spirit of God. This change comes by prayer and gospel power. Pray for the lost and tell them of God's grace before it is too late and the opportunity is gone.

Do you know for sure that you are saved by grace? Are you able to trust in God's goodness to see you through suffering? For whom can you pray and share the gospel with this week?

Those who gladly submit to God live with peace.

2 Chronicles 22-23; Revelation 10; <u>Zechariah 6</u>; John 9

When God is on the move, eternal power from heaven is being exerted to bring change to the world. This happens in seemingly small and big ways. It happens when a person is saved, when there is restoration in a relationship through biblical peacemaking, and when an entire society is transformed by a great awakening. The power of God is unmistakable. In Zechariah 6, the Lord's army is on the move and God's will is revealed.

Four chariots are seen being led by horses of different color: red, black, white, and dappled (vv. 1-3). The mountains represent God's judgment. These chariots are representative of the Lord's army. God was bringing His presence to influence the happenings on earth. The angel explains what each chariot was responsible to do (vv. 4-6). What we can ascertain from this is that God has a plan. He has the power to accomplish that plan. Nothing is outside of His reach. The Lord has complete supremacy over all things – with plenty to spare. The chariots with white, black, and dappled horses were on a mission. The red horses and chariot were held in reserve (vv. 7-9). They were all willing to serve God. That is how it is with all of God's heavenly servants.

While God was on the move in the world, He was also active within His chosen people. The exiles who had returned from Babylon were supposed to build the temple, but they had not engaged in that project. God renewed His call and consecrated the leadership to do His will (vv. 10-15). This calling spoke not only of the plan for that season in Jerusalem, but also of the eternal plan that was yet to be accomplished. The *Branch* is Jesus. He is the priest who would be crowned as king and would come to build a temple that would influence the world. The temple is the church that Jesus lives in and through to accomplish His will. Now that Christ has come, those who are far off have been called to build the church. This biblical text is a reminder of the plan and ultimate power of God.

How have you seen the Lord at work recently in your life and in the world? Are you being faithful to join God in the work He is doing? Are you making disciples of Jesus to build God's church?

Those who join God in His eternal plan will see God do
great things and will experience peace in the process.

2 Chronicles 24; Revelation 11; Zechariah 7; John 10

To help us understand who He is, God provides many wonderful descriptions and metaphors. One is that of a shepherd. In John 6, Jesus describes Himself as the Good Shepherd.

There has never been and there never will be anyone like Jesus. It is easy to understand why people were often confused by what Jesus said. When He said He was the Good Shepherd and the Door of the sheepfold, the Pharisees and crowds did not understand what He was saying (vv. 19-21). The Pharisees could tell that Jesus was in opposition to them (John 9:40). Jesus made it clear that He alone was the means of salvation. To make His point, Jesus used an image that was well known (John 10:1-6). A good shepherd was one who would care for the sheep and would be trusted by them. Jesus cares for His people, and they follow Him and His Word.

He is not like the religious leaders He spoke to or like the leaders of other religions of the world who destroy and rob people of peace (vv. 7-8). Instead, Jesus explained that He is the only means of salvation (vv. 9-18). All other forms of religion are destructive because in those other religions, people are expected to earn salvation. That is impossible. The salvation of Jesus brings life that is eternal by grace. It is a life that is full and abundant, beyond anything humanly possible. It is a life that is provided by Jesus' sacrifice and love. His followers know Him and trust Him. This pleases God the Father and reveals the true heart of God.

Jesus and the Father are one (vv. 22-38). The religious leaders asked Jesus, and He spoke plainly about His identity. What He said was blasphemy to them. Jesus claimed to be the Son of God. They wanted to kill Him right then and there, but Jesus reminded them of the miracles He had done. They would not believe Him, but sought to kill Him. Jesus escaped to where John had baptized, and many followed and believed in Him (vv. 39-42).

Do you believe that Jesus is the Son of God? Is Jesus your personal Shepherd and Savior? Are you following Jesus and telling others about Him?

Those who trust Jesus to shepherd them live with peace.

Pride is very seductive and destructive. The Lord calls His people to live with humble confidence in Christ alone. The confidence of the Lord's people is humble because they know that every good thing comes from God, and they are humbled by His grace to them. His grace gives us hope. If our confidence is not humble, it will often turn into pride. Amaziah became proud. The story of his seduction and destruction is told in 2 Chronicles 25.

Amaziah's reign began well. At the age of twenty-five, he was a man who did what was right in the eyes of the Lord, even though he did not do so with his whole heart (vv. 1-4). It is crucial for Christians to keep Christ as their treasured delight and avoid the traps of the flesh by obeying the Bible. Although Amaziah was not completely committed to the Lord, he trusted God and fought the men of Seir without the hired help of the Ephraimites (vv. 5-10). Amaziah and his men took courage and were victorious (vv. 11-13). God does not need the help of darkness. He can accomplish His will for His people.

Rather than rejoice in the Lord, Amaziah was seduced by the idols of Seir, and he worshipped in wicked ways (v. 14). This roused the wrath of God, who was gracious and sent a prophet to instruct him to repent – but Amaziah rejected the message of God (vv. 15-16). We can know that pride has set in when we refuse to listen to and consult the Word of God with prayer. We say we are busy and we make other excuses, but the core issue is pride.

Full of pride, Amaziah challenged the king of Israel to war (vv. 17-19). God had hardened Amaziah's heart. That is what pride does. It blinds us to danger (vv. 20-21). Amaziah and his army were defeated, the city was looted, many leaders were captured, and the nation was humiliated (vv. 22-26). Because Amaziah had turned against God in his pride, the people put him to death. That is the consequence of sin. It always leads to death and shame. Only those with humble confidence are blessed by God.

Are you humbly confident in the blessings that God has bestowed upon you? Do you seek to honor God in your decision-making? Is the Word of God your guide, and is the Holy Spirit your strength in your daily battle against sin and idolatry?

Those with humble confidence in Christ live and die with peace.

2 Chronicles 26; <u>Revelation 13</u>; Zechariah 9; John 12

Counterfeits are not always easy to spot. Given enough time and resources, a con artist can easily manipulate images and products to make them seem to be the real thing. Satan is the ultimate con artist. He desires, but cannot have, God's throne. His goal now is to rob God of the glory that is due to His holy name. To do that, Satan appears to be something he isn't in order to deceive humanity. This is what happened at the beginning in the garden of Eden. It is what will continue to happen until the end of time. Revelation 13 reveals the tricks of Satan's trade and equips the saints to stand strong against him.

Satan often raises up a dynamic person and provides the opportunity for that individual to have much success. Enveloped with pride and afraid to fail, this person will do anything to maintain power, popularity, possessions, and pleasure. This person becomes like a beast (vv. 1-2). These individuals come from different places of influence, but their story is the same. They appear to be weak and vulnerable so that people will identify with them, and then they have much success that makes people worship them (v. 3). A culture's worship of the beast ultimately gives praise to Satan, the dragon that authored their success (v. 4). One of Satan's great goals is to rob God of glory.

Meanwhile, the beast also gains power by turning against God. The ultimate beast will have a limited time of authority, but all beasts are limited in their time of success (v. 5). The true saints of God do not worship Satan's puppet (vv. 6-10). It takes courage and genuine faith to remain loyal to God.

While some beasts blaspheme God, other beasts pretend to be godly in order to deceive the faithful (vv. 11-14). The final beast, like those that will come before it, may have some power, but the beast is not all-powerful as God is (v. 15). The final beast will limit commerce to the enemies of God (vv. 16-18), but even before this beast comes, there will be other beasts that will persecute God's people. We must not be surprised by this. We must remain steadfast in our faith.

Can you spot idols and spiritual fakes? Are you willing to stay faithful to God no matter what? Is Christ your source of peace?

Those who worship Christ alone sustain a sense of peace.

Godly leaders recognize that their position and authority have been given to them in order for them to serve. True Christian leaders are servant leaders. They feel burdened to care for God's flock. Their model for leadership is Jesus. Jesus is the Good Shepherd. All who follow Him and serve like Him enjoy His pleasure and peace. Zechariah 10 points out the difference between God's good shepherds and worldly shepherds who are not of God.

God's good shepherds look to God to provide for their needs and the needs of God's people (v. 1). Worldly shepherds do not trust in God. They look to idols and created things that have limited power (v. 2). Idols and false prophets cannot provide what is ultimately needed. They seduce deceived people with promises that they cannot keep.

God's good shepherds are affirmed and blessed by God, while worldly leaders suffer God's wrath (v. 3). God is not slow to keep His promises. The plan of God will come at the right time and in the right way. Those who do not serve the Lord will be punished. The good shepherds will be rewarded and renewed with God's strength for God's glory. They will be like warhorses.

This renewal that God's good shepherds enjoy is described with many wonderful metaphors. While these descriptions apply specifically to those whom God raised up to lead the exiles who returned from Babylon, these qualities are also seen in Christlike leaders. These leaders provide security and strength (v. 4). They are mighty warriors who stand for God (v. 5). They are empowered by God (v. 6). Their followers also become like warriors, and the children rejoice because of the blessings they live with (v. 7).

The exiles were whistled back to Judah just as the redeemed are called out of darkness into Christ's marvelous light (vv. 8-12). God provided for Judah. God has provided for Christians by raising up Jesus and calling the redeemed to worship Him.

Are you using your influence for the glory of God? Can you sense that God is pleased with how you are living and serving? Do you see the blessings God gives to good shepherds?

Those who serve the Lord with a heart like the heart of Jesus will be rewarded with His pleasure and peace.

2 Chronicles 29; Revelation 15; Zechariah 11; <u>John 14</u>

God has made wonderful promises to His people. Over many millennia, God has proven faithful to do what He said He would do. Throughout the Old Testament, God said He would do many amazing things. Saints can now read the New Testament and look back at our own lives and see how God did what He said He would do. John 14 is filled with some of the greatest promises of all.

Jesus promised He would go to heaven and prepare a place for all of His people (vv. 1-4). One of the responsibilities of a husband is to provide a dwelling for his family. When a man proposes marriage, he is offering a woman a life under his care. Jesus offers to His bride, the church, a home and a life of great blessing. He proposes a life that is eternal and glorious.

Thomas did not understand what Jesus meant (v. 5). In a broken world, it is hard to imagine and believe that Jesus could care for and love us. Jesus reminded His disciples of who He is (vv. 6-11). Jesus is the only means of salvation. He is truth revealed and life eternal. He gives Himself to all who believe in Him. Those who receive Him receive God.

This glorious gift is made possible by the Father's grace, the Son's sacrifice, and the Spirit's empowering. Jesus promised that the Holy Spirit would come and that those who would be made alive by Him would be able to do greater works (vv. 12-14). The power of God would soon come to live in the saints of God. This supernatural power among so many would transform lives, families and cultures! This was the plan of God and it has been and is being carried out by His Spirit-filled people.

Those who believe in Jesus are compelled to love Jesus. Because they love Jesus, they obey Jesus (John 14:15-31). The Holy Spirit enables us to believe. Our belief inspires the love to obey. Our obedience honors God and enables us to know God's peace. It is a peace that lasts forever.

Have you trusted in Jesus and been made alive by the Holy Spirit? Do you live in loving obedience to God? Are you counting on Jesus to keep His promises?

Those who trust in Jesus to keep His promises have God's peace.

Merry Christmas! The God of heaven was born of the virgin in Bethlehem and was celebrated by angels and shepherds. God calls us to worship Jesus today. He is the hope of ages. He is the promised one. God calls us to remember the sacrifice that was made by His Son and to celebrate this holy gift that gives eternal life to all who receive Him. In 2 Chronicles 30, Hezekiah's call to God's people reminds us of the call of God to us today.

Hezekiah had restored the temple, and he invited Judah and all who remained of Ephraim and Manasseh to come and celebrate Passover (v. 1). Passover was a celebration that commemorates God's salvation of His people who were enslaved in Egypt. On that Passover night, the people took the blood of a lamb and put it over their doors so that when the angel of death came, he would pass by their homes. Jesus is the Lamb of God who takes away the sin of the world. He provides salvation to all who receive Him.

Hezekiah consulted with other leaders, and they formed a plan to consecrate those who were needed in order to provide for the celebration. They then called on the people to come and honor God (vv. 2-8). The offer came with great motivation – to gain God's favor for themselves and for those who had been taken captive by Assyria (v. 9). When God's people worship the Lord and celebrate Jesus, not only are they and their families blessed, but also a message of hope is provided to the culture that is enslaved in sin. The celebration of the birth of Christ tells sinners there is hope. This hope gives peace to all who believe.

Many people mocked Hezekiah and ignored his invitation, but some did come (vv. 10-11). Not everyone can believe in the goodness of God. Not everyone will receive God's gift. Those who did come to celebrate were blessed (vv. 12-27). God was honored, and the prayers of the people were heard in heaven. Those who celebrate Jesus and worship Him gain heaven's reward. There is great joy and peace that fills the hearts of those who believe in Jesus.

Do you celebrate Jesus today as the Lamb of God who has come to save sinners? Is it your desire to worship Him and to make known to the world what He has done? How will you remember Jesus and celebrate Him today?

Those who celebrate and worship Jesus enjoy His peace.

2 Chronicles 31; Revelation 17; Zechariah 13:2-9; John 16

The world is not as God designed it to be. God created the world to be full of harmony and peace. Human beings were given the authority to care for the garden of Eden so that it filled the whole earth. They were also to populate paradise with other human beings who would live to honor God. When we sinned, the world fell into chaos. That chaos will continue until Christ returns. Revelation 17 pictures the chaos that consumes our world.

One day God will bring judgment to the evil that has deceived and destroyed so many lives (v. 1). This evil permeates the planet, and only those who are filled with the Spirit of God by the grace of God can escape its grip. This evil is pictured as a prostitute who overcomes sinners with temptation that leads them to sensual sin (v. 2). Without the Holy Spirit, the flesh will always contaminate the desires of a person and cause destruction.

John was carried away by the Spirit to a place of spiritual protection and physical scarcity so he could see beyond the surface beauty and into the sick sin of the woman (v. 3). She was arrayed in power and riches (v. 4). She personifies all the worldliness of those who hold power without Christ (v. 5). Without Christ, people in power will fear godliness and will seek to destroy it (v. 6). The power of Christ protects saints from the seduction of worldliness, which is a threat to those with worldly power. Saints are not easily seduced.

The angel explained to John that this evil power would not reign forever (vv. 7-13). There were and would still be rulers who would come and serve the evil that now permeates the planet, but one day they will all be brought down. Worldly leaders who live to gain worldly pleasure have made and will continue to make war on Jesus and His saints, but Jesus will win in the end (v. 14). He is Lord of Lords and King of Kings. He has overcome, and He will win in the end.

Evil is its own worst enemy. It can never get enough blood and power. Like fire, it devours. God will allow the forces of evil to destroy themselves (vv. 15-18). This is the plan of God.

Can you discern the evil around you? Do you delight in holiness and hate the sin that so easily entangles? Are you looking forward to the return of Christ and His eternal reign in righteousness?

Those who choose Christ may suffer, but they will have peace.

The Bible tells of the majesty of God, the fall of humanity, the rescue by Jesus, and the restoration of creation. Throughout the Scriptures, God tells this story in different ways. It may be through a character, a song, or a difficult situation. Regardless of the means, the story is the same. In Zechariah 14, the story is told through prophecy. God's glory, humanity's pain and salvation, and creation's renewal are revealed.

God is holy and loving. His desire is for His people to trust and obey Him. The inhabitants of Jerusalem in Zechariah's vision turned away from God (v. 1). That is what humanity did in the beginning. God was kind to provide the garden of Eden, but we sinned. The inhabitants of Jerusalem in Zechariah's vision were plundered and forced to flee (v. 2). Humanity lost the peace of God and was thrust into chaos.

God did not abandon Jerusalem, and He has not abandoned humanity. He promised to fight for Jerusalem and win them back (vv. 3-6). God promised to come and save a people for Himself, and He did. Just as He promised to save Jerusalem one day, so He has come to save humanity through the life, death, and resurrection of Jesus Christ. Jesus has won the victory, and now the picture of salvation that Zechariah described is reality for those who trust in Jesus (vv. 7-8). God brings peace to the souls of believers.

One day God will bring peace to all of the earth (vv. 9-21). This great day will be a day of ultimate victory. There will be justice in all of creation. Those who refused to submit to God by grace through faith in Christ alone will be judged for their sin. Those who looked to Jesus for salvation will live and reign with the Lord forever. This will be a time of great celebration. God will restore the world to its glory. The saints will shout with joy and sing the songs of victory. Everything will be as it should be. The people and their places will be holy because heaven and earth will be one.

Are you a faithful servant of Jesus Christ, having repented of sin and trusted in God's grace? Do you pray for Christ's return? How will the final judgment go for you?

The story of God is unfolding, and those who have entrusted themselves to Jesus and live for His glory will know His peace.

2 Chronicles 33; Revelation 19; Malachi 1; John 18

The rescue of sinners by God is both sad and glorious. It is sad that the Son of God would have to suffer for sin He never committed and be unjustly killed by those He loved. It is glorious because this was the plan of God before the foundation of the world. Everything happened according to God's will. John 18 traces the last steps of the Savior as He prepared to rescue sinners through His sacrificial death.

Jesus went to the Mount of Olives on the night before His death (v. 1), which was the very place mentioned in our text from yesterday (Zechariah 14:4). Hundreds of years separated these two writings, but the ultimate author is the same. God is the author of all Scripture and is sovereign over all things. Judas knew the place, and his betrayal was realized when he brought the soldiers to arrest Jesus (John 18:2-11). God's plan is perfect. God's people can always be at peace because God is in control.

The soldiers took Jesus to the religious leaders of that time (vv. 12-14). While John went in with Jesus, Peter remained outside in the courtyard warming himself and making His first denial of Jesus (vv. 15-18). Meanwhile, Jesus was questioned and abused, and then He was sent to the official high priest of the day (vv. 19-24). Peter was still outside being questioned. He denied Jesus two more times, which made a total of three, as the rooster began to crow (vv. 25-27). This happened just as Jesus said it would (John 13:38).

Jesus was taken from the high priest to the headquarters of the Roman government (John 18:28). The religious leaders made it clear that they wanted the Roman government to kill Jesus (vv. 29-32). Pilate then had an amazing conversation with Jesus about the kingdom of God and truth (vv. 33-38a). Pilate knew that Jesus was innocent and did not deserve to die, and he tried to set Jesus free with political maneuvering – but God's plan would not be stopped (vv. 38b-40). God's plan cannot be stopped. The story of God is written, and all that God has promised will come to be.

Do you trust God to accomplish His purpose for your life? How has God intervened in the past to get you where you are today? What do you think eternity is like for Pilate?

God's people are guided by providence and can live with peace.

<u>2 Chronicles 34</u>; Revelation 20; Malachi 2; John 19

We cannot choose the family we are born into or undo the hurt and harm that they may have caused, but we can choose to live a life that honors Jesus. Not everyone comes from a loving, godly family. However, those who do not are still without excuse for their sin. We all make our own choices in life. By nature, we choose to sin, but Christ has come to give us a new nature. In 2 Chronicles 34, we see how Josiah chose to honor God.

Josiah was a young boy when he became king of Judah. He reigned for thirty-four years (v. 1). At the age of sixteen, he began to make God-honoring decisions for himself and for the nation (vv. 2-7). Unlike his father, Josiah did what was right in the sight of the Lord. This is a reminder that a family heritage does not need to determine a person's destiny. There are many people, like Josiah, who have been raised by godless parents, yet have found hope and obeyed God. Some who were raised in godly homes have turned away from God.

Josiah was blessed to gain access to the Bible and to rightly respond to the truth (vv. 8-21). Given the number of years that his father and grandfather had rejected God, it is not surprising that God's Word was lost. It is also not surprising that God still held the people responsible for their sin. It is easy to get away from God's Word and miss its blessing. There is a cost to our lack of devotion. God is just. He holds people accountable.

Josiah knew that about God, and he repented. The Lord was gracious to him (vv. 22-33). God is gracious and desires to do good to those who love and fear Him. It is not His desire to bring down His wrath. Rather, He desires to be gracious and loving. When God saw Josiah's humility and repentance, He showed His favor. Jesus, the Word, became flesh (John 1:14). He has dwelt among us and has gained victory over sin and death. All who look to Him by faith and choose to repent and believe the gospel will be saved from God's wrath and will be made pure by the presence of His Spirit.

Have you made the choice to be a disciple of Jesus? Are you faithfully studying the Bible and seeking to obey God's commands by the power of the Holy Spirit? What blessings have you gained from God by choosing to walk humbly with Him?

Those who choose to love and live for Christ gain God's peace.

2 Chronicles 35; Revelation 21; Malachi 3; John 20

The restoration of creation is the final reality that is yet to come. God has created all things. Humanity has fallen. Jesus has come to rescue sinners. The next and final step is the second coming of Christ, when heaven and earth will become one. Harmony will be restored. Justice will be served. All will be as it should be. Revelation 21 describes how the restoration of creation will take place.

First, the old heaven and earth will pass away (v. 1). The world we know will be no more. The heaven where the souls of the saints have gone to be with Jesus will be changed. The dead in Christ will rise, and those who are left will be raised. We will meet the Lord in the air, and our souls will be united with new, resurrected bodies (1 Thessalonians 4:13-18). We will descend with the new heaven (Revelation 21:2-4). God will dwell with us forever.

Second, Jesus will sit in judgment of all people (vv. 5-8). Those who have repented and believed the gospel will be saved. Those who died while still under the penalty and responsibility of their sin will be sentenced to hell with Satan and all of the demons. Theirs will be an everlasting judgment in the presence of God's wrath.

Third, the church will be married to Jesus (vv. 9-21). We will be perfect. We will be joined to Christ. We will live in the new heaven and the new earth with Him. Everything will be as it should be and will be measured out in exactness and holiness. The beauty and majesty of it is hard to describe with fallen language. It will take all of eternity for us to fully delight in all that has been and will be.

Finally, the whole world will be at peace (vv. 22-27). The city of God will always be available to all who come. Those who live in distant lands will inhabit a world of beauty and peace. There will be no more death, pain, suffering, or crying. People will live with perfect love. The angels will rejoice at the splendor of the bride and her groom. Every creature in heaven will be happy!

Do you believe that Jesus will return and restore creation? Are you living every day in light of the second coming of Christ? Is it your aim to be among the redeemed who live for eternity in the new heaven and earth as the bride of Christ?

All who are part of the bride of Christ will one day know perfect peace.

2 Chronicles 36; Revelation 22; Malachi 4; John 21

As we prepare to enter into a new year, it is good to reflect on the good that God has done and to look forward to what God has in store. The Lord has provided for you. The fact that you are reading this means you have survived another year. You may not feel blessed or be in the circumstance of your choosing, but you are blessed, and God has a plan for you. God has a plan for this next year. God's plans never fail. Malachi 4 provides insight into some of the great plans of God that have come and are yet to come.

Jesus is coming to restore His creation. We learned about that yesterday. Before the new heaven and earth are a reality, the old world will pass away. It will pass away by fire and divine judgment (v. 1). Those who lived to gain power, pleasure, popularity, and possessions in this world will be left with nothing. All of their pursuits will be lost. Everything they had hoped to gain will no longer exist.

Those who fear the name of God and submit to the authority of Jesus by grace through faith will be rewarded (vv. 2-3). The saints of God will experience complete healing in Christ. There will be spiritual, emotional, mental, and physical effects of sin. The wicked will be defeated, and there will be no more temptations to overcome. We will be holy. We will be with God.

Until that time and in light of the coming of Jesus, we are to live in obedience to the Word of God (v. 4). Like the people of God who were saved from Egypt, the redeemed of Christ have passed through the waters of baptism and have been given the law of God. This is meant to be a blessing for all who believe.

Elijah came before Christ was made manifest as the Son of God (vv. 5-6). John the Baptist served as the forerunner who prepared the people for Christ's coming, and Elijah himself showed up on the Mount of Transfiguration. His coming announced the day of the Lord – the last era before the restoration. We who believe are called to live in light of and for that great day.

Do you live in awe and wonder at the greatness of God? Are you able to trust in God's plan for your life in this upcoming year? How can you best prepare to engage in God's will for your life?

Those who look forward in Christ have peace about their future.

Without the help of Holli McDaniel, I would have never finished this book. Thank you for your help and encouragement!

About the Author

Jason Pettus has served as an ordained pastor since August 1993. His wife, Carrie, led him to saving faith when he was fifteen. They married six years later, and they now have three children: Mackenzie, Jackson, and Asher. He has degrees from Belmont University (BA in Religion), David Lipscomb University (MDiv), and Reformed Theological Seminary (DMin). His passion is to make disciples who know the Word of God and have a deep love for Jesus.

Connect with Jason Pettus

www.pastorjasonpettus.com

CPSIA information can be obtained
at www.ICGtesting.com
Printed in the USA
BVHW041050301121
622865BV00020B/988